FEMINIST PEDAGOGY IN HIGHER EDUCATION

FEMINIST PEDAGOGY

CRITICAL THEORY
AND PRACTICE

IN HIGHER EDUCATION

Tracy Penny Light, Jane Nicholas and Renée Bondy, editors

 WILFRID LAURIER
UNIVERSITY PRESS

This book was published with the help of a grant from the Canadian Federation for the Humanities and Social Sciences, through the Awards to Scholarly Publications Program, using funds provided by the Social Sciences and Humanities Research Council of Canada. Wilfrid Laurier University Press acknowledges the financial support of the Government of Canada through the Canada Book Fund for our publishing activities. This work was supported by the Research Support Fund.

Library and Archives Canada Cataloguing in Publication

Feminist pedagogy in higher education : critical theory and practice / Tracy Penny Light, Jane Nicholas and Renée Bondy, editors.

Includes bibliographical references and index.
Issued in print and electronic formats.
ISBN 978-1-77112-114-9 (pbk.).—ISBN 978-1-77112-097-5 (pdf).—
ISBN 978-1-77112-098-2 (epub)

1. Feminism and higher education. 2. Critical pedagogy. I. Nicholas, Jane, 1977–, author, editor II. Penny Light, Tracy, 1970–, author, editor III. Bondy, Renée, 1966–, author, editor

LC197.F35 2015   370.11'5   C2015-900223-0
                                          C2015-900224-9

Cover design by hwtstudio.com. Text design by Daiva Villa, Chris Rowat Design.

© 2015 Wilfrid Laurier University Press
Waterloo, Ontario, Canada
www.wlupress.wlu.ca

This book is printed on FSC® certified paper and is certified Ecologo. It contains post-consumer fibre, is processed chlorine free, and is manufactured using biogas energy.

Printed in Canada

Contents

For Wendy

Acknowledgements

First and foremost we would like to thank our contributors for entrusting us with their fine essays. Lisa Quinn at Wilfrid Laurier University Press has been enormously supportive of this project from its inception and we thank her for her enthusiasm and guidance along the way. Thank you to Rob Kohlmeier for steering the book and the editors smoothly through production. Thank you to the copy editor, Matthew Kudelka, for his detailed work. The anonymous reviewers were rigorous, thoughtful, and generous. Their feedback strengthened the collection and their support of it was critical.

In preparing the manuscript we appreciated the financial support provided by St. Jerome's University and the work of Alisha Pol in compiling it. Colleagues assisted in various ways along the way and we thank Steven Bednarski, Diana Parry, and Kristin Burnett.

The origins of the book date back to the Canadian Committee of Women's History conference held in Vancouver in 2010, and we would like to acknowledge the work of the organizers of that conference in bringing us together. In the long road from the initial discussions in 2010 to the final product we were supported by our families. We thank them here for all the quiet and thoughtful ways they make our work possible. Finally, this book is dedicated to Wendy Mitchinson, with much gratitude.

Introduction: Feminist Pedagogy in Higher Education

Renée Bondy, Jane Nicholas, and Tracy Penny Light

Dr. Emily Howard Jennings Stowe, one of the first women to practise medicine in Canada and a tireless advocate for women's education and suffrage, was denied entry to classes in chemistry and physiology at the University of Toronto in 1869. She then wrote to the president of University College remarking that "these university doors will open some day to women." His reply? "Never in my day, Madam" (Feldberg). Of course, Stowe was correct in her prediction.

Through the efforts of many early women reformers and academic feminists, the past century has witnessed drastic changes to higher education (Prentice and Theobald; Smyth and Bourne). Once privileged institutions accessible to an elite few—mostly white men of the upper classes—many of today's universities are arguably more diverse and inclusive. In fact, 56 percent of university students in Canada are women, a statistic that mirrors the trend in many developed countries (AUCC, 5, 12). Women and other groups once excluded from higher education now participate more fully in many capacities.[1]

But inequities, especially as they intersect with class and race, remain. Access to higher education in Canada continues to be at best uneven. Students whose parents went to university are more than two times more likely to attend university than those whose parents did not. In the widespread complaints about Millennials, the persistent gap in participation in higher education—especially acute when intersecting with immigration—was rendered invisible. One popular and sensationalist book linked democratization of the academy to "dumbing it down" and, unfortunately, conflated access with unrelated issues like grade inflation and the lowering of entrance requirements. The same authors also argued that changes in the curriculum to make it more inclusive—changes that began in the 1960s but that they presented as recent developments—were decentring the "core curriculum" (Cote and Allahar, 119). This argument was not only misguided and ideologically driven but also historically incorrect. In History, for example, Bonnie G. Smith's work has shown how that "core" (code for white, middle-class, and male) was a product of a particular time that became naturalized in the emerging structures of the modern university. Women's contributions, like those of people of colour, were suppressed, appropriated, or dismissed because of racism and/or sexism (Smith). Yet in the recent critique, white, middle-class, and masculine was deemed to be natural and anything else an academic interloper.

Disproportionate funding for children on First Nations reserves is one persistent problem leading to structurally based inequities in education, from kindergarten to university. For Aboriginal peoples in Canada, education is haunted by the history of residential schools ("Funding gap plagues education of First Nations, says AFN"). Blair Stonechild, in documenting the long history of universities' failure to respectfully include Aboriginal peoples as well as appropriate content and pedagogies, argues that postsecondary education must be part of a wider discussion about self-government. Other challenges are important to note. Gender imbalances remain, especially in so-called STEM (science, technology, engineering, and math) disciplines (Alphonso). Yet at the turn of the twenty-first century, widespread concern was expressed at the perceived failure of white, middle-class boys. As Christopher Greig's work suggests, the discourse of boys' failing was based largely on uninterrogated assumptions about certain boys' expected privilege and success. Such trends, concerns, and debates continue to echo across institutions of higher education; changes are being made in admissions strategies to counteract the "fear" of the feminization of the university, or at least specific programs, such as medicine (Greig).

Since the 1970s, as feminist scholars have established themselves in universities, feminist pedagogy has emerged as a way for educators to "walk the talk," that is, to bring their philosophical, political, and—to use bell hooks's term—*gender justice* ideals to the classroom (hooks 2000, 23). Critical to this has been the development of Women's Studies as a discipline with a permanent academic presence and with its own theories, methodologies, and debates supported by specific journals and learned societies (Cuthbert

Brandt et al., 538–39). Intersectional analysis has been a key development within the discipline. Intersectionality requires the use of multiple categories of analysis, including purposeful reflection on how those categories intersect, work in conjunction, or grind against one another uneasily. A full account of the complex development of intersectionality is beyond the scope of the discussion here, but a few key points are important. Criticisms of feminism as a white, middle-class women's movement brought other categories of analysis into discussions about women's lives historically and contemporarily. Socialist and Marxist feminists argued for the significance of studying the dynamics of class and gender, even while some acknowledged the uneasy relationship between Marxism and feminism in practice. Black, Latina, and Indigenous women's voices brought issues of race as well as class and sexuality together in feminist debates (see for example hooks; Anzaldúa; Green). As early as the late 1970s, Audre Lorde was calling attention to difference with regard to age, race, class, and sexuality, thus marking out what would become some of the key discussions of the 1980s and 1990s. Those discussions would continue to focus on three main categories of gender, race, and class; meanwhile, other scholars sought productive ways to more fully engage with multiple differences and categories of analysis. Adding to the "holy trinity" of race, class, and gender, other scholars have called for feminists to study how sexuality, age, ethnicity, immigration status, citizenship, and dis/ability intersect (see, for example, Kosofsky Sedgwick; Thobani, Garland Thomson). Robust debates within academic feminism continue to reverberate across the university, despite the fact that sometimes, the discussions are deemed unwelcome by some colleagues, administrators, and students (Bobba). While we celebrate the changes brought by academic feminism within the academy, we are reminded of the need to be vigilant. Academic feminism has challenged the university with regard to everything from institutional practices like admissions to issues of curriculum and pedagogy. It has contributed substantively to making the university more inclusive, diverse, and responsive. As noted above, however, significant challenges remain to ensuring full inclusivity and accessibility.

Despite some advances in access to and diversity within higher education in recent decades, the metaphor of the "ivory tower" persists, likening the university to a privileged and protected fortress, distanced from the mundane preoccupations of everyday life. Professors, students, and others often speak of the "real world" outside the university, reinforcing notions of the university as a rarefied and artificial space. But as those who teach in higher education know, in few places is the "real world" more evident than in the university classroom. Professors and students ask tough questions and craft complex answers, wrestle with timely problems and posit innovative solutions, and grapple with ethical dilemmas for which they seek just resolutions. If it is a privilege to have the time to work through issues based on research and evidence, the practice of critical thinking about problems and issues is not distant from "real world." University campuses are places of discussion, debate, elucidation, interpretation, and consolidation of learning. And in some circumstances, these processes happen outside the traditional classroom space. To twenty-first-century universities, participants bring diverse experiences, interests, and perspectives, as well as various teaching and learning styles, and all of these things necessitate inventive and evolving pedagogical approaches.

Building on critical advances in feminist theory, feminist scholars have developed innovative ways of teaching and learning that place issues of social inequality and difference at the centre of the curriculum. These inclusive approaches to teaching engage learners in the process of constructing knowledge. Feminist pedagogy has embraced open debate and discussion in ways that are meaningful yet safe for all students and that take into account the great variations in social location within student populations. Students struggle with course material in order to challenge traditional assumptions, ask critical questions about the world around them, and make connections between and among their learning experiences, often with a view to generating social change. This requires that they be afforded opportunities to engage and explore their own interests, while being taught ethical and feminist practices for conducting research. Feminist pedagogy typically critiques traditional received wisdom, recognizes the existing knowledge of students, challenges the hierarchy of ways of knowing (e.g., book versus experiential learning), renegotiates and re-forms the relationship between teacher and student, and respects and values the diversity of the personal experiences of all students while relating the learning in academic classrooms to the "real world." Feminist pedagogy also values the development of self-reflexivity in both learning and research practices. Striking a balance between these facets of feminist pedagogy leads to differences and debates across the academy. Does feminist pedagogy open professors to criticisms that they are "biased" or "pushing an agenda"? Does empowering students lead to problems with discipline and entitlement? How can college and university teachers maintain the authority they often require for job security (especially prior to receiving tenure) while at the same time challenging traditional power structures? These questions are arguably more pressing for sessional and contract faculty, who lack the security of tenure or the tenure track. Thus, discussions of feminist pedagogy require a wider lens, one that examines broader trends in higher education, including neoliberalism, corporatization, and the fracturing of the job market, which places greater reliance on contingent (disproportionally female) labour.

Research in feminist pedagogies looks at everything from the dynamics of student–student and student–professor interactions in the classroom, to institutional concerns about funding, direction, and priorities. *Feminist Pedagogy in Higher Education: Critical Theory and Practice* brings together educators from across the disciplines to interrogate the state of feminist pedagogy today. In so doing, they ask and answer some essential questions: How do we define feminist pedagogy in the twenty-first century? Or are we better off speaking of pedagog*ies*? What do feminists bring to teaching? What constitutes the feminist classroom and feminist teaching strategies? In what ways has teaching spurred feminist thought and action? What are some of the new and innovative strategies currently employed in university teaching? What are the challenges inherent in implementing feminist pedagogies? What are the rewards and triumphs of such efforts?

This collection is intentionally cross-disciplinary and includes writing and research from Education, English, History, Law, Philosophy, Psychology, Sexuality, Marriage and Family Studies, Sociology, and Women's and Gender Studies. Many of the contributors to this collection come from interdisciplinary fields or view their work as interdisciplinary, in that they draw on varied and innovative methodological and theoretical frameworks. As such, the essays extend beyond individual disciplinary borders. Well-established scholars with decades of teaching experience in universities and other educational institutions are featured alongside innovative emerging scholars. We note, however, the absence of scholars in the STEM disciplines, as well as the distinctly Western bias. As editors we ran into serious roadblocks in attempting to mediate these limitations; unfortunately, they remain.

The essays in this book showcase the celebrations and successes, as well as the struggles and pitfalls, of feminist pedagogies. All are theoretically sophisticated analyses of and reflections on feminist pedagogy, and many offer practical classroom tools—including assignments, teaching strategies, and assessment and evaluation techniques—along with teacher and student reflections. We have eschewed the traditional dichotomy between theory and practice in favour of an approach rooted in feminist praxis. We toy quite deliberately with the traditional categorization of theory versus practice. We call upon scholars to be self-reflexive while integrating different perspectives and analytical frameworks. While some of the essays collected here spend more time on theory, and others more on practice, all of the contributors demonstrate keen awareness of the interplay between theory *and* practice, testament to their thoughtful application of feminist praxis.

Several of the contributors ground their evolving understandings of pedagogy in the works of second-wave feminist writers and thinkers, especially the American feminist bell hooks, whose work, which emerged from critical feminist debates in the late 1970s and early 1980s, has informed generations of scholars as they grapple with questions of power and privilege in education. hooks' interrogation of the power dynamics between students and teachers, and the questions her findings have raised regarding issues of equity, affect both classroom practices and curricular design. Her thinking also affects teachers on a more personal level. Her caveat that "teachers must be actively committed to a process of self-actualization ... if they are to teach in a manner which empowers students " is reflected in the ways in which writers in this collection share their first-hand experiences in the classroom—both their successful teaching strategies and those failures that have led them to reassess and revise their practices (hooks 1994, 15).

Many salient themes emerge in this collection. A timely issue explored in several of the essays is how the recent corporatization, or marketization, of the university has affected teaching and learning. In particular, the authors in this book express concern over how a climate of corporatization often thwarts the implementation of feminist pedagogies. Llewellyn and Llewellyn explore the potential of a "restorative approach" to university education, one that would counter the current neoliberal model and seek "to protect the conditions of relationships that allow communities and the individuals within them to flourish." Silva Flores sets a broad study of feminist teaching practices in the United Kingdom against the backdrop of recent reforms to higher education, including those that have devalued the arts, humanities, and social sciences and have cut their funding. Briskin's discussion of "privileging agency in troubled times" through the implementation of activist feminist pedagogies confronts shifts in the university climate and culture, which include "the promotion of the university–corporate nexus, unprecedented attacks by some university administrations on the liberal arts and critical theorizing, the marketization of education, and the neoliberal invocation of clientalist and consumerist attitudes among students."

Another theme common to many of the essays is *reflexivity* as a central component of the learning process. De Santis and Serafini bring reflexive process to a practicum seminar and investigate the multiple ways in which both students and professors engage in self-reflection. Gullage discusses the theoretical underpinnings of Fat Studies; she and her students seek to disrupt and challenge dominant understandings of fat bodies. Bondy shares how her frustrations with the limitations of traditional lecture halls motivated the development of a class book club; her strategy was designed to foster meaningful engagement with curriculum and to stimulate a desire for lifelong learning. Dorney explores how she and her students in an undergraduate course on Women and Anger experience and reflect on the concepts of resonance and dissonance in their quest to locate feminist voice. Using her own strategies in teaching Philosophy, Gotlib challenges the persistent issue of masculinized abstract thinking by using embodied gender narratives. While Gotlib's focus is particular to Philosophy, the challenge to abstraction is a pertinent reminder of the ongoing struggles that feminist pedagogues continue to face across the disciplinary divides. Iverson's exploration of "the power of the imagination-intellect" offers an in-depth examination of theoretical and practical aspects of reflexive learning.

Among the more exciting aspects of this collection is that it provides an opportunity to highlight new questions and directions emerging in feminist scholarship, many of which challenge traditional structures and conventional approaches to teaching and learning. Srigley offers readers an insider view of innovative teaching in Canadian history and suggests how professors "might alter the Eurocentric trajectory of first-year history classrooms by putting the challenges of feminist pedagogy and Indigenous methodologies into practice." Nicholas and Baroud draw attention to the legacy of exclusion in the history of Canadian education and apply Bartky's theory of shaming to their appeal for a rethinking of the contemporary student body, the so-called Millennials. Both Browdy de Hernandez and Wilson engage visual culture in innovative ways—the former by using film and literature to teach about female genital mutilation, the latter by exploring how her use of the visual culture of prisons in teaching gender history contributes to overcoming anti-feminist attitudes and stereotypes. Penny Light takes a slightly different spin on the use of visual culture as a way to engage students in thinking about the myriad ways that the media may undermine feminism and how such post-feminist thinking could be used to open up new spaces to consider broader analyses of gender, sexuality, and power. Labinski's paper on sexuality in the classroom will surely spark discussion on a taboo yet almost ever-present issue.

This book had its origins in a panel presentation by Penny Light, Nicholas, and Bondy at the Canadian Conference of Women's History (CCWH–CCHF) August 2010 conference, "Edging Forward, Acting Up: Gender and Women's History at the Cutting Edge of Scholarship and Social Action," held in Vancouver. Our essays were adapted from that event. The collective vision for the CCWH conference panel and for this book began, at least in part, at our alma mater, the University of Waterloo, where we pursued doctoral studies under the direction of esteemed Canadian women's historian Wendy Mitchinson. Mitchinson, adamant that teaching and research are not separate entities, mentored her students to see the mutually reinforcing value of both, and, significantly, of approaching both from a feminist perspective. The volume is dedicated to her in the hope that we might preserve the important understanding that teaching and research are mutually dependent, each informing the other, and that we must be cognizant of this in our work as feminist scholars and teachers.

Over the years, as the three of us moved on to teach at different Canadian universities, our overlapping scholarly interests and feminist commitments, combined with our passion for teaching, led to ongoing discussions and debates. These conversations ultimately inspired us to invite others to join in an ongoing exchange through participation in this edited collection. We hope this volume will spark many fruitful conversations about and inspire further engagement with feminist pedagogy. There is a long history of feminist struggles to make higher education more accessible, diverse, and humane. The twenty-first century offers new challenges and opportunities to continue the struggle.

Note

1 For faculty, there are ongoing issues as many women continue to serve as sessional instructors and the numbers of women academics decrease the higher up the academic chain (assistant, associate, dean, VP, President, etc.). In addition, there continue to be issues regarding the privileging of certain parts of the academic job so that women disproportionately carry heavier teaching and service loads. See, for example, the essays in *Not Drowning but Waving: Women, Feminism and the Liberal Arts,* edited by Susan Brown, Jeanne Perreault, and Jo-Ann Wallace (Edmonton: University of Alberta Press, 2011), as well as "Strengthening Canada's Research Capacity: The Gender Dimension" Council of Canadian Academies, November 2012, and Joya Misra, Jennifer Hickes Lundquist, Elissa Holmes, and Stephanie Agiomavritis, "The Ivory Ceiling of Service Work," *Academe,* January–February 2011.

Works Cited

Alphonso, Caroline. "Early Engagement Key to Getting Girls into Science Careers, Canadian Study Says." *Globe and Mail,* 22 January 2014. http://www.theglobe andmail.com/news/national/education/early-engagement-key-to-getting-girls -into-science-careers-canadian-study-says/article16461308

Anzaldúa, Gloria. *This Bridge Called My Back: Writings by Radical Women of Color.* Watertown: Persephone Press, 1981. Print.

AUCC (Association of Universities and Colleges of Canada). *Trends in Higher Education,* vol. 1: *Enrolment.* Ottawa: 2011. http://www.aucc.ca/wp-content/ uploads/2011/05/trends-2011-vol1-enrolment-e.pdf

Bobba, Anuhya. "'Women Against Feminism' Generates Backlash Against Students," *USA Today*, 18 July 2014. http://college.usatoday.com/2014/07/18/women-against-feminism-generates-backlash-among-students/

Cote, James E., and Anton L. Allahar. *Ivory Tower Blues: A University System in Crisis.* Toronto: University of Toronto Press, 2007. Print.

Cuthbert Brandt, Gail, Naomi Black, Paula Bourne, and Magda Fahrni. *Canadian Women: A History*, 3rd ed. Toronto: Nelson Education, 2011. Print.

Feldberg, Gina. "Emily Howard Jennings." *Dictionary of Canadian Biography*, vol. 13. Toronto: University of Toronto/Université Laval, 2003. http://www.biographi.ca/en/bio/jennings_emily_howard_13E.html

"Funding gap plagues education of First Nations, says AFN" *CBC News*, 8 April 2014. http://www.cbc.ca/news/canada/manitoba/funding-gap-plagues-education-of-first-nations-says-afn-1.2602274

Garland Thomson, Rosemarie. *Extraordinary Bodies: Figuring Physical Disability into American Culture and Literature.* New York: Columbia University Press, 1997.

Green, Joyce. *Making Space for Indigenous Feminism.* Black Point: Fernwood, 2007.

Greig, Christopher J. *Ontario Boys.* Waterloo: Wilfrid Laurier University Press, 2014.

hooks, bell. *Ain't I a Woman: Black Women and Feminism.* Boston: South End Press, 1981.

———. *Teaching to Transgress: Education as the Practice of Freedom.* London: Routledge, 1994.

———. *Feminist Theory: From Margin to Centre,* 2nd ed. Boston: South End Press, 2000.

Kosofsky Sedgwick, Eve. *Epistemology of the Closet.* Berkeley: University of California Press, 1990.

Lorde, Audre. *Sister Outsider.* Darlinghurst: Crossing Press, 1984.

Prentice, Alison, and Marjorie R. Theobald, eds. *Women Who Taught: Perspectives on the History of Women and Teaching.* Toronto: University of Toronto Press, 1991.

Smith, Bonnie G. *The Gender of History.* Cambridge, MA: Harvard University Press, 1998.

Smyth, Elizabeth M., and Paula Bourne, eds. *Women Teaching, Women Learning: Historical Perspectives.* Toronto: Inanna Publications, 2006.

Stonechild, Blair. *The New Buffalo: The Struggle for Aboriginal Post-Secondary Education in Canada.* Winnipeg: University of Manitoba Press, 2006.

Thobani, Sunera. *Exalted Subjects: Studies in the Making of Race and Nation in Canada.* Toronto: University of Toronto Press, 2007.

CHAPTER ONE

A Restorative Approach to Learning: Relational Theory as Feminist Pedagogy in Universities

Kristina R. Llewellyn and Jennifer J. Llewellyn

This essay examines the need for feminist pedagogy in universities that is based on a restorative approach to learning. A restorative approach to learning is often associated with restorative justice, or the redress of negative behaviours, in elementary and secondary schools. But disciplinary issues are not the core of this approach. A restorative approach is attentive to the promotion and protection of positive relationships within a learning community. The core of this approach is relationality. Relational theory holds that as human beings we live in and are constituted by relationships (Nedelsky 1989; see also Whitbeck, 68). Relational theory challenges the inadequacies of liberal and neoliberal social theory, which characterizes the self as individualistic (Downie and Llewellyn). A restorative approach seeks to protect the relationships that allow communities and individuals within them to flourish (Llewellyn). It is antithetical to the market-driven objectives and standardized accountability measures that are increasingly defining the university classroom, including conceptions of effective teaching. Instead, a restorative approach makes interconnectivity key to engaged teaching and learning (e.g., Boler).

A restorative approach is not a feminist pedagogy that calls for a recognition of caring relationships as an essentialist model of teaching, as might be interpreted from some of the "ethic of care" literature (e.g., Gilligan, 1982; Noddings; Porter). Nor is it a feminist pedagogy that is assumed to be liberatory on the basis of collaborative learning (Gore). Rather, a restorative approach to feminist pedagogy is attentive to the range of private and public relationships that support, or potentially thwart, human flourishing (Downie and Llewellyn; see also Tronto; Code). It is a perspective, as bell hooks would say, that lies on the margins of education. It is a vantage point, however, that *is* critical in order to allow students and teachers to see and understand the connectedness of people and thus the relations of power that define and mobilize knowledge. Drawing upon feminist pedagogy literature, feminist relational theory, and teaching experiences, this essay illustrates that a restorative approach provides no definitive model of practice; rather, it offers principles that are capable of responding to contexts for learning. These principles embrace, but are not limited to, relationality, contextualism/subsidiarity, dialogism, and future-orientation. A restorative approach, reflective of such principles, supports pedagogies that facilitate engaged and inclusive learning, including relational truth and relational judgment. Such practices potentially challenge neoliberal ideological effects in universities, as they shift the pedagogical emphasis away from the rational individual learner toward the interactive aspects of learner communities that are essential to socially just education (Arnot; Kennelly and Llewellyn).

Neoliberal Learning: The Critiques of Critical and Feminist Pedagogy
Liberalism has a long history in Western nations. Founded on the eradication of the caste system, the roots of liberal ideology are individual freedom based on reason and law and the right to property and the sale of labour in a free market (e.g., Mill; Locke). Neoliberalism gained a grip on liberal democratic nations like Canada in the 1980s. At that time, governments sought to reduce the welfare state, and in so doing they legitimized free market economies and encouraged political individualism (Kennelly and Llewellyn, 898–900; Brown). Despite protests well before the Occupy Movement, the centralization of political power in the hands of transnational corporations—and accompanying deregulation, downsizing, and labour intensification—eroded social policies (McLaren and Farahmandpur, 137). What is new about liberalism today is its strong emphasis on self-regulation, an emphasis that has spread far beyond the economy (Ong). Wendy Brown argues: "Neoliberal rationality, while foregrounding the market, is not only or even primarily focused on the economy; it involves *extending and disseminating market values to all institutions and social action*, even as the market itself remains a distinctive player" (Brown, 39–40, as quoted in

Kennelly and Llewellyn, 899). Private corporations and market discourse have come to define democratic practices and public institutions.

The effects of neoliberalism on public education are well documented. Increased standardized testing seemingly proves that poorly run schools and incapable teachers, rather than inequitable social structures and underfunding, are to blame for underachievement (Hyslop-Margison and Sears, 14). The school choice movement sells increased competition, privatization, and accountability as the correctives for the academic failure of public schooling (Hyslop-Margison and Sears, 12–16; e.g., No Child Left Behind legislation in the United States). For universities, Sheila Slaughter and Larry Leslie (1997) label the outcome as "academic capitalism." Although their study positioned Canada as a potential resister to university privatization in comparison to Australia, the United Kingdom, and the United States, scholars have demonstrated Canada's capitulation (e.g., Metcalfe). Governments have cut back funding to universities, encouraged private source revenue, and emphasized institutional competition through increased performance measures (Torres and Schugurensky, 437–38). The University of Waterloo, where one of the authors teaches, serves as an ideal example: corporations are providing capital in exchange for influence over the direction of research (e.g., CAUT). Across Canadian universities, knowledge is now a form of production that requires global marketplace value. Despite high unemployment, universities guarantee themselves a prominent place in the expansion of capitalist accumulation by making curricular promises of career-applied learning. Students are positioned as astute consumers to whom faculty must effectively sell their wares for the sake of security of tenure and grants (Davies and Guppy; Aronowitz; Giroux and Giroux).[1]

Dewey's vision of lifelong learning, inclusive of personal and social development, is displaced by this model. Likewise, Marshall's vision of education serving to develop social citizenship is undermined. According to Rose, neoliberalism involves the "regulated choices of individualized citizens" so as to detach systems of authority from political rule, locating them instead "within the market governed by the rationalities of competition, accountability, and consumer demand" (Rose, 285, as quoted by Kennelly and Llewellyn, 899). A higher education is no longer defined in terms of the knowledge and skills of democratic citizenship, but rather in terms of the "attainment of the 'complex skills' necessary for individual success in a global economy" (Mitchell, 399, as quoted in Kennelly and Llewellyn, 899). For students and professors alike, good judgment and critical thinking are seen as dependent upon individual capacity, and as instrumental for personal capital, rather than as emerging from community and for human rights. Appreciative inquiry is subsumed by technical reasoning that requires individual students to accept means–end thinking with regard to global, economic "problems" (Brookfield, as cited by Hyslop-Margison and Sears, 18). And replicable information or fixed truths are provided for autonomous living, instead of complex, multifaceted truths being generated for civic engagement (Barber, 241). Neoliberal ideology conceptualizes the student citizen in dehumanizing fashion. Universities, Carlos Torres and Daniel Schugurensky write, are guided by "a new set of values that appeal to individual self-interest rather than collective rights" (439).

Concomitant with the rise of neoliberalism in the 1980s was the field of critical pedagogy. Critical pedagogy, building in large measure on the work of Paulo Freire (e.g., 1973; 1978), was founded on a project of liberation from the ruling classes. The aim for schools, and their teachers, was and remains to help students discover through cultural meanings and lived experience those ideological frameworks, inclusive of liberalism/neoliberalism, that encourage uncritical acceptance of exploitation. Education helps students construct counter-hegemonic identities for themselves and then act as public citizens against individual and collective oppression. Peter McLaren explains that "a critical pedagogy must assist students in developing a language of critique ... from the standpoint of understanding what is necessary for the capitalist social structure to sustain its most oppressive social relations: e.g. ... an inurement to discourses which encourage subject positions uncritical of racism, sexism, and class exploitation" (McLaren, 9, as quoted in Luke, 35). For critical pedagogues, student voice, reflexivity, and self-empowerment are primary tools of social justice learning and democratic transformation and must be developed (e.g., Giroux 1988; Apple).

Feminist pedagogy theorists have expressed skepticism about these critical perspectives.[2] Feminists share with critical pedagogues a desire to create "emancipatory" and "democratized" classrooms that challenge relations of domination. Feminist theorists express uneasiness, however, about the metanarratives of liberation promised through critical pedagogy. Carmen Luke argues:

> In the discourse of critical pedagogy, the educational politics of emancipatory self- and social empowerment, and of emancipatory rationality and citizenship education, have been articulated in epistemic relation to liberal conceptions of equality and participatory democracy. These, in turn, are located squarely in (male) individualism constitutive of the public sphere. (29)

Feminist theorists contend that critical pedagogy calls upon a universal, common "human" interest to disrupt oppression within the public world of politics. Furthermore, they maintain that critical pedagogy envisions an androgynous, singular subject who feels empowered to rationally provide answers to inequality. In other words, critical pedagogy is based on "liberal notions of disembodied, dispassionate subjects capable of equal and impartial (perspectiveless) normative reasoning" (Luke, 39; e.g., Young; Fraser). On these terms, political consciousness continues the historical privilege of the individual, bourgeois male (e.g., Pateman; Coole). Carole Pateman discusses that in liberal democratic theory, conceptions of egalitarianism and public participation are premised on the rational male to the exclusion of the personal, private, and domestic. The knowledge-bearing, rational, autonomous subject is conflated with dominant notions of masculinity. When the foundation is self-disclosure for public agency, critical pedagogy ignores the contextual relations that position women and marginalized "others" within an abstract, illegitimate place from which to speak (Walkerdine and Lucey). Critical pedagogy, at least theoretically, reinstates the individualist ethic central to liberal/neoliberal social theory, albeit with extension to the collective and for liberation.

What many feminist theorists pursue, often without explicitly naming it, is the recognition of relationality and its significance to the learning process. They call for classrooms to be spaces in which student and teacher have sustained encounters with each other and with the oppressive formations in which social relations are invested (Ellsworth 1992, 100). Influenced by post-structuralism, they seek pedagogy that treats knowledge, and thus curriculum, as provisional and uncertain, and student and teacher identities as partial and contextual. This does not mean that truth is relative and that, as such, students have nowhere from which to speak or (more importantly) are unable to engage in political struggle. Rather, classrooms are spaces for contradictory standpoints and embodied realities that provide for "transgressive boundaries, potent fusions, and dangerous possibilities" (Haraway, 154). It is the responsibility of a teacher not to assume the power to empower but rather, as Diana Fuss proposes, to take on the "responsibility to historicize, to examine each deployment of essence, each appeal to experience, each claim to identity in the complicated contextual frame in which it is made" (118). Despite such goals, which are some two decades old, feminist scholars in the field have not provided an explicit theoretical framework of relationality. Nor have they been attentive to the institutional practices of a restorative approach as feminist pedagogy. In the following two sections we will provide a theoretical account of a restorative approach rooted in relational theory. We will then envision what that framework means for a restorative approach to university teaching and learning.

An Overview of Relational Theory

Relational theory offers an important and informative framework for feminist pedagogy. It starts from the claim that the human self is fundamentally relational. Relational theorists recognize not only that human beings enter into and live in a range of relationships that influence and shape the course of their lives directly or through socialization,[3] but also that relationship and connection with others is essential to the self. The human self is constituted *in and through* relationship with others (Whitbeck, 68; Llewellyn and Howse; Llewellyn). As Jennifer Nedelsky explains it,

> we come into being in a social context that is literally constitutive of us. Some of our most essential characteristics, such as our capacity for language and the conceptual framework through which we see the world, are not made by us, but given to us (or developed in us) through our interaction with others. (1989, 8)

Catriona Mackenzie and Natalie Stoljar contend that this conception of the self proceeds from the understanding "that persons are socially embedded and that agents' identities are formed within the context of social relationships and shaped by a complex of intersecting social determinants, such as race, class, gender and ethnicity" (4).

Relational theory recognizes the intrinsically relational nature of the self without denying the meaningful existence of individuals and the notion of agency. It does, however, challenge the conception of the individual as distinct and apart from relationship and thus the view of relationship as simply the coordination of individual component parts. A relational view does not simply situate individuals in the context of relationships; it revises the very notion of the individual relationally. The choice of the expression *in* and *through* relationship to describe the constitution of the individual, rather than *by* relationship, is intended to reflect the continued presence of an agent, who is able to reflect and choose but who cannot do so alone. As Diana Tietjens Meyers describes, this view of the self stands in contrast to

> the view of the self that has dominated contemporary Anglo-American moral and political philosophy[, which] is that of homo-economicus—the free and rational chooser and actor whose desires are ranked in a coherent order and whose aim is to maximize desire, satisfaction. This conception of the self isolates the individual from personal relationships and larger social forces. (2)

This individualist picture of the self is at the core of liberalism and neo-liberalism as described above. Marilyn Friedman identifies it as abstract individualism, which "considers individual human beings as social atoms, abstracted from their social contexts, and disregards the role of social relationships and human community in constituting the very identity and nature of individual human beings" (143). Christine Koggel suggests that it "is not that liberals deny the relationality of selves, but that they do not take these aspects to be relevant to an account of what it is to be a person or to treat people with equal concern and respect" (128). In contrast to liberal/neoliberal individualistic accounts of the self, feminist relational theorists assert the importance and centrality of relationships.

Feminist relational theory is sometimes mistaken for the ethic of care, care feminism, or relational feminism. Indeed, it owes a significant debt to the insights offered by ethic-of-care theorists (Gilligan 1982; Noddings; Held). Through her influential work, Carol Gilligan initially brought attention to the significance of relationships for human selves and their moral reasoning. Relational theory shares this view of the significance and centrality of relationships; but it does not share what is often attributed to ethic-of-care scholarship—namely, the affirmation of certain models or types of relationship or activities as inherently valuable. Instead, feminist relational theory affirms the significance of the *fact* of relationship and signals the importance of attending to what is required within relationship to ensure well-being and flourishing. The focus, then, is not on particular types of relationships as might be assumed by some versions of care feminism as models of relationship (i.e., mother/child, same-sex, opposite-sex, or, in the case of universities, professor/student). Rather, the focus is on the dynamics or characteristics of relationship that need to be supported and encouraged in order to foster human flourishing. Sue Sherwin clarifies that the emphasis in feminist relational theory is not on interpersonal relationships, but rather on the full range of influential relationships, personal and public, in which we exist and are constituted as human selves (2011, 19).

For relational theory, then, relationship is not a "good" in and of itself, to be valued and promoted. Rather, relational theory contends that relationships *are* and thus attention must be paid to the nature and implications of our connections. Such attention reveals that our connectedness can be a source of pain and devastation as much as promise and hope. It reveals that for as much as we need each other to be well and flourish, we can equally be undone and profoundly harmed by one another (Llewellyn).

This relational conception of human beings grounds a feminist commitment to address injustice. Oriented relationally, justice aspires to *equality of relationship* (Llewellyn). It seeks equality in the basic elements required for peaceful and productive human relationships—namely, equality of respect, dignity, and mutual care/concern for one another (Llewellyn and Howse;

Llewellyn). The equality sought by this account is *relational* equality, which cannot be achieved by measure of treatment or result alone. Rather, as Koggel, in her foundational work on the idea, explains:

> we need people with all of their encumbrances and in all their embeddedness in social and political contexts engaged in critical thinking about difference and perspective to know what equality requires. Impartiality, in the sense of the ability to treat each person with equal concern and respect, is achieved not through the monological thinking of a solitary and isolated moral reasoner but through a communicative process of an ongoing dialogue among different points of view. (5)

These elements of just relationship are evident—and perhaps most clearly accessible—from our experiences of injustice. We can come to know what is required for equality of relationship by what is clearly missing from the unjust relationships that surround us—those of oppression, violence, neglect, racism, discrimination. Relational equality differs from the notion of equality underpinning liberal justice in that it rejects abstraction and is concerned with equality as it is realized in actual relationships among people. Achieving this equality requires attention to particular contexts, to the people involved, and to what will be required to ensure respect, care/concern, and dignity in relations between and among people.[4]

A Restorative Approach to Learning

Relational theory is the conceptual framework for a restorative approach to learning that supports feminist critiques of liberal/neoliberal effects on education. Some readers will be familiar with the term *restorative* in the context of the justice system, which has garnered significant attention over the past two decades.[5] Increasingly, restorative justice is expanding beyond the justice realm into other social and political contexts including labour, community services, child welfare, and education. As it has expanded, some have worried that it represents a possible extension of the justice system's reach. To assuage this concern, particularly in education, some purveyors of restorative models for schools began using the term "restorative practices" (Costello et al.). The phrase was intended to narrow the terrain shared with restorative justice to a particular set of practices or techniques. As a result, the exposure of educators to restorative ideas has generally been limited to a set of practices aimed at securing certain behavioural results (i.e., disciplinary measures). At present, the restorative practices movement in schools obscures the significant connection with restorative justice, which is not first and foremost about practices that are transferable, but about what such practices reflect and seek to achieve. What is important about restorative justice for schools is, we suggest, that it is a *relational approach* to justice. It is the relational theory that animates a restorative approach to justice, and this has implications for approaching other social and political institutions and processes, including university pedagogy.

Knowing this broadens our focus beyond particular practices or techniques to encompass a deeper and richer understanding of the principles of a restorative approach to learning. Understanding a restorative approach as more than a discrete set of practices has implications for how such an approach should be implemented. Perhaps most significantly, it cannot be achieved by "training" models of education. A neat package of abstract practices is being sold to educational institutions in Canada that are seeking justice-centred learning. For example, the International Institute for Restorative Practices offers discrete training models that are currently being used in some schools in Canada, the United States, Australia, and Europe.[6] Decontextualized practices have their appeal in our neoliberal context but are antithetical to restorative learning. By contrast, a restorative approach based on relational theory is grounded and contextual. The only standard answer one can offer from a restorative approach as to what is required in practice is "it depends." It depends on the relationships at stake and on the context. Thus, "it depends" does not mean we cannot know that upon which it depends. Indeed, a starting point for implementing a restorative approach is to be attuned to the principles that emerge from its relational grounding.

The principles of a restorative approach to learning include, but are not limited to, relationality, contextualism/subsidiarity, dialogism, and future-orientation. At its core, as previously explained, a restorative approach is relationship focused. Learning cannot focus only on individuals; it must also direct attention to the relationships between and among the people involved. The experiences, needs, and perspectives of all learners, including educators, matter and are central, not in contrast to or in competition with one another, but in *relation* to one another. Relationship in the university classroom is not a dualistic model of professor/student or student/student. Relationship transcends multiple one-on-one encounters in the classroom to include what Elizabeth Ellsworth refers to as the "unconscious" (1997, 63). The pedagogical situation includes "social and cultural norms and prohibitions," showing that learning does not develop linearly from ignorance to knowledge, but rather, as Ellsworth suggests, through "substitutions, displacements, dreams, and slips of the tongue" (1997, 64). A focus on relationships requires pedagogies that are flexible and responsive to the conscious and unconscious and to the knowable and unknowable in the educational context. It defies cookie-cutter or "add water and stir" pedagogical models, which cannot take account of the nature of the relationships at stake and the people involved. A professor cannot fully know, for example, how to teach about human rights before working with students to understand the different subject positions, histories, and experiences of oppression that may produce fear, ambition, and/or hope in the classroom. There are requirements in terms of cultural practices or safety concerns, or the complexity or breadth of the particular issues involved in encouraging healthy learning relationships. All of these need to be considered in crafting a restorative approach.

The concept of contextualism is equally important to a restorative approach to learning. This principle, which is well known to feminist pedagogues, may be best explained in the context of a restorative approach through the less familiar principle of subsidiarity. Found at the core of Canadian Confederation, and a key principle for the European Union, the subsidiarity principle "is intended to ensure that decisions are taken as closely as possible to the citizen and that constant checks are made as to whether action at Community level is justified in the light of the possibilities available at national, regional or local level" (European Commission, Article 5).[7] Framed relationally, this speaks to the importance of involving those with intimate knowledge of the contexts and relationships at stake if we are to have the knowledge and capacities needed to foster equality of relationship. The principle of subsidiarity points to the importance of inclusion and participation for a restorative approach to learning. Relational perspectives invite different views of who is connected and ought to be involved in restorative processes. It is not enough, however, to *include* all those with a stake in a situation. It is not enough, for example, to "give" students a voice in the design of learning objectives and assessments. Their inclusion must be meaningful to the process and its outcome. Does their inclusion actually open up new modes of thought, providing "reality checks," or the possibility of disrupting oppressive relations inside and outside the university? A restorative approach is not based on the simple ideal of participatory democracy in the classroom, as envisioned by some critical pedagogues. In other words, it is a pedagogy that seeks not to create a consensus of identities among students, but rather to find coalitions or affinities that acknowledge power relations and the differential standpoints of professors, students, administrators, and others involved in the university community (Haraway, 197). The focus is on the politics of the local, which are inextricable from "teaching of the politics of global structures and justifying narratives of oppression" (Luke, 49). Only by means of this politics of disruption through the principle of subsidiarity can university education invoke the hopes of democratic pedagogy.

Such a pedagogical stance necessitates communicative processes through which those involved can participate. This principled commitment is often expressed within restorative literature as a commitment to dialogical processes. Many feminist pedagogues argue that communicative dialogue, in its conventional sense, assumes individualized subjects coming to mutual understanding based on absolute political principles (e.g., Ellsworth 1997, 125; Luke, 38). The result is often the status quo or, in our context, the neoliberal order of our institutional lives. We agree that invoking the principle of dialogue as "mutual understanding" and "direct communication" obscures that all voices in the classroom "cannot carry equal legitimacy, safety, and power" (Ellsworth 1992, 108). Ellsworth notes, for example, when she was teaching a course on Media and Anti-Racist Pedagogies at the University of Wisconsin–Madison, the classroom was not a safe space for all students to "talk back" to oppression. She also notes that things were not said for many reasons: being too vulnerable, resentment that other oppressions were marginalized, feeling the burden as a minority to "educate" students and the professor, and concerns about distorted communication (107–8). Based on the work of Shoshana Felman, Ellsworth calls for analytic dialogue or an analysis of the paths used to arrive at interpretation (1997, 125). Such communication needs to acknowledge "that we are not interacting in class dialogue solely as individuals, but as members of larger social groups, with whom we shared common and also differing experiences of oppression, a language for naming, fighting, and surviving that oppression" (Ellsworth 1992, 109).

A restorative approach similarly calls for communication and its mechanisms to ensure a powerful encounter and participation with one another as well as with our social positions inside and outside the classroom. Restorative theorists acknowledge furthermore that non-verbal communicative modes may be used in the classroom as well. For example, silence, or the right to listen more than tell, is critical to any learning process. Students and teachers need time to deliberate on the relational spaces in which they exist, and part of this includes reading the body language and emotions of others *before* (or *if*) expressing their ideas and positions on a given subject. Dialogue in a restorative approach is connected to the principles of democratic deliberation in the sense that those principles connect the legitimacy of decision making to inclusive processes through which decision-making can take place.[8] This necessitates appreciative inquiry. Some who have sought to implement restorative practices in schools have focused on inquiry as a means of inclusion through the use of "restorative questions."[9] A restorative approach, however, requires more than a strategic deployment of inquiry as a move to make learners *feel* included. Inquiry within the classroom must be about more than mere inclusion of issues and people; it must be undertaken with a genuine appreciation for what is said and not said, and in that the "answers" might make a difference to the outcome.[10] A restorative approach reveals that processes must be comprehensive and holistic if such processes are to be able to understand and respond to the relational nature of the world. It is insufficient then, with a restorative approach, to focus narrowly on an issue without attention to its causes, contexts, and implications.

With reference particularly to this broader attention to addressing causes, contexts, and implications, a restorative approach is oriented toward the future. This approach is oriented toward pedagogy as a way of seeking understanding of what has happened or is happening in order to assess what needs to happen in the future in order to create or sustain conditions for restored relationships. It is thus concerned with more than personal empowerment; as discussed earlier, it is also aimed at a broader realignment of power for the purpose of achieving equality of relationship. It measures its success not by modifications in behaviour but by the change in social relationships that results (Llewellyn et al.). This approach shares the goals of most critical and feminist pedagogues in that it seeks to produce oppositional discourses and social movements against oppression through the educational project (e.g., Shor; Shor and Freire; Lewis). It rejects, however, the grand narrative of self-empowerment in much critical pedagogy literature (Luke and Gore, 5). It also rejects association with feminist pedagogy rooted in post-structuralism as pure deconstruction. In both instances, whether through a reaffirmation of individualism or a slippery slope to relativism, pedagogy becomes a form of "political inertia ... where educators remain frozen in the zone of 'dead'" (e.g., McLaren, 71–72, as cited by Lather, 125). A restorative approach is future-oriented because it requires collective action. Educational objectives are not limited to right relationship within the classroom. A restorative approach—one that is attentive to *all* relationships—necessitates a perspective consciousness rooted in considering what is required for participation in healthy social and political communities. Students cannot simply consider what an anti-oppressive classroom means and feels like, but must consider the very mission of the university. For example, at Dalhousie University, where one of the authors teaches, students, faculty, and administrators are considering the implications of a restorative approach for equality and access policies, responses to academic offences, and residence life on campus (e.g., Sniderman).

Standardized testing and lecturing to masses of students—increasingly the reality in university classrooms—do not lend themselves to the principles of a restorative approach. In these circumstances, the purpose of assessment is "for a student to get it, comprehend it, be 'conscious' of it; even if she didn't want to get it, didn't enjoy it, or does not intend to use it" (Ellsworth 1997, 46). The principles of a restorative approach are more apt to be reflected in processes such as critical questioning, narrative inquiry, conferencing, circles, and living curriculum. Many of these practices are quite familiar to, and have been promoted by, the critical pedagogy movement and some feminist pedagogues. But reliance on these methods as inherently liberatory, anti-oppressive, or progressive has rightfully attracted criticism from feminist pedagogy (e.g., Gore; Ellsworth, 1997). We agree with suspicions of these claims— that processes could be a panacea—and agree with the potential danger of resting so much faith in the transformative effects of a single method. Liberal/neoliberal pedagogy that focuses on the rational, individual learner to the detriment of "Others" is not challenged by virtue of, for example, opening up the syllabus to the voices of students (e.g., a living curriculum) or creating assignments that necessitate peer review (e.g., conferencing papers). Nor is democratic education or conceptions of social citizenship achieved by changing the seating arrangements in a classroom (e.g., circles) or by altering the way questions are asked (e.g., critical questioning). Indeed, this is our very point in emphasizing that relational theory leads us to adopt an approach that is not simply concerned with doing things in a different way, but with paying attention to the reason we are doing things.

It is this reason, the commitment to promote and support equality of relationship, which needs to animate pedagogy. We are compelled to play with pedagogy or do things differently, as suggested by this collection, because we are thinking differently about who we are and what we need from one another to be well and to flourish. Methods become tools or mechanisms for promoting, nurturing, fostering, and sustaining the equality of relationship required for healthy and productive learning communities. This is a restorative approach to feminist pedagogy.

Concluding Thoughts: A Restorative Approach as Feminist Pedagogy

What is the potential of understanding a restorative approach as feminist pedagogy? What are the implications for a socially just education and against liberal/neoliberal effects on universities?

The potential of this approach is vast. As Ellsworth states:

Pedagogy as a social relationship is very close in. It gets right in there— in your brain, your body, your heart, in your sense of self, of the world, of others, and of possibilities and impossibilities in all those realms ... It's a relationship whose subtleties can shape and misshape lives, passions for learning, and broader social dynamics. (1997, 6)

The limits on a restorative approach are primarily the structures that continue to encourage self-marketing, global competitive models for teaching and learning. In fact, detailed examples of the implementation of a restorative approach are hard pressed because of the neoliberal effects on learning that the approach seeks to undermine. When assigned upward of five hundred students to a class or, as is increasingly the case, to an online course, educators are challenged to move beyond didactic teaching. Furthermore, the concept of a restorative approach is relatively new in the area of education and has not yet found substantial articulation in the field of higher education—an issue we are trying to address with this chapter. For as much as neoliberalism has made such examples harder to develop, it also structures the desire and demand for neat examples that can be modelled and replicated. The problem with generating such examples of a restorative approach to learning is not a data problem; rather, it reflects the approach's resistance to the simplicity and decontextualism required for such examples. Examples cannot be conveyed for quick and easy digestion and dissemination. Instead, illuminating a restorative approach requires an appreciation not only of what is being done and why, but of the effects on relationships in the context of learning. From our teaching experiences, in which we have implicitly and explicitly taken a restorative approach, we have found that this pedagogy has the potential to create more inclusive learning communities that "enlarge the minds" of their members. Specifically, a restorative approach develops a sense of relational truth and good judgment that can challenge the "inevitability" of neoliberal effects on education.

For example, a restorative approach challenges the idea of knowledge as fixed or as an abstract commodity waiting to be mobilized. This approach recognizes and accommodates the complexity and nuance of truth understood relationally. Fixed truth claims are seductive in our universities for the ease with which they can be conveyed, examined, and commodified. As previously described, the commodification of knowledge, which is at the heart of neoliberalism, is dangerous for equity in education. Universal truths found through abstract moral reasoning imply that individualism is the path to learning and public citizenship. And the individual moral reasoner is associated with dominant masculinity. Those persons with cultural identities that "associate them with the triviality of particularized interests, with the savagery of emotions, desire, the body, and with relational rather than abstract moral reasoning abilities," are marginalized (Luke, 39; see also Gilligan 1987; Benhabib 1987). At the core of a restorative approach is shared or shareable knowledge rather than what is "already" knowable. It is an approach to knowledge that resists the market orientation of current pedagogical practices, which fail to equip students with the capacity to question the known and to participate in the creation of new ideas—essential capabilities for lifelong learning and democratic citizenship. The potential result is a greater diversity of students who see themselves *as* the curriculum and thus as part of a larger political community that struggles for justice.

Similarly, a restorative approach provides the cornerstone for successful learning—good judgment. Good judgment is often considered difficult to teach. In large measure, this is because judgment has been rendered by neoliberalism as an individual's ability to assert an unbiased position over another. Judgment is as such an individual capacity and the exercise of it is domination. Nedelsky, drawing on the work of Hannah Arendt, argues for a relational redefinition:

> What makes it possible for us to genuinely judge, to move beyond our private idiosyncrasies and preferences, is our capacity to achieve an "enlargement of mind." We do this by taking different perspectives into account. This is the path out of the blindness of our subjective private conditions. The more views we are able to take into account, the less likely we are to be locked into one perspective, whether through fear, anger or ignorance. It is the capacity for "enlargement of mind" that makes autonomous, impartial judgment possible. And Arendt makes it clear that impartiality is not some stance above the fray, but the characteristic of judgments made by taking into account the perspectives of others in the judging community. (1997, 107)

This relational approach to judgment revises liberal/neoliberal ideas of impartiality as lacking perspective. In its stead, good judgment requires impartiality grounded in the capacity to conceive of different perspectives and to judge fully interested and engaged in the matter—not from a distance. It is to judge, as the Supreme Court of Canada has affirmed (*R. v. R.D.S.* 1997 as per Justice Cory), with an open mind, not an empty mind. Students, then, are taught that to learn is to be embedded, partial, and empathetic. It is not to be autonomous in the sense of being alone; rather, it is the ability to choose in one's best interest, something that is possible only within healthy and supportive relationship (Sherwin 1998; Sherwin 2011; Mackenzie and Stoljar).

This exchange is the very definition of pedagogy. Patti Lather, building on the work of David Lusted, argues that pedagogy means addressing "the transformation of consciousness that takes place in the intersection of three agencies—the teacher, the learner and the knowledge they together produce" (Lusted, 3, as quoted by Lather, 121). We would argue that other relationships need to be added to the pedagogical act, depending on the context. Nonetheless, we agree with Lather that "pedagogy refuses to instrumentalize these relations, diminish their interactivity, or value one over another" (121). Lusted argued in his well-known article "Why Pedagogy?" that pedagogy was undertheorized and thus failed its emancipatory objective (3). In large measure, thanks to the work of critical and feminist theorists, this is no longer the case. Yet we remain far from the emancipatory ideals set out by educators like Dewey and Freire. This may be because the fundamental relationality of pedagogy remains grossly undertheorized. And it is the "interactive productivity, as opposed to the merely transmissive nature of what happens in the pedagogical act," that is at issue in the struggle against neoliberalism's grip on universities and a movement toward right relations in the world (Lather, 121).

Notes

1 Funding for university research is increasingly awarded based on demonstrated value to business and marketable "innovation." Recent examples include the changes to the Social Sciences and Humanities Research Council of Canada and funding for National Research Centres. Such policies are a commodification and capitalization of social research.

2 It is important to acknowledge that within critical and feminist pedagogy there are various strands of thought and disagreement. There are, of course, many commonalities, which are emphasized in this chapter. For more detailed information regarding the central and differential claims made by critical and feminist pedagogues, see Gore, 15–49.

3 This is similar to what Mackenzie and Stoljar refer to as the claim that selves are "causally relational." This is juxtaposed with constitutively or intrinsically relational conceptions of the self, which reflect the metaphysical claim we take to underlie relational theory (Mackenzie and Stoljar, 22).

4 For a fuller discussion of the relationship between this relational account of justice and liberal conceptions of justice, see Llewellyn.

5 See, for example, Johnstone and Van Ness, and Archibald and Llewellyn.

6 The International Institute for Restorative Practices is headquartered in the United States but licenses its model through subsidiaries in Canada (IIRP Canada), the UK and Ireland (IIRP UK and Ireland), Australia (Real Justice

Australia), Hungary (Community Service Foundation of Hungary), and Latin America (Centro de Prácticas Restaurativas para Centroamérica, El instituto Latino Americano de Prácticas Restaurativas). See http://www.iirp.edu.

7 The European Commission offers this definition of subsidiarity as delineated in Article 5 of the Treaty on European Union. See http://europa.eu/legislation_summaries/glossary/subsidiarity_en.htm.

8 Here we refer more specifically to the deliberative democratic theory of Seyla Benhabib, as a great deal of literature in the field reaffirms conceptions of individual rationality as the cornerstone of deliberation. Benhabib's theory focuses on the legitimacy brought by participation but also on the conditions required for that legitimacy, including the ability to question the topic of discussion and to challenge the way in which dialogue happens (Benhabib 1996).

9 For the most part, such questions are adapted from those originally identified by Howard Zehr in his description of the orientation of a restorative lens on crime and justice (Zehr).

10 The International Institute for Restorative Practices' training is illustrative of the failure to make this distinction between inclusion and meaningful participation and between questioning and appreciative inquiry. The reliance on the idea of "fair process" (Kim and Mauborgne) and the "social discipline window" (adapted from Glaser) in their training modules deploys the notion of relationality as a strategic "means to an end" (Costello, Wachtel, and Wachtel). Not always apparent in their materials, these ideas are deeply rooted in the liberal/neoliberal tradition. The idea of fair process advanced by Kim and Mauborgne, now of the Blue Ocean Strategy Institute (online at http://www.insead.edu/blueoceanstrategyinstitute/home/index.cfm), was introduced as a means of producing effective outcomes in business organizations. It is an implementation principle for leaders to deal with, among other things, keeping employees committed to implementing new strategies. They claim that "individuals are most likely to trust and cooperate freely with systems—whether they themselves win or lose by those systems—when fair process is observed" (Kim and Mauborgne). Here we can see fair process is being deployed for compliance rather than for the difference it might make to the outcomes of the relationships at stake. Similarly, their adaptation of the "social discipline window" rooted in Glaser's work in prisons reveals the stark contrast in the significance of relationships in their model contrasted with a restorative approach grounded in relational theory. The orientation of the model to discipline and to assisting those with authority to manage relationships in order to produce desired behavioural results reflects an individualist frame. Interestingly, its original source in Glaser's work utilized a much more contextualized and relational approach than is reflected in the adaptation of his insights to secure discipline in the IIRP model.

Works Cited

Apple, M. *Teachers and Texts*. London: Routledge & Kegan Paul, 1986.

Archibald, B., and J.J. Llewellyn. "The Challenges of Institutionalizing Comprehensive Restorative Justice: Theory and Practice in Nova Scotia." *Dalhousie Law Journal* 29 (2006): 297–343.

Arnot, M. *Reproducing Gender? Critical Essays on Educational Theory and Feminist Politics*. New York: Routledge Falmer, 2002.

Aronowitz, S. *The Last Good Job in America*. Lanham: Rowan and Littlefield, 2001.

Barber, B.R. *An Aristocracy of Everyone: The Politics of Education and the Future of America*. New York: Ballantine Books, 1992.

Benhabib, S. "The Generalized and the Concrete Other." In *Feminism as Critique*. Ed. S. Benhabib and D. Cornell. London: Polity, 1987.

———. "Toward a Deliberative Model of Democratic Legitimacy." In *Democracy and Difference: Contesting the Boundaries of the Political*. Ed. S. Benhabib. Princeton: Princeton University Press, 1996.

Boler, M. *Feeling Power: Emotions and Education*. New York: Routledge, 1999.

Brookfield, S. *The Power of Critical Theory: Liberating Adult Learning and Teaching*. San Francisco: Jossey-Bass, 2005.

Brown, W. *Edgework: Critical Essays on Knowledge and Politics*. Princeton: Princeton University Press, 2005.

CAUT (Canadian Association of University Teachers). "Wilfrid Laurier and Waterloo Universities Face Academic Censure." April 2012. http://www.caut.ca/news/2012/04/30/wilfrid-laurier-waterloo-universities-face-academic-censure

Code, L. *What Can She Know? Feminist Theory and the Construction of Knowledge*. Ithaca: Cornell University Press, 1991.

Coole, D. *Women in Political Theory: From Ancient Misogyny to Contemporary Feminism*. Hertfordshire: Harvester Wheatsheaf, 1993.

Costello, B., J. Wachtel, and T. Wachtel. *The Restorative Practices Handbook for Teachers, Disciplinarians, and Administrators*. Bethlehem, PA: International Institute for Restorative Practices, 2012.

Davies, S., and N. Guppy. "Globalization and Educational Reforms in Anglo-American Democracies." *Comparative Education Review* 41.4 (1997): 435–59. http://dx.doi.org/10.1086/447464

Dewey, J. *Experience and Education*. New York: Macmillan, 1938.

Downie, J., and J. Llewellyn. "Introduction." In *Being Relational: Reflections on Relational Theory and Health Law and Policy*. Ed. J. Downie and J. Llewellyn. Vancouver: UBC Press, 2011.

Ellsworth, E. "Why Doesn't This Feel Empowering?: Working Through the Repressive Myths of Critical Pedagogy." *Feminisms and Critical Pedagogy*. Ed. C. Luke and J. Gore. New York: Routledge, 1992.

———. *Teaching Positions: Difference, Pedagogy, and the Power of Address*. New York: Teachers College Press, 1997.

European Commission. "Treaty on European Union, Article 5." http://europa.eu/legislation_summaries/glossary/subsidiarity_en.htm

Felman, S. *Jacques Lacan and the Adventures of Insight: Psychoanalysis in Contemporary Culture.* Cambridge, MA: Harvard University Press, 1987.

Fraser, N. "What's Critical about Critical Theory?" In *Feminism as Critique.* Ed. S. Benhabib and D. Cornell. London: Polity, 1987. 31–55.

Freire, P. *Pedagogy of the Oppressed.* New York: Seabury Press, 1973.

———. *Education for Critical Consciousness.* New York: Seabury Press, 1978.

Friedman, M. "Feminist and Modern Friendship: Dislocating the Community." In *Feminism and Political Theory.* Ed. C.R. Sunstein. Chicago: University of Chicago Press, 1990.

Fuss, D. *Essentially Speaking: Feminism, Nature, and Difference.* New York: Routledge, 1989.

Gilligan, C. *In a Different Voice: Psychological Theory and Women's Development.* Cambridge, MA: Harvard University Press, 1982.

———. "Woman's Place in Man's Life Cycle." In *Feminism and Methodology.* Ed. S. Harding. Bloomington: Indiana University Press, 1987.

Giroux, H. *Schooling and the Struggle for Public Life.* Minneapolis: University of Minnesota Press, 1988.

———. *Schooling and the Struggle for Public Life: Democracy's Promise and Education's Challenge.* Boulder: Paradigm Publishers, 2005.

Giroux, H.A., and S.S. Giroux. *Take Back Higher Education: Race, Youth, and the Crisis of Democracy in the Post–Civil Rights Era.* New York: Palgrave Macmillan, 2004. http://dx.doi.org/10.1057/9781403982667

Glaser, D. *The Effectiveness of a Prison and Parole System.* Indianapolis: Bobbs-Merrill, 1964.

Gore, J. *The Struggle for Pedagogies: Critical and Feminist Discourses as Regimes of Truth.* New York: Routledge, 1993.

Haraway, D. "A Manifesto for Cyborgs: Science, Technology, and Socialist Feminism in the 1980s." In *Feminism/Postmodernism.* Ed. L. Nicholson. New York and London: Routledge, 1990. 190–233.

———. *Simians, Cyborgs, and Women: The Reinvention of Nature.* New York: Routledge, 1991.

Held, V. *Justice and Care: Essential Readings in Feminist Ethics.* Boulder: Westview Press, 1995.

hooks, bell. *Feminist Theory: From Margin to Centre.* Cambridge, MA: South End Press, 1984.

Hyslop-Margison, E.J., and A. Sears. *Neo-Liberalism, Globalization, and Human Capital Learning: Reclaiming Education for Democratic Citizenship.* New York: Springer, 2006.

Johnstone, G., and D.W. Van Ness, eds. *Handbook of Restorative Justice.* Devon: Willan, 2007.

Kennelly, J., and K.R. Llewellyn. "Educating for Active Compliance: Discursive Constructions of Active Citizenship." *Citizenship Studies* 15.5–6 (2011): 891–914.

Kim, W.C., and R. Mauborgne. "Value Innovation—the Strategic Logic of High Growth." *Harvard Business Review* 75 (1997): 103–12.

Koggel, C. *Perspectives on Equality: Constructing a Relational Theory*. Lanham: Rowman and Littlefield, 1998.

Lather, P. "Post-Critical Pedagogies: A Feminist Reading." In *Feminisms and Critical Pedagogy*. Ed. C. Luke and J. Gore. New York: Routledge, 1992.

Lewis, M. "Interrupting Patriarchy: Politics, Resistance, and Transformation in the Feminist Classroom." *Harvard Educational Review* 56.4 (1990): 467–88.

Llewellyn, J.J. "Restorative Justice: Thinking Relationally about Justice." In *Being Relational: Reflections on Relational Theory and Health Law and Policy*. Ed. J. Downie and J. Llewellyn. Vancouver: UBC Press, 2011.

Llewellyn, J.J., B.P. Archibald, C. Clairmount, and D. Crocker. "Imagining Success for a Restorative Approach to Justice: Implications for Measurement and Evaluation." *Dalhousie Law Journal* 36.2 (2013): 281–316.

Llewellyn, J.J., and R. Howse. *Restorative Justice—a Conceptual Framework*. Ottawa: Law Commission of Canada, 1998.

Locke, J. *Two Treatises of Government*. Cambridge, MA: Cambridge University Press, 1993.

Luke, C. "Feminist Politics in Radical Pedagogy." In *Feminisms and Critical Pedagogy*. Ed. C. Luke and J. Gore. New York: Routledge, 1992.

Lusted, D. "Why Pedagogy?" *Screen* 27.5 (1986): 2–16. http://dx.doi.org/10.1093/screen/27.5.2

Mackenzie, C., and N. Stoljar. "Introduction: Autonomy Revisited." In *Relational Autonomy: Feminist Perspectives on Autonomy, Agency, and the Social Self*. Ed. C. Mackenzie and N. Stoljar. Oxford: Oxford University Press, 2000.

Marshall, T.H. "Citizenship and Social Class." In *Citizenship and Social Class*. Ed. T.H. Marshall and T. Bottomore. London: Pluto Press, [1950]1992.

McLaren, P. "Language, Social Structure, and the Production of Subjectivity." *Critical Pedagogy Networker* 1.1–2 (1988): 1–10.

McLaren, P., and R. Farahmandpur. "Teaching Against Globalization and the New Imperialism: Toward a Revolutionary Pedagogy." *Journal of Teacher Education* 52.2 (2001): 136–50. http://dx.doi.org/10.1177/0022487101052002005

Metcalfe, A.S. "Revisiting Academic Capitalism in Canada: No Longer the Exception." *Journal of Higher Education* 81.4 (2010): 489–514. http://dx.doi.org/10.1353/jhe.0.0098

Mill, J.S. *On Liberty*. 1859. London: Penguin, [1859]1988.

Mitchell, K. "Educating the National Citizen in Neoliberal Times: From the Multicultural Self to the Strategic Cosmopolitan." *Transactions of the Institute of British Geographers* 28.4 (2003): 387–403. http://dx.doi.org/10.1111/j.0020-2754.2003.00100.x

Meyers, D.T. "Introduction." In *Feminists Rethink the Self*. Ed. D.T. Meyers. Boulder: Westview Press, 1997.

Nedelsky, J. "Reconceiving Autonomy: Sources, Thoughts and Possibilities." *Yale Journal of Law and Feminism* 1 (1989): 7–36.

———. "Embodied Diversity: Challenges to Law." *McGill Law Journal / Revue de Droit de McGill* 42 (1997): 91–117.

Noddings, N. "An Ethic of Caring and Its Implications for Instructional Arrangements." *American Journal of Education* 96.2 (1988): 215–30. http://dx.doi.org/10.1086/443894

Ong, A. *Neoliberalism as Exception: Mutations in Citizenship and Sovereignty.* Durham: Duke University Press, 2006. http://dx.doi.org/10.1215/9780822387879

Pateman, C. *The Sexual Contract.* Cambridge: Polity, 1988.

Porter, E. "Women and Friendships: Pedagogies of Care and Relationality." In *Feminism and Pedagogies of Everyday Life.* Ed. C. Luke. Albany: SUNY Press, 1996.

R. v. R.D.S. 1997: 3 S.C.R. 484.

Rose, N. "Government, Authority, and Expertise in Advanced Liberalism." *Economy and Society* 22.3 (1993): 283–99.

Sherwin, S. *No Longer Patient: Feminist Ethics and Health Care.* Philadelphia: Temple University Press, 1992.

Sherwin, S., ed. "A Relational Approach to Autonomy in Health Care." In *The Politics of Women's Health.* Ed. S. Sherwin. Philadelphia: Temple University Press, 1998.

———. "Relational Autonomy and Global Threats." In *Being Relational: Reflections on Relational Theory and Health Law.* Ed. J. Downie and J.J. Llewellyn. Vancouver: UBC Press, 2011.

Shor, I. *Critical Teaching and Everyday Life.* Boston: South End Press, 1980.

Shor, I., and P. Freire. *A Pedagogy for Liberation: Dialogues on Transforming Education.* Westport: Bergin and Garvey, 1987.

Slaughter, S., and L. Leslie. *Academic Capitalism: Politics, Policies, and the Entrepreneurial University.* Baltimore: Johns Hopkins University Press, 1997.

Sniderman, A.S. "Crime and the New Punishment for University Students: Dalhousie Takes Kinder Approach If Students Are Arrested." *Maclean's,* 12 December 2012. http://www2.macleans.ca/2012/12/12/crime-and-the-new-punishment/

Torres, C.A., and D. Schugurensky. "The Political Economy of Higher Education in the Era of Neoliberal Globalization: Latin America in Comparative Perspective." *Higher Education* 43.4 (2002): 429–55. http://dx.doi.org/10.1023/A:1015292413037

Tronto, J. "Creating Caring Institutions: Politics, Plurality, and Purpose." *Ethics and Social Welfare* 4.2 (2010): 158–71. http://dx.doi.org/10.1080/17496535.2010.484259

Walkerdine, V., and H. Lucey. *Democracy in the Kitchen: Regulating Mothers and Making Daughters.* London: Virago, 1989.

Whitbeck, C. "A Different Reality: Feminist Ontology." In *Women, Knowledge, and Reality: Explorations in Feminist Philosophy.* Ed. A. Garry and M. Pearsall. Boston: Unwin Hyman, 1989.

Young, I. *Justice and the Politics of Difference.* Princeton: Princeton University Press, 1990.

Zehr, H. *Changing Lenses: A New Focus for Crime and Justice.* Scottsdale: Herald Press, 1990.

CHAPTER TWO

Feminist Pedagogy in the UK University Classroom: Limitations, Challenges, and Possibilities

Jeannette Silva Flores

In this essay, I analyze how feminist academics in the United Kingdom view the notion of feminist pedagogy and its application in their teaching practices in contemporary higher education (hereafter HE). Hence, this essay includes feminist academics' critical thoughts about the possibilities, limitations, and challenges related to feminist pedagogy. This essay is based on interviews with academics who define themselves as feminist, as well as on observations I have made in different types of feminist classrooms. Analysis of feminist pedagogy in HE is pertinent to the current academic environment in the UK, especially with new developments in academia: new governance, managerialism, inspection, and accountability (Deem, Hillyard, and Reed; Lucas; Lambert, Parker and Neary); structural transformations and changes in resource allocation and conditions of service for academics (Blaxter, Tight, and Hughes; Black); and the recently implemented HE cuts.

This essay has five parts. In the first part, I present the methodology of this study, including the sampling methods, techniques and tools, and characteristics of the participants. In the second part, I describe the current academic context in the UK and how this has affected feminist pedagogy. In the third part, I discuss feminist pedagogy and its main aspects. In the fourth part, I describe the feminist classroom sessions observed over the course of this study. In the fifth and final part, I reflect on the limitations, possibilities, and challenges for feminist pedagogy and its practice in contemporary UK.

Methodology

This study is based on a feminist approach; it views academia as a gendered social reality and attempts to understand how this has affected the experiences of feminist women academics. According to Ramazanoglu and Holland, "feminist research is politically for women; feminist knowledge has some grounding in women's experiences, and in how it feels to live in unjust gendered relationships" (16; emphasis in original). I concur with Briskin (in this book) on the need to acknowledge differences among feminisms; nonetheless, the focus in this chapter is on women's experiences as feminist academics. "Experience" is a key concept in feminist theory as well as in research and the development of feminist politics (Hughes; Weedon). It has also been a crucial concept for feminist critiques of knowledge production—in particular, for feminist critiques of objectivity and neutrality; of the position of the knower, what can be known, and what valid knowledge is; and of the relationship between epistemology and ontology (Harding; Haraway; Maynard and Purvis; Stanley; Stanley and Wise; Weedon). I argue that experience is key to a better understanding of how feminist academics perceive and reflect on their own practices in the contemporary UK academy, especially with regard to feminist pedagogy.

A non-probability sampling method, the "snowball" method, was applied for the purpose of this study. The participants had to meet the following criteria:

- Identify as women
- Currently work in universities in the UK
- Define their academic practices as feminist
- Hold different positions and ranks such as assistant professor, lecturer, reader, senior lecturer, or professor
- Be active members of feminist organizations such as the Gender and Education Association (GEA), the Feminist and Women's Studies Association (FWSA), or the Feminist Academics Network

I conducted both participant and non-participant observations of different activities led by participants in this study, such as lectures, seminars, Ph.D. supervision meetings, a reading group, workshops, and conferences. With regard to classroom observations, it is worth noting that I observed only lectures and seminars led by participants with teaching responsibilities whose home institutions and students allowed me to observe their classrooms. In these cases, informed consent was obtained from both the participants and the students.[1] Each participant was observed for two to six teaching hours.

I refer to ten participants in this study; they reflect the diversity of the broader study. With each of the ten, I conducted two interviews. I applied a semi-structured interview guide that covered various aspects of their academic life; that guide included a special section on feminist pedagogy and its applicability in today's university classrooms. The interviews were conducted at different universities in England and lasted for one hour, on average. Each interview was recorded and transcribed using the verbatim system.

The participants were women currently working in UK universities; their ages varied from early thirties to early sixties. According to their own understanding of ethnicity, they identified themselves as white. With regard to sexual identity, they defined themselves as heterosexual. Most were married and had children, but not all lived with their children. Two participants were single mothers with young children. The rest either were single or had a partner.

Some participants had completed their undergraduate studies in countries outside the UK because they were foreigners, but all had been awarded a doctorate from a British university and had worked in the UK for a while. The subjects of their university education varied, but included Political Science, Literature, Sociology, History, Film Studies, Education, and Construction Management. Their current research projects covered a wide range of interests: feminist theories and methodologies, feminist history, gender representations in media, gender and technology, gender in medical education, women's labour and history, and cultural studies. The participants had held between one and four academic appointments during their academic career.

The Current Context of Higher Education in the UK

HE in the UK has faced profound changes over the past few decades. Since the 1960s, there has been a transformation from an elite university system to a mass HE sector (Tight; Blaxter, Tight, and Hughes), owing to the expansion of student enrolment in HE. The 1990s can be considered the tipping point in this transformation. According to the Higher Education Statistics Agency (HESA), student enrolment rose from 100,000 students in the 1960s to around 2.5 million in 2012–13.[2]

The current situation has been shaped by important developments dating back to the late 1970s (i.e., during the Thatcher era), when a restrictive plan of public expenditure was imposed and policies for the marketization of HE began to be implemented (Black; Furedi; Brown; Brown and Carasso). Shattock describes how universities faced significant budget cuts and how this led to a profound transformation from private to public governance. There have also been cultural changes as a consequence of the marketization of HE. These changes have led not only to new approaches to governance, managerialism, inspection, and accountability (Deem, Hillyard, and Reed; Lucas; Lambert, Parker, and Neary) but also to structural transformations and changes in resource allocation and conditions of service for academics (Blaxter, Tight, and Hughes; Black).

In 1992, the Further and Higher Education Act gave university status to all polytechnics and required them to audit their procedures for teaching and research. In the late 1990s, when the New Labour government was in power, most of the HE policies implemented during the Thatcher era were carried forward (Shattock; Jarvis) and more attention was paid to issues such as the quality of teaching and learning processes; also around this time, universities began to internalize a corporatized managerial ethos (Deem and Brehony; Deem, Hillyard, and Reed; Gopal). After a national review of HE in 1997 (the Dearing Report), tuition fees for British undergraduate students were introduced and the Quality Assurance Agency was established. Also, the government promoted "widening participation" as an important goal, and student loans were reduced (Shattock; Black). Widening participation is a specific policy aimed at providing access to HE to students from disadvantaged groups (visit http://www.hefce.ac.uk/whatwedo/wp/currentworktowidenparticipation).

Academics have faced a variety of challenges since the 1980s—for example, the consequences of increased student enrolment. Casualization, the abolition of tenure positions, more intensive work practices, a slippage in salaries relative to other professions, and the implementation of external audits have also affected academics (Black, 127). External audits and increased regulation have introduced tensions, constraints, competitiveness, individualization, pragmatism, and some inequalities within academia as well as some changes in working conditions (Black; Blaxter, Tight, and Hughes). Also, the academic culture now emphasizes research and publication, sometimes at the expense of teaching (see Coate, Barnet, and Williams; Barnett; Parker; HEA).

As a result of these widespread changes, academic careers now tend to be less linear, secure, and straightforward than in the past (Blaxter, Tight, and Hughes). Research and teaching posts are increasingly based on fixed-term contracts, with more mechanisms of assessment. Also, the current structure of HE promotes inequalities, particularly related to funding, student characteristics, and institutional status. This difference is especially sharp between traditional universities and post-1992 institutions (Black, 128).

The current Conservative–Liberal Democrat coalition government has implemented major HE cuts that are affecting teaching activities, especially in the arts, humanities, and social sciences. Research and teaching in science, engineering, technology, and maths will be the priorities in the HE budget in the coming years. This has raised questions about the future of HE. In the American context, Nussbaum argues that education needs to prepare students for meaningful lives and democratic citizenship (9) and impart skills of critical thinking and imagination (10). It follows that education, rather than focusing solely on economic growth, should be reconnected with the humanities (143). In the UK context, feminist academics are concerned about similar issues but in particular about the future of feminism and feminist practices in British universities.

Feminist Pedagogy
In the mid-1980s, Stanford Friedman pointed out that the premises of feminist pedagogy included "a non-hierarchical classroom; validation and integration of the personal; commitment to changing students' attitudes toward women, most particularly women's images of themselves and their potential; recognition that no education is value-free and that our field operates out of a feminist paradigm (as opposed to the patriarchal paradigm of most classrooms)" (204). Yet in the current UK academic context, feminist academics are still concerned about issues of gender equality and power relations in the classroom. As stated by a participant in this study:

> It is like trying to create a feeling of equality in the classroom. I don't want the power division between me and the students ... But it also means that if I notice any behaviour that I think is unacceptable, for example, male students dominating female students or international students not participating in the discussion as fully as I'd like them to, I make sure that is addressed. [Pauline]

As Culley and Portuges reflect, feminist university teachers are "aware of the ways in which the pedagogical situation may reproduce discriminatory, even destructive, attitudes and expectations about women." Those teachers "enact a conscious (and unconscious) array of behaviours and attitudes that bear in important ways on the issue of gender" (2). As Srigley and Nicholas and Baroud (in this book) point out, issues of gender are always complicated by race, ethnicity, class, age, and other facets of intersectional identity.

The UK feminist academics who participated in the study emphasized that feminist pedagogy also had to do with equality, diversity, and inclusion:

> [Feminist pedagogy] is [about] creating safe spaces for people to talk about inequalities, to reflect on their practices, to talk about themselves and

develop your different identities ... It also means commitment to feminism and feminist ideas and promoting feminist ideas about equality, diversity, and inclusion in every aspect of teaching, learning, and interpersonal relationships within the classroom. [Gloria]

In addition, they saw the classroom not only as a space for debating and reflecting on one's practices and experiences but also as a space for relating and interacting with different people. Clearly, issues related to difference and identities are at the heart of the current understanding of feminist pedagogy in the UK.

This study highlights the different ways of being a feminist academic based on the diversity of lived experiences informed by different theoretical underpinnings and situated in particular institutional contexts. Feminist academics practice feminism as they understand it (Moss and Pryke, 368; Wickramasinghe, 606), and as Leathwood argues, their viewpoints vary with their emotional and theoretical identifications with feminism (455). Thus, individual feminist academics have different approaches to feminist pedagogy and its applicability to contemporary university classrooms in England. Given these differences between individuals, the existence of different feminist pedagogies informed by different theoretical perspectives should be recognized, as Briskin argues in this book.

Webb, Allen, and Walker assert that the feminist university teacher embraces some of the following principles: "the reformation of the relationship between professor and student; empowerment; building community; respect for the diversity of personal experiences; challenging traditional views" (68). In this study, I found that feminist teachers assumed that challenging dominant discourses and issues related to discrimination and exclusion, both inside and outside classrooms, was a valid part of their teaching practice. This indicates the extent to which the feminist university teacher can open up new ways of thinking for students and themselves. This point was articulated by one participant:

To bring into the classroom multiple perspectives to decentre the dominant perspectives ... Decentring these dominant forms and opens up possibilities for other voices, for other practices and possibilities to emerge in our understanding and practices inside and outside the classroom. The commitment to multiplicity and marginalized subjects, and to other ways of knowing different from theorizing, produced from arts, social movements ... multiple forms of producing knowledge. [Elisa]

The participants in this research described the feminist university teacher as one who has particular personal politics (her feminist point of view) as well as a critical understanding of the academic world and of her various roles. Those roles included the pursuit of knowledge, "pastoral" care of students,[3] and mentorship of younger colleagues, especially women and those interested in feminist pedagogy, research, theories, and methodologies.

In other words, the participants in this study felt obligated to meet a variety of demands related their academic and intellectual pursuits (e.g., research) as well as to the institution itself (e.g., attending meetings, sitting on committees). In this context, the feminist university teacher has to shape her own experiences while dealing with various constraints. She has to contend with dominant systems of knowledge and academic production, dominant systems of thought and gendered academia, the labour market, and society as a whole. All along, she needs to be critical and reflexive about her own feminist academic practices. In particular, with regard to her role as an educator, there is an assumption that a feminist teacher who desires liberation and social change has to guide others, raise their awareness, and promote ideas, rather than simply try to indoctrinate students (see the following section).

My research indicates that feminist academics hold the view that the feminist university teacher tries to relate to students in a particular way; this is an inherent part of how they understand feminist pedagogy. It is important to highlight that they understand students not only in a holistic manner—as composed of body and mind, affects and emotions—but also as embedded, situated, and embodied subjects. The situated and contextualized subjectivity of students has been emphasized by bell hooks, who points out that "students want us to see them as whole human beings with complex lives and experiences rather than simply as seekers after compartmentalized bits of knowledge" (15). bell hooks also points out that feminist teachers should "interrogate constantly the mind/body split that was so often taken to be a given" (18), precisely because "any classroom that employs a holistic model of learning will also be a place where teachers grow, and are empowered by the process" (21). Furthermore, as summed up by one participant in this study:

> It's important to take the whole person into consideration and not have a narrow sense of the relationship between the student and the teacher ... It isn't only about the reason, the rational side of us. It draws on our whole being, our emotions, and our body. So ... instead of having a strict public/ private and reason/emotion divide, I think in teaching it's very important to cross those boundaries. [Louise]

Also, students are seen as active learners who sometimes disagree with the feminist university teacher or criticize her thoughts and make their own choices (hooks). The intersection of axes of differentiation among students is important too for the feminist teacher in the UK; her students come from different social and cultural backgrounds and have different lived experiences, so they have different points of view, learning styles, sexual orientations, age, ethnicity, and so forth. This is especially true in current times, with the rise in the international student population. Therefore, as stated by hooks, "students [have] to be seen in their particularity as individuals and interacted with according to their needs" (7). However, this approach has some limitations, especially when feminist university teachers have to teach large and diverse classrooms where closer and deeper interactions become more difficult.

Currently, feminist university teachers in the UK, as in Canada, try to encourage students to further their own ways of thinking. In doing so, they are putting into practice "education as the practice of freedom" because "everyone [can] claim knowledge as a field in which we all labor" (hooks, 14). In that sense, participants in this study are enthusiastic, as highlighted below:

> You allow people to form their own opinions, often by the end of an academic year I've had people come up to me and say, "Thank you for introducing me to things that I had never thought about before." And the way that's being done is through debate and discussion and I'm allowing them to come to their own opinions by talking with their peers ... I'm there to allow people to start thinking about things in different ways. [Mary]

Feminist university teachers in the UK also believe that they are empowering their students by giving them tools for challenging ideas, people, and everything they may find questionable. As stated by one participant:

> We are here to encourage them. And to let them know, particularly for young women, that their opinions are valued and they matter and they should be able to express them without fear. [Elaine]

Indeed, the issue of empowerment is essential to our discussion about feminist pedagogy, in particular in this edited book. Most of us contributors have reflected on or referred to that issue in our teaching and learning practices. Consequently, we also help students develop their confidence and strengthen their motivation and self-esteem. Furthermore, feminist university teachers promote student social engagement as they analyze different social problems in class and through readings, case studies, or a variety of assignments (for specific examples in this book, see Briskin, De Santis and Serafini, and Bondy). When possible, they also motivate students' interest in feminist research topics, although this can be a big challenge for feminist teachers because there is resistance to understanding feminist issues—very often, among both male *and* female undergraduate students. It is worth noting that in this study, the feminist university teacher is defined in relation to others: oriented not only in relation to students but also in relation to institutions, social structures of oppression and inequality, dominant discourses and systems, and society as a whole. This orientation to others helps make her work as a teacher meaningful and rewarding.

Feminist Classroom Sessions in the UK
In the UK, feminist academics can apply a variety of teaching and learning practices and activities within the courses they teach. However, these practices and activities are restricted by the boundaries of university classrooms and by limited contact time with students. There are also some institutional constraints, such as term time limits (usually ten weeks), class time limits (often one lecture and one seminar per week), and departmental and/or discipline content requirements, but above all the standardization of different procedures such as for student assessment. Generally, assessment consists of student essays and oral or written exams.

The participants in this study who have taught feminist issues recognized that their main taught content has been, in a broad sense, women. That content can be taught from various theoretical perspectives, using different disciplinary and/or interdisciplinary approaches, including women's history, women's television, women's lives, women's health, women's movements, and women's literature. Some of the participants specifically have taught feminist theories, epistemologies, and methodologies, whereas others have taught a particular topic from a gender perspective (e.g., human resources management from a gender perspective). A number of the participants analyzed issues of gender, equality, diversity, and inclusion within specific fields of study such as education, international relations, and politics.

A strong case can be made that, in the current academic context in the UK, university classrooms are problematic for both students and academics (Furedi, 2), and especially for feminist university teachers. In the past few decades, the ideological shift in HE has inclined toward a more instrumental view of education, which is currently understood as a provision of services, degrees, and credentials (Olssen, and Peters, 325), with students perceived as consumers (Neary and Winn; McMillan and Cheney). Students, then, have a wide range of motives for enrolling in HE institutions, and they are not necessarily interested in feminist pedagogy, theory, and critique. Other scholars have analyzed students' resistance to understanding feminism and the lack of critical reflexivity on gender issues among the student population (Hughes; Lee; Thompson and McGivern).

But some university teachers are "committed to an emancipatory pedagogy for education" and so are opposed to the marketization of higher education (Canaan, 368). Canaan notes: "It seemed to me that the changes students and I instigated resulted in more lively and engaged seminar discussions. In addition, student attendance remained relatively high throughout the course and student engagement with social theory generally was fuller than it ever had been" (377). One participant in my study referred to her current classroom as follows:

> It's trying to create ... a two-way exchange ... It's not me just standing up on a podium and lecturing them ... There's some reciprocity in the lecture ... I join a small group and then we feedback and have a larger discussion about it. I try to ... be involved ... I try to give them responsibility for their learning rather than to position myself as the expert ... My teaching just falls awry if I put myself as the expert. [Lorena]

The current feminist classroom challenges instrumental views of teaching and learning and traditional hierarchies between university teachers and students as it promotes other ways of thinking about and relating to people.

Critical observations can be analyzed to reveal how these broader patterns take shape in the classroom. The observed undergraduate feminist class analyzed here took place in the Midlands at a university that is a member of the Russell Group.[4] Students in this course were in the final year of their bachelor's degree course. The sessions held in January 2012 during spring term were observed. The observed sessions consisted of two lectures and three seminars, each lasting one hour. The two observed lectures presented a broad picture of the "three waves of feminism," and the seminars focused on a post-feminist reading list that included Rosalind Gill, Angela McRobbie, and Christine Gledhill.

Lectures and seminars were held in the same room, a space with comfortable chairs, a big screen, and an audio system, but no tables. Around sixteen students attended the lectures, and smaller groups attended the seminars. Most students were female; only six were male. During the feminist lectures, most students played a passive role. Most female students took notes by hand; only one male student made notes on his netbook. The feminist teacher led the sessions, delivered the content, gave examples, and asked the students questions to encourage discussion. She was seated in front of the students while presenting the content, stood up while showing slides and explaining contents, and sat among the students during discussions. She introduced herself as a feminist and told them why.

During the observed lectures, all the male students sat together at the back of the room, where they persistently challenged the content by chatting with one another, laughing, and disturbing the lectures; sometimes, their behaviour annoyed other students. Some of the male students did not attend the seminars. In one seminar, two male students dominated the discussion and only one female student played a more active role. These two male students were disruptive during the lectures, yet during the seminar, they were active, referred to the feminist issues presented, and posed interesting questions. These behaviours and attitudes are consistent with what Titus has described as resistance to the feminist perspective.

The other two seminars were different: most students were well-prepared for discussion and participated in the debate. In these seminars, female students were more active and showed interest in feminist theory and critique. When the feminist teacher asked the students about the usefulness of feminism for understanding the analyzed subject matter in England, most students in these seminars supported feminism as a means to understand not only these materials but also why and how current society works. Two male students, however, disagreed. In the other seminar, the male students recognized the topic as interesting but stated that they would not engage in a feminist perspective; the female students were silent.

Teaching feminist issues has been consistently reported as one of the most challenging aspects of being a feminist university teacher at the undergraduate level, as articulated by a participant in this study:

> Students used to say: "oh she's always going on about women." Which on one level is quite funny and you just have to take it with a pinch of salt. But on the other ... it's not just young men, it's young women as well who think these battles are won and that we don't really need to talk about women any more. And we certainly don't need to talk about women's inequality 'cause there isn't any. And they would argue that they're proof that there isn't any. When I talk about the pay differential, for example, and the fact that women earn less than men, they just refuse to accept that ... So the hardest and my biggest challenge is with students. [Mary]

These kinds of challenges are faced by feminist university teachers beyond the national borders of England. Indeed, Langan and Morton indicate that feminist academics in Canadian universities have experienced a "chilly climate," including different forms of violence (398). Canadian authors in this volume have also reported difficulties and expressions of resistance.

In spite of the challenges, and the fact that we cannot predict the impact of these feminist lectures, seminars, and other activities on students' minds, a feminist academic may still be seen as an agent of change (Culley, 211; Morley and Walsh, 1). Empirical evidence in this study shows that by teaching feminism, the feminist university teacher can positively influence students' lives. The observed postgraduate feminist class in this subsection took place in a university in northern England that is a member of the Russell Group. The students in this course were master's students in the Department of Education. The sessions held in March 2012 during spring term were observed. Each observed session consisted of two one-hour lectures and a two-hour seminar.

During the lectures, the feminist university teacher provided students with an overview of basic concepts and current debates in the field of Education. She presented gender inequalities through a feminist lens and discussed the scope and limitations of policy measures, which are not necessarily aimed at generating cultural change. During the lectures, she interacted with the students, trying to engage them with the topic, highlighting relevant issues on the local *and* global scale and asking them for their opinions and personal experiences. In one of these lectures, one student presented an experience-based story. The story was sad and full of emotion; it was a personal account contextualized in the intimacy of her family and in direct relation to the society she lived in. The audience seemed engaged in the story, and I was also affected. From my point of view, this was a classroom that acknowledged "a connection between ideas learned in university settings and those learned in life practices" (hooks, 15).

Afterwards, the feminist university teacher suggested that the students think about ways to present and produce knowledge and highlighted issues of stigmatization. She also suggested that students be critical of notions of neutrality and objectivity in the context of knowledge production. During the seminars, the students took part in a practical exercise in small working groups, which consisted of analyzing a research-based article they had read. They were asked to analyze the article's methodology, scope, and limitations and to give an account of what they had gained from it. After working in small groups, there was a plenary led by the feminist teacher, who was available for answering queries, and the students gave an account of their group work.

The other observed session was the final one in the course module. In that session, there were only chairs and no tables. The chairs were placed in a circle so that all were looking at one another. This session was split into three parts. In the first part, the feminist teacher asked students for their course module assessments and reminded them of the importance of answering the online university survey.[5] She also asked them what they had gained from the course and for their suggestions for improving it. Most students said they had never thought of inequality and education in this way before, and that this was the main benefit from the course.

In the second part, the chairs were rearranged so that each student could deliver an oral presentation. Each student presented a plan for his or her final essay and received feedback both from the teacher and from the other students. The teacher clarified aspects that seemed to be incorrect or misunderstood and provided students with guidance for writing their essays. Immediately after the class, she arranged extra appointments with students who needed more assistance.

In the third part, the feminist teacher organized a friendly and interesting end-of-course activity. Students experienced recognition of their different cultures and ways of living, and these differences were recognized as highly valuable. Indeed, I observed the intersection of various axes of differentiation among participants in this class (teacher, students, and myself) and how they work within the boundaries of a feminist postgraduate classroom.

I also observed an inaugural lecture in southeast England in March 2012, where one participant in my study had just been appointed a professor. This event was open to a wide audience and was attended by a variety of people, from undergraduate and postgraduate students and academics, to men and women of different ages and from different institutions and social backgrounds.

This inaugural lecture focused on the lecturer's own academic journey as a feminist and her ways of knowing. She highlighted her personal experience living and working in different countries, including her political activism. She also described the stages in her research journey, some turning points, and how these were related to her life. She emphasized how all of these things had shaped her methodological and theoretical approaches and research interests. She pointed out that "individual choices constitute the social world we make, so we can change it." She clearly identified how, for her, "the personal is political."

The audience seemed engaged and enthusiastic. Although there were neither comments nor questions afterwards, there were opportunities for social interaction between the lecturer and members of the audience during the reception that followed, where refreshments and live music were provided. It seemed to be a great celebration of feminism and feminist scholars and their triumphs in these difficult times.

Limitations, Challenges, and Possibilities for Feminist Pedagogy
In this final section, I emphasize the limitations, challenges, and possibilities for feminist pedagogy in the UK. These are difficult times for feminist pedagogy; however, the findings of this study show that there is still room for the feminist university teacher.

Stigmatization and marginalization are social processes, often painful ones. The participants in this study are aware of the negative consequences of being labelled as feminists. Feminist university teachers worry about negative reactions from their students and colleagues when they teach feminist content, apply feminist teaching practices, or study feminist issues—after all, they have already experienced being labelled, rejected, marginalized, stigmatized, or misunderstood:

> I still think in many areas if you'd positioned yourself as a feminist academic you would be probably accused of compromising your scholarly standards, your research objectivity, something like that. And maybe being seen also as old fashioned. [Ruby]

Feminist university teachers may be seen as biased, especially when course reading lists are based on feminist research or theories. This perception is particularly likely among students (men and women) who do not feel inclined toward feminism and/or are openly against it. This perception has usually been reported by students through anonymous course evaluations. The participants in this research have found it especially difficult to bring into the classroom discussions of some issues that are relevant to feminism (e.g., the masculine managerial norms) or to teach certain materials inspired by feminism (e.g., women's history):

> There is a connection between a resistance of students towards local history and a resistance towards women's history. And they tend to go hand in hand. Because a lot of young men students ... like the grand and the big and the international and the diplomatic type of histories. So they think that local history is soft. They think that women's history is soft. Social history is soft. These aren't things that they wish to study. [Mary]

Those who see the value of non-hierarchical and close relationships with students seem more concerned about the diverse demands made by students because students tend to see them as more approachable, friendly, and trustful than other members of the academic staff. Also, there is a kind of institutional expectation that they are more capable of providing caring roles, leading to a high workload. This concern is most often mentioned by those who are already in pastoral roles, such as tutoring undergraduate students or supervising research students.

Feminist university teachers are not always successful in creating learning communities, in grasping students' experiences and ways of knowing, or in relating to them. Our teaching methods fail at times (Sánchez-Casal and Macdonald, 4).

HE in the UK, especially in England and Wales, has experienced profound changes that can be linked to national and global neoliberal trends. One such change has been the marketization of HE, which has had practical consequences, as described in the introductory section of this chapter. Marketization is particularly challenging for feminism and feminist pedagogy and its practitioners, as one participant in this study pointed out:

> It's also worrying that I think in new situations it's harder to apply feminist pedagogy in a university context where universities either see themselves as world class research establishments that are terribly exclusive. Or they see themselves as completely market driven organizations that are effectively commercial training organizations that respond to customer demand. It's very difficult to keep the idea of alternative challenges open. [Ruby]

Other issues include working conditions, institutional, disciplinary, and departmental demands, and the standardization of academic procedures such as term time limits, lecture time, contact time with students, and student assessment. Regarding the latter, Motta comments: "The increasing professionalization and standardization of teaching methods and of our relationships with students create mechanisms of surveillance. Such mechanisms discipline the educator and researcher but also the student who is ranked and valued against pre-established criteria of assessment, ranking of universities and grade evaluation predetermined performance criterion" (5). Standardization, then, is seen as a menace to feminist pedagogy and its practices, as expressed by the feminist university teacher:

> There's an increasing move to standardization. And that standardization is occurring in the context of marketization and commercialization of higher education. So it's not necessarily standardization on the basis of ... any sort of real engagement with existing studies of pedagogy. [Beatrice]

Some participants in this study feared they would jeopardize their careers by declaring themselves to be feminists. Several reported that they had planned to teach optional courses based on feminist perspectives, but because these courses attracted too few students, their department cancelled them. They have also been asked to rename their courses in order to make them "more attractive" to students. As a result, they had not had courses to teach or they have been asked to teach other courses that are more economically profitable but not necessarily based on critical perspectives such as feminism.

In addition, because most of the participants do not teach or conduct research on mainstream issues, they face problems fitting into the Research Excellence Framework (REF).[6] If they do not fit into the REF, their academic recognition is under threat. Moreover, their work is seen as having no impact—specifically, no economic impact (Nussbaum, 128)—so it can be difficult for them to gain promotions as well as funding. This situation appears more pronounced for those working in post-1992 institutions.

Furthermore, the practice of teaching itself is becoming undervalued within universities, among students, and even among academics themselves. The current academic culture tends to overemphasize research and publication, with the result that teaching receives less recognition (Coate, Barnett, and Williams; Barnett; Black, 132–33; Parker; HEA).[7] In line with this, hooks writes that "teaching is seen as a duller, less valuable aspect of the academic profession" (12). Also, students tend to dismiss the study of critical ideas such as feminist ones:

> The first time I mentioned feminism to MSc students, so postgraduates, there's this row of people just groaned and put their heads in their hands. So, yeah, they weren't too receptive of it. [Pauline]

There is an ongoing risk that feminist pedagogy and its practitioners will be co-opted by other pedagogical perspectives such as social constructivist ones; even neoliberal discourse can pervade feminist pedagogy.

Meanwhile, the population of international students is growing. Feminist university teachers find it especially challenging to teach feminist issues or to apply feminist teaching and learning practices to students from Asian, African, or Middle Eastern countries because of the cultural implications of these issues for students from those parts of the world. Several of the study participants noted that these students can easily view the teaching of feminist ideas as an attempt to colonize them instead of liberating them.

Feminist classrooms in the UK—the ones I observed and the ones that have been experienced by the feminist university teachers who participated in this research—have generated myriad experiences, from student resistance to student engagement in feminist topics and/or feminist teaching practices. Nonetheless, feminist classrooms are spaces where feminist university teachers can inject alternatives into mainstream content and practices, negotiate student responses and issues of power relationships within classrooms, and challenge the current marketization of HE in England.

According to hooks in *Teaching to Transgress,* "the classroom remains the most radical space of possibility in the academy" (12). She points out that classrooms need to be understood as places where everyone can learn, where "we can think and re-think, and create new ideas, and celebrate teaching that enables transgressions and makes education the practice of freedom" (12). "Teaching as the practice of freedom" seems to be a possible scenario for feminist teachers: students and teachers can be conceived as active learners; their learning can be based on respect and care for their souls; room can always be found for mutual recognition between students and teachers. There will also be recognition of the way they live in this world (hooks, 13). One participant in this study reported:

> People in my class don't take advantage of other people's vulnerability, they accept each other, they respect each other and they are very supportive; they are creating a feminist classroom by building relationships, intellectual but also affective relationships, caring relationships among all of us. It is not competitive, it is not about trying to get power over others ... It is also an emotional space. [Elisa]

These participatory and respectful spaces can be led by feminist university teachers precisely *because* there are plenty of students interested in other ways of thinking as well as those from marginalized groups seeking identity politics, as one participant stated:

> Usually, in my optional courses there are few dominant students, few from upper middle class ... Male students don't come to my optional courses, to the compulsory they have to ... It is really interesting that year after year I get the black women, non-white men, people from working-class background ... So, how they identify with my courses and choose them is something I find fascinating. [Elisa]

The participants in this study also stated how well international students fit into the feminist classroom and how they appreciate their inclusion led by the feminist teacher:

> Well, in terms of the international students, I've always had very positive ratings from the international students. They've rated my teaching very highly

and commented how much they appreciate my efforts to ensure that international students are integrated into the classroom. [Pauline]

It was also mentioned that some overseas students seem willing to question their own experiences when they come to the feminist classroom in the UK:

> Particularly students from the Indian Subcontinent, particularly women who, they all want to do their dissertations on arranged marriages. And why arranged marriages are a bad idea or a good idea depending on their perspective. But certainly they question, a lot of them question the whole notion of arranged marriage. And that's, that's, I think from my Western feminist perspective, that's a good thing. [Elaine]

In some of the postgraduate feminist classrooms I observed, international students and women accounted for most of the student population. These students seemed to be enthusiastic about the way they were taught, especially those who were seeking a better understanding of their own cultures. One feminist university classroom in the north of England impressed me because all but one of the attendees (including the feminist teacher, the feminist observer, and the students) were non-British women. This group composition showed me that the feminist classroom in England can have a group of women from all over the world (Europe, Asia, Latin America, the Middle East) learning and critically thinking about education and inequality from a feminist perspective.

We live in a world (at least in this part of the world) in which critical thinking is not always encouraged and may be seen as problematic by students, staff, and institutions. However, the ability to think and act critically is at the heart of feminist pedagogy. That is why hooks, an advocate of feminism, emphasizes "engaged pedagogy" in the feminist classroom is "an expression of political activism" (203). Furthermore, hooks argues that the pleasure of teaching is itself "an act of resistance" (10).

Academia can be a challenging environment for feminist pedagogy. As hooks argues, "the [university] classroom, with all its limitations, remains a location of possibility" (207). This way of understanding university classrooms shows that there is room for thinking and rethinking the feminist project, deconstructing hegemonic and hierarchical structures both within and beyond academia, nurturing feminist politics, and challenging the whole notion of education as a marketplace and the way we relate to one another and to the world. Motta adds to this point: "We are opening spaces of possibility for thinking, acting and being otherwise against the logic of a commodification of social relationships and subjectivities in the neoliberal university ... We have begun therefore to politicise the crisis in higher education as a moment of possibility" (11; emphasis in the original). By opening affective and intellectual spaces of possibility we make "the other" possible and decentre the dominant discourse and regime of the neoliberal university, which is inherently a political transgression (Motta, 17). As hooks argues, we should celebrate "teaching that enables transgressions" (12). We should celebrate teaching that enables thinking of a better world. In doing so, we are enacting a small but necessary political and ethical act of resistance.

Notes

1 This study follows the ethical guidance of the University of Warwick.
2 For more details, see https://www.hesa.ac.uk/stats.
3 Most of the participants perceive pastoral and caring roles as "expected roles" for them to fulfill in their institutions. These expectations come from both their male colleagues and students (male and female). Since these perspectives are taken for granted, these expectations are seen as problematic from a feminist point of view. However, it does not mean that all of them neglect these roles. It seems to be a more complex area that probably merits deep discussion although it is not the main topic in this chapter.
4 The Russell Group represents twenty-four UK universities, which by their own definition "are committed to maintaining the very best research, an outstanding teaching and learning experience and unrivalled links with business and the public sector." For more details, visit http://www.russellgroup.ac.uk/home.
5 A key issue for the market-led university and external audit in the UK is students' evaluation surveys, for instance, the own university assessment surveys, the National Student Survey (NSS), and the International Student Barometer (ISB).
6 The Research Excellence Framework (REF) is the new system for assessing the quality of research in HE institutions in the UK. It replaces the Research Assessment Exercise (RAE) and will be completed by autumn 2014. The REF is undertaken by the four UK higher education funding bodies. For more information, visit http://www.ref.ac.uk.
7 In addition, see the Russell Group papers, Issue 4 (2012), where research rather than teaching is emphasized as a strategic policy for the group; see also Gravestock for the Canadian context.

Works Cited

Barnett, Ronald. *Beyond All Reason: Living with Ideology in the University*. Buckingham: Society for Research into Higher Education and Open University Press, 2003.

Black, Paula. "Class Matters in UK Higher Education." *Women's Studies International Forum* 28.2–3 (2005): 127–38. http://dx.doi.org/10.1016/j .wsif.2005.04.003

Blaxter, Loraine, Malcolm Tight, and Christina Hughes. "Writing on Academic Careers." *Studies in Higher Education* 23.3 (1998): 281–95. http://dx.doi.org/ 10.1080/03075079812331380256

Brown, Roger. "The March of the Market." In *The Marketisation of Higher Education and the Student as Consumer.* Ed. Mike Molesworth, Richard Scullion, and Elizabeth Nixon. Oxford and New York: Routledge, 2011. 11–24.

Brown, Roger, and Helen Carasso. *Everything for Sale? The Marketisation of UK Higher Education.* London: Society for Research into Higher Education and Routledge, 2013.

Canaan, Joyce. "Theorizing Pedagogic Practices in the Contexts of Marketization and of September 11, 2001 and Its Aftermath." *Anthropology and Education Quarterly* 33.3 (2002): 368–82. http://dx.doi.org/10.1525/ aeq.2002.33.3.368

Coate, Kelly, Ronald Barnett, and Gareth Williams. "Relationships Between Teaching and Research in Higher Education in England." *Higher Education Quarterly* 55.2 (2001): 158–74. http://dx.doi.org/10.1111/1468-2273.00180

Culley, Margo. "Anger and Authority in the Introductory Women's Studies Classroom." In *Gendered Subjects: The Dynamics of Feminist Teaching.* Ed. Margo Culley and Catherine Portuges. Boston: Routledge and Kegan Paul, 1985. 209–17.

Culley, Margo, and Catherine Portuges. "Introduction." In *Gendered Subjects: The Dynamics of Feminist Teaching.* Ed. Margo Culley and Catherine Portuges. Boston: Routledge and Kegan Paul, 1985. 1–7.

Deem, Rosemarie, and Kevin Brehony. "Management as Ideology: The Case of 'New Managerialism' in Higher Education." *Oxford Review of Education* 31.2 (2005): 217–35. http://dx.doi.org/10.1080/03054980500117827

Deem, Rosemarie, Sam Hillyard, and Michael Reed. *Knowledge, Higher Education, and the New Managerialism: The Changing Management of UK Universities.* Oxford: Oxford University Press, 2007. http://dx.doi.org/10.1093/acpr of:oso/9780199265909.001.0001

Furedi, Frank. "Introduction to the Marketisation of Higher Education and the Student as Consumer." In *The Marketisation of Higher Education and the Student as Consumer.* Ed. Mike Molesworth, Richard Scullion, and Elizabeth Nixon. Oxford and New York: Routledge, 2011. 1–8.

Gopal, Priyamvada. "How Universities Die." *South Atlantic Quarterly* 11.2 (2012): 383–91. http://dx.doi.org/10.1215/00382876-1548284

Gravestock, Pamela. "Does Teaching Matter? The Role of Teaching Evaluation in Tenure Policies at Selected Canadian Universities." Ph.D. diss., University of Toronto. 2011. https://tspace.library.utoronto.ca/bitstream/1807/31764/6/ Gravestock_Pamela_S_201111_PhD_thesis.pdf

Haraway, Donna. "Situated Knowledges: The Science Question in Feminism and the Privilege of Partial Perspective." *Feminist Studies* 14.3 (1988): 575–99. http://dx.doi.org/10.2307/3178066

Harding, Sandra. "Introduction: Is There a Feminist Method?" *Feminism and Methodology: Social Sciences Issues.* Ed. Sandra Harding. Bloomington: Indiana University Press, 1987.

———. *Whose Science? Whose Knowledge? Thinking from Women's Lives.* Ithaca: Cornell University Press, 1991.

HEA (Higher Education Academy). *Reward and Recognition of Teaching in Higher Education: A Collaborative Investigation.* Interim report. York: HEA and GENIE Centre for Excellence in Teaching and Learning, University of Leicester, 2009. https://www.heacademy.ac.uk/sites/default/files/Reward_and_Recognition_Interim_2.pdf

———. *Reward and Recognition of Teaching in Higher Education: Institutional Policies and Their Implementation.* York: Higher Education Academy and GENIE Centre for Excellence in Teaching and Learning, University of Leicester, 2009. https://www.heacademy.ac.uk/sites/default/files/Reward andRecognition_2_2.pdf

HESA (Higher Education Statistics Agency). Statistics—Students and Qualifiers at UK HE Institutions, 2014. https://www.hesa.ac.uk/stats

hooks, bell. *Teaching to Transgress: Education as a Practice of Freedom.* New York: Routledge, 1993.

Hughes, Christina. *Key Concepts in Feminist Theory and Research.* London: Sage, 2002.

———. "Pedagogies of, and for, Resistance." In *Gender, Teaching, and Research in Higher Education.* Ed. Gilliam Howie and Ashley Tauchert. London: Ashgate Press, 2002. 99–110.

Jarvis, Simon. "Phantasmal Disestablishment." *South Atlantic Quarterly* 11.2 (2012): 402–11. http://dx.doi.org/10.1215/00382876-1548302

Lambert, Catherine, Andrew Parker, and Mike Neary. "Entrepreneurialism and Critical Pedagogy: Reinventing the Higher Education Curriculum." *Teaching in Higher Education* 12.4 (2007): 525–37. http://dx.doi.org/10.1080/13562510701415672

Langan, Debra, and Mavis Morton. "Through the Eyes of Farmers' Daughters: Academics Working on Marginal Land." *Women's Studies International Forum* 32.6 (2009): 395–405. http://dx.doi.org/10.1016/j.wsif.2009.09.002

Leathwood, Carole. "Doing Difference in Different Times: Theory, Politics and Women-Only Spaces in Education." *Women's Studies International Forum* 27.5–6 (2004): 447–58. http://dx.doi.org/10.1016/j.wsif.2004.09.002

Lee, Deborah. "Students and Managers Behaving Badly: An Exploratory Analysis of the Vulnerability of Feminist Academics in Anti-Feminist, Market-Driven UK Higher Education." *Women's Studies International Forum* 28.2–3 (2005): 195–208. http://dx.doi.org/10.1016/j.wsif.2005.04.007

Lucas, Lisa. *The Research Game in Academic Life.* London: McGraw-Hill Education and Open University Press, 2006.

Maynard, Mary, and June Purvis. *Researching Women's Lives from a Feminist Perspective.* London: Taylor and Francis, 1994.

McMillan, Jill, and George Cheney. "The Student as Consumer: The Implications and Limitations of a Metaphor." *Communication Education* 45.1 (1996): 1–15. http://dx.doi.org/10.1080/03634529609379028

Morley, Louise, and Val Walsh. "Introduction." In *Feminist Academics: Creative Agents for Change.* Ed. Louise Morley and Val Walsh. Abingdon: Taylor and Francis, 1985. 1–6.

Moss, Dorothy, and Julie Pryke. "Creating Space and Time for Feminist Approaches in Higher Education." *Women's Studies International Forum* 30.5 (2007): 367–79. http://dx.doi.org/10.1016/j.wsif.2007.07.002

Motta, Sara Catherine. "Teaching Global and Social Justice as Transgressive Spaces of Possibility." *Antipode: A Radical Journal of Geography* 45.1 (2012): 80–100.

Neary, Mike, and Joss Winn. "The Student as Producer: Reinventing the Student Experience." In *The Future of Higher Education: Pedagogy, Policy, and the Student Experience.* Ed. Les Bell, Howard Stevenson, and Mike Neary. London: Continuum, 2000. 126–38.

Nussbaum, Martha. *Not for Profit: Why Democracy Needs the Humanities.* Princeton: Princeton University Press, 2010.

Olssen, Mark, and Michael A. Peters. "Neoliberalism, Higher Education, and the Knowledge Economy: From the Free Market to Knowledge Capitalism." *Journal of Education Policy* 20.3 (2005): 313–45. http://dx.doi.org/10.1080/02680930500108718

Parker, Jonathan. "Comparing Research and Teaching in University Promotion Criteria." *Higher Education Quarterly* 62.3 (2008): 237–51. http://dx.doi.org/10.1111/j.1468-2273.2008.00393.x

Ramazanoglu, Caroline, and Janet Holland. *Feminist Methodology: Challenges and Choices.* London: Sage, 2002.

Sánchez-Casal, Susan, and Amie A. Macdonald. "Feminist Reflections on the Pedagogical Relevance of Identity." In *Twenty-First-Century Feminist Classrooms: Pedagogies of Identity and Difference.* Ed. Susan Sánchez-Casal and Amie A. Macdonald. New York and London: Palgrave Macmillan, 2002. 1–28. http://dx.doi.org/10.1057/9780230107250

Shattock, Michael. "The Change from Private to Public Governance of British Higher Education: Its Consequences for Higher Education Policy Making 1980–2006." *Higher Education Quarterly* 62.3 (2008): 181–203. http://dx.doi.org/10.1111/j.1468-2273.2008.00392.x

Stanford Friedman, Susan. "Authority in the Feminist Classroom: A Contradiction in Terms." In *Gendered Subjects. The Dynamics of Feminist Teaching.* Ed. Margo Culley and Catherine Portuges. Boston: Routledge and Kegan Paul, 1985. 203–8

Stanley, Liz. "Feminist Praxis and the Academic Mode of Production: An Editorial Introduction." In *Feminist Praxis: Research, Theory, and Epistemology in Feminist Sociology.* London: Routledge, 1990. 3–19.

———. "On Academic Borders, Territories and Tribes." *Knowing Feminisms: On Academic Borders, Territories, and Tribes.* Ed. Liz Stanley. London: Sage, 1997. 1–17.

Stanley, Liz, and Sue Wise. "Method, Methodology and Epistemology in Feminist Research Processes." In *Feminist Praxis: Research, Theory, and Epistemology in Feminist Sociology.* Ed. Liz Stanley. London: Routledge, 1990. 20–60.

Thompson, Jane, and Janet McGivern. "Sexism in the Seminar: Strategies for Gender Sensitivity in Management Education." *Gender and Education* 7.3 (1995): 341–50. http://dx.doi.org/10.1080/09540259550039040

Tight, Malcolm. "Higher Education as a Field of Research." In *The Routledge-Falmer Reader in Higher Education.* Ed. Malcolm Tight. London: Routledge-Falmer, 2004. 1–14. http://dx.doi.org/10.4324/9780203464045

Titus, Jordan. "Engaging Student Resistance to Feminism: How Is This Stuff Going to Make Us Better Teachers?" *Gender and Education* 12.1 (2000): 21–37. http://dx.doi.org/10.1080/09540250020382

Webb, Lynne M., Myria W. Allen, and Kandi L. Walker. "Feminist Pedagogy: Identifying Basic Principles." *Academic Exchange Quarterly* 6.1 (2002): 67–72.

Weedon, Chris. *Feminist Practice and Poststructuralist Theory.* Oxford: Blackwell, 1987.

Wickramasinghe, Maithree. "An Epistemology of Gender—an Aspect of Being as a Way of Knowing." *Women's Studies International Forum* 29.6 (2006): 606–11. http://dx.doi.org/10.1016/j.wsif.2006.10.010

CHAPTER THREE

Activist Feminist Pedagogies: Privileging Agency in Troubled Times

Linda Briskin

"Canada's Government fundamentally believes that women are equal."
This misguided statement by then Status of Women Minister Bev Oda in
2006 was coincident with the removal of the word "equality" from government programs and policies, and a cut of more than 37 percent from the
modest $13 million budget of Status of Women Canada. This decision was
justified with reference to "fiscal responsibility and 'efficiency savings,' as
well as an argument that the unit's mission had been fulfilled ... Funding
guidelines were altered so that organizations engaged in advocacy, lobbying or research work became ineligible for support" (Bashevkin, 4; see also
Muzak).

The systematic campaign by the Conservative government to erode
equality initiatives is part of a larger pattern of troubled times for social
justice initiatives. Globalization and neoliberalism have drastically restruc-
tured the labour market and increased the long-term prospects of pre-
carious work. The intensification of radical individualism is legitimizing
attacks on equality-seeking by marginalized groups, blaming the victims of
inequality, and reshaping the practice and meaning of citizenship. Increasingly, protest has been criminalized; a particularly egregious example was
the behaviour of the police toward G20 resistance in Toronto in 2010. At
the same time, widespread corruption in governments and corporations
has increased cynicism about democratic and electoral processes.

Inside universities, the promotion of the university–corporate nexus, unprecedented attacks by some university administrations on the liberal arts and critical theorizing, the marketization of education, and the neoliberal invocation of clientalist and consumerist attitudes among students are prompting dramatic shifts in culture and climate (see also Wilson in this book). Equity-seeking around organizational practices, affirmative action, and curricular development is facing mounting challenges. Heightened surveillance, the micromanaging and policing of faculty, and the increased use of quantifiable performance measures reflect the infusion of corporate values that threaten the traditional mission of higher education.

Women's Studies programs face reduced resource allocation,[1] challenges to their credibility and legitimacy, and unparalleled attacks in the Canadian media. In a CBC radio segment on 12 January 2010, *National Post* columnist Barbara Kay claimed that Women's Studies is "hopelessly biased" and raised concerns that such programs encouraged "students to take their work out of the classroom and into their communities" and participate "in political action" (quoted in Cole, 15).[2] Many of the letters responding to Kay's attacks took on the false binary between activism and academics.[3]

> Whether we teach in women's studies or in other fields throughout the academy, feminist scholars and teachers should not have to apologize for motivating many students to work toward social change. (Gillian Creese, Director, Centre for Women's & Gender Studies, University of British Columbia)[4]

> We train engineers to build bridges and roads; medical professionals to help the sick and prevent illness; and women's studies graduates to enable our society's social, political and economic institutions to function with greater efficiency, effectiveness, equality and inclusiveness. (Hans Rollman, Doctoral Studies, Women's Studies, York University)[5]

These troubled times offer a profound rationale for privileging agency as a pedagogical approach. In previous work, I explored the privileging of agency through a focus on women's organizing as a subject of study. A curricular focus on women's organizing provides ways to work with students around the complex intersections of theory, practice, and experience; it also offers a unique vantage point to teach about the meaning of fluid identities and the importance of contextual and historical analysis (Briskin, 2004).

This essay considers a second way to privilege agency: through activist feminist pedagogies that focus on students seeking to make change in their own communities—work, peer, family, community, and university— as well as in the spaces and microspaces they inhabit such as classrooms, shopping malls, workplaces, fast food restaurants, public streets, and buses/subways. This pedagogical approach emphasizes the local and recognizes the university as community. It also redefines politics and activism and promotes intersectional awareness. Such pedagogies teach toward activism and help empower students as change agents.

The next sections clarify privileging agency as a conceptual frame; examine the limits and possibilities of Community Service Learning (CSL), with attention to concerns about service, charity, volunteerism, and "helping"; consider the contribution of Women's Studies to CSL; and explore the alternative approach of activist feminist pedagogies.

Privileging Agency

Agency refers to the ability to act to shape one's own life, to resist victimization, and to improve the communities and societies in which we live. Two threads are key to unpacking the concept. The first is the relationship between agency and structure, which recognizes structural constraints in the exercise of agency while simultaneously acknowledging that some degree of agency is always possible. This approach resonates with Marx's understanding that humans make history but not in circumstances of their own choosing (Marx).[6]

The second thread speaks to the dynamic tensions between individual and collective agency. In the most limited sense, individual agency is often linked to taking charge of one's life, having a life plan, and making effective personal choices. What might be called an *ideology of individualism,* prevalent in Western countries, focuses on individuals changing themselves as the solution to social problems. Commonsense thinking, as promoted by right-wing governments and employers, endorses the view that improving one's educational qualifications—that is, increasing one's human capital—is not only the key to self-improvement but also a solution to poverty and pay inequities.[7] Individualism, then, prizes the rights of individuals over collective or group rights, presupposes meritocracy, conflates social progress with individual advancement, and disavows the significance of social identities. But commonsense beliefs that the development of individual potential depends on individualism, and that agency begins with changing the self, are problematic. In fact, it may well be that acting to change our communities is the key to personal transformation.

The conceptualization of agency invoked in the following discussion does appreciate forms of individual agency, but it also moves beyond this frame to highlight individuals as political actors. Privileging agency emphasizes the significance, possibility, and necessity of collective agency and counters both widespread individualism and antagonism to collective action.[8]

Community Service Learning
Experiential education (EE), whose roots are in the outdoor education movement (Smith, Knapp, and Seaman), is currently the term of choice for "any structured learning experience outside the traditional classroom" (Bojar and Naples, 3). This essay will focus on one aspect of EE—what is often called Community Service Learning (CSL)—which routinely takes the form of internships, practicums, and volunteering with community organizations and services:

> [CSL] integrates service in the community with intentional learning activities ... CSL programs and courses assist students to make meaning from their community experiences, to connect experience outside of the classroom to more theoretical study, and to develop as individuals in relation to their values, their sense of social responsibility, and their leadership skills.[9]

Williams and McKenna identify the following rationale for CSL programs: "to complement conventional academic learning with applied knowledge and practical experience ... to affirm an institutional ethos around public service or to promote and nurture the idea of a caring citizenry ... [and to] stimulate consciousness about diversity and ethical issues" (136–37). Walker also points to the high ideals of CSL: "Service, combined with classroom learning, has become the supposed solution to making education more meaningful, reminding young people of their obligations as citizens, making students 'more human,' teaching the skills necessary to live in a democratic society, rebuilding an ideal of national cohesion, and saving communities in need" (26). As the Canadian CSL website demonstrates, there has been an explosion of interest in such initiatives across many academic disciplines.[10] Paradoxically, the increase in CSL initiatives in universities has been sadly coincident with unprecedented attacks by university administrations on the liberal arts and critical theorizing.

Despite the enthusiasm for CSL and its apparent benefits for students, social justice, multicultural, and feminist scholars have raised concerns about the limits of service, charity, volunteerism, and "helping." Pearson argues:

> Service is typical of agencies ... Unfortunately, it usually just perpetuates the inequality and privileges of the caregiver who, it is assumed, has superior resources and knowledge ... In most service-learning ... projects, the instructor and the students have no interest in initiating changes in social or economic power. Fitting neatly with academia's goal of creating experts

through higher levels of learning, they assume the students are merely providing services to those less fortunate than themselves. (101–2)

Service-learning projects assume that students have the wherewithal and
inclination to "help." Furthermore, the power relationship between those
helping and those being helped is rarely problematized, and neither is the
value of such "helping." "In an almost colonialist way, the student was positioned as the 'knower' who brought 'enlightenment' to the 'natives'" (Webb,
Cole, and Skeen, 240). As a result, many service-learning projects that send
students into various communities "devolve into a cultural safari into the
jungle of 'otherness.'" Undoubtedly, such othering is problematic:

> Community service is at best an exercise in observing otherness and at worst
> a missionary expedition … The community service requirement was envi-
> sioned as a way for students to obtain "real-world" experience with people
> different from themselves. Those people deemed "different" … were groups
> such as Southeast Asian refugees and Mexican American migrant laborers.
> (Forbes et al., 158, 162)

CSL projects, then, can resonate with traditional charitable and philanthropic endeavours. In their social foundations course in a teacher education program, Tinkler, hannah, Tinkler, and Miller developed a qualitative
and quantitative study to assess the degree to which service learning fosters
a charitable or a social justice perspective.

Despite the heightened sensitivity of the authors to the problems of
service-learning and charitable orientations, and their own overt commitment to social justice, Tinkler, hannah, Tinkler, and Miller found that the
service-learning project they designed for pre-service teachers who tutored
Job Corps students (the majority of whom were from low socioeconomic
backgrounds, male, and African American) still "foster[ed] paternalistic
attitudes, reinforce[d] stereotypes, or allow[ed] pre-service teachers to
blame students for their lack of achievement" (95).

Walker (30) discusses the individualization of the social problems of
hunger and homelessness, arguing that "the focus tends to be on how this
one student can make a difference without necessarily understanding or
addressing larger social conditions." The emphasis on individual efforts
contributes to the commonsense view that "misfortune can always be overcome by a bootstraps attitude or that homelessness is inevitably the result
of individual circumstances" (Bickford and Reynolds, 243). "The server's
stereotypes or preconceptions about the individual and the source of his or

her problems are maintained or strengthened, since there is no emphasis on the structural causes of problems" (Moely and Miron, 63).

Concerns about the lack of structural analysis of inequalities in CSL projects are widespread: "Students in service learning courses without prior understanding of social inequalities on a structural level may create racist conclusions about the population(s) they're serving. Students often view social problems though a culturally deterministic approach or see them as the product of individual character deficiencies" (Hondagneu-Sotelo and Raskoff, as quoted in Bubriski and Semaan, 93).

In their research on student responses to service learning, Espino and Lee distinguish among racial/class complicity, racial/class consciousness, and racial/class action. With regard to the first, they usefully differentiate among feeling pity, the reproduction of deficit models, defensiveness, and distancing. They found that the "emphasis on self-determination" made it difficult for students of colour participating in the CSL project to identify with the students they mentored (144).

Bickford and Reynolds argue forcefully that service projects should be grounded in social structural analysis:

> One of service learning's biggest limitations, admittedly, is that it induces students to ask only, "How can we help these people?" instead of the harder question, "Why are conditions this way?" ... If students are asked to observe, they will see trash on a beach; if they are asked to "do something about it," generally speaking, they may pick it up. The next step must be to ask them to figure out where the trash came from and why it is found on the beach. (241)

Without a grounding in a critique of social structures, an interrogation of the subject positions of students and the power relations between students and communities, and a commitment to social justice and social change, CSL projects can bolster stereotypes about personal responsibility, blame the victims of poverty and homelessness, reinforce deeply rooted beliefs in individualism, and parallel traditional forms of charity and philanthropy. These concerns offer reference points for examining feminist engagement with and alternatives to CSL.

Community Service Learning and Women's Studies
Despite the limits of the CSL model, many scholars and commentators have noted its parallels with aspects of feminist pedagogies (see De Santis and Serafini, in this book). However, as Webb, Cole, and Skeen point out, "feminism and service-learning come out of different social experiences (feminism starting outside the university as activism and service-learning starting in

the university as pedagogy)" (241). Trigg and Balliet remark that "women's studies ... grew out of a social movement" (98). In a 2011 report, the National Women's Studies Association (NWSA) in the United States argued that

> as higher education re-dedicates itself to its longstanding commitment to promote civic purposefulness ... Women's Studies is a valuable resource ... Women's Studies has developed a vast body of scholarship and a collection of pedagogical approaches that bridge theory and practice for students at institutions seeking to bolster their roles as a citizen educators ... The discipline of Women's Studies ... highlights social justice frameworks that distinguish engagement from "service" or "volunteering" where too often issues of power and privilege go unquestioned. (Orr, 4)

Women's Studies, then, addresses the structural roots of inequality, is sensitive to questions of power and authority, uses an intersectional analysis within which gender is positioned, and is committed to social change and social justice; thus it has the potential to address some of the limits of the CSL paradigm. Unlike the "charity model," the "social justice model" of service learning "is community-based, views the community as a partner, empowers the community while simultaneously advocating student learning, and views society through a conflict model in which social structures need transformation. This model acknowledges oppressive inequalities" (Lewis, as quoted in Bubriski and Semaan, 93). However, even as "problem-solving learning and internship programs have received renewed legitimacy within the academy," activist learning initiatives in Women's Studies are "often viewed with suspicion" (Naples, 387). The goal of social change embedded in Women's Studies initiatives is undoubtedly a key factor in the heightened suspicion.

The desire to maintain and reclaim Women's Studies as a vehicle for social change has prompted increased interest in practicums, placements, and internships. The *2000 Resource Guide for Women's Studies Practica: Students Linking Academe and Community* (Estable and Meyer with Ng), prepared for the Canadian Research Institute for the Advancement of Women (CRIAW),[11] offers the most recent overview of the Canadian situation. In the discussion of what students learned through practicums, the CRIAW guide emphasizes learning "rooted in real experience, in comparison to learning that takes place exclusively in an academic setting" (29); "raising individual consciousness and increasing awareness around many feminist concerns" (30); "developing practical life-skills and basic work experience" (32); and "discovering how to establish working relationships across class and racial differences" (31).

Undoubtedly, such practicums offer a wide range of pedagogical and political possibilities, for students and for Women's Studies programs. They help establish links to a variety of sites that impact women's lives; they also build institutional and activist relationships between the community-based women's movement and Women's Studies. At the same time, Women's Studies faces considerable barriers to adopting a CSL model: few feminist and women's organizations are available for placements; resources to run such programs are lacking; and a common cluster of resistant student values interfere.

Institutional and Resource Barriers
In recent decades, in Canada and elsewhere, cutbacks have dramatically reduced the number of women's organizations and the extent of women's mobilization. Many of the remaining organizations lack the resources to adequately train and supervise practicum students: "for a lot of feminist organizations, a lot of poorly supervised students seeking practicums would present an intolerable burden" (McKenna, 128). Furthermore, "organizations understandably are reluctant to invest in educating and training student volunteers only to have them leave after completing twenty hours of work" (Forbes et al., 165). Many organizations are so short of resources that they may find themselves using students as free clerical labour. Although such maintenance work is critical to the survival of organizations, "some students have found themselves expected to do little more than receptionist work, paperwork, or leafleting" (Tice, 131). A 2001 workshop at the Canadian Women's Studies Association[12] "addressed the market value of women's studies practica. For instance, if students are expected to provide free labour and women's groups are expected to supervise students for free, are we perpetuating the devaluing of women's work instead of giving the real market value?" (Torres, 12).

Bubriski and Semaan (2009) point out that in the United States—and this is also true in Canada—many women's organizations, especially those that work on domestic violence, face serious restrictions on advocacy as a result of their dependence on government funding: "With those funds came strings which forced battered women's agencies to focus on providing professionalized services and banned certain political activities" (95). Professionalization favours "growth, formalization, and service delivery over advocacy" (Tice, 128). Muzak comments on the impact of this shift for student placement: "because these government-mandated changes depoliticize the responsibilities and roles of many women-centred non-profit organizations in Canada, students have fewer opportunities to experience feminist activism in their service-learning placements" (97).

Many Women's Studies programs lack the resources to set up and supervise practicum programs with external organizations, and those that do may be able to accommodate only small numbers of students. Practicums, internships, and community placements require institutional resources from both university and community partners—a serious problem not only for feminist and social justice organizations but also for Women's Studies programs.

Time resources are also significant for students, many of whom lead "intensely pressured lives ... desperately trying to juggle school, job, and family responsibilities, often on very limited incomes" (Bojar, 55). In this regard, CSL-style projects may have implicit class and race biases. In fact, student populations at large urban universities in Canada are ethno-racially very diverse, and many students are the first in their families to attend university.[13]

Student Values

Although generalizations are problematic (see Nicholas and Baroud, in this book), in my experience at a large urban university in Ontario most students—including some in Women's Studies—have internalized commonsense naturalism and biologism. By extension, students assume that social structures are unchangeable and endorse the pessimistic mantra "That's just the way it is". They have few skills to envision alternatives to current social configurations; accept negative stereotypes of feminists, activists, and organizing; understand little about the macrostructural realities of inequalities; have an unquestioned and deep-rooted commitment to individualism and meritocracy; and lack experience in social movements. A recent study found "a 48-per-cent decrease in empathic concern ... between 1979 and 2009 among students ... Young adults today comprise one of the most self-concerned, competitive, confident, and individualistic cohorts in recent history."[14] In fact, "whereas more education has previously been associated with higher rates of civic participation, that trend has reversed with this generation" (Orr, 5).

Forbes and colleagues point out that "rather than ask what they can contribute to the organization, many students look for what they can personally gain from volunteering and complain that their valuable time is being wasted" (165). Indeed, the positioning of CSL projects in the university curriculum encourages an emphasis on what Himley has called the "exchange value" of service learning (in Muzak, 102): "Students benefit professionally from service-learning; they are well aware that they are volunteering (at least initially) for a grade, and they often acquire highly commodifiable skills through service-learning" (Muzak, 102). The difficulties outlined above of sending students into "other" communities are undoubt-edly exacerbated by such values.

Research also shows that students prefer service to advocacy and activ-ism. In a study of students recruited from service-learning courses in a variety of disciplines, Moely and Miron found an overall preference for the charity orientation (following Morton's paradigm), especially among women. "Students showed a strong and consistent preference for the Char-ity orientation. Students appear to be more comfortable with the activities involved in 'helping' than with activities that attempt societal change" (74; see also Bickford and Reynolds; Bojar). In a context in which equity gains are under serious attack, demoralization, disempowerment, disengage-ment, and antagonism to "politics" are often the norms among Canadian students. Clearly, this cluster of student values and attitudes affect their participation in CSL and what they learn from it.

Activist Feminist Pedagogies (AFP)

The final parts of this essay explore an alternative approach to CSL—what I call activist feminist pedagogies (AFP). It is beyond the scope of this chap-ter to explore the range and substance of feminist pedagogies themselves; suffice it to say that assuming a singular meaning to feminist pedagogy is, in my view, problematic. Just as there are multiple feminisms, so there are multiple feminist pedagogies—for example, anti-racist feminist ped-agogies, liberal feminist pedagogies, socialist feminist pedagogies, queer pedagogies, and intersectional feminist pedagogies.[15] Drawing out such distinctions opens up potentially innovative ways of thinking about fem-inist pedagogical practices. Such an approach not only positions multiple feminist pedagogies with reference to feminist political projects but also encourages a move toward empowerment and agency and away from a narrow focus on techniques.

Activist feminist pedagogies focus on students seeking to make change in their own communities—work, peer, family, community, and univer-sity—and in the spaces and microspaces they inhabit, such as classrooms, shopping malls, workplaces, fast food restaurants, public streets, and buses/subways. AFP teach analytic and conceptual tools as well as the leadership, organizational, and interventionist strategies students require to be effec-tive political actors. Such pedagogies privilege agency and "teach toward activism," to adopt a phrase used by Gilbert (135).

AFP offer a contrast to CSL practicums and internships. CSL encourages students to go into *other* communities to provide assistance and expertise, and/or to gain experience, and often relies on or prompts the volunteerist, helping, and charity mentality described above. Even the many excellent feminist CSL projects that deliberately resist the philanthropic approach often focus on helping "others" and solving their problems (see, for example, Walker; Bickford and Reynolds). A similar frustration with CSL prompted Forbes and colleagues "to offer a class on feminist activism that teaches students how to create their own feminist responses—to events, injustices, and institutional oppression—while providing experience in coalition building among our very diverse student body" (158).

Williams and McKenna note that feminist service learning "asks students to move beyond their own experiences, to see life from other points of view in order to gain a critical perspective on how they have understood their own lives" (142). In contrast, AFP encourages students to immerse themselves in their own experiences in order to see their lives from new vantage points, to reconceptualize the meaning of agency and recognize their own potential as agents. These projects help to position students as agents and activists in their own lives rather than in the lives of "others" and to heighten their belief that they can intervene in their own contexts— and, by extension, change social structural realities. Abena Busia observed: "Only when we are taken out of our own comfortable context do we learn by experience" (as quoted in Shattuck, McDaniel, and Temple). However, it is not necessary to move out of our own communities to unsettle our commonsense assumptions. AFP can penetrate and unsettle the commonsense values internalized by many students, highlight the positionalities of students, and support intersectional awareness. Finally, AFP avoids some of the organizational problems associated with CSL since these more modest activist learning projects do not depend on university or community resources, nor do they require extended time commitments from students.

The following discussion of AFP identifies three characteristics of this pedagogical approach: emphasizing the local and recognizing the university as community; redefining politics and activism; and promoting intersectional awareness. The final section of the chapter will offer some specific examples of AFP assignments.

Emphasizing the Local: University as Community

Much though not all of the discussion about CSL assumes a divide between the university and the community, and a persistent dichotomy of activism and academic. In fact, the university is comprised of multiple communities struggling for voice, as evidenced by the development of Women's Studies itself and the ongoing debates about equity and academic freedom. Universities are sites of activism and political practice confirmed by numerous strikes of unionized full-time and contract faculty, graduate students, and cafeteria and maintenance workers; student organizing around access to space, accommodation issues, tuition fees, violence and harassment on campus, and homophobia, transphobia, and racism; student organizations such as women's centres; and campus electoral politics. Universities are also arenas in which to negotiate relationships across class, race, gender, ability, and sexuality.

Bickford and Reynolds suggest that the American university offers excellent terrain for mapping "geographies of exclusion." They conclude, as I do, that

> sending students away from the university may simply reinforce the notion of the ivory tower ... or lead them to believe that, while the community may need their services, the university does not. Students do not need to leave the college or university to engage in acts of dissent. Neither do they need to take part only in large-scale, long-term projects to learn something about social change practices that we might call activism. (243–44)

The practicum goal, then, to transform "the theory of women's studies into the practice of community activism" (Estable and Meyer with Ng, 30) is possible on university and college campuses. Challenging the binary of activist and academic, community and academy *inside* the university opens up discussion of activist learning in women's studies that is not necessarily linked to practicum experiences.

Re-Defining Activism and the Realm of the Political. CSL is often criticized for its sometimes overt, often implicit individualism. Rejecting individualism needs to be differentiated from the importance of individuals acting to make change in the everyday microspaces and realities of their own lives. Bickford and Reynolds point to the fact that many of their students

> recognize activism only as participation in huge events planned by global or national organizations: marches, rallies, and the like. They imagine activists as heroes, courageous and dedicated in ways that seem impossible to emulate. They do not recognize grassroots efforts as activism, and they do not see themselves as potential actors in either local or larger arenas. They also cannot identify actions they take in their daily lives as activist, for example, their challenging a friend's use of sexist language. (238)

Students also commonly assume that politics refers only to the electoral system, and, by extension, that politicians are the quintessential and possibly only agents of change. In contrast, the women's movement and other social movements are firmly committed to the recognition that we are all political agents and that politics happens in the streets, in classrooms, in community organizations, and in social movements as well as in parliaments and leg-islatures. AFP projects help students challenge their perceptions of what constitutes politics and deconstruct those ideologies that confine the polit-ical to the electoral. Students are encouraged to interrogate the apparently neutral stance of "not being political"—which many of them claim with a certain vigour—and to recognize themselves as political actors. As a result, activism is repositioned from a marginal to a mainstream activity.

As Bickford and Seaman conclude, students "need a broader under-standing of activism to see both that they are often activists already, albeit unwittingly, and that they can decide to be activists" (238). This approach also resonates with the work of Martin, Hanson, and Fontaine, who point to "a definition of activism as everyday actions by individuals ... that often start from small, local-scale, and immediate daily personal connections ... Activism always involves creating change, but creating change can mean simply intervening when and where one happens to be" (79, 90).

Promoting Intersectional Awareness Muzak argues that "service-learning encourages students to realize their various privileges, often through ... an encounter with the Other ... and to understand more fully the diversity of women's experiences" (98). Espino and Lee are also explicit on this front: "By establishing relationships with community members through service-learning, college students can gain an understanding of themselves in relation to the Other and can confront their assumptions about communities in need, particularly those with whom they do not per-sonally identify" (137). However, relying on the Other to heighten aware-ness of privilege can be problematic, as this American example suggests:

> If predominantly white upper-middle-class students are only exposed to
> Latino men in a jail, or to African American women in a women's shelter,
> or to gay men in an AIDS hospice, or to the "poor" in the lines of a soup
> kitchen, there is a real risk of affirming pre-existing stereotypical views. Their
> encounter with "others" may well serve to reproduce rather than alter their
> personal investment in race, class, and gender privilege ... If left unchecked,
> a course with an experiential component can yield a situation where preju-
> dicial perceptions of privilege and power are fortified and enhanced by "an
> experience" made legitimate by a given academic course of study. (Williams
> and McKenna, 140)

In contrast, the goal of AFP is for students to achieve that sense of other-ness in relation to their own lives and communities; to recognize their mul-tiple positionalities with regard to class, race, gender, ability, and sexuality; and to support intersectional awareness.[16] One might say that AFP proj-ects create the conditions for doing auto-ethnography—that is, for using cross-cultural distancing not to study another community but to make deeper sense of one's own, to study one's own positionality as "other," and to invoke cognitive dissonance. In this way, such projects can help students understand who they are, how they are positioned, and the relevance of their identities.

To fully appreciate such intersectional mapping, absence is as important as presence. In all-white classrooms, the global village data that examine human ratios in relation to location, gender, race, religion, sexuality, distribution of wealth, literacy, and education can help students insert themselves into a larger context and thereby challenge commonsense Euro- and ethnocentrism.[17]

Embedding Agency and Activism in Women's Studies Assignments

Given the difficulties implementing practicum-based approaches and CSL, I have struggled with operationalizing an alternative practice of AFP in my Women's Studies courses. Here are a few examples of accessible projects that speak to the themes of university as community, redefining activism, and intersectional awareness. They are premised on students working in the microspaces and communities they inhabit. Such projects require considerably fewer faculty and community resources than formal practicums. They are also less likely to invoke the charitable and philanthropic focus of CSL.

Political Interventions   In my third-year course Women Organizing, the goal of the project "Organizing a Political Intervention" is for groups of students to organize and analyze a political intervention. This project, which offers an opportunity to bridge the activist and the academic, has been very successful—indeed, transformative for those students who choose this option over the more conventional essay assignment, which is also available to them. I describe this assignment to students as follows: "Action projects make connections between theory (what we think), practice (what we do), and reflection (how our experiences impact what we know)."[18] Furthermore,

> the goal is not just for your group to join or help organize events that are already happening. Rather your group should decide on a political intervention to organize. For example, you might decide that you wish to organize an event for International Women's Day (IWD) which targets women students in the Faculty of Science or first year women students; to organize dialogues between white and black women for Black History Month; to organize events to publicize an initiative of the women's movement and perhaps to set up a York organizing committee; to plan forums to publicize Canada's commitments to women under the United Nations Treaties. These are just some examples.

First, students develop a contract around the goal of their political intervention; second, they research the area of intervention, interview activists,
develop a plan of action, and write a report. After their intervention, they do
a class presentation and write a group evaluation. The instructions for the
assignment emphasize that students will not be marked on the success of
their intervention but on their thoughtful planning, their class presentation,
and their written reflections on it. Unlike with practicums where students
join an already existing group, in this assignment students constitute their
own group and experience both organization and organizing in microcosm.

One student who worked on a project to expose the lack of wheelchair
accessibility in the York University Fine Arts building sent me an email
commenting on her experience with the single word "Awesome!" When
the news came that, as a result of their organizing, the university administration was planning an additional elevator, another student wrote, "I am
speechless ... It is amazing what six women can do with a petition." To the
delight of the students and myself, three projects that same year—on the
Fair Share campaign to increase funding to Canadian women's groups, on
labour standards for homeworkers in Canada, and on accessibility—were
written up in the York student newspaper *Excalibur*.[19] For a more modest
version of this intervention assignment in which students were asked as
individuals or in groups to carry out and analyze an action aimed at challenging sexism, racism, and/or homophobia, see Box 3.1.

BOX 3.1
Action Project

i) Describe your planned action. Explain how and why it challenges
sexism, racism and/or homophobia.
   Include in your discussion when and where the action will
happen; what you hope the outcomes will be, that is, your goals;
if relevant, who your allies will be; who you expect will witness
your action; and what problems/resistance/opposition you antic-
ipate and how you plan to deal with them.
ii) Consider the incident/pattern of sexism, racism and homophobia
you plan to protest. Analyze why such incidents occur. To answer
this question, do not try to present a macro theory of sexism or
racism, but consider the particulars of the situation you hope to
challenge. The better your micro-analysis of the situation, the more
effective your strategic response or political intervention will be.

(Continued)

iii) Embedded in your plan of action are some assumptions about how you think change happens. In order to make them explicit, describe and critically analyze these assumptions.
iv) In general, do you see yourself as an agent of change? If yes, in what ways? If no, why not?

Over the years, I have also attempted a variety of AFP projects in my first-year lecture course Women and Society. Students can choose to engage in a protest—that is, "to challenge and/or protest an incident or pattern of sexism, racism and/or homophobia"—or to participate in an act defying gender norms—that is, "to step (ever so slightly) across gender boundaries and to act for a brief moment in a way that is contrary to others' and/or your own gender expectations in order to upset the normal functioning of gender."[20] After the first try with this assignment, what became clear was that first-year students had great difficulty imagining either gender defiance or protest; this was likely connected to their lack of vision regarding alternative ways of organizing everyday life and their inability to recognize gender as a social construct. They did not see themselves as agents, nor did they believe that the world can be changed by social intervention. In subsequent revisions to the assignment, I added a section on imagining, and student engagement improved considerably (see Box 3.2).

BOX 3.2
Imagining

You may have difficulty imagining a protest or gender defiance. You may not be used to challenging the gender order, and perhaps you have little experience of acting as an agent and trying to change the world around you.

EXERCISE
Make a list of all the arenas in which you live your life. So, for example, family, school (classrooms, student centre), work, shopping mall, buses/subway etc.

i) Gender Defiance
Identify a gender expectation that operates in each arena. Or to put it another way, consider the moments when gender norms are enforced,

regulated and policed, often unconsciously. For example, in some of your families, daughters might be expected to do considerably more housework than sons, thus reinforcing the norm that domestic labour is women's work. Once you have identified a gender expectation, ask how you might challenge it. In the housework example, you might take out the garbage (if this is your brother's responsibility) and refuse to do the dishes. Witness the responses of family members.

ii) Protest
Begin by listing a variety of examples of racism, sexism and homophobia that have been directed at you or that you have witnessed, for example, at work, in the subway, at a club. For each example, try to identify what would need to change in order to address this discrimination. What might you do to effect such a change? For a protest around housework, your goal is to change the division of labour in your family. You might raise this issue at a family dinner and indicate that you will no longer do more than your brother. Or you might make a picket sign which says "Division of Labour Unfair: On Strike For Fairness" and refuse to do your chores until there is a change. In this example, the goal of the "protest" is to change the way that housework is organized.

From "Action Assignment," Women and Society, York University (Canada)

Group Process as Activist Feminist Pedagogy
Central to the success of social change interventions is the capacity to work effectively in groups. The intervention assignment described above includes this comment about the importance of process:

> Effective interventions are built on the foundation of strong and cooperative group work. Groups include members with different perspectives, personalities, and degrees of commitment as well as different academic abilities. Learning to work with these differences is an important skill, and working effectively with groups is a critical part of any political practice. Do not underestimate the importance of group process to the success of your intervention.

Both in their class presentation and in their final group evaluation, students are asked to comment on their group process as an instance of organizing and to assess how effectively their group functioned with respect to leadership, communication and decision-making.

Structured classroom activities can also teach students directly about different approaches to working in groups. In a Simulation Exercise, student were divided into groups, each with the same task of developing an action plan to address cuts to funding for the University Women's Centre. However, one group was directed to use an organizational structure based on elected leadership, and the second group was told to work with a consensus model. The second part of the exercise asked each group to assess the efficacy of their structure and process and to share their findings with the class as a whole group. These findings provided the basis for a discussion about various approaches to collective organizing. (See Box 3.3.)

BOX 3.3
**Simulation: Learning about
Organizational Strategies**

The York Federation of Students (YFS) is threatening to cut the funding for the York Women's Centre. The YFS has received complaints (from both male and female students) that the Centre is anti-male because of a December 6 campaign, and a number of women-only events that have been held. Internally, the Women's Centre is also in crisis: a group of women of colour have argued that the Centre is unwelcoming to their concerns and that it has failed to integrate an anti-racist analysis and practice into their work. You are the co-ordinating committee for the Women's Centre. Your task is to develop a plan of action to prevent the proposed cuts, as well as to address the concerns raised by women of colour. Since you are a non-profit organization, remember that you have a limited budget, and that the members of your group are volunteers.

**ORGANIZATIONAL STRUCTURE: INSTRUCTIONS
FOR GROUP ONE**

1) Elect a leadership:
Take nominations for a chair-person, vice-chairperson, and secretary. Have an election. Decide positions by majority vote. Due to time constraints, vote by raising your hand. Once the positions have been filled, the chairperson should facilitate the discussion.

2) Responsibilities of those elected:

CHAIRPERSON: Takes a speakers' list, facilitates the discussion and plays a leadership role in trying to formulate an action plan. All decisions should be made by majority vote.

VICE-CHAIRPERSON: Supports the chair, aids in facilitating discussion, and counts votes. Monitors the time to ensure that the group is ready to report.

SECRETARY: Takes minutes of the discussion. These minutes will be used to present proposal to the class. Normally the Chair reports (using the minutes of the secretary), but your group may decide that the secretary should report.

ORGANIZATIONAL STRUCTURE: INSTRUCTIONS FOR GROUP TWO

All decisions are to be made by consensus, that is, everyone has to agree on each element of your proposal. Each member of your group should speak freely, but should also respect the rights of others to speak, that is, do not interrupt one another and ensure that all members of your group are participating. Make sure all communication is respectful. If you have a problem with the way someone is speaking, raise this as a process issue. Each member may take notes individually. No "secretary" should be elected or chosen. Present your proposal as a group. Share the responsibility of monitoring the time so you are ready to report.

PART TWO: ASSESSING ORGANIZATIONAL STRATEGIES

1 Describe your organizational structure and process to the other group. In particular, your approach to leadership, group communication and decision-making.
2 How did your group handle differences of opinion?
3 What elements of your organizational structure and process facilitated your discussion and the development of an effective proposal? Hindered your discussion and the development of an effective proposal?
4 What changes would have made your structure and process more effective?
5 What is the significance of organizational structure and process to effective political work?
6 Relate your experience in this simulation to what you learned from the articles you read.

A qualitative study of fifteen students who participated in a mandatory community organization project (e.g., conducting a rape awareness campaign, lobbying at a state legislature, community education on housing) examined the impact of community activism on the personal development of female social work students. Galambos and Hughes concluded that the project "appeared to have a clear influence on [students'] perceptions of themselves as effective leaders and team members. Many emphasized their belief that they had made a difference" (29). This study was also interested in collaborative leadership:

> When asked to describe the benefits of this project, those working collaboratively mentioned the unity of purpose, common goals, learning and working as a team, and the focus on getting things done ... In contrast, when the activities were individual efforts or coordinated by a strong somewhat autocratic leader, the participants experienced frustration with disorganization, minor details, and interpersonal conflicts. When asked about the strongest aspects of this project, the participants in these situations focused only on outcomes rather than interaction and team work. (29)

A rich literature explores women's experience in groups (Briskin, "Negotiating"). Gilbert describes an activity called *A Collective of Our Own*

> in which students begin thinking about the ways in which they have worked in groups before. They usually note that they have been either leaders or followers, and describe situations where they have taken on too much work, not enough work, or have slacked off entirely. Over and over again women say that they often feel silenced in groups and "choose to sit back and let others make the decisions" ... Students begin to see the gendered aspects of their prior group work and decide that they want to do something different ... We end this activity by taking out a long piece of paper, taping it to the blackboard, and writing out our "Ground rules for the Collective." These usually include rules such as "Respect the experiences of others," "Trust other women," "Keep secrets," "Don't silence yourself," "Share all tasks equally," "Take responsibility for your actions," and "Negotiate authority." (For more on the setting of ground rules, see Briskin, "Negotiating Power in the Classroom.") (125–26)

Advocacy and Sharing Expertise

Another project introduced students to lobbying strategy and the writing of advocacy letters. This assignment focused on the defence of provocation in Canadian law, which allows those convicted of homicide—often men who have brutally murdered their ex-wives—to claim they were provoked by their victims and thus to receive reduced sentences.[21] At the time of this intervention, the Canadian justice minister was considering changing the law. Based on our discussions, each student wrote a personal letter during class time to the prime minister, the justice minister, and/or the secretary of state for women's issues during class time. The students all eventually received replies, much to their surprise. The experience dramatically increased their sense of their own agency and voice; it also reconfigured their thinking about who is a political agent. Following this project, a group of students and myself wrote an article about it for *Jurisfemme: Newsletter of the National Association of Women and the Law.*[22]

Advocacy letters were also part of an assignment for first-year students in a large lecture course, Women and Society (200 students). As part of their involvement in the Women's Economic Equality Campaign sponsored by the Canadian Labour Congress (CLC), students wrote their Members of Parliament. They were prompted to raise their concerns about the issues highlighted in the CLC campaign and to ask questions about their MPs' views on these issues and their parties' future policy directions. Students also shared, in a structured fashion, their newly developed expertise on economic equality with friends, co-workers, or family members, thus strengthening the authority of their own voices and their experience of agency within their communities.[23]

Sharing expertise with a larger community is at the centre of an assignment described by Cattapan in which her students "undertook the project of editing, updating, and expanding ... the Wikipedia page 'Feminism in Canada.'": According to Cattapan,

> the direct relationship between author-editors and readers on which Wikipedia is based can do the sort of bridging between classroom and community that feminist teachers strive for ... Wikipedia's dedication to challenging conventional scholarship by putting the onus of knowledge formation in the hands of users advances feminist pedagogical commitments to empowering students to be the experts; taking on the dual role of learner and knower. (129–30)

In my fourth-year Feminist Thought class, activist learning was not part of the planned curriculum; rather, it was a redirection of unanticipated student anger toward enhanced agency. When I returned assignments in which students had theorized the construction of themselves as gendered, raced, and classed subjects in the university, the room was filled with an almost palpable resentment. What emerged was that students felt very angry about coming to "know" and reinterpret their university experience. When they realized how, as white women, Black women, and women of colour, their experiences, knowledge, concerns, and questions had been marginalized, many felt cheated of a full university education. The hostility of students was initially directed at me; through discussion, it was collectivized and politicized. Out of this energy, a group of students took responsibility for constructing an article based on students' essays. The publication of "Gender, Power and Silence in the Classroom" was an empowering moment for both the students and myself.[24] The article was sent to all Women's Studies programs in Canada and generated a very positive response. It is still one of the few pieces on these issues written entirely in student voices.

The range of activist learning activities with the capacity to enhance students' sense of agency is limitless. I am intrigued by the possibilities of senior Women's Studies students offering workshops on feminism or Women's Studies to students in their first year (Yaffe) and in local high schools and community centres; of students organizing actions through theatre and graffiti in order to interrupt business-as-usual in public campus spaces (Ellsworth); and of students publicizing women's movement campaigns on campus, such as my students did around the Fair Share campaign. Such activities reveal to students their unproblematized assumptions about how change occurs and invite them to reconfigure their understandings based on their own political practice.[25] Finally, AFP projects move away from the charitable and philanthropic focus of CSL and are much less likely to invoke a helping and service orientation. Some students do resent what they see as prescribed activism; but in my experience, these resentments are most salient *before* they have engaged in AFP projects.

Conclusion

AFP focus on students seeking to make change in their own communities—work, peer, family, community, and university—and in the spaces and microspaces they inhabit such as classrooms, shopping malls, workplaces, fast food restaurants, public streets, and buses/subways. This pedagogical approach emphasizes the local and recognizes the university as a community; it also redefines politics and activism and promotes intersectional awareness. Such pedagogies privilege agency and teach toward activism.

Privileging agency helps reposition activism from a marginal to a mainstream activity; it also challenges individualism, encourages students to understand and experience themselves as political actors and change agents, and contributes to empowering them to resist in their everyday lives. For those students who have internalized negative stereotypes of feminists, activists, and organizing, this is an important shift. Activist inter-ventions help students see that change is possible, both on a large scale and in everyday life; they also challenge student resignation and pessimism. In response to an assignment titled "Theory–Practice Pedagogy" developed by Kimmich, one of her students said: "What was so great was that I found hope. I learned what I could do about all of these problems" (65). Kimmich notes that many students "came to see themselves as capable subjects" and concludes that the assignment "gave many students a confidence and au-thority whose transformative potential I cannot even begin to measure" (65). In these troubled times when equity gains are under serious attack and demoralization, disempowerment, disengagement, and antagonism toward "politics" are often the norm among students, it is not insignificant that an AFP approach inspired students.

Peet and Reed did a content analysis of the self-reflection papers writ-ten for an activist project that asked students this question: "Do you see yourself as actively confronting oppression ... either now or in the future?" They examined papers from one hundred students, fifty of whom chose the action project and fifty of whom did a conventional research project:

> Of the fifty students who did not complete an action ... twenty-six said they felt empowered but expressed confusion about how to act on their new per-ceptions and feelings. Fifteen students stated that they did not see them-selves confronting injustice directly ... However, forty-three of the forty-nine students who completed the action project stated that they felt empowered and offered examples of how they intended to use their new knowledge and experience from the course. (31)

Peet and Reed conclude: "They [the students] begin to see others and them-selves not as passive recipients of historical moments but as social actors that create, shape and give meaning to the world around them" (23).[26]

Courses in Women's Studies, especially introductory ones, which often focus on women's *experience*, may inadvertently encourage a view of women as victims and, as a result, heighten students' sense of powerless-ness. As students come to understand the discrimination women face, and to recognize the extensive violence against women that pervades our soci-ety, many feel discouraged and disempowered. Their new knowledge comes to be connected to feelings of victimization rather than agency. In contrast, privileging agency helps students develop an informed resistance that may encourage them to interrupt hegemonic coherence, disorganize consent, and unsettle everyday common sense. It offers unlimited possibilities for advancing social justice, invigorating new generations of feminist activists and leaders, enhancing the relevance of academic studies, building links across social identities, and developing ties with communities both inside and outside universities.

Notes
This chapter draws on "Troubled Times, Privileging Agency, and Women's Studies in Canada." Invited paper presented at the conference on Women's Studies North and South, Bellagio Center, Italy, September, 2011.

1 An instructive case is the 2009 closing of the Women's Studies program at the University of Guelph (Ontario), despite considerable protest. The program was apparently sacrificed in the name of "fiscal belt-tightening," but "in reality it saved only 0.17 percent of the university's budget shortfall" (Bondy, 18). Professor Helen Hoy, the former coordinator of the program, commented: "Having tried to use money as the reason, and finding it was quite a limp explanation, [the administration] moved to arguments about it being outdated and at an impasse" (quoted in Bondy, 18).

2 The audio broadcast is available at http://www.cbc.ca/thecurrent/episode/2010/01/12/january-12-2010. An Editorial in the *National Post*, "Women's Studies Is Still with Us" (26 January 2010), included the following: "If the reports are to be believed, Women's Studies programs are disappearing at many Canadian universities. Forgive us for being skeptical. We would wave good-bye without shedding a tear, but we are pretty sure these angry, divisive and dubious programs are simply being renamed to make them appear less controversial. The radical feminism behind these courses has done untold damage to families, our court systems, labour laws, constitutional freedoms and even the ordinary relations between men and women. Women's Studies courses have taught that all women—or nearly all—are victims and nearly all men are victimizers. Their professors have argued, with some success, that rights should be granted not to individuals alone, but to whole classes of people, too. This has led to employment equity—hiring quotas based on one's gender or race rather than on an objective assessment of individual talents ... There would be little of rational worth left even if Women's Studies were to disappear ... While we'd like to cheer and say 'Good riddance,' we're certain such celebration would be premature."

3 http://www.wgsrf.com/uploads/9/2/7/1/9271669/cbccurrentwsletters.doc

4 http://www.wgsrf.com/uploads/9/2/7/1/9271669/cbccurrentwsletters.doc

5 http://www.wgsrf.com/uploads/9/2/7/1/9271669/cbccurrentwsletters.doc

6 "Men make their own history, but they do not make it as they please; they do not make it under self-selected circumstances, but under circumstances existing already."

7 Llewellyn and Llewellyn (in this anthology) also highlight the limits of the rational individual learner. They argue for the importance of relationality rather than individualism.

8 This approach to agency both reflects and resists dominant Western notions. But it may well be less applicable in other cultures. In intensely nationalist contexts, resisting nationalism may rest on invoking the individual. Cockburn's notion of "coerced identities" may offer a relevant framework. She examines the often-coercive and always essentializing nature of collective identities in nationalist struggles: "Many (sometimes it seems most) identity processes are coercive. We are labeled, named, known by identities that confine us, regulate us and reduce our complexity. The subtleties in our sense of self are difficult to convey in the terms available to us. We often feel misunderstood and misrepresented" (216). Similarly, in countries where the oppression of collective identities based on religion and gender is widespread, highlighting individual identities may well be central to both personal and collective agency.

9 http://www.communityservicelearning.ca/en. This website lists university CSL programs in each Canadian province. For example, at York University, experiential education (EE) is seen as "a form of engaged learning that blends theory and coursework with practical, hands on experience" and takes three distinct forms: "In-class Experiential Education: Learning through Project Consultation," "Community Based Learning (CBL): Bridging the Community with the Classroom," and "Community Service Learning (CSL): Serving the Community Through Outreach and Engagement." http://www.yorku.ca/laps/ee/index.html.

In the United States, Campus Contact is a national coalition of more than 1,100 colleges "who are committed to fulfilling the civic purposes of higher education ... [It] promotes public and community service that develops students' citizenship skills, helps campuses forge effective community partnerships, and provides resources and training for faculty seeking to integrate civic and community-based learning into the curriculum ... These institutions put into practice the ideal of civic engagement by sharing knowledge and resources with their communities, creating local development initiatives, and supporting service and service-learning efforts." Visit http://www.compact.org. The National Service-Learning Clearinghouse is a searchable database of programs and resources in the United States. Visit http://www.servicelearning.org/about-nslc.

10 Ibid.

11 http://criaw-icref.ca

12 CWSA is now called Women's and Gender Studies et Recherches Féministes (WGSRF); see http://www.wgsrf.com.

13 For example, the citizenship profile of York University's 2011 undergraduate student body included 170 different countries. Those from outside Canada

represented almost 20 percent. *York University Factbook,* visit http://www
.yorku.ca/factbook/factbook.asp?Year=2011+%2D+2012.

14 http://www.theglobeandmail.com/life/work/todays-college-kids-are-40-per
cent-less-empathetic-study-finds/article1587609. See also Konrath, O'Brien,
and Hsing.

15 My own work has focused on analyzing, theorizing and strategizing about
the negotiation of power inside classrooms, and about patterns of speaking
and silence, also infused with power. I have developed some concrete proac-
tive strategies for intervening into classroom dynamics around power and silence. For example, see Briskin, *Feminist Pedagogy,* "Using Groundrules," and
"Power in the Classroom."

16 In their article on linking second-language learners with communities that
need their language skills, Orban and Thompson (125) highlight the importance of language in relation to intersectional realities and privileges. "Language was identified as a key to appreciating the unique social locations of
each woman, building community, and encouraging resistance to oppressive
situations. Within the context of intersectional theory, it is crucial for women
to choose the language in which they want to work, [and] to avoid privileging
English over other languages."

17 See the data at http://www.miniature-earth.com.

18 This line comes from Peet and Reed (23).

19 3 March 1999.

20 The original idea for a gender violation assignment and some of this language
is from Shattuck, McDaniel, and Temple.

21 http://www.nawl.ca/en/allissues/violence-against-women/defenceprovocation

22 http://www.nawl.ca/ns/en/jf_summer03_en.html

23 The assignment can be found at http://www.yorku.ca/lbriskin/courses/1185/
assignment2.htm.

24 It was originally published in the March 1991 issue of the York student paper
Lexicon. It has since been reprinted (Fleming et al).

25 There is a rich literature on activist, interventionist, and Community Service
Learning projects in Women's Studies and other disciplines. In addition to the
many articles referenced in this piece, see Karen Dugger's collection, which
includes extensive teaching materials and course syllabi, and Nancy Naples
and Karen Bojar's anthology *Teaching Feminist Activism.* Although my experiences using activist feminist pedagogies were in Women's Studies courses, it
is my view that it is possible to adopt such an approach in all disciplines. See
for example, Webb, Cole, and Skeen (242) on creating "rhetorical spaces in
public spheres" in composition and writing classes.

26 Washington explores the impact of CSL on her Women's Studies students in
four areas; this might provide a paradigm for future research on the impact
of activist feminist pedagogies: impact on stereotypical beliefs and attitudes;
participants' abilities to connect service learning to course objectives; impact

on participants' understanding of intersectionality; and impact on social awareness and personal growth.

Works Cited

Bashevkin, Sylvia. "Regress Trumps Progress: Canadian Women, Feminism, and the Harper Government." Washington: Friedrich Ebert Foundation, 2012. http://library.fes.de/pdf-files/id/09205.pdf

Bickford, Donna, and Nedra Reynolds. "Activism and Service-Learning: Reframing Volunteerism as Acts of Dissent." *Pedagogy* 2.2 (2002): 229–52. http://dx.doi.org/10.1215/15314200-2-2-229

Bojar, Karen. "Teaching Feminist Activism: Probing Our Assumptions, Analyzing Our Choices." *Teaching Feminist Activism: Strategies from the Field*. Ed. Nancy Naples and Karen Bojar. New York: Routledge, 2002. 54–67

Bojar, Karen, and Nancy Naples. "Introduction." In *Teaching Feminist Activism: Strategies from the Field*. Ed. Nancy Naples and Karen Bojar. New York: Routledge, 2002. 1–6

Bondy, Renee. "Women's Studies: Is It Time to Change Course?" *Herizons* 24.2 (2010): 16–19.

Briskin, Linda, Louise Hamelin, Christina Hollingshead, michelle elle pettis, and Elizabeth Taylor. *Feminist Pedagogy: Teaching and Learning Liberation*. Ottawa, Feminist Perspectives Monograph Series of the Canadian Research Institute for the Advancement of Women (CRIAW), 1994. Reprinted in *Sociology of Education in Canada: Critical Perspectives in Theory, Research, and Practice,* ed. Lorna Erwin and David MacLennan. Toronto: Copp Clark Longman, 1994. 443–70.

———. "Using Groundrules to Negotiate Power in the Classroom." In *Centring on the Margins: The Evaded Curriculum*. Proceedings of the Second Biannual Canadian Association for the Study of Women and Education CASWE. Ottawa: International Institute, 1998. 25–32, 49, 80.

———. "Negotiating Power in the Classroom: The Example of Group Work." *Canadian Woman Studies / les cahiers de la femme* [Issue on Women and Education] 17.4 (1998): 23–8. Reprinted in *Canadian Woman Studies: An Introductory Reader,* ed. Nuzhat Amin et al. Toronto: Inanna Publications, 1999. 359–69.

———. "Power in the Classroom." In *Voices from the Classroom: Reflections on Teaching and Learning in Higher Education*. Ed. Janice Newton et al. Toronto: Garamond Press and Centre for Support of Teaching, York University, 2001. 25–39.

———. "Agency and Urgency: An Advocacy Project on the Defence of Provocation." *Jurisfemme: Newsletter of the National Association of Women and the Law* 22.2 (2003): 1–4. http://www.nawl.ca/en/jurisfemme/entry/agency-and-urgency-an-advocacy-project-on-the-defence-of-provocation

————. "Privileging Agency and Organizing: A New Approach to Women's Studies." In *Feminisms and Womanisms: Foundations, Theories, and Praxis of the Women's Movement.* Ed. Althea Prince and Susan Silva-Wayne. Toronto: Women's Press, 2004. 343–58.

Bubriski, Anne, and Ingrid Semaan. "Activist Learning vs. Service Learning in a Women's Studies Classroom." *Human Architecture: Journal of the Sociology of Self-Knowledge* 7.3 (2009): 91–98.

Cattapan, Alana. "Rewriting 'Feminism in Canada': Wikipedia in the Feminist Classroom." *Feminist Teacher* 22.2 (2012): 125–36. http://dx.doi.org/10.5406/femteacher.22.2.0125

Cockburn, Cynthia. *The Space Between Us: Negotiating Gender and National Identities in Conflict.* London: Zed, 1998.

Cole, Susan. "Women's Studies under Attack." *Herizons* 23.4 (2010): 15.

Dugger, Karen, ed. *Handbook on Service Learning in Women's Studies and the Disciplines.* Towson: Institute for Teaching and Research on Women, 2008.

Ellsworth, Elizabeth. "Why Doesn't This Feel Empowering? Working Through the Repressive Myths of Critical Pedagogy." In *Feminisms and Critical Pedagogy.* Ed. Carmen Luke and Jennifer Gore. New York: Routledge, 1992. 90–119.

Espino, Michelle, and Jenny Lee. "Understanding Resistance: Reflections on Race and Privilege Through Service-Learning." *Equity and Excellence in Education* 44.2 (2011): 136–52. http://dx.doi.org/10.1080/10665684.2011.558424

Estable, Alma, and Mechthild Meyer, with Roxana Ng. *A Resource Guide for Women's Studies Practica: Students Linking Academe and Community.* Ottawa: Canadian Research Institute for Advancement of Women, 2000.

Fleming, Markita, et al. "Gender, Power, and Silence in the Classroom: Our Experiences Speak for Themselves." In *Voices from the Classroom: Reflections on Teaching-Learning in Higher Education.* Ed. Janice Newton et al. Toronto: Garamond Press and Centre for Support of Teaching, 2001. 7–17.

Forbes, Kathryn, Linda Garber, Loretta Kensinger, and Janet Trapp Slagter. "Punishing Pedagogy: The Failings of Forced Volunteerism." *Women's Studies Quarterly* 3–4 (1999): 158–68.

Galambos, Colleen, and Sherri Hughes. "Using Political and Community Activism to Develop Leadership Skills in Women." *Race, Gender, and Class* 7.4 (2001): 18–35.

Gilbert, Melissa Kesler. "Educated in Agency: Student Reflection on the Feminist Service-Learning Classroom." In *The Practice of Change: Concepts and Models for Service-Learning in Women's Studies.* Ed. Barbara J. Balliet, Kerissa Heffernan, and Edward Zlotkowski. Washington: American Association for Higher Education, 2000. 123–38.

Kimmich, Allison. "'I Found Hope,' or Reflections on Theory/Practice Pedagogy." *Women's Studies Quarterly* 3–4 (1999): 59–69.

Konrath, Sara, Edward O'Brien, and Courtney Hsing. "Changes in Dispositional Empathy in American College Students over Time: A Meta-Analysis."

Personality and Social Psychology Review 15.2 (2011): 180–98. http://dx.doi
.org/10.1177/1088868310377395

Martin, Deborah G., Susan Hanson, and Danielle Fontaine. "What Counts as
Activism?: The Role of Individuals in Creating Change." *Women's Studies
Quarterly* 35.3–4 (2007): 78–94.

Marx, Karl. "The Eighteenth Brumaire of Louis Bonaparte." 1852. http://www
.marxists.org/archive/marx/works/1852/18th-brumaire/ch01.htm

McKenna, Katherine. "Violence Against Women: Students Working in Community Agencies." *Atlantis* 22 (1997): 127–30.

Moely, Barbara E., and Devi Miron. "College Students' Preferred Approaches
to Community Service." In *Improving Service-Learning Practice: Research on
Models to Enhance Impacts.* Ed. Jane Callahan, Susan Root, and Shelley Billig.
Charlotte: Information Age Publishing, 2005. 61–78.

Muzak, Joanne. "Women's Studies, Community Service-Learning, and the
Dynamics of Privilege." *Atlantis* 35.2 (2011): 96–106.

Naples, Nancy. "Negotiating the Politics of Experiential Learning in Women's
Studies: Lessons from the Community Action Project." *Women's Studies on
Its Own: A Next Wave Reader in Institutional Change.* Ed. Robyn Wiegman.
Durham: Duke University Press, 2002. 383–415. http://dx.doi.org/10.1215/
9780822384311-022

Naples, Nancy, and Karen Bojar, eds. *Teaching Feminist Activism: Strategies from
the Field.* New York: Routledge, 2002.

Orban, Clara E., and Martha E. Thompson. "Building Bridges against Violence:
Service-Learning for Second Language Students." *Feminist Teacher* 17.2 (2007):
122–35.

Orr, Catherine M. *Women's Studies as Civic Engagement: Research and Recom-
mendations: A Teagle Foundation White Paper.* Prepared on behalf of the
Teagle Working Group on Women's Studies and Civic Engagement and
the National Women's Studies Association, 2011. http://082511c.member
-shipsoftware.org/files/WomensStudiesasCivicEngagement2011Revised_
Finalpdf-1.pdf

Pearson, Nelda K. "Social Action as Collaborative Transformation." *Women's
Studies Quarterly* 3–4 (1999): 98–113.

Peet, Melissa, and Beth Glover Reed. "Activism in an Introductory Women's
Studies Course: Connected Learning Through the Implementation of
Praxis." *Women's Studies Quarterly* 3–4 (1999): 21–35.

Shattuck, Sandra D., Judith McDaniel, and Judy Nolte Temple. "The Outra-
geous Act as Gender Busting: An Experiential Challenge to Gender Roles."
In *Teaching Introduction to Women's Studies: Expectations and Strategies.* Ed.
Barbara Scott Winkler and Carolyn DiPalma. Westport: Bergin and Garvey,
1999. 201–11.

Smith, Thomas E., Clifford E. Knapp, Jayson Seaman, et al. "Experiential Education and Learning by Experience." In *Sourcebook of Experiential Education:*

Key Thinkers and Their Contributions. Ed. Thomas E. Smith and Clifford E. Knapp. New York: Routledge, 2011. 1–11.

Tice, Karen. "Feminist Theory/Practice Pedagogies in a Shifting Political Climate." *Feminist Teacher* 14.2 (2002): 123–33.

Tinkler, Barri, c. lynne hannah, Alan Tinkler, et al. "Analyzing a Service-Learning Experience Using a Social Justice Lens." *Teaching Education* 25.1 (2014): 82–98. http://dx.doi.org/10.1080/10476210.2012.744742.

Torres, Sara. "Reflections About the CWSA Annual Meeting." *CRIAW Newsletter* (Summer 2001): 12.

Trigg, Mary, and Barbara J. Balliet. "Learning Across Boundaries: Women's Studies, Praxis, and Community Service." *The Practice of Change: Concepts and Models for Service-Learning in Women's Studies.* Ed. Barbara J. Balliet, Kerissa Heffernan, and Edward Zlotkowski. Washington: American Association for Higher Education, 2000. 93–108.

Walker, Tobi. "A Feminist Challenge to Community Service: A Call to Politicize Service-Learning." In *The Practice of Change: Concepts and Models for Service-Learning in Women's Studies.* Ed. Barbara J. Balliet, Kerissa Heffernan, and Edward Zlotkowski. Washington: American Association for Higher Education, 2000. 34–47.

Washington, Patricia A. "The Individual and Collective Rewards of Community-Based Service Learning." In *Teaching Feminist Activism: Strategies from the Field.* Ed. Nancy Naples and Karen Bojar. New York: Routledge, 2002. 166–82.

Webb, Patricia, Kirsti Cole, and Thomas Skeen. "Feminist Social Projects: Building Bridges Between Communities and Universities." *College English* 69.3 (2007): 238–59.

Williams, Tamara, and Erin McKenna. "Negotiating Subject-Positions in a Service-Learning Context." In *Twenty-First-Century Feminist Classrooms: Pedagogies of Identity and Difference.* Ed. Amie A. Macdonald and Susan Sanchez-Casal. New York: Palgrave Macmillan, 2002. 135–54.

Yaffe, Debby. "A Good Idea Takes Form: Practising Feminism for Fun and Profit." *Atlantis* 22 (1997): 131–34.

CHAPTER FOUR

Classroom to Community: Reflections on Experiential Learning and Socially Just Citizenship

Carm De Santis and Toni Serafini

This essay offers our interpretation of, and commitment to, socially just, anti-oppressive, feminist-informed pedagogies, and describes our attempts to realize these values as predominantly "white" women teaching in an undergraduate university. We focus our discussion on how feminist and anti-oppressive practices serve as lenses through which we facilitate (and have team-taught) an undergraduate service-learning Practicum-Capstone course in the Department of Sexuality, Marriage, and Family Studies (SMF) at a small, liberal arts, Catholic, undergraduate university. We will illustrate how several themes congruent with post-structural feminist pedagogies play out in this Practicum-Capstone course. On one level, we are a work-in-progress—continuously working on becoming teachers who practise in ways that are congruent with the social justice and feminist ideologies we embrace. On another level, we engage in a political process (hooks 1994, 37; Manicom, 365) by creating a learning community in which students and instructors are invited to engage in dialogues, activities, and assignments that require all of us to critically analyze and challenge ourselves and one another on our positioning and practice as learners, educators, and responsible citizens. As ongoing learners ourselves, we include in this chapter our reflections on the challenges associated with performing our

identities as "white" women, post-structural feminists, and critical pedagogues in this university classroom, and our efforts to move alongside our
students, and each other, through the teaching and learning processes.

Locating Ourselves as Persons

As is customary for us in our roles as teachers and advocates of post-structural feminism (which we discuss later in this essay), we practise the
importance of transparency and positionality by locating ourselves as
people as well as pedagogues. We are both professionally trained relational postmodern therapists, university educators, researchers, and "not
quite white" women. We are women whose Mediterranean and Latin ethnicities, although from European descent, are not part of the dominant
culture. Because we have each experienced first-hand discrimination and
oppression based on our ethnicities, we often refer to ourselves as "beige"
(Carm, a Brazilian-born Italian who immigrated to Canada as a child) or
"off-white" (Toni, a first-generation Canadian child of Italian immigrants)
women to capture how we experience "whiteness" differently. Among people of colour, we are seen as white; among other groups (who continue to
hold political, social, and economic power), we are sometimes treated as
"not white enough." This fluctuation of power across contexts based on
race and/or ethnicity affords us privileges that are not experienced by our
sisters of colour.

As feminist teachers, it is important for us to be responsible regarding
the privileges and power we hold, while simultaneously honouring our
experiences of oppression, marginalization, and less privilege. Furthermore, our differences in sexual orientation, marital status, and educational
attainment uniquely position us in our individual experiences of power
and marginalization across contexts. Thus our social locations and personal experiences of power, oppression, and immigration become part of
who we are in the classroom and the relationships we develop with students
and with each other. When we teach this Practicum-Capstone course, we
mindfully position our identities as professors to include these personal
parts of who we are, and we use our experiences to locate ourselves in relation to the students in the room and the content of the course.

As educators, we are influenced primarily by social justice and feminist pedagogies. Our "advocating feminism" (hooks 2000, 31) from a
post-structural position is one of many ways to *be* feminists and *do* feminisms, as feminism is defined, theorized, and practised in many ways
(Forrest and Rosenberg, 180; Tisdell, 140). At this time in our lives, we
both find that post-structural feminist theories (see hooks 1994, 70; hooks

2000, 6; Manicom, 374; Tisdell, 146–47) best capture how we engage as instructors and researchers to practise our commitment to social justice and to "eradicate the ideology of domination" (hooks 2000, 26). As such, our pedagogy is rooted in Freire's notion of education that liberates, and hooks's ideas about education as a "practice of freedom" (1994, 12), where education challenges the oppression that results from maintaining the status quo.

Feminist Pedagogy

Our understandings and practices of feminist pedagogy in higher education align with the work of several feminist scholars. Tisdell reviews the history of post-structural feminism as emerging from structural models that emphasize the effects of social structures or systems on learning, rather than the role of individual agency (142). In structural models, "individualistic understandings of learning are downplayed, and issues of psychological safety in the learning environment are underplayed or ignored" (142); whereas in post-structural approaches, individual agency and the learning environment play more central roles. Tisdell emphasizes that post-structural feminism includes a strong focus on "the intersections of gender with other systems of oppression and privilege" (146) and pays particular attention to the "positionality of all participants" (145) and to "deconstructing dichotomies such as the safe–unsafe learning environment, [and] rationality-affectivity in working for social justice" (145). Like us, she believes in the importance of forming connections between who we are as people and the social structures—such as class, race, ethnicity, and gender—that impact our movement through the world (from thinking to action). Similar to Tisdell, Larson (136–38) poses a feminist pedagogy that emphasizes a systems approach to understanding oppression and individual/collective action. She underscores the importance of recognizing personal experience as a legitimate form of knowledge, focusing on analysis (or what we call critical self-reflection) and incorporating process as well as content in the learning environment (136). These principles of feminist pedagogy play central roles in how we engage as feminist educators and facilitate the Practicum-Capstone course in SMF.

Among the various approaches to feminist pedagogy, Sinacore, Healy, and Justin identify characteristics of a "united feminist pedagogy" (340) that capture much of Tisdell's and Larson's perspectives and that resonate for us as feminist pedagogues. These include: "a) addressing power and authority; b) establishing equality; c) confronting and incorporating diversity; d) promoting collaboration and leadership; e) valuing personal

and academic experiences; and, f) integrating cognitive and affective learning" (340). As such, our pedagogies also align with bell hooks' (1994, 18)
and Paolo Freire's (48) ideas of emancipatory education, which emphasize social and political actions inside and outside the classroom that create
opportunities for educational transformation. These ways of understanding feminism and applying feminist principles to the practice of education
help us to mindfully contribute to the ongoing critical interrogation of
individual and social inequities and to engage in actions that contribute to
a more socially just world.

Experiential Learning and Capstone Course
The practicum course was first offered in 2005 by other faculty with
diverse theoretical and ideological perspectives; but it remains founded
on experiential learning theory (Kolb, 38) and on inquiry-based learning
principles rooted in John Dewey's notion of "learning by doing" (Spronken-
Smith and Walker, 724). Over time, the course has changed to intentionally
reflect the evolution of the SMF program and its values, which are
grounded in ideologies of social justice, gender theory, and postmodern/
post-structural world views. Once solely a service-learning course, it
now also serves as the Capstone course for the honours program in SMF.
According to Hensheid and Barnicoat, a Capstone course in higher education takes the form of "senior seminars [that] offer undergraduate students nearing graduation the opportunity to summarize, evaluate, and
integrate some or all of their college experience" (*Gale Encyclopedia of
Education*, first paragraph). The Capstone piece provides students and
instructors with the opportunity to unpack knowledge construction from
a post-structural feminist position that includes multiple forms of knowing (Tisdell, 146–47), thereby integrating academic learning with service
learning and lived experience.

During the first class, we introduce the course format and content, with
an emphasis on the social justice, power, and anti-oppression frameworks
that emerge from our post-structural feminist pedagogies. We share with
students that our teaching practices focus on facilitating an environment
wherein they may identify and address their comfort zones, learning edges,
and triggers (Hardiman, Jackson, and Griffin, 54). Although "requirements," "goals," and "objectives" are clearly laid out in the course syllabus,
as part of our commitment to feminist pedagogy and to the students whom
we teach, we also deliberately engage the group in a facilitated conversation
where together we co-construct guidelines for a meaningful, empowering,
and respectful learning experience.

At the forefront of our teaching practices is our commitment to inter-rogating perceived wisdom and dominant discourses, while ensuring that we create space for subjugated ways of knowing. As feminist educators, we hope to invite class members into what Kuhn calls a "critical paradigm shift" (85), one that encourages both educators and students to critique traditional models of education (Freire, 75; Tisdell, 152), thereby creating opportunities to experience learning that is consciousness-raising, gen-erative, more egalitarian, and empowering. A facilitative learning process invites students to be holistically involved in their learning experience and engages them to find meaningful ways to hold, interpret, and apply the mul-tiple sources of knowledge they have been part of constructing. We believe that this type of facilitated learning not only invites students to make a paradigm shift but also allows them to be more authentically involved in their learning experience. Engaging the student as a whole person who is in relationship with multiple learning processes (formal education, work, service-based, and life experience) has the potential to deepen not only students' understanding of knowledge construction but also their human citizenship and compassionate investment in their world. As such, we hope the learning environment in this course is conducive to empowering us all to be critical consumers of knowledge in an effort to become more socially just citizens who are reflective, critical thinking, social change agents.

Feminist Pedagogies and Community Service Learning
The Canadian Alliance for Community Service Learning defines Commu-nity Service Learning (CSL) as "an educational approach that integrates service in the community with intentional learning activities." Critical thinking and reflection are presented as key elements of this approach as they are used to facilitate students' meaning-making and to connect aca-demic learning to community experiences, personal values, and a sense of social responsibility. This definition echoes our university's position on CSL as a form of experiential education that integrates "relevant com-munity service experiences with reflective exercises for a powerful learn-ing experience that aligns with course curriculum" (Centre for Teaching Excellence). The design and delivery of the Practicum-Capstone course in SMF integrates these notions of CSL with post-structural feminist peda-gogies that deconstruct and reconstruct valued knowledge to include both personal and affective knowledge domains and that weave intersections among gender, race, class, dis/ability, sexuality, and so on into the critical analysis and reflection components of both the practicum (experiential/service learning) and classroom experiences.

The Practicum-Capstone course is a one-term/semester (four-month) required course for all fourth-year honours SMF students. They may then choose one of two follow-up courses: a thesis course (with a research focus) or a second Practicum course (extending the applied field experience from four to eight months). The Practicum-Capstone course is designed to promote integration and closure across all forms of learning as students "end" their undergraduate degrees and studies in SMF. The Practicum service-learning component provides an opportunity for students to apply and expand their learning to the human services field and to process their own values around social justice and community citizenship. Carbine refers to Community-Based Learning (CBL) as promoting a "meaningfully engaged citizenship identity rather than a narrow careerist identity" (321). She underscores "the person-shaping ability of CBL to often resist (but still sometimes reinscribe) unequal power relations along race, gender, class, ethnicity, and other social as well as sexual hierarchies" (321) and how "a feminist approach to CBL enables transformative education" (321). The students' practicum experience is a complex political and social interaction that brings together various groups of people with diverse social locations and power (e.g., agency staff and supervisors, agency clientele, students, university professors), while balancing the experience of the learner as part of the dynamic.

The practicum placement serves as an opportunity for praxis, an embodiment of learning in an applied environment (Mayberry and Rees, 106), and for continued learning. Students apply (and often interview) for unpaid placement positions (100 hours per semester) across a wide array of human service agencies. Practicum placement agencies in SMF include those who work with street-involved youth, children and families, or persons with disabilities; counselling and women's crisis centres; and sexual health education and advocacy agencies. Placement opportunities change annually depending upon a myriad of factors, including a rise in experiential learning placement needs in the community where we teach. Through the field practicum, students experience a learning-by-doing that builds on and adds to their existing learning foundations.

Briskin (in this book) examines concerns raised by feminist scholars around various Community Service Learning models, especially those that privilege a charity or helping model that places expertise in the hands of the student "volunteer," thereby reinforcing the domination, oppression, and colonization of marginalized groups. As feminists, we need to problematize this helping approach, especially in terms of how *helping others* reinforces an oppressive structural power dynamic paralleling colonizing practices. As Briskin notes, CSL placements may "bolster stereotypes about personal responsibility, blame the victims of poverty and homelessness, reinforce deeply rooted beliefs in individualism, and parallel traditional forms of charity and philanthropy." A CSL approach that is grounded in post-structural feminist ideologies and social justice principles can mitigate such unwanted outcomes. A framework that critically addresses the dangers associated with helping or charity models and engages students to recognize and understand the systemic structures that may (albeit unintentionally) replicate oppressive practice is the foundation on which the Practicum-Capstone course in SMF is built.

We thus position ourselves alongside our students as lifelong learners. None of us is an expert, especially in the lived experiences of others with whom we interact, across both academic and Community Service Learning environments. Drawing upon this "non-expert" stance, we invite students to consider how our different life experiences (including, but not limited to, educational attainment) contribute to our varied knowledges. We apply a braid metaphor (De Santis and Serafini) to capture how feminist ideologies problematize traditional understandings of knowledge construction, and we draw upon this metaphor to invite students to recognize, analyze, and integrate three equally important strands of their own learning process (their personal learning braid): academic, experiential (service learning), and personal (lived experiences). In doing so, we hope to challenge, as many have done before us, traditional discourses about knowledge acquisition and learning that privilege academic learning as more *legitimate* than other forms of learning that are grounded in personal experience and action (Freire, 87; hooks 1994, 6; Shor, 12). Drawing upon this braid metaphor, we actively invite students to value and integrate all forms of learning across contexts and over their lifespans. The braid then captures students' *process* of learning: each strand has value and legitimacy on its own, and, when woven with the others (integrated), they create a more holistic learning narrative that promotes a discourse of lifelong learning.

Students thus enter their practicum placements as learners as well as "knowers"—learners who bring with them various forms of knowledge in tandem with an awareness of the limitations of this knowledge. Through "bookends of supervision" (De Santis and Serafini) conjointly provided by the practicum site supervisor and the course instructor(s), students are supported from both sides of the CSL experience (from classroom to community). It is in the classroom that we facilitate and support discussions of power, authority, privilege, and intersectionality as they relate to students' experiences in the practicum. By doing so, we challenge what Briskin (in this book) has identified as problematic consequences of some service-learning experiences. Here our post-structural feminist positioning informs how we facilitate class discussions that encourage "learners [to] examine the impact of social systems of privilege and oppression on their own identity, including their beliefs and values, [so that] the 'discourse' is disrupted, thus shifting their identity, as well as increasing their capacity for agency" (Tisdell, 146). In doing so, we ask students to challenge "stereotypes about personal responsibility, blame[ing] the victims of poverty and homelessness, ... [and their own] deeply rooted beliefs in individualism" (Briskin, in this book). By increasing students' capacity for agency, the Practicum-Capstone promotes social action and social change. A CSL experience situated in critical feminist pedagogies thus provides opportunities for students to enact change through/within their practicum placements.

Power and the Collaborative Learning Process

Many scholars (e.g., Crabtree and Sapp, 133–36; St. Germaine-Small, Walsh-Bowers, and Mitchell, 138–40; Tisdell, 151–53) have written about the challenges associated with applying feminist pedagogical practices to the teaching environment. Attending to power as it connects to the position and authority of the instructor, for example, has been discussed extensively by Crabtree and Sapp (135–36). They highlight the use of self-introductions and naming practices involving titles as a way to mindfully address this aspect of power in the teaching environment. Expanding student narratives about instructors to include personal aspects of the teacher's identity, and inviting students to address instructors by their first names are two of many feminist pedagogical practices aimed at reducing hierarchies and creating more egalitarian power relationships within the classroom.

These naming and self-introduction practices are embedded in our own pedagogies and are consistent across the introductory to senior level courses we teach. Mindful of the power, privilege, and authority associated with our roles as professors, we introduce ourselves in ways that invite students to see beyond our titles and status to include other aspects of our identities. By positioning ourselves alongside our students as lifelong learners who embody diverse layers of social location, we situate learning as a collaborative rather than top-down process. As noted by Crabtree and Sapp (136), however, such disclosures may unintentionally strengthen power differences associated with title/position (where power and legitimacy are associated with those who are called by their "Dr./Professor" title, rather than their first name) and create space for misinterpretations of roles and relationships.

For example, traditional gender roles are pervasive, and regardless of their professional status, teachers are gendered beings. Students may therefore be inclined to view female instructors, especially those whom they know on a first-name basis, as nurturers or objectified erotic objects (Crabtree and Sapp, 135–36). While naming and self-introduction practices may serve to decrease hierarchies and create space for more egalitarian relationships, this context of "familiarity" may be a dangerous one in terms of boundary negotiations and professional interactions. The gendered experiences of instructors who adopt these practices are important to consider; the risks are not gender neutral. Despite these and other possible challenges, we are committed to the use of self to address power and privilege. When we suspect misinterpretations or blurring of boundaries, we address them as learning opportunities with our students. These practices are integral to our feminist pedagogies; therefore, we continue to invite students to call us by our first names rather than our titles and to integrate our personhood into our identities as educators—and we deal with the consequences that may ensue!

By the time students enter the Practicum-Capstone course in their senior year, they have witnessed our self-introduction and naming process as a consistent feature of how we embody our teaching roles, and they appear comfortable enough to communicate with us (and about us) using our first names. That being said, we are aware that our efforts to decrease hierarchies in the classroom do not eliminate power positioning altogether; we evaluate students with grades, and they evaluate us with institutional course evaluations. Honouring the feminist pedagogical practice of positioning (Tisdell, 147–50) and the need to transparently address power and authority (Forrest and Rosenberg, 184–85; Manicom, 379–81; Sinacore et al., 348, 352), we integrate the personal parts of who we are into our identities as professors; invoke power as a unit of analysis and facilitate discussions that name and analyze power; and use our own personal experiences to locate ourselves in relation to students, practicum agency partners, and course content. By the end of the course, students' disclosures of "who they are" do not exist in isolation. They exist alongside our own disclosures of self-locations. Knowing that hierarchies cannot be eliminated, we aim here to make space for a more collaborative learning environment—one in which power is named, owned by both instructors and students, and recognized as socially, institutionally, and historically located.

Shrewsbury (10–11) and others (hooks 1994, 84; hooks 2003, 78; Wånggren and Sellberg, 545–47) discuss the experience of empowerment for students, who together with the instructor are part of establishing a collaborative learning community where all members engage in creating, interrogating, and exchanging knowledge in multilayered learning processes. For our students, this begins with the Practicum placement process, which is set in motion during the spring term prior to the start of the course. Our goal is to set up students, agencies, and agency supervisors for a match that fosters learning and potential transformation. In doing so, we consider student interests, needs, personalities, and skill sets, as well as agency structure, milieu, and supervisory approach. Because we each have individual experiences with the students from previous courses, we strive to bring our understandings of "who they are" as people and learners into the placement equation. This is not intended to direct students' learning experiences; rather, it is meant to create a safer (less anxiety-provoking) environment wherein they can build on the knowledges and experiences they bring to the placement. For example, if students who have previous experiences working in a particular domain and/or with a particular group apply for a placement in a similar field, we will likely invite them to consider a placement that fills a gap in their learning history or that will propel them forward in their desired professional direction. These mark the initial stages of collaborative relationship development.

Drawing upon collaboration and attention to power and authority as hallmarks of feminist pedagogies (Briskin 2001, 1–15; Forrest and Rosenberg, 184–85; Manicom, 379–81; Sinacore et al., 340), we dialogue with students about ideas for their placement and reach a mutual conclusion about what type of placement would/could be a good fit for them. All of this is done in consultation with the partnering agencies, who interview students and make final determinations regarding how many students (and which ones) they will accept as practicum interns. In this way, a course facilitation process that is consultative and collaborative is introduced well before the first day of class. Our hope is that this tone is carried into the learning environment when the course officially begins.

The pairing of weekly three-hour class seminars with time spent at the practicum placement is essential for integrating critical perspectives with Community Service Learning. We propose a structure to these seminars that invites students to value the learning that occurs through and from one another, rather than solely from us as instructors (hooks 1994, 158). As we indicated earlier, our position on power is more egalitarian than in traditional lecture-style courses (or perhaps even some traditional seminar classes). The organizational design of our in-class time together can thus be characterized as a *facilitated dialogue*. Students use class time to check in about their practicum placements, highlighting their struggles, challenges, and celebrations. The dialogues that emerge from these disclosures serve several purposes. First, they provide students with the opportunity to learn from and through one another's experiences. Second, they intentionally make space for analyzing and reflecting on the practicum and classroom interactions from an intersectional lens of power, values, and practices that reinforce oppressive social structures. Third, these discussions open up space for further practising our feminist pedagogies by "confronting and incorporating diversity ... valuing personal and academic experiences ... [and] integrating cognitive and affective learning" (Sinacore et al., 340). These critical dialogues are integral to creating a Community Service Learning experience that addresses and moves beyond the limitations and dangers noted by Briskin (in this book).

These facilitated discussions are not always generative and balanced, however. At times, they may replicate an oppressive social structure and process. For example, we once had an experience where we both noticed a complex dynamic forming—one that included individual ways of being (e.g., different personality traits, such as introversion/extroversion) and personal preferences or learning styles (e.g., processing orally or in writing)—in the context of having/using one's voice in the classroom. What was most disconcerting about the dynamic that had formed was that it appeared to replicate our current socio-cultural-political context, which affords some people more privileges than others based on their social location. Students who were more representative of the dominant power culture (e.g., white, Christian, Canadian-born from British ancestry) seemed both to have a voice and to feel comfortable using it regularly (e.g., sharing frustrations or celebrations). This was in stark contrast to the silence (little to no involvement in discussion) exhibited by the only students of colour in the room. Our awareness of this dynamic moved us to reflection followed by action.

Many feminists have examined the concept of having voice and the meanings of silence (Briskin 2000; hooks 1994, 11; Manicom, 377–79; Tisdell, 150–51). We thus wondered what meanings this unequal division of space in class discussions might hold. Was the silence an act of resistance (Briskin 2000; Manicom, 377–78) that can facilitate control and power, especially for people who have experienced abuse or other forms of oppression? Alternatively, was this silence an outcome of the processes taking place in the room that either intentionally or unintentionally misused location and power? Given that historically dominant groups have used silence to control marginalized groups and further oppress them (Freire, 33; hooks 1994, 179), we wondered if that was happening here, knowingly or unknowingly.

Our inclination to respect personality differences among group members was strong, yet we felt compelled to name the imbalance or inequality we observed. After much consultation and reflection, we brought these wonderings to the group and engaged in a facilitative dialogue that invited each of us to consider our social locations and how they influenced the roles we played in this dynamic. We navigated this carefully in order to not "blame the victim" or shame any students, while holding all members of the group, including ourselves as instructors, accountable—after all, we were members of the learning environment that we had co-created (Larson, 137; Forrest and Rosenberg, 185).

This was a difficult dialogue to have, *and* one that was well worth having. As the people with the most power (authority) in the room, we began the discussion by owning and processing the ways in which we may have inadvertently contributed to the dynamic. We reflected, wondered aloud, and attempted to make space for others to process their own roles and contributions. Some students became defensive, claiming that they intentionally waited to speak so that they did not take space away from their colleagues. Others drew upon reasons such as fatigue or a sense of obligation to contextualize their contributions to either the silence or the discussion. We acknowledged students' responses while also challenging them to "dig deeper" and engage with us in a reflexive analysis of how our actions (and decisions to not act) can reinforce dominant power positions and discourses, even when this may not be our intention. This facilitated conversation invited students to experience and know themselves differently in the classroom context and to consider how they position themselves in other contexts when they have more or less power. Knowing oneself in a different way, an outcome of critical self-reflection, is the key to transformational learning so that, as Hackman has noted, "the self [becomes] a site for change" (170).

Privilege, Emotions and (the Importance of) Process

The Capstone course is comprised of various reflective, research, and applied assignments; these make up the more concrete parts of the course. That said, much of the classroom "teaching" occurs organically—we facilitate a culture known to our students as "processing the process," and attend to what is happening in the room, among a diverse group of students with varied backgrounds and placement experiences. In many ways, the course readings unite the class by serving as fodder for critical and often emotionally charged discussions. In collaboration with students, we unpack the readings and invite students to critically analyze, deconstruct, and reconstruct their own ways of moving through the world and how they may subtly (or not so subtly) engage in actions that endorse "isms" and oppressions individually and/or systemically.

In our most recent co-teaching of this course, we chose Narda Razak's book, *Transforming the Field: Critical Antiracist and Anti-Oppressive Perspectives for the Human Services Practicum,* as the main text alongside supplementary readings grounded in feminist and anti-oppressive practices (e.g., "White Privilege: Unpacking the Invisible Knapsack" by Peggy McIntosh). We select readings that we hope will disrupt and provoke students to think outside their spheres of experience and comfort, especially given that for most students, the practicum placement exposes them to a world of variation and diversity that may not be part of their lived experience. This approach is deliberately provocative and connects to the course goals, which focus on students examining their "learning edges" and moving outside their comfort zones. It aligns with bell hooks's (2000, 66) feminist ideology and practices, which may be considered intentionally confrontational, yet still feminist.

We have often used the phrase *being comfortable with being uncomfortable* to describe the process of honestly and critically examining one's privilege and power. Both in class discussions and in private talks with each of us, students have shared that this process of interrogating their own privilege—especially among a group of students with so many layers of privilege (e.g., education, class, race, language, ability)—makes them feel "uncomfortable," "bad," and "guilty." Many of these feelings of discomfort stem from a lack of awareness of one's own privilege and power; becoming aware requires recognizing one's own dominant position relative to those who are marginalized. Making space for such affective components of learning is an important feminist pedagogical principle (Larson, 138) and one we believe is central to a critical CSL experience.

This process of emotional expression in response to increased awareness of oppressive structures and experiences is key to what hooks referred to as "building a culture of community" (1994, 40). We tend to move carefully in response to these sensitive situations by intentionally maintaining connection with the students who have more privilege, while taking care that students whose social locations are marginalized are not silenced in the process. As noted by Tisdell, "poststructural feminist educators maintain directive roles as challengers of unequal power relations" (151). We thus move between *inviting* and *directing* discussions that challenge students to consider how they may perform their privileged identities in ways that are socially just and that contribute to social change.

Because most student cohorts have been predominantly female and white, with one or two persons of colour, males, and/or queer-identified students in each group, ideas about "white privilege" are not easily received and have been very difficult for some students to understand and own. We have noticed what Griffin and Ouellett describe as "dissonance," "anger," and "immobilization" as common themes when facilitating social justice education (106). As feminist pedagogues, we believe it is important to name and make space for the processing of emotions in the learning context (Lempiäinen and Naskali, 201–2; Larson, 137). Over the years, we have become better skilled at facilitating and promoting conversations that address feelings of guilt, shame, powerlessness, and fear, recognizing that these emotional reactions are often part of the learning process. Validating these reactions in some way (by naming and making space for them in the academic environment) is crucial to maintaining students' engagement in the learning dialogue and to practising our feminist pedagogy, because "the feminist classroom is decisively one in which tears, anger, silence, joy, and enthusiasm co-exist and are normalized as part of the learning process" (Larson, 138).

Admittedly, our own graduate education (including but not limited to our training as relational therapists) and experiences as students in feminist classrooms have been instrumental in shaping how we balance support with challenge and stay grounded in sometimes very emotionally charged environments. We practise what one of our own mentors described as being "a calm presence in an anxious field." Although each of us in the class has a shared and collective responsibility to move respectfully through the process, power imbalances still exist. As instructors who are committed to a socially just learning process, when the learning environment becomes emotionally charged, we take a more active role in facilitation. Between pacing the dialogue, and at times actively directing it, we create a safer space within which students may examine and articulate their feelings, biases, assumptions, and perspectives. For the most part, the facilitative skills and positions we employ are not limited to therapists; they are, in fact, feminist principles in practice and can be applied by anyone who shares these values. This type of facilitative practice moves us toward one of the goals of feminist pedagogy: "to bring about personal transformation that inspires and compels individuals to take action—regardless of their gender—in response to what they have learned, and critically, as part of a group that has a collective understanding of oppression" (Larson, 138).

Our personal backgrounds, including our graduate training, help us stay curious, compassionate, and supportive in the classroom. This has been our intention, and student feedback (from mid- and end-of-term evaluations, emails, and conversations) suggests that this has been our overall impact. For example, students have reported that they appreciate our feedback and facilitation of the class environment in these ways: "continue giving feedback—I appreciate your honesty," "[feedback] helps me process my process," "prompt me with questions to go deeper," "encourage and foster my inner reflection ... probe me to dig deeper," "facilitate meaningful class discussions," "co-teaching ... allows for ... two supports ... the unique strengths of two professor to guide the classroom experience."

Intersectionality and Critical Self-Reflection

The adult learning literature positions critical self-reflection at the heart of transformative learning (see Cranton, 33; Mezirow 2000, 8, 20). According to Mezirow (2000, 8, 20; "Contemporary Paradigms of Learning," 162–65), critical self-reflection invites learners to engage in a process of questioning assumptions, values, and perspectives they encounter in their world. The Community Service Learning literature also underscores the value of self-reflection (Mitchell, 61), and the questioning of assumptions and critical analysis of dominant discourses are congruent with most feminist pedagogies (Larson, 138; Lempiäinen and Naskali, 198).

To be fair, however, this focus on critical self-reflection does not begin in the Practicum-Capstone course. In fact, students in SMF have been exposed to this type of analysis throughout their studies. Reflective papers are common across several second- and third-year courses. In the Practicum-Capstone course, we expect greater depth of analysis; therefore, intersectionality—how race, gender, sexuality, and other social locations intersect with social structures (Crenshaw 1991, 1244; 1989, 139)—is a focus of many of the reflective assignments. Together, positionality (Tisdell, 147) and intersectionality—that is, where the "connections between the individual and the intersecting structural systems of privilege and oppression that affect how participants construct knowledge, discuss their own experience, and interaction in the classroom [and in the practicum setting]" (Tisdell, 146)—are the foundational elements of critical self-reflection.

Keeping process journals and writing reflections about field experiences are key assignments in the Practicum-Capstone course. We implement directed reflections as a way to invite students to critically analyze particular aspects of their placement experiences, drawing upon layers of social location, social justice, and social change as they do so. Our feedback on these papers asks students to consider how their social locations and identities (e.g., gender, race, age, ability) intersect with other layers of privilege and systems of oppression, and how these intersections apply to the students' experiences in or with the Practicum. Consideration of these intersections is key to a post-structural feminist pedagogy (Tisdell, 146) and to differentiating reporting from analysis. Through reflective (and reflexive) classroom discussions and papers, the principles of post-structural feminist pedagogy come to life in this course. These varied and diverse reflective practices are pivotal to the type of transformative learning advocated by hooks and others (e.g., see Iverson and Dorney in this book).

Earlier in this essay, we shared a selection of student responses regarding how we structure and facilitate the course. Generally speaking, students seem to value the reflective focus of the course: "Keep encouraging and fostering inner reflection"; "I really liked them because they allowed me to fully understand why I may have been feeling the way I was during my practicum placement"; "writing the reflection papers was the first time during my undergraduate schooling where my experience was important ... It provided an opportunity and space to ... debrief and essentially helped me to process the practicum experience." Some identified a learning curve: "My reflections at the beginning of the term were often related more to the tasks I was completing at my practicum and not on my own personal growth ... This was something that was identified early on in my reflections, and was something I did have to work on." Others expressed a desire for direction: "Ask us to specifically reflect on something, especially in the first couple of weeks because at first I didn't know what to reflect on." One student captured the feminist principles behind reflection in this way: "It is through constant reflection that we are able to gain understanding of the ways in which we interact with the world and why. To reflect on past experiences is to build a personal self-awareness which becomes a useful tool in informing our actions, choices, values, belief systems or even how we interpret research." We sometimes hear students in the SMF program groan about the constant reflection across courses, yet as these comments suggest, when they leave the Practicum-Capstone course at the end of their studies, they do so with an appreciation for the significant and transformative role that critical self-reflection has played in their educational experience. Self-reflection provides "a place to enact social change and growth ... [where] the self [becomes] a site for change" (Hackman, 107).

Construction of Knowledge
Including personal experience as a valued source of knowledge and as a site for knowledge construction is common among feminist pedagogies (Sinacore et al., 347; Tisdell, 146–47). How regularly is this approach put into practice in higher education? This statement by a former SMF student suggests that the emphasis on personal experience is not common: "Writing the reflection papers was the first time during my undergraduate schooling where my experience was important." Valuing personal experience as a legitimate form of knowledge is central to the Practicum-Capstone course;

critical self-reflection is expected, as is integration among diverse learning contexts. Here we intentionally use our authority as course instructors to direct how aspects of the course are structured and facilitated. We engage in teaching as a political act (Forrest and Rosenberg, 180; hooks 1994, 35) by challenging students to view their learning as partial when it rests exclusively on academic knowledge and the status quo. We position personal experiences and field practicum experiences alongside academic knowledge via the Capstone Electronic Portfolio project (see Penny Light, Chen, and Ittelson for a discussion of the use of ePortfolios in higher education). It is here that students explicitly process their *learning braid* (De Santis and Serafini) by interrogating the ways in which their current beliefs, values, and assumptions have been created over time and across contexts.

Along with other course assignments, the in-class discussions and written reflections serve as catalysts for the type of critical reflexivity and processing that is showcased in the ePortfolio. The final ePortfolio presentation allows students to share, and classmates and instructors to bear witness to, the integrated learning braid they have woven. What they create is a marker that celebrates their accomplishments, honours their personal process, and integrates all forms of knowing into a coherent whole. The process of presenting the ePortfolio is thus a powerful one for both the student presenter and the witnesses. Student feedback suggests that this Capstone project has succeeded in helping them make connections. One student shared that "it enabled me to take a step-back and make connections between course material and how it has affected me as an individual." Another student shared that it "allowed me, and my classmates, to showcase our individuality with the metaphorical framework behind the assignment." It also provides a vehicle through which students can demonstrate their growth as people and learners. As one student stated: "It showed me how much I had grown during my undergrad." In these ways, the ePortfolio Capstone project serves as a catalyst for shifting identities and transformative learning. Students shared that "doing this ePortfolio really allowed me to see how I have transformed from a student into para-professional" and that "ultimately, the project really wrapped up my experiences in the program and had me identify the aspects of the program that challenged me, enlightened me, and helped me grow."

Team Teaching
It likely seems clear at this point that we see our primary role in this fourth-year Practicum-Capstone course as facilitators and collaborators more than instructors. Our aim is to facilitate critical self-reflection, analysis, and

integration, but we do not do this in isolation. We believe that part of what enables us to practise our feminist pedagogy in the way that we do stems from our team-teaching approach. Of course, team teaching (or co-teaching) is a position of privilege in higher education. It is not fiscally efficient, and it is often not supported by academic institutions. At our university, team teaching typically involves either dividing course content across two (or more) instructors (the equivalent of teaching a portion of the course) or sharing every component of the course equally. The latter describes how we team-teach this course—we both attend and actively facilitate every class and co-evaluate every student assignment. We firmly believe that part of what makes this Practicum-Capstone course so impactful is the dynamic process of course facilitation that our team-teaching arrangement affords us.

How have we come to believe this so strongly? As many would agree, team teaching is most successful when the instructors work well together. For us, working well together does not mean being duplicates; rather, we draw on the similarities in our teaching philosophies, pedagogies, and core values, as well as on our unique skills or strengths that complement each other in some way. Open communication and trust are what make our co-teaching relationship work. We have consistently engaged in frank and reflective discussions with each other about our team teaching. Hackman argues that this type of reflection is essential for teachers: "reflect[ing] critically on themselves and the personal qualities that inform their practice" (106), especially for those who wish to create an "effective social justice teaching environment" (106). We include in these dialogues what makes us good partners in the classroom, what areas we need to work on, how we can support each other by drawing on our individual strengths, and so on. What we have come to realize, and genuinely appreciate, is the level of trust that is necessary to form a strong teaching partnership. We make ourselves vulnerable when we teach, and even more so when we co-teach with a colleague. Trust and respect are integral to the formation of a successful teaching relationship and have allowed us to work through any differences or difficulties in a collaborative way, one that is sensitive to power and diversity.

Students benefit from our unique team-teaching approach. Because the course can be personally challenging for students and often evokes strong feelings and reactions, working as a team allows us greater opportunities to notice patterns and themes emerging from class discussions and to act upon them. When one of us challenges, the other reframes and supports. We intentionally move back and forth in these roles. This is not a "good cop bad cop" dichotomy; rather, it is a performance of roles that allows us to encourage students while simultaneously challenging them to stretch outside their comfort zones and explore their learning edges. It enables us to support students' learning processes more fully, and it keeps us accountable to our beliefs and pedagogy. Students have described our team-teaching approach as "cohesively dynamic," "helpful for understanding content," "allow[ing] for the unique strengths of two professors to guide the classroom experience," and "essential in a course like this."

Our students may also appreciate witnessing our interactions with each other in the classroom, and our individual and unique ways of wrestling with ethical dilemmas and practices of oppression and marginalization in the institution and in the community. They have described us as "playing off each other" in terms of how we perform our roles as co-facilitators. For example, both of us engage in transparent processing of the material that is generated during classroom dialogues. Of course, this processing may be different for each of us, and we may grapple with challenging material or situations in the classroom in unique ways. Despite our differing levels of institutional and structural power, we intentionally practise "not holding back" when our perspectives differ, thus demonstrating how to challenge respectfully, extend and expand ideas, and assert one's voice. We hope that this serves to deconstruct some of the top-down knowledge and power discourses that oppress more than they free.

Furthermore, our classroom interactions model how communication breaches the boundaries of speech, as students witness how we communicate with each other through our bodies, our silences, and our voices. We draw upon our group facilitation skills and years of teaching in higher education to "read the room" and attend to process as well as content. As feminist pedagogues, both of us are sensitive to classroom dynamics that replicate the oppressive power structures in the larger society, and when we notice these patterns taking shape, we sometimes signal to each other— non-verbally first—so that we can support each other as we interrupt the dynamic and engage students in a dialogue to process the process. Many cohorts of students have told us how surprised they are at our ability to communicate without words. We respond openly and transparently to such observations, using them to highlight how important it is for students *and* instructors to understand the complexities of communication. We use these discussions and teachable moments to highlight the importance of processing how our bodies and our ways of interacting with others (beyond speech) may invite and free, or silence and oppress, and how this applies to students' Practicum and future work experiences.

Our Learning Edges

As female university teachers, we have sometimes felt constrained in our ability to name feminism as an ideological lens, especially in courses (and institutions) that may on the surface appear to ascribe to authoritarian ways of understanding knowledge. The difficulty does not lie in our personal values but rather with the term *feminism* itself and how it is received by students. As Practicum-Capstone course facilitators, we have noticed what seems to be a contemporary backlash against feminism—what others call "resistance" (see Bondestam 2011, 140, 144; Sharp et al., 538; Sinacore, Healy, and Justin, 350)—among our female, middle-class students, in particular. What is happening among young adult women when the word *feminism* tends to silence and indeed evoke resistance to any type of feminist ideology?

We have noticed that when we use the term feminism early in class discussions, students respond by actively denying that they are feminists (thus treating feminism as "the f-word"). Yet when we facilitate classroom discussions about inequality, marginalization, oppression, voice, power, and diversity (all feminist concepts), students seem more willing to engage in critical discussions that draw upon feminist and anti-oppressive principles and to express owning those principles as personal values. We wonder what must happen for young adults, especially women, to freely embrace the word *feminism* without shame, anger, or resistance.

Our attempts to address this resistance dynamic have led us to the following tentative observations. First, for some students, the term *feminist* conjures up "man-hating separatist women" who want to hold power over men. Students may thus oppose feminists and feminisms because they do not support one group having power over another under the guise of gender equality. Second, the women in the class may not view gender inequality as a current issue because they are privileged in other ways (see Silva Flores in this book). All of them have access to higher education and are able to choose to have a career and a family. In some ways, the benefits they experience from what hooks refers to as "bourgeois feminism" (2000, 21) have left them in a dominant position. Because they need not question gender inequalities, which they themselves have not experienced, they tend to replicate the dynamics of the domination ideology (hooks 2000, 36) in relation to women whose intersections of class, race, sexuality, dis/ability, and so forth does not make gender equality possible. Third, our students' dominant analysis of oppression is not centred on gender as a binary construct; it is more likely to be focused on sexuality, especially the subjugation of transgender and queer people, followed by some analysis of race, and a little on class. More typically, we hear them argue that the word feminism tends to privilege women and therefore is not inclusive of all the "others" (including gender-variant and gender-queer people), and hence does not represent their idea of social justice. In many ways, their arguments parallel hooks's analysis (2000, 11) of why Black poor women did not call themselves feminists. For these students, awareness of the lived experiences of marginalized sexualities offers them the opportunity to critically question and problematize feminism; thus, they "resist" identifying with the word, and by consequence, with the movement itself.

As teachers, we have spoken often about how to address this backlash issue. We wonder how to address the discomfort in the room without entering into a power struggle with students, and how to honour the contradictions that come with advocating feminism. We try to harness the energy it takes students to resist the term and use it to work through their discomfort so that they can reach a different place of knowing. This invites an interrogation of feminism into the dialogue. As a result of our efforts to draw the energy away from oppositional and defensive positionings toward the course content (be it feminism, white privilege, ableism, etc.) and/or course process (critical and reflective analysis), those students who hold a feminist identity have space to speak more freely, and they tend to ask questions that move the dialogue forward without blaming or shaming their classmates. Safety and trust within the classroom are vital for these types of critical consciousness dialogues.

We proceed cautiously, and we hope respectfully, to link the values students have expressed, analyzed, and owned with those of feminism and social justice. In doing so, we explicitly connect social justice principles and post-structural feminist ideas to the context of students' practicum placements to create space for bringing to life the connections between feminist principles and being socially just, responsible citizens. It appears that when social justice concepts are introduced prior to the term feminism, students are more receptive to critically questioning how their expressed values converge with feminist and anti-oppressive practices. Students are initially surprised (or shocked) by these connections, which may have a destabilizing effect on them, causing them to rethink how they have come to know themselves and the values they adopt. Through facilitated dialogues, students may revisit their perceptions and biases about feminism and begin to pay closer attention to the discourses that subjugate feminist ideas. In turn, they may be better equipped to begin to critically interrogate and problematize feminisms and the nuances of knowledge construction in socio-political and academic contexts. With diverse opportunities to engage in critical self-reflection worked into the course, some students do shift and claim feminism (the word/label) as an identifier. Our hope is to empower students of this generation to challenge the backlash and recognize the feminist and anti-oppressive values they hold as congruent with *being* feminists. *Doing* feminism—with an emphasis on social justice—is promoted through the responsible citizenship focus of the course and the service-learning experience. The journey to becoming socially just citizens is not an easy one; however, in the safer class environment, students may internalize and value the practice of challenging structural barriers that may perpetuate social injustices, and, in doing so, they may accept (or even embrace) the idea of *being* feminists.

Closing Comments: Coming Full Circle

Our goal with this essay has been to share our reflections about the process of teaching as feminists committed to social justice and anti-oppressive practices in the context of a senior undergraduate Practicum-Capstone course. This is our pedagogical dance, choreographed collaboratively by two "white" female university professors whose lived experiences constitute a valuable and important way of knowing. This is our story of our experiences, reflections, commitments, and struggles around performing feminist values in the teaching context.

The Practicum-Capstone course is constructed and delivered in a way that situates "knowledge as a process not product" (Lempiäinen and Naskali, 198). We apply the braid metaphor (De Santis and Serafini) to illustrate the process of knowledge construction as drawing on three knowledge domains: academic, experiential (service learning), and personal. Historically, personhood and lived experiences have been treated as marginalized ways of knowing in academia. Therefore, we actively and intentionally deconstruct assumptions that place more or less value on certain "types" of knowledge, and instead emphasize the *process* of integrating all forms of knowledge. Through active and mindful critical self-reflection, students work to weave a new understanding of what they know and how they have come to know it. As a "pedagogy of liberation" (Manicom, 367), feminist pedagogy pays attention to the "transformation of both relations among people in the classroom, and of relations of power in the world at large" (367). Through praxis and taking learning outside the classroom, students are called to be ethical citizens by living their values, challenging injustices, and being agents of social change. In this way, the classroom and fieldwork placements are "a place of passion and possibility, a place ... where all that we learn and know leads us into greater connection" (hooks 2003, 183) with one another and our communities.

Note
Both authors were equally involved in the development and writing of this chapter. Its authorship reflects a collaborative effort between two women who have differing abilities and strengths, and who together have sought to present their best work. Therefore, the order of authorship is strictly alphabetical, and not reflective of contributions.

Works Cited
Bondestam, Fredrik. "The Challenge of Classroom Silence." *Core: Newsletter of the Centre for Support of Teaching* 10.1 (2000): 6–7. http://pi.library.yorku.ca/ojs/index.php/core/article/view/2706/1911

———. "Resisting the Discourse on Resistance: Theorizing Experiences from an Action Research Project on Feminist Pedagogy in Different Learning Cultures in Sweden." *Feminist Teacher* 21.2 (2011): 139–52. http://dx.doi.org/10.5406/femteacher.21.2.0139

Briskin, Linda. "The Challenge of Classroom Silence." *Core: Newsletter on University Teaching* 10.1 (2000). http://core.journals.yorku.ca/index.php/core/article/view/2706/1911

———. "Power in the Classroom." *Voices from the Classroom: Reflections on Teaching and Learning in Higher Education.* Toronto: Broadview Press, 2001. 10–47.

Canadian Alliance for Community Service Learning. 5 November 2012. http://www.communityservicelearning.ca/en/welcome_what_is.htm

Carbine, Rosemary P. "Erotic Education: Elaborating a Feminist and Faith-Based Pedagogy for Experiential Learning in Religious Studies." *Teaching Theology and Religion* 13.4 (2010): 320–38. http://dx.doi.org/10.1111/j.1467-9647.2010.00645.x

Centre for Teaching Excellence, University of Waterloo. 5 November 2012. https://uwaterloo.ca/centre-for-teaching-excellence/teaching-resources/teaching-tips/alternatives-lecturing/other/incorporating-service-learning-university-courses

Crabtree, Robbin D., and David Alan Sapp. "Theoretical, Political, and Pedagogical Challenges in the Feminist Classroom: Our Struggles to Walk the Walk." *College Teaching* 51.4 (2003): 131–40. http://dx.doi.org/10.1080/87567550309596428

Cranton, Patricia. *Understanding and Promoting Transformative Learning: A Guide for Educators of Adults.* 2nd ed. San Francisco: Jossey-Bass, 2006.

Crenshaw, Kimberlé. "Demarginalizing the Intersection of Race and Sex: A Black Feminist Critique of Antidiscrimination Doctrine, Feminist Theory, and Antiracist Politics." *University of Chicago Legal Forum* (1989) 140: 139–67.

———. "Mapping the Margins: Intersectionality, Identity Politics, and Violence Against Women of Color." *Stanford Law Review* 43.6 (1991): 1241–99. http://dx.doi.org/10.2307/1229039

De Santis, Carm, and Toni Serafini. "Weaving the Capstone Braid: Intersections among Classroom Learning, Practicum Experience, and Personal Life." Fifth Annual Windsor-Oakland University Teaching and Learning Conference, Windsor, Ontario, May 2011. Conference Presentation.

Dewey, John. *How We Think: A Restatement of the Relation of Reflective Thinking to the Educative Process.* Boston: D.C. Heath, 1933.

———. *Experience and Education.* New York: Collier Books, 1938.

Forrest, Linda, and Freda Rosenberg. "A Review of the Feminist Pedagogy Literature: The Neglected Child of Feminist Psychology." *Applied and Preventive Psychology* 6.4 (1997): 179–92. http://dx.doi.org/10.1016/S0962-1849(97)80007-8

Freire, Paolo. *Pedagogy of the Oppressed.* New York: Seabury, 1970.

Griffin, Pat, and Mathew L. Ouellett. "Facilitating Social Justice Education Courses." In *Teaching for Diversity and Social Justice*, 2nd ed. Ed. Pat Griffin and Mathew L. Ouellett. New York: Routledge/Taylor & Francis, 2007. 89–113.

Hackman, Heather W. "Five Essential Components for Social Justice Education." *Equity and Excellence in Education* 38.2 (2005): 103–9. http://dx.doi.org/10.1080/10665680590935034

Hardiman, Rita, Bailey Jackson, and Pat Griffin. "Conceptual Foundation for Social Justice Education." In *Teaching for Diversity and Social Justice*, 2nd ed. Ed. Maurianne Adams, Lee Ann Bell, and Pat Griffin. New York: Routledge, 2007. 35–66.

Hensheid, Jean M., and Lisa R. Barnicoat. "Capstone Courses in Higher Education." In *Gale Encyclopedia of Education,* 5 November 2012. http://www.answers.com/topic/capstone-courses-in-higher-education

hooks, bell. *Teaching to Transgress: Education as the Practice to Freedom.* New York: Routledge, 1994.

———. *Feminist Theory: From Margin to Centre,* 2nd ed. 1983. Cambridge, MA: South End Press, 2000.

———. *Teaching Community: A Pedagogy of Hope.* New York: Routledge. 2003.

Kolb, David. *Experiential Learning: Experience as the Source of Learning and Development.* New York: Prentice Hall, 1984.

Kuhn, Thomas. *The Structure of Scientific Revolutions.* Chicago: University of Chicago Press, 1962.

Larson, Laura M. "The Necessity of Feminist Pedagogy in a Climate of Political Backlash." *Equity and Excellence in Education* 38.2 (2005): 135–44. http://dx.doi.org/10.1080/10665680590935115

Lempiäinen, Kirsti, and Päivi Naskali. "Feminist Researchers Learning to Teach: A Finnish Case of University Pedagogy in Women's Studies." *Women's Studies International Forum* 34.3 (2011): 195–205. http://dx.doi.org/10.1016/j.wsif.2011.01.008

Manicom, Ann. "Feminist Pedagogy: Transformations, Standpoints, and Politics." *Canadian Journal of Education* 17.3 (1992): 365–89. http://dx.doi .org/10.2307/1495301

Mayberry, Maralee, and Margaret Rees. "Feminist Pedagogy, Interdisciplinary Praxis, and Science Education." In *Feminist Pedagogy: Looking Back to Move Forward.* Ed. Robbin D. Crabtree, David Alan Sapp, and Adela C. Licona. Baltimore: Johns Hopkins University Press, 2009. 94–113.

McIntosh, Peggy. "White Privilege: Unpacking the Invisible Knapsack." *Gender Through the Prism of Difference.* Ed. Maxine Zinn, Pierrette Hondagneu, and Michael Messner. New York and Oxford: Oxford University Press, 2005.

Mezirow, Jack. "Contemporary Paradigms of Learning." *Adult Education Quarterly* 46.3 (1996): 158–72. http://dx.doi.org/10.1177/074171369604600303

———. "Learning to Think Like an Adult." In *Learning as Transformation: Critical Perspective on a Theory in Progress.* Ed. Jack Mezirow and Associates. San Francisco: Jossey-Bass, 2000. 3–34.

Mitchell, Tania D. "Traditional vs. Critical Service-Learning: Engaging the Literature to Differentiate Two Models." *Michigan Journal of Community Service Learning* 14.2 (2008): 50–65.

Penny Light, Tracy, Helen Chen, and John Ittelson. *Documenting Learning with ePortfolios: A Guide for College Instructors.* San Francisco: Jossey-Bass, 2012.

Razak, Narda. *Transforming the Field: Critical Antiracist and Anti-Oppressive Perspectives for the Human Services Practicum.* Halifax: Fernwood, 2004.

St. Germaine-Small, Melissa, Richard Walsh-Bowers, and Terry L. Mitchell. "Exploring the Relevance of Feminist Pedagogy to Community Psychology: Continuing the Dialogue." *Journal of Community Psychology* 40.1 (2012): 129–44. http://dx.doi.org/10.1002/jcop.20482

Sharp, Elizabeth J., J.M. Bermudez, W. Watson, et al. "Reflections from the Trenches: Our Development as Feminist Teachers." *Journal of Family Issues* 28.4 (2007): 529–48. http://dx.doi.org/10.1177/0192513X06297473

Shor, Ira. *Empowering Education: Critical Teaching for Social Change.* Chicago: University of Chicago Press, 1992.

Shrewsbury, Carolyn. "M. "What Is Feminist Pedagogy?" *Women's Studies Quarterly* 15.3–4 (1987): 6–14.

Sinacore, Ada, Patricia Healy, and Monica Justin. "A Qualitative Analysis of the Experiences of Feminist Psychology Educators: The Classroom." *Feminism and Psychology* 12.3 (2002): 339–62. http://dx.doi.org/10.1177/ 0959353502012003007

Spronken-Smith, Rachel, and Rebecca Walker. "Can Inquiry-Based Learning Strengthen the Links Between Teaching and Disciplinary Research?" *Studies in Higher Education* 35.6 (2010): 723–40. http://dx.doi.org/10.1080/030750709 03315502

Tisdell, Elizabeth J. "Poststructural Feminist Pedagogies: The Possibilities and Limitations of Feminist Emancipatory Adult Learning Theory and Practice." *Adult Education Quarterly* 48.3 (1998): 139–56. http://dx.doi.org/10.1177/074171369 804800302

Wånggren, Lena, and Karin Sellberg. "Intersectionality and Dissensus: A Negotiation of the Feminist Classroom." *Equity, Diversity, and Inclusion: An International Journal* 31.5–6 (2012): 542–55. http://dx.doi.org/10.1108/ 02610151211235514

CHAPTER FIVE

Fat Lessons: Fatness, Bodies, and the Politics of Feminist Classroom Practice

Amy Gullage

This paper examines how certain identities and bodies are validated or silenced, normalized or rejected within the university classroom and through teacher/student interaction. This theme is explored by many other essays in this collection, such as those by Jeannette Silva Flores and Jane Nicholas and Jamilee Baroud. Like Judith A. Dorney's and Maggie Labinski's contributions, I describe an application of academic interests to feminist pedagogical interventions. Specifically, I explore an intersection between theorizing about fatness and feminist pedagogical practice. I also explore the complexity of teaching about the politics of fatness and the social implications this has both in the classroom and within the broader university culture. I examine this complexity by reflecting on my teaching on the subject of bodies and representations in an Introduction to Women and Gender Studies class and by examining three interactions between students and myself on the topic of fatness in the classroom.

The Importance of Fatness in Feminist Pedagogy

What exactly is meant by feminist pedagogy is complex, and there is great diversity in teaching methods and approaches that claim to espouse feminist values or ideologies. As Berenice Malka Fisher has noted, "how feminist academics and other teachers define and respond to the problems that arise in teaching is shaped in great part through the conjunction of a teacher's political and educational values, the models of teaching and learning she has encountered and adopted, and the institutional and social conditions under which she teaches" (25). The writings of feminist pedagogical theorists such as Elizabeth Ellsworth, Patti Lather, and Carmen Luke have especially shaped my approach to teaching. Their work demonstrates the complexities of power relations within the classroom.

Ellsworth contends that notions of empowerment, student voice, and dialogue are based on myths that reinscribe relations of domination in the classroom (298). Her assertions can be used to interrogate how educators, often unintentionally, reproduce and reinforce systems of power and oppression with their students. She argues that it is important to acknowledge the institutionalized power imbalances between educators and their students as well as the essentially paternalistic project of education itself (306). Lather places critiques of empowerment within a broader theoretical framework of postmodernism, questioning whether educators can liberate their students from oppression and domination, given that their very position reinforces the position of the educator as the possessor of knowledge and authority. Luke takes to task the universal student and teacher subjects that are assumed, using the notion of empowerment (25). She suggests that these assumptions produce metanarratives that perpetuate and reinforce gendered and oppressive systems of power and privilege. By applying a feminist pedagogical approach that interrogates power on institutional and individual levels, I attempt to challenge normalized understandings of body size and to construct a teaching space that values and embraces corporeal difference.

To challenge how particular bodies are normalized in the classroom, it is important, first of all, to acknowledge how the bodies of both educators and students are regulated and policed by institutional power structures (see also Wilson, in this book). As I have argued elsewhere (Gullage), through both course curricula and the structure of the university space, universities perpetuate and reproduce dominant understandings of fat bodies, often relying on stereotypical and marginalized discourse. For example, Ashley Hetrick and Derek Attig have argued that classroom desks, particularly those in lecture halls that have hinged writing surfaces attached to individual seats, demonstrate "simultaneous punishment and ignorance of fat existence in higher education's crafting of the ideal student body" (198).

As feminist pedagogy attempts to challenge power structures, educators using a feminist teaching framework should be aware of how both their students' bodies and their own are regulated, surveyed, and/or marginalized by the institution. Furthermore, to various degrees, universities can be sites of intense surveillance of students and their bodies, given that many students live on or near campus, spending time at university not only studying but also eating, socializing, drinking, playing sports, and participating in social clubs. Such surveillance can make fat student bodies prone to heightened forms of regulation and policing (Gullage). Deborah Britzman discusses the possibility of "articulating pedagogies that call into question the conceptual geography of normalization" (1995, 152). I understand Britzman's term "geography of normalization" to mean those spaces, both physical and abstract, wherein practices and discourses both explicitly and implicitly reify particular bodies and identities as normal and others as flawed or deviant. It is crucial to examine the work that bodies do in the space of Women and Gender Studies classrooms and how these classrooms can be important sites where the dominant social and political understandings of bodies and fatness can be challenged: where the geography of normalization can be questioned.

There is no requirement that Women and Gender Studies instructors apply a feminist pedagogical approach to their courses. However, Women and Gender Studies instructors who take a feminist approach to pedagogy are uniquely positioned to challenge dominant understandings of the body and fatness in their courses. As Susanne Luhmann notes, "from the beginning WGS [Women and Gender Studies] has asked us to think differently about education, even if it has not always lived up to its own promise" (66). Early disciplinary approaches to Women and Gender Studies positioned feminist learning as a result of feminist teaching (Luhmann, 66). However Luhmann argues that "learning turned out to be a more complex intellectual, to say nothing of affective, process, the result of which cannot be presumed in advance" (66). Feminist pedagogical approaches in Women and Gender Studies aimed at producing critical independent thinkers should, Luhmann writes, attempt to foster "a love of the processes of thinking and learning" (79). Women and Gender Studies classes, premised on a feminist pedagogy that fosters an engagement with and attachment to learning processes, are ideally suited to discussions of how dominant understandings of fatness and the body are produced.

Teaching Fatness

I gave the annual lecture on "Bodies and Representation" to the Introduction to Women and Gender Studies undergraduate class for which I was a teaching assistant for three years. As a TA, I facilitated weekly tutorials over the course of eight months. The examples in this essay were drawn from the 2010–11 school term, the last time I was a TA for the course. The course instructor positioned the students as active knowers and producers of knowledge rather than as consumers. As such, students were positioned against what Paulo Freire has called the "banking model of education."

I approached my lecture on fatness by using a feminist pedagogy that did not attempt to free students from oppressive ways of thinking, but rather conveyed knowledge and skills, which students could then use when critiquing dominant discourses that marginalize bodies through practices of normalization. What might teaching from a position of fatness involve? This is a different question than one that requires acknowledgement of fat identities and oppression in universities and classrooms. Asking to evoke a position of fatness does not mean asking to create classrooms that are safe, inclusive, and fat positive. This question asks something more. It speaks to the social and political of fatness. It requires working with and through differences, including corporeal difference as a feminist pedagogical approach.

A fat feminist pedagogical approach is centred on helping students learn the processes through which ideals, norms, and histories shape our social and political worlds and in turn shape our understandings of our bodies and the bodies of others. Britzman asks whether education can be a site of "deconstructive revolts" and whether pedagogy can provoke responses that refuse normalizing terms (1995, 79). Corporeality could be an educational site of these deconstructive revolts wherein the body could be explored, unthought/rethought, and negotiated. Thinking and teaching about the body explicitly opens up a space in which commonsense assumptions and dominant discourses can be critiqued and challenged.

I imagined a fat feminist classroom as one that challenges dominant understandings of fat while simultaneously acknowledging the importance of these understandings in our everyday lives. It is not necessary for an educator to identify as fat to employ these techniques, as the emphasis is on learning how understandings of fatness shape all our lives. That said, it would be important for an educator who would be read as "fit" or slender to discuss explicitly the power related to having their body read in that way. For those educators who do have a fat body, fat feminist pedagogy might require that they draw on their own body in order to question the assumptions it creates both in the classroom and more broadly in their everyday lives. This is no simple task. Requiring that bodies be understood as embedded in social and political processes can be particularly challenging for educators, as demonstrated by some of the moments I experienced when I attempted to apply a fat feminist pedagogy.

In the classroom, I sought to disrupt students' investment in dominant understandings of fatness and health in an attempt to locate this knowledge within broader social practices laden with power structures that oppress particular bodies (such as fat bodies) while valuing other bodies (such as slender ones). The central goal of both the lecture I gave and the tutorials I facilitated was to encourage students to question how hegemonic notions of health and desire become mapped onto bodies—particularly white, slender, active bodies—and to demonstrate how bodies that do not fit this representation get constructed as the Other. It was not my intention to empower students through these discussions; instead, I wanted students to have an opportunity to think about bodies in ways that would let them examine the social and political implications and how those implications are intricately related to systems of power.

To achieve this pedagogical goal in the lecture, I drew on feminist Fat Studies scholars, such as April Herndon, Eve Sedgwick, Le'a Kent, and Kathleen LeBesco, to provide concrete examples of how to examine commonsense understandings of bodies and the implications these understandings have for peoples' lives regardless of their body size. I also wanted to demonstrate how discourses that challenge notions of healthy and desirable bodies get silenced, ignored, and rendered illegitimate; I did so by emphasizing that body size and perceptions of who is deemed healthy are related to contemporary understandings of gender, race, class, ability, and age. Fatness is not isolated from other social identities. Indeed, it is directly related to gender and race as well as to class, age, and ability.

Fat is not a new feminist concern. Indeed, since Susie Orbach famously declared "Fat Is a Feminist Issue," feminist theorists have been engaged in understanding the politics of women's bodies and fatness. S. Bear Bergman, who identifies as a butch with a transmasculine identity, describes how fatness shapes the ways in which gender is read. When Bergman is taken to be a man, hir[1] body is not understood as fat and does not experience negative social consequences of fatness (141). For example, ze can easily purchase fashionable clothing and is not harassed in public by strangers. Conversely, when Bergman is taken to be a woman, ze is frequently harassed on the street and is shamed when ordering foods such as french fries (141). Bergman's personal accounts of negotiating gender and fat identity underscore the different social consequences of fatness in relation to gender. Linking gender with fatness may foster an understanding of how body size is related to other identity hierarchies of power.

To demonstrate how hierarchies function, I listed a series of traits typically assumed to be related to fat people such as laziness, gluttony, and sloppiness. I then related these traits to the broader understandings of the history and production of "Otherness"—a central notion in the class. Particular attention was given to examining fatness as represented in popular culture. I illustrated how fat bodies are often marginalized and/or demonized by using images from popular films and television programs, such as *Gilmore Girls* (2000–7), *Mike and Molly* (2010–), *Harry Potter and the Prisoner of Azkaban* (2004), and *The Little Mermaid* (1989). Furthermore, I demonstrated how our understandings of fatness need to be placed in relation to other identities. For example, I used the characters of Roseanne and Dan Connor from the television show *Roseanne* to show how gender, class, and fatness interlock.

I spent the remaining time in the lecture discussing how fat feminist activists intervene and challenge the dominant understandings of fatness. Although specific reasons and outcomes for fat activism vary widely, in general fat activism seeks to challenge and change stereotypical and stigmatized understandings of fat. The purpose of drawing on fat activism was to encourage students to reframe dominant discourses of fatness by presenting them with numerous, diverse examples of how others intervene in popular discourses of fatness.

I presented the students with a variety of fat activist projects and discussed the various forms and uses of different media. For example, I described the book *Fat!So?* by Marilyn Wann, a long-time fat activist, and shared some of the ways such activist interventions could be taken up in the Women and Gender Studies classroom. One such intervention is "L.B. O'Fat, a globetrotting pound of lost fat" (Wann, 26). L.B. is a plastic replica of a pound of fat that was originally created as a motivational tool for weight loss. However, Wann has resignified L.B.'s purpose. She shows L.B. touring the world and meeting up with other lost pounds of fat (27). When first confronted with L.B., it is difficult not to rethink knowledge of fat and its role in the body.

Another example of fat activism is "FemmeCast," a podcast[2] that speaks to the complexity of fatness, corporeality and the construction of subjectivities. "FemmeCast," hosted by Bevin Branlandingham, uses interviews with queer fat femmes to present multiple subjectivities to raise questions of fatness and subjectivity. The discussion of fatness and how it interlocks with other subjectivities is the main focus of the show. "FemmeCast" problematizes the notion of stable identity categories by enabling discussions that speak to identifications in local and historically specific sites. The premier episode, broadcast in April 2008, featured narratives of self-identified queer, fat femmes describing how they came to claim their particular subjecthood through corporeality and sexuality. The narratives are not used to present the "right" way to be a queer fat femme or to present a unified voice of fatness. Rather, these narratives are used to present the multiplicity and diversity of fat identifications. This approach toward understanding fatness, bodies, and subjectivity is an important facet of fat pedagogy. As

Kathleen LeBesco argues, "underlying the project of retheorizing corpulence is an understanding of communication as the primary process by which identities are negotiated and narratives are constructed, such negotiation and construction both scrambling traditional views of what it means to be a political subject" (83). The approaches used in FemmeCast conceptualize subjectivities related to fatness as unstable, fluid, and multiple. They offer approaches to understanding the body by negotiation with and through difference.

Lastly, I discussed the "Illustrated BMI." The "Illustrated BMI" project was created by feminist blogger Kate Harding and attempts to subvert and reclaim the body mass index (BMI) through photos that feature self-portraits of individuals under a caption that states their name and their BMI classification (e.g., underweight, normal, morbidly obese). The project challenges viewers' concept of healthy bodies and normativity by having individuals upload photos of themselves along with their BMI classification: "underweight," "normal," "overweight," "obese" or "morbidly obese." These images, often featuring individuals actively using their bodies by engaging in activities such as yoga and/or showing smiling and happy individuals, challenge the dominant medicalized image of the fat body as lazy and/or unhappy. Furthermore, the project shows a diversity of bodies and their BMI classifications, and this juxtaposition helps raise questions about the usefulness of this classification system, in that many bodies appear to be of a similar size even though they have radically different labels attached to them.

The Illustrated BMI challenges the normalized, medicalized understanding of the body by associating the medical label with an active, human subject rather than clinical photography. Understandings of the truth claims associated with the medical classification are most dramatically called into question when viewers are confronted with the label "morbidly obese" attached to a photo of an individual expressing her vitality through either the actions or positions of her body. The self-portraits and their captions also suggest a certain reclaiming of the BMI classification, given that the participants are unashamed by their classification and call into question the purpose of such a label.

Each fat activist project has its own risks and pitfalls. As I prepared to teach with the projects, three key concerns arose about using them in the class I was teaching: (1) How might such projects serve to establish a new norm? If the bodies represented get taken up as "acceptable," what bodies are rendered unacceptable? I was cautious of what unthinkable and abject bodies such an approach would enable. (2) Would I be constructing or perpetuating a good fattie / bad fattie binary, in which fat bodies that uphold contemporary notions of health, such as physical activity and healthy eating, are understood as "good," while other fat bodies, primarily those that fail to uphold notions of health, are rendered as "bad" or deserving of poor treatment? (3) Would I be privileging the visual? Would seeing a fat body in a particular way confirm or deny particular knowledge?

It is dangerous to raise questions and open spaces for critique of the dominant discourse, for these discourses are used to make sense of our bodies and ourselves. Educators can never ensure that students receive and comprehend the message or critique that such activist interventions offer. The intention of teaching fatness by applying a feminist pedagogy is not to espouse a "right" or proper understanding; rather, such teaching attempts to create educational spaces in which corporeality, fatness, and understanding of the body can be discussed, challenged and critiqued. There is no question that these techniques require both the student and the teacher to confront difficult knowledge of the body. However, fear of such confrontation should not be an excuse to allow fat phobia and the dominant discourses of the body in Women and Gender Studies and/or feminist classes to go unchallenged.

Working Toward Fat Feminist Pedagogy

Three notable moments arose during my attempt to teach critical understandings of fatness to Women and Gender Studies students. These moments underscored not only my personal challenges of discussing fatness in the classroom but also the politics of classroom practice. Two of these moments occurred during a tutorial I facilitated; the third, at the final examination for the course after students had submitted their exam booklets. All three moments underscore the challenge of teaching from a position of fatness.

Moment #1: The Word "Fat" Is the Problem
During the discussion of bodies and representations in tutorial, a student raised an unanticipated concern to the group. She claimed that the real problem was not bodies; rather, it was the word "fat." The student stated that the word was insulting and that a new one was needed to define fat bodies. The student's comment identified the importance of language in relation to bodies. While I had attempted to create a fat-positive space in tutorial and in the lecture, the comment demonstrated that the Women and Gender Studies classroom is a space that is always embedded in these discourses and, importantly, is not disconnected from the realities of students' lives beyond the class.

The student's concern underscored the power of the word in her social world. It also led to a tutorial discussion about reclaiming words and why doing so is important. Kathleen LeBesco has argued that new understandings of fatness can be created through words. Students in the tutorial had the space to discuss the uses and meanings ascribed to the word fat and were able to debate the importance of challenging how we understand our bodies through the language we use to describe them. I was pleased with the discussion that resulted from the student's concern, for it provided an opportunity to develop and practise a critical understanding of fatness.

Moment #2: Calling Me Fat

Politically, I attempted to teach fatness through feminist pedagogy by critically interrogating normalizing practices and how, through engaging with these practices, we construct our bodies and our selves. This approach was initially destabilizing and perhaps difficult for students to engage fully, as demonstrated by an interaction I had with a student in tutorial. The student claimed that "it was okay for PhD students to 'let themselves go' but as undergrads there is no excuse for not being healthy." My initial response was "Okay, she's not talking about my body." Then I heard the shocked gasps from the students sitting next to me and realized that yes, she was intentionally trying to insult me by calling me out as fat in front of the class.

This was an emotionally challenging moment for me as a tutorial instructor. The student's comment brought my body back into the class or, more specifically, served to remind me that my body was always there. Her comments underscored my own vulnerability in the classroom and demonstrated that the bodies of Women's Studies instructors are read as manifesting their feminist politics and practices. Sharon Rosenberg discusses how her students responded to her changing her hair colour. Rosenberg's example demonstrates how "bodies are never neutral in or outside of classroom spaces ... how [teacher's] bodies do a certain kind of work with, for, and against 'us' in the dynamics of teaching and learning" (88).

I could have used this opportunity in class to discuss expectations of Women's Studies instructors or even to question why the student believed that fatness is allowable if you are a PhD student but not an undergrad. Instead, I chose to deflect the question by asking if anyone else had another comment. I believe some students did question her statements, but unfortunately I was too busy retreating into my head in an attempt to gain control over my body (i.e., to stop blushing) and to come to grips with what had just happened in front of the class. Initially, I was disappointed by my reaction to the student's comment; however, my response demonstrates the challenge of teaching fatness. My desire to provide a response that challenged this student's understandings of fatness was trumped, in the moment, by my own emotional reactions regarding the body.

This student's behaviour could be interpreted as an attempt to challenge my authority or power in the class. However, the questioning of power and authority is a crucial aim of my feminist pedagogical approach. On reflection, her comments demonstrated an attempt to engage and challenge power (in this case the power I held in the class) while simultaneously calling into question the neutrality of the bodies in the space. Ultimately, her comments are reflective of the goals of fat feminist pedagogy.

Moment #3: "Lookin' Good!"

The last of the moments happened toward the end of term. On two different occasions, students came up to me to tell me how great I was looking: one student asked if I had been losing weight; another declared that I *had* lost weight. These innocent off-the-cuff comments once again brought up uncomfortable feelings as they demonstrated to me that my body was very much part of my teaching. At the time, I interpreted their comments as a failure in my teaching. I wanted students to question the idea that losing weight equates to "looking good." I will never know the motivation behind their comments. Perhaps they were trying to compliment me before I went and graded their exam; but just as likely, their understanding of what it means for women to "look good" had changed. Regardless of their motivation, their comments made me feel very uncomfortable.

My response was to brush off the comments. This response was inadequate. It does, however, reflect the contradictions I encountered when I attempted to teach fatness through a feminist pedagogical approach. Challenging the neutrality of the body in the classroom can be risky. Both Susan Bordo and Yofi Tirosh highlight the importance of the educator's body and its relationship to classroom authority. Bordo admits how losing weight and achieving a thinner, normalized body may have limited her capacity to be an alternative role model for her students and that her body is likely viewed "as confirmation that success comes only from playing by the cultural rules" (31). Similarly, Tirosh describes her struggle to address body size in the classroom and suggests that a teacher's authority is inseparable from how her students understand her personal experience, background, and body (275). Rather than providing a "'voice-over' to dub the body," Tirosh leaves her body to do its own expressive work in her classrooms (276). Tirosh's approach is potentially problematic as the bodies of educators are simultaneously understood by and construct discourses in the classroom.

Despite my goal to have frank conversations about the body in the context of the class, these interactions with students demonstrated how I continued to be deeply uncomfortable with having my body talked about in the classroom or in casual conversations with students. In the future, I would explicitly discuss this contradiction with my students and explain that I too am still learning how to go about challenging dominant understandings of fatness in everyday interactions as an educator. This kind of response may serve to emphasize the process of learning related to challenging understandings of fatness as well as the power related to the position I hold in the classroom.

Conclusion

Importantly, fat as an identity must not be understood as distinct from other identities that can be written on the body, including but not limited to gender, sex, race, class, ability, and age. It is not up to individuals who are marginalized or marked as Other to fix the problems related to social and political oppressions. As Kevin Kumashiro argues, merely adding difference requires the voice or presences of the different to do double duty by simultaneously being required to speak to difference and to be the solution to the problem (11). Kumashiro points out that the quest for full knowledge conceptualizes the problem as a lack of diversity, in which the inclusion of more diverse voices renders the problem solved (11). Simply adding concerns related to fat feminist pedagogy should not be expected to give fat individuals "voice" in their classes, nor can fat individuals be expected to perform the task of challenging their own marginalization based on body size.

A fat feminist pedagogy should seek to question the very processes of normalization that serve to define bodies. It requires students and educators to confront the social and political processes that serve to construct idealize bodies by examining how power functions both in our classrooms and in our social worlds. Furthermore, this approach aims to emphasize the process of learning rather than the achievement of the correct understanding. A fat feminist pedagogy approach can challenge and intervene into the "geography of normalization." Through this approach to teaching, educators can help to create a space for students to rethink (and unthink) how they understand bodies and explore new possibilities for understanding their bodies and themselves. For me, applying fat feminist pedagogy will continue to bring up uncomfortable but important conversations. This pedagogy serves as a constant reminder of what bodies do in the classroom.

Notes

I would like to thank Professor Joan Simalchik and the students in her 2010–11 Introduction to Women and Gender Studies course for helping me learn these "fat lessons." I also would like to thank Allison Burgess, Kristin Smith, and Marie Vander Kloet for their thoughtful feedback on early drafts of this essay. I am very grateful to Dr. Heather Sykes and fellow students in Queer Theory, Bodies and Curriculum at the Ontario Institute for Studies in Education of the University of Toronto (Winter 2009) for the fruitful discussion we had regarding topics addressed in this chapter.

1 Bergman does not identify as male or female and prefers the pronouns hir or ze in place of gender-specific pronouns.
2 Podcasts are online radio shows available through music-purchasing websites such as iTunes as well as directly through websites associated with the individual podcast.

Works Cited

Bergman, S. Bear. "Part Time Fatso." In *The Fat Studies Reader*. Ed. Esther Rothblum and Sondra Solovay. New York: NYU Press, 2009. 139–42.

Bordo, Susan. *The Unbearable Weight: Feminism, Western Culture, and the Body*. Berkeley: University of California Press, 1993.

Branlandingham, Bevin. *FemmeCast: The Queer, Fat Femme Podcast Guide to Life*. Episode 1. 2008. http://www.femme-cast.com. Podcast.

Britzman, Deborah. "Is There a Queer Pedagogy? Or, Stop Reading Straight." *Educational Theory* 45.2 (1995): 151–65. http://dx.doi.org/10.1111/j.1741-5446.1995.00151.x

———. "Queer Pedagogy and Its Strange Techniques." In *Lost Subjects, Contested Objects: Toward a Psychoanalytic Inquiry of Learning*. New York: SUNY Press, 1998.

Ellsworth, Elizabeth. "Why Doesn't This Feel Empowering?: Working Through the Repressive Myths of Critical Pedagogy." *Harvard Educational Review* 59.3 (1989): 297–324.

Fisher, Berenice Malka. *No Angel in the Classroom: Teaching Through Feminist Discourse*. Lanham: Rowman & Littlefield, 2001.

Gullage, Amy. "An Uncomfortable Fit: Fatness, Femininity, and the University." *Atlantis: A Women's Studies Journal* 34.2 (Spring 2010): 66–76.

Harding, Kate. "Illustrated BMI." http://kateharding.net/bmi-illustrated

Hetrick, Ashley, and Derek Attig. "Sitting Pretty: Fat Bodies, Classroom Desks, and Academic Excess." *The Fat Studies Reader*. Ed. Esther Rothblum and Sondra Solovay. New York: NYU Press, 2009. 197–204.

Kumashiro, Kevin. "Queer Students of Color and Antiracist, Antiheterosexist Education: Paradoxes of Identity and Activism." In *Troubling Intersections of*

Race and Sexuality: Queer Students of Color and Anti-Oppressive Education.
Ed. Kevin Kumashiro. Lanham: Rowman & Littlefield, 2001. 1–25.

Lather, Patti. "Post-Critical Pedagogies: A Feminist Reading." In *Feminisms and Critical Pedagogy*. Ed. Carmen Luke and Jennifer Gore. New York: Routledge, 1992. 120–37.

LeBesco, Kathleen. "Queering Fat Bodies/Politics." In *Bodies Out of Bounds*. Ed. Jana Evans Braziel and Katherine LeBesco. Berkeley: University of California Press, 2001. 74–87.

Luhman, Susanne. "Pedagogy." In *Rethinking Women's and Gender Studies*. Ed. Catherine M. Orr, Ann Braithwaite, and Diane Lichtenstein. New York: Routledge, 2012. 65–82.

Luke, Carmen. "Feminist Politics in Radical Pedagogy." In *Feminisms and Critical Pedagogy*. Ed. Carmen Luke and Jennifer Gore. New York: Routledge, 1992. 25–53.

Orbach, Susie. *Fat Is a Feminist Issue*. New York: Berkeley Books, 1978.

Rosenberg, Sharon. "Que(e)r(y)ing the Teacher's Body: Femme Corporeality, Vulnerability, and Play." *Journal of Curriculum Theorizing* 20.2 (2004): 87–96.

Tirosh, Yofi. "Weighty Speech: Addressing Body Size in the Classroom." *Review of Education, Pedagogy, and Cultural Studies* 28.3–4 (2006): 267–79. http://dx.doi.org/10.1080/10714410600873183

Wann, Marilyn. *FAT!SO?: Because You Don't Have to Apologize for Your Size.* Berkeley: Ten Speed Press, 1998.

CHAPTER SIX

Engaged Pedagogy Beyond the Lecture Hall: The Book Club as Teaching Strategy

Renée Bondy

A significant challenge I face teaching in the university setting is facilitating meaningful, productive discussion among students in large classes. One of the main barriers to this is a practical one—in most standard lecture halls, the seats are fastened to the floor! It is almost impossible for students to discuss, debate, and learn from one another when, confined to immovable chairs and further encumbered by flip-down desktops, they cannot engage in face-to-face conversations. Several semesters ago, in 2007, standing at the lectern and looking out at a sea of more than one hundred eager first-year students, I knew there had to be a solution to this dilemma. I couldn't take bolt cutters to the chair legs, and relocating to occupy the student centre commons during our class time simply was not a realistic option—but somehow we had to escape the lecture hall.

The aforementioned course is a first-year Women's Studies offering titled Gal Pals: Women and Friendship. This interdisciplinary study of women's friendships examines the topic through the lenses of history, literature, philosophy, psychology, and popular culture.[1] With its rich subject matter and thought-provoking ideas to which I knew almost all students could relate, it is for this course in particular that I have struggled to find ways to facilitate productive small group discussion. Building in weekly or biweekly tutorials offers students some opportunity to discuss the assigned readings in small groups, but the staid tutorial format really doesn't meet my vision of "engaged pedagogy," which I will expand upon in a later section of this chapter (see hooks, 13–22).

As a result of my quest for new and innovative discussion formats, the use of a class book club has become a key teaching strategy in the Gal Pals course, and a celebratory culminating event for the semester. The Gal Pals Book Club not only takes us out of the lecture hall but also increases student engagement, bolsters their sense of efficacy, facilitates reflexive learning, and builds relationships both among the students and with the larger Women's Studies community. In its close attention to the dynamics of one particular event—the classroom book club—this chapter resembles those by Browdy de Hernandez, Dorney, and Gullage, each of which analyses the pedagogy employed in a discrete class or course exercise. By exploring the practical and theoretical underpinnings in the planning and execution of a classroom book club, and offering reflections on this process (see also Iverson in this book), I aim to chart a roadmap for others who wish to adopt the book club as a teaching strategy in the university setting.

Engaging a History of Women's Book Clubs
The history of women's book clubs is one topic studied in our course. This learning, paired with active participation in the Gal Pals Book Club, encourages *reflexivity;* that is, it enables students to make meaningful connections between the content of their learning and their lived experiences, including active participation in and personal reflection on the pedagogical process. For this reason, before expanding on the theory and practice of the classroom book club, brief examination of the historical significance of book clubs for women is warranted.

The recent increase in the popularity of book clubs in North America began in the late twentieth century and is often attributed to the Oprah Book Club phenomenon. Since its inception in 1996, the Oprah Book Club has grown to a whopping two million members, comprising television viewers, readers of *O* magazine, and online devotees.[2] Oprah's book endorsements have brought fame and fortune to previously unknown authors and, more importantly, turned countless non-readers into avid readers of classic and contemporary literature. Two decades later, and subsequent to the termination of her long-running popular television show, bookstore and library shelves remain lined with books bearing the Oprah Book Club insignia. Of course, there are some people who feel that Oprah's impact is not altogether positive, arguing that the commercialization of literature detracts from it somehow. Yet, despite cynicism about the endemic influence of Oprah—the so-called "Oprahfication" of Western culture (see Hall; Cotten and Springer)—it is impossible to deny that she has affected the popularity of book clubs in the late twentieth and early twenty-first centuries.

Of course, well before Oprah's influence, book clubs served as important sites of socializing and engagement with literature, particularly for women. In North America, the nineteenth-century Woman Movement spurred a rapid increase in the number of women's organizations. These ranged from reform bodies with national and international renown, like the Women's Christian Temperance Union (WCTU) and the Young Women's Christian Association (YMCA), to local, lesser-known women's groups and clubs, among which book clubs (often referred to as literary societies) were especially popular. Canadian historian Heather Murray records the existence of more than three hundred literary societies between 1820 and 1900 in the province of Ontario alone—and those are just the ones for which archival materials or other historical evidence are available (Murray, 17). While some of these were mixed-gender book clubs, women-only clubs were very common, sometimes because of restrictions barring women from exclusive men's groups.

Histories of women's book clubs reveal that from the nineteenth to the mid-twentieth centuries, book clubs served multiple purposes for women. Perhaps most importantly, these clubs were sites where women might extend their educations, with book clubs compensating for the lack of access to institutions of higher learning for most women. In her documentation of American book club members' experiences, Elizabeth Long includes a fitting insight from a Dubuque Iowa Conversation Club member, who remarked in 1898, "Our universities must be in our homes" (36). This statement likely reflects the sentiments of many women at a time when higher education was the privilege of an elite few. Even for those women who benefited from advanced levels of education, it would often have been the case that the limitations placed on women's access to ongoing studies and to the professions curtailed opportunities for further learning. For some women, book clubs picked up where formal education left off.

Book clubs also allowed women to come together in semi-public spaces to hone their skills in public speaking, organizing, and leadership—skills that, once developed, might then be used in the public sphere (Long, 59). The structured format of the nineteenth-century book club lent itself to the development of such skills. Stringent club protocols, such as membership requirements, elected officers, constitutions, bylaws and parliamentary procedure for meetings, required leadership and organization. In many book clubs, discussion proceeded in an orderly manner, following presentation of one or more formal essays on the literature by club members (39–40). Guest speakers on topics of interest to members were common, and in this way book clubs became a venue for women reformers and suffragists to relay their messages (52).

The best-known example of the nineteenth-century book club model in the Canadian context is the Toronto Women's Literary Club (TWLC). Founded in 1877 by Emily Howard Stowe, the TWLC, as a result of the politicization of its members, become the Canadian Women's Suffrage Association in 1883 (Murray, 107–8). Many women's book clubs, including the TWLC, advocated for higher education and other rights for women. Some hosted open lectures on topics of interest to women, and some sponsored scholarships and advocated for women's educational rights. These efforts stand in stark contrast to the apolitical tenor of most book clubs today.

In the past several decades, as women's access to education has increased significantly, along with their participation in public life, book clubs have maintained their social value but have relinquished their political involvements. Today's book clubs are much less formal in structure and pose no real challenge to the social order. They are also so casual as to meet almost anywhere—from living rooms to cafés to big-box stores, or even online. No longer crucial venues for women's education, today's book clubs are primarily recreational, a chance to gather over a cup of coffee or a glass of wine and chat about the latest bestseller or a recent Oprah pick.

When students compare the book clubs of the nineteenth and early twentieth centuries to those of the late twentieth and early twenty-first centuries, they can readily see that contemporary book clubs seem to have lost the mandate for women's advancement and social reform held by women's book clubs in the past. At the same time, the students in Gal Pals recognize some similarities between today's book clubs and those of generations past: book clubs continue to offer women opportunities for community, support, friendship, and self-reflection through literature, and they provide a safe context for exploring ideas about women's issues and identities. The fact is, however, that very few undergraduates belong to book clubs and therefore they have no lived experience by which to evaluate those ideas.

Since our Gal Pals course already incorporated the reading of a novel, *The Color Purple* by Alice Walker, it seemed feasible to build an event that would offer the students a book club experience. In this way, they might compare their own experience of the book club to that of other women, past and present. This would also be a reason to gather outside the lecture hall and to experiment with a new and innovative discussion format. After much planning and negotiating for space, the teaching assistants,[3] students, and I launched our first Gal Pals Book Club in 2007. Today, seven years and more than two thousand students later, participation in the Gal Pals Book

Club provides an opportunity for students to explore salient themes and ideas in the novel, as well as to consider new and innovative purposes for book clubs in the twenty-first century.

It is important to note that the practice of classroom book clubs has its own precedents. The literature on education reveals that outside the post-secondary realm, book clubs have been used effectively for various purposes. Examples of book clubs in elementary and secondary school classrooms in recent decades are numerous, and many of these target specific demographics, including "reluctant readers" and students with learning disabilities and other special education needs (see Berkeley; Lesperance). Experiments in girls-only and boys-only book clubs in school settings are also noted in the literature (see Broughton; Stevenson; Weih). Also, teachers at the elementary and secondary levels have used book clubs as forums for professional development (see Galloway; Goldberg and Pesko), and parent–teacher groups use them to build parent and community engagement in education (see Dail; Zaleski et al.). In alternative education settings, such as the Humanities 101 course at Lakehead University (see Nicholas and Baroud in this volume), as well as in prison education programs (see Geraci), book clubs offer unique learning opportunities for students with limited access to traditional educational settings or negative prior experiences in them. The employment of book clubs as teaching strategy in these contexts leads me to believe that their use at the post-secondary level might be both justified and productive.[4]

The Gal Pals Book Club as Feminist Teaching Strategy

My use of a book club in a university Women's Studies course is inspired by bell hooks's observation that the feminist classroom is one in which professors strive to "create participatory spaces for the sharing of knowledge" (15). hooks extends this to include the caveat that professors must "be actively committed to a process of self-actualization ... if they are to teach in a manner that empowers students" (15). Therefore, before attempting to create the "participatory space" hooks suggests, I had to first ask this question: What in my own experience, my own awareness, might I bring to the learning situation?

Over the years I have accrued many experiences that, taken together, approximate hooks's vision of the professor's "process of self-actualization." My use of the book club as a teaching strategy has its genesis in my personal curiosity about women's book clubs, which began in the mid-1990s. Although this is the same era in which the Oprah Book Club hit its stride, it wasn't the Oprah phenomenon that drew my attention to them. Actually, it was my neighbour, Sara, and her experiences with her book club that piqued my curiosity. Sara and I met in 1996 when I bought a house in the downtown area of a small city and we became backyard neighbours. Over our shared chain-link fence we discovered that, despite our vast difference in age (at the time, she was in her late eighties and I was in my late twenties), we had a lot in common. We were both teachers by training, and we shared many interests, like gardening, baking, and a passion for books and reading. When I discovered that Sara had belonged to the same book club for almost fifty years, I was intrigued! Sara's book club, affiliated with the Canadian Federation of University Women, shared some of the characteristics of book clubs of earlier eras, including the practice of preparing formal research essays to read at meetings. Over the years I had the opportunity as an invited guest to observe this women's book club in action, and noticed that it seemed to bridge the characteristics of women's book clubs of nineteenth- and early-twentieth-century North America and those of more recent decades. This experience, and my own participation in reading groups and book clubs,[5] has fuelled my passion for the topic and led me to include the study of book clubs in the Gal Pals course.

As mentioned previously, Walker's novel *The Color Purple* had been an assigned text for the Women and Friendship course before the advent of the Gal Pals Book Club.[6] *The Color Purple* had long been one of my favourite books, and I originally chose it for the course because of its exploration of the complexities of women's friendships. This, together with another central theme in this epistolary novel, "empowerment through literacy," served as inspiration for the Book Club. The central character in *The Color Purple* is Celie, a young Black girl in the American South at the turn of the twentieth century who survives incest and years of physical and emotional abuse and isolation. She maintains a tenuous relationship with God and with her sister Nettie, a missionary in Africa, by writing letters. For the most part, Celie's letters go unanswered, yet they sustain her. Over time, they form a narrative that reveals not only Celie's increasing ability to read and write, but also the confidence she gains through her friendship with women and, in particular, her love affair with blues singer Shug Avery. *The Color Purple* is a story of Celie's journey from illiteracy, enslavement, and isolation to literacy, freedom, and relationship. Literacy and friendship are Celie's salvation. As a fan of the novel and a teacher on the subject of women's friendships, I appreciated the parallel between the ways in which literacy and friendship together transformed Celie and the ways in which women's book clubs preserve and honour both literacy and friendship.

The emphasis on the relationship between literacy and friendship in the course seemed to suit a social event, like a book club. My translation of this idea into pedagogical practice was informed by Vygotsky's social constructivist learning theory. Simply put, this is the notion that knowledge is constructed in a social context and therefore that learning is essentially a social process. If optimal learning occurs when students are actively engaged in social exchange, then the classroom must be a place that facilitates this. The most common learning space for large university classes—the lecture hall, which accommodates one hundred or more students in rows with fixed, often tiered, seating facing a lectern and projection screen—ensures by design the practice of all-eyes-on-the-professor-at-all-times and is hardly amenable to meaningful social interaction. This arrangement is appropriate for traditional lecture-style delivery but is not conducive to active social exchange among students. While the idea of learning as a social process made good sense to me, I had a hard time seeing how this could be realized in a lecture hall.

Perhaps simply because the subject of study in the course is women's friendships, and therefore might attract students with specific interests in or commitments to friendship, as we near the end of the semester many students in the class seem to form close bonds with one another. On a practical level, the friendships among the students help facilitate an easy transition from the lecture and tutorial formats to the less formal book club space. The Gal Pals Book Club is held in a conference facility on the university campus with round tables and chairs for six to eight people, a set-up especially conducive to productive discussion. Thanks to the generosity of the Women's Studies program, the club enjoys refreshments and small table favours, such as bookmarks, and this contributes to a warm and celebratory environment. Participants are encouraged to wear name tags, and seating is not assigned, which encourages students to sit where they are comfortable and also to interact with guests from the campus and community. While these seem like small details, they help establish the book club as a welcoming and egalitarian space.

Planning for the Gal Pals Book Club, I wanted to ensure that the event embedded hooks's notion of "engaged pedagogy," which emphasizes "mutual participation between teacher and student" (204). To achieve this, I ask students not just to read the novel but also to prepare for the club by considering certain themes that might connect their reading to theories studied in the course and then to create questions that might be pertinent to their discussions. In a traditional tutorial format, the discussion is often guided by the teaching assistant or professor; in the book club, the students take on this role. They organize and synthesize their questions in advance of the event so that they can draw on a broad and diverse bank of questions. Also, students are encouraged to volunteer to prepare and present author biographies and readings of key passages from the novel; in this way, they shape and direct the discussion. All of this takes responsibility for the content and direction of learning out of the hands of the professor and places it into the hands of the students.

I also wanted to ensure that the Book Club challenged what hooks dubs the "banking system" of education, which assumes that "memorizing information and regurgitating it represent[s] gaining knowledge that [can] be deposited, stored and used at a later date" (5). I was confident that the Gal Pals Book Club, because of how it was structured, would undermine the banking system—that it would "create participatory spaces for the sharing of knowledge" and give students a unique opportunity to bring their own experiences and interpretations as readers to bear. Ideally, the evaluation process would include much more than simply reiteration of their understandings of the novel. Indeed, the students would go beyond interpretive assessments of the novel and engage in what might be considered a reflexive exercise, comparing and evaluating their own book club experiences with those of other women in other book clubs. Initially, this was unsettling for me and required some faith on my part that if I let go of the lecture format and left the students to learn in this collaborative environment, the formative assessment outcome (in this case, student performance on a final exam) would not suffer. My fears around this turned out to be unfounded; compared to results in previous semesters, the students who participated in the first Book Club demonstrated superior ability to connect the novel to the literary and film theories examined in the course readings and lectures.

Perhaps the most unique aspect of our Gal Pals Book Club is that it takes the course beyond the lecture hall and opens participation to the larger campus and community. At the beginning of the semester, the students extend invitations to their friends, sisters, mothers—anyone who has read or agrees to read the novel by the date of the Book Club. We also send invitations to women connected to the Women's Studies program—students, professors, alumna, and affiliated community women. This ensures that our Book Club discussions incorporate not only the students' learning but other perspectives and experiences as well, further diversifying and democratizing the learning space.

Reflections and Moving Forward
Since its inception in 2007, the Gal Pals Book Club has become a much anticipated culminating event for the Women and Friendship course. Its success has confirmed my initial hunch that the Book Club would be a good fit with my vision of feminist pedagogy; it has also challenged me to think about how I might incorporate similar strategies and approaches in

other classes. While I have not used the book club strategy in other courses as yet, as a result of its use in the Women and Friendship course I am open to the possibility that it could be used effectively in other classroom situations. Generally speaking, my teaching has improved as a result of this experience: I am more open to possibilities for student planning and leadership in class discussions, and more willing to venture outside the assigned lecture hall. "Engaged pedagogy" is no longer an abstract notion but a lived reality in my classes. I now echo hooks's claim that "my voice is not the only account of what happens in the classroom" (20).

A few years ago I was invited to take the Book Club on the road, guest-hosting a session with the students in the Humanities 101 course at Lakehead University. It was encouraging to see that this strategy had relevance beyond the Women and Friendship course, for which the club had close ties to course content and served as an extension of our historical study of book clubs.

To me, one of the most important outcomes of the Book Club—and an unanticipated one—is that class activities and discussions can be shaped by and have a profound impact on people outside the course. An especially revealing and rewarding moment occurred a few years ago at the conclusion of a particularly lively Book Club. One of our invited guests from the local community, the mother of a student in the Gal Pals class, approached me to say thank you for offering the event. This woman, who appeared to be in her mid-fifties, was visibly moved as she told me that she had lived in the city her entire life and had never visited the university campus. She seemed to imply that she had not viewed the university as a welcoming place and that she had not seen herself as having anything to offer in such a setting. Extending our Gal Pals Book Club to the community not only enriched the students' experience by expanding the range of perspectives shared, but benefited others as well. In this way, it could be said that the Book Club affects social change and thus has both personal and political significance for participants. To fully explore the reach of this claim, a more in-depth qualitative study of participants is warranted.

The use of the Book Club as a teaching strategy has led me to take a much longer view of the outcomes of the Women and Friendship course. Prior to my experience using the Book Club as a teaching strategy, I would have identified a few specific purposes for a first-year Women's Studies course, including introducing Women's Studies as an interdisciplinary scholarly field and teaching key terminology, ideas, and feminist theories. Using the Book Club in the classroom not only meets these short-term objectives but also engages students in an activity that has the potential to affect their lives and their learning in the long term. While most students probably will not continue to read scholarly articles and textbooks after graduation, they will read for pleasure and perhaps even as a means to social engagement, allying them with generations of book club members. It is my hope that, in addition to the learning in the course, participation in the Gal Pals Book Club will inspire some of them to found or join book clubs after graduation, encouraging their ongoing love of reading and fostering lifelong learning.

Notes

1 For a course description, visit www.uwindsor.ca/womensstudies.
2 Visit http://www.oprah.com/pressroom/About-Oprahs-Book-Club.
3 Although this essay offers my personal analysis of and reflections on the use of the book club in the Gal Pals: Women and Friendship course, much credit is due to the many teaching assistants assigned to the course who have contributed to this event, semester after semester. These women are too numerous to name, but special thanks is extended to Carol Reader, a long-serving assistant for the course, whose teaching support and friendship have contributed immeasurably to the students' lives and my own.
4 There are few documented examples of the use of book clubs in university courses. One example is Addington's study of the use of book clubs in university English classes. See Addington, "Talking about Literature." See also Chuppa-Cornell, "Watch Out, Oprah!"
5 From 2003 to 2006 I belonged to a graduate students' Gender Reading Group at the University of Waterloo, founded by a co-editor of this volume, Jane Nicholas. At present, I belong to the Sunday Morning Book Club, a casual group of friends who share a passion for contemporary fiction.
6 Over the past several semesters, the Gal Pals Book Club has read other novels about women's friendship, including Otto, *How to Make an American Quilt*; Flagg, *Fried Green Tomatoes at the Whistle Stop Café*; Kidd, *The Secret Life of Bees*; and Stockett, *The Help*.

Works Cited

Addington, Ann H. "Talking about Literature in University Book Club and Seminar Settings." *Research in the Teaching of English* 36.2 (2001): 212–48.
Berkeley, Sheri. "Middle Schoolers with Reading Disabilities in Book Club?" *TEACHING Exceptional Children Plus* 3.6 (2007): 13.
Broughton, Mary. "The Performance and Construction of Subjectivities of Early Adolescent Girls in Book Club Discussion Groups." *Journal of Literacy Research* 34.1 (2002): 1–38. http://dx.doi.org/10.1207/s15548430jlr3401_1
Chuppa-Cornell, Kim. "Watch Out, Oprah! A Book Club Assignment for Literature Courses." *Teaching English in the Two-Year College*, 30 vols., 2003.

Cotten, Trystan T., and Kimberly Springer, eds. *Stories of Oprah: The Oprahfica-tion of American Culture*. Jackson: University Press of Mississippi, 2010.

Dail, Alanna Rochelle, Lea M. McGee, and Patricia A. Edwards. "The Role of Community Book Club in Changing Literacy Practices." *Literacy Teaching and Learning* 13.1 (2009): 32.

Flagg, Fannie. *Fried Green Tomatoes at the Whistle Stop Café*. New York: Random House, 1987.

Galloway, Nicole H. "Sources of Information Used by Teachers in Professional Development Book Club Discussions." Ph.D. diss., University of North Carolina at Chapel Hill.

Geraci, Pauline M. "Promoting Positive Reading Discourse and Self-Exploration through a Multi-Cultural Book Club." *Journal of Correctional Education* 54.2 (2003): 54–59.

Goldberg, Shari M., and Ellen Pesko. "The Teacher Book Club." *Educational Leadership* 57.8 (2000): 39–41.

Hall, R. Mark. "The 'Oprahfication' of Literacy: Reading 'Oprah's Book Club.'" *College English* 65.6 (July 2003): 646–67. http://dx.doi.org/10.2307/3594275

hooks, bell. *Teaching to Transgress: Education as the Practice of Freedom*. New York: Routledge, 1994.

Kidd, Sue Monk. *The Secret Life of Bees*. New York: Penguin, 2003.

Lesperance, Gerald. "A Different Kind of Book Club." *American Educator* 26.1 (2002): 42–46.

Long, Elizabeth. *Book Clubs: Women and the Uses of Reading in Everyday Life*. Chicago: University of Chicago Press, 2003.

Murray, Heather. *Come, Bright Improvement: The Literary Societies of Nine-teenth-Century Ontario*. Toronto: University of Toronto Press, 2002.

Otto, Whitney. *How to Make an American Quilt*. New York: Random House, 1991.

Rooney, Kathleen. *Reading with Oprah: The Book Club That Changed America*. Fayetteville: University of Arkansas Press, 2005.

Stevenson, Sara. "My Bluford High Boys: How a Book Club for Reluctant Read-ers Proved the Naysayers Wrong." *School Library Journal* 55.5 (2009): 34–36.

Stockett, Kathryn. *The Help*. New York: Penguin, 2009.

Vygotsky, L.S. *Mind and Society*. Cambridge, MA: Harvard University Press, 1978.

Walker, Alice. *The Color Purple*. New York: Simon & Schuster, 1982.

Weih, Timothy G. "A Book Club Sheds Light on Boys and Reading." *Middle School Journal* 40.1 (2008): 19–25.

Zaleski, Joan, Lori Duvall, and Chris Weil. "Parents and Teachers as Readers: The Book Club as Meeting Place." *Language Arts* 77.2 (1999): 118–24.

CHAPTER SEVEN

Teaching a Course on Women and Anger: Learning from College Students about Silencing and Speaking

Judith A. Dorney

A good anger acted upon
is beautiful as lightning
and swift with power.
A good anger swallowed,
A good anger swallowed
clots the blood
to slime.

—Piercy, 88

For as we begin to recognize our deepest feelings, we begin to give up, of necessity, being satisfied with suffering and self-negation, and with the numbness which so often seems like their only alternative in our society. Our acts against oppression become integral with self, motivated and empowered from within.

—Lorde, 58

Perhaps we can at last devise reflective communities in the interstices of colleges and schools. Perhaps we can invent ways of freeing people to feel and express indignation, to break through the opaqueness, to refuse the silences. We need to teach in such a way as to arouse passion now and then … These are dark and shadowed times, and we need to live them, standing before one another, open to the world.

—Greene, 111–12

This essay describes some of my learning from the Women and Anger course I created and teach at a state university in the United States. The course emerged from my research with women teachers in public schools exploring their experiences of anger in their work lives. I developed the course in part to learn whether and how a younger generation of women might have different understandings and experiences of anger than the teachers, who ranged in age from their late twenties to early sixties. Unfortunately, my experiences in the Women and Anger course confirm that the problematizing and pathologizing of girls' and women's anger continues and inhabits the psyches of many young women.

The Women and Anger course explores the emotion of anger and its gendered development as well as the nature of aggression, both indirect and direct, and its implications for the development of girls and women and their relationships. The course is an interdisciplinary undergraduate course offered through the Women's Studies program at the college. The readings present a largely feminist standpoint and are drawn primarily from the disciplines of Psychology, Philosophy, Ethics, Cultural Studies, and History. The intention is to assist college women in recognizing, scrutinizing (Lorde, 57), and claiming the knowledge signalled by their anger and to promote the practice of positive, creative aggression in their interpersonal and civic relationships. The primary data sources for the analysis I offer include texts from the course, student comments, papers, and emails from students.

In any consideration of women and anger, the theme of voice is central. In *The Feminist Classroom,* Maher and Thompson Tetreault offer an insightful perspective that extends more conventional ideas on voice. They note their own movement from an understanding of voice as the "ability [for students] to speak for themselves, to bring their own questions to the material," to a sense that voice is "fashioned" rather than found and that students use the material in a course, along with their own knowledge and experiences, to "shape a narrative of an emerging self" (18). I would add to this organic process of shaping one's self the process of becoming more socially engaged, or as Maxine Greene states, more "open to the world" (112). This notion of voice is something these authors identify as central to a feminist pedagogy. My sense of the "voices" shared here, including my own, is that they are illustrative of emerging selves being fashioned in part as a response to our experiences of material that is both resonant and dissonant in the Women and Anger course and to dialogue with others. These concepts of resonance and dissonance offer a framework for understanding students' reactions to the course and to their development within the course. The final section of this essay describes some of my own emerging sense of self in response to a dialogue with a transgender student. I hope this work will bring us all more fully into an active encounter with the world.

Rationale and Overview of the Women and Anger Course

Central to the development of this course is research conducted during the last three decades examining the ways that girls and women often learn to silence their anger and aggression and the developmental and relational consequences of this silencing.[1] The researchers argue that when anger is claimed and reflected upon as a source of relational information it can be used to determine whether and how to take action to address the source of the anger in order to move relationships forward. Expressions of aggression become pertinent in this arena as one considers the question of how to respond to anger. Dana Jack offers ways of thinking about the forms of indirect and direct aggression that women express in response to anger, illuminating the fact that women do exercise aggression in relation to anger, albeit often unconsciously and ineffectively (1999, 180–232).

It must be noted that much of the philosophical and psychological work investigating the suppression and silencing of anger has been done by middle- and upper-middle-class white women, who in their research have largely drawn upon the experiences of women like themselves. While these experiences and investigations are meaningful and critical, there are other female cultural experiences of anger that suggest alternative understandings and reactions. For example, Sharon Welch's identification of an "ethic of risk" in African American women's literature illuminates an ethical perspective dependent upon the presence of anger and the practice of positive aggression. In the work of these writers, anger is acknowledged as a fact of life due to the racism suffered by African Americans in the United States. The anger that arises in response to subordination and abuse serves as both a source of analysis and a catalyst for action to redress injustice (39–48). While the approach to anger that Welch outlines challenges a dominant white, middle-class understanding of girls and women's anger as silenced, it is critical to acknowledge that the dominant culture is governed by this conventional interpretation that women's anger is problematic. Therefore, while there may be alternative cultural perspectives on anger and aggression, they have not taken hold in prevailing social institutions.[2]

Given this cultural backdrop, the course was designed to offer students an overview of the research background, some critique of the research based on class and race, and an exploration of political anger and creative aggression as tools of personal and social change. The trajectory of the course begins with a psychological and philosophical examination of power in relationships between dominants and subordinates, moves to a consideration of how these power dynamics create and shape anger and influence individual and institutional development, and closes with an exploration of the power of anger and aggression to create personal and civic relationships based on mutuality and social justice.

Methods and Analysis

For much of this essay I draw on student essays from a final writing assignment in one particular class in which students wrote autobiographies of their own anger. In addition to excerpts from these papers, I include comments and emails from students in that class, as well as from a few students from other classes.

There were twenty-one students in the targeted class. It appeared that the majority of students were white. Two of the female students identified themselves as Latina. I did not ask students to reveal their socioeconomic class status, but through their stories in the course, two female students identified themselves as growing up in an environment that was poor to working class. Five female students lived with their mothers for all or most of their childhood, and four female students admitted to experiencing or witnessing physical abuse in their homes. Three additional females revealed that their fathers were verbally abusive. Students' ages ranged between nineteen and mid-thirties. All but two students were female, or at least presented themselves as such. The male students tended to relate the material to women they knew and to their relationships with women (one of the males in this class was a boyfriend of one of the female students), but there were also times when they examined their own relationship to anger and aggression, especially in the final paper.

The final assignment asked the students to address several questions. The following are a few of the questions used to focus their analysis:

• What in the course speaks in a special way to your developing understanding of anger and aggression?
• Where do you see a need for change in your relationship to anger and aggression?

- How is your anger both personal and political?
- How would you like to use your anger and aggression interpersonally (in personal relationships) and politically (as a citizen)?

I read the final papers three times. The first reading was for an overall understanding of the development of each student's experiences of anger and aggression, both her/his own and those of others. The second and third readings focused on identifying commonalities in their experiences and naming them. For example, I noted the number of students who revealed experiences of physical abuse in the home and their tendency to identify or conflate those experiences with anger. This conflation was significant in that it led these women to see anger as a negative, "dangerous," and destructive emotion. One student, for example, admitted to repressing her anger, fearing that her expression of anger would lead to her become a batterer like her father. She lamented that this repression led her to difficulties with intimacy and to binge eating. It was in these second and third readings that I began to identify resonances and dissonances with the material; these became my conceptual framework for this chapter.

Students' names have been altered, with the exception of Zach, who gave permission for his name to be used. I received permission from all students whose words are used. I also met with two students from this class, Olivia and Isabelle, in order to discuss and check out some of the overall themes (the resonances and dissonances) I had identified in the students' writing. In addition, I invited these two students to respond in writing with regard to whether and/or how they could see the course as an intervention, negatively and/or positively, in their development. If they felt the course had not influenced their development, they were to suggest what was missing or what more might have been helpful for them. A portion of Isabel's reflection is included in this chapter.

Learning from the Students: Resonances

In *Silencing the Self: Women and Depression,* Dana Jack discusses the inner dialogue of depression that takes place between two parts of the self. Jack identifies them as the "authentic self" and the "Over-Eye." The "authentic self" is a first person voice that speaks from experience, trusts its observations, and acknowledges the power of its first-hand knowledge. The "Over-Eye" emanates from cultural traditions and conventions. It speaks to the authentic self from a place of judgment. "The Over-Eye carries a decidedly patriarchal flavor, both in its collective viewpoint about what is "good" and "right" for a woman and in its willingness to condemn her feelings when they depart from the expected 'shoulds'" (94).

There were several students who connected with the concept of the "Over-Eye," explaining how it had played a direct part in their own lives, or who identified it in their mothers and admitted to learning it from them. Bianca wrote about how her mother would never talk back to her father and how, if she did, she would be punished by him "physically and emotionally." Bianca continues:

> So as much as my mother did not enjoy being treated poorly, this other voice was telling her that she should stay in this relationship because she needs a husband in her life to help her raise her children. This voice was telling her that it was bad for a wife to disobey her husband. This voice was telling her that it was against her family beliefs to ever get a divorce because it makes them look bad. So she had two different voices in her head telling her what to do, and she didn't always listen to the right one. She experienced a loss of self for a long time in her life. As shocking as it was for me to realize this was the case for my mother, it also made me realize that I have this Over-Eye in my head all the time that I am constantly listening to.

Nina also speaks to the power of her mother's example in her discussion of the "Over-Eye." Nina identified strongly with Jack's claim that girls learn from their mothers' relationships with men, often seeing capitulation and inequality. These observations of how adult women behave with adult men become part of the injunctions of the "Over-Eye." "In this way, girls learn images and ways of relating to men that differ from their primary experience of intimacy with their mother but that grow out of identification with her" (Jack, 109). Even though Nina's parents were separated, she had learned deference to males:

> Even though my father was not physically the dominant one within our household, he still had a dominant presence over my mother. My mom still forced me to "please" my father all the time, whether it was a simple phone call to not "acting up" when we visited him ... As I look back, I can see myself performing in front of my father, playing the role of "good girl" for him, as if he was the judge [of] my overall personality and behavior as not just a daughter, but as an overall person. My mother's unequal relationship with my father carried on into my own relationship with my father, and I have learned to tend to his and other men's needs. Even now I still worry about what my father and other men think of me now as an adult.

Nina and Bianca were two of several students who wrote about the "Over-Eye" as a force in their lives, and the lack of mutuality signalled in the relationships they describe is disturbing and suggests how depression and an overreliance on the "Over-Eye" can be linked. Because the "Over- Eye" resonated so commonly for these women, it seems important for girls and young women to be provided with more opportunities to identify the presence of the "Over-Eye" in their lives and to critically examine its influence on them as they develop. Part of the power of the "Over-Eye" is that it works to prevent girls and women from distinguishing and exploring their feelings. This restriction informs their knowledge and their capacity to act on those feelings. Naming the ways in which they see the "Over-Eye" as a force in their lives can be a first step for girls and women in claiming their emotional knowledge, especially the knowledge connected to their anger.

A second theme that resonated with students was the relational dynamic of triangles. Harriet Lerner writes about this issue in *The Dance of Anger*. In describing the phenomenon of triangle formation in human relationships, Lerner says that "we reduce anxiety in one relationship by focusing on a third party, who we unconsciously pull into the situation to lower the emotional intensity in the original pair" (156). Triangles are common in multiple relational worlds such as work, family, and friendships and may initially be helpful in the short term by assisting in thinking through a problem or concern in a relationship. However, triangles can prevent movement and growth in relationship by sidetracking or undermining legitimate differences and sources of conflict, especially when they become entrenched. The third person allows for displacement of feelings so that the conflict between the original two people is never addressed directly.

Again, many students spoke in class and wrote in their papers about their experiences of both creating and being drawn into relational triangles. Karen, one of the mothers in the class, identified a triangle that existed between herself, her husband, and her children. She ultimately told her husband that he had to speak to their children directly and not draw her into their conflicts. Olivia shared her experience of the triangle that existed between herself, her boyfriend, and his mother:

> I'm uncomfortable and angry that my boyfriend and his mother have made me a part of their triangle, why don't I express to them how I feel? Unfortunately, I feel that my inability to remove myself from the triangle between my boyfriend and his mother is due to my impression that as a woman I serve as the role of peacemaker. Although I have no problem expressing to my boyfriend when he makes me angry, I don't like the thought of him and his mother being angry at each other. Therefore, I stay in their triangle hoping that I can somehow avoid anger between them. It amazes me that even though I can acknowledge that my own experience of anger and aggression

is positive and constructive, for some reason when I think of my loved ones expressing their anger towards each other I continue to view anger as negative and destructive.

In a conversation with Olivia after the course ended, she mentioned this triangle again. "The triangle I'm still finding a little bit of difficulty with. I feel I have to be very respectful [toward his mother]. I have found a way to tell him [boyfriend] he needs to talk to her. I haven't found a way to tell her she needs to speak to him."

Olivia has made some progress in her efforts to disentangle herself from this threesome. She is able to speak to her boyfriend directly about the situation. But because of her sense of respect for his mother, and perhaps because of some of her own discomfort with the anger her boyfriend's mother feels toward him, she remains in the triangle. While it can be quite difficult to extricate oneself from these relational patterns, the fact that Olivia can identify the triangle and has spoken to her boyfriend about it is a step in making their communications clearer and more direct. Whether she will ultimately be able to remove herself altogether is yet to be seen.

Although many of the women struggled with the idea that women could and/or should be aggressive, almost all of the students found that the examples of indirect aggression, cited by Dana Jack, rang true. They could identify instances in which they masked their anger or aggression by manipulation, sweetness, a stare, or the "silent treatment." Jack notes that these are forms of expressing anger or opposing others that "allow for a hasty retreat if one is confronted." This indirect aggression is, according to Jack, "culturally prescribed, socialized at home and in schools, yet, at the same time, is culturally condemned and seen as proof that women are more devious and less principled than men" (1999, 188).

Female students spoke and wrote about their expressions of indirect aggression, for example, giving a boyfriend the silent treatment or a stare. They also wrote about observing this form of aggression in other women. Gina wrote that in response to her dad's yelling, her mother would "give off clues like slam things or mumble under her breath" or complain to an "outside party," thus creating a triangle. Caroline described how, when her parents were angry with her, her mother would be silent and let her father be the one who yelled at and punished her. In this case the mother serves as the silent witness to overt aggression by the father and does not have to express it herself. Because of their encounters with such covert aggression on the part of women, the female students initially resisted the idea that women regularly express or exercise aggression. In fact, it wasn't until we read the chapter in Dana Jack's book on "Masking Aggression" that the women in the class could comfortably acknowledge their exercise of aggression, indirect as it might be.

"Over-Eye," relational triangles, and indirect aggression highlight just a few of the ways girls learn both to deny their own knowledge and lived experiences and to subvert or silence their will, desire, and anger. They observe women they often love and admire listen to and grant authority to the voice of cultural conventions and mores rather than trust what the women themselves want and know. They see women mask their aggression and deflate their anger by creating triangles. Such examples communicate both subtly and directly their subordinate status and the taboo of anger and direct constructive aggression for women.

Dissonances: Aggression and Defensive Anger

The exploration of aggression in our class comes largely in response to discussions of Dana Jack's book, *Behind the Mask: Destruction and Creativity in Women's Aggression*. The initial examinations of aggression were challenging for the students because many of the women were reluctant to consider aggression either as something that could be used positively or as something that women would exercise. Because aggression has been a central dimension of the definition of masculinity (29), and because male aggression is used to subordinate women verbally and physically, the women in the class argued that aggression is only negative and destructive and that it is a capacity exhibited by men, not by women. The students' position emerges from a deeply embedded cultural understanding of gender. As Jack notes, "Underlying these long-standing issues around gender and aggression is a fear woven deeply into the human psyche. What the culture fears, wants to control, and denies is women's intent to do harm" (30). Jack's comment underscores the assignment of an exclusively negative interpretation of aggression as "harmful" and destructive.

As the analysis of aggression continued, and we used Jack's definition of aggression—"forcefully bringing one's will, desires, and voice into relationship to oppose or displace those of another, for either constructive or destructive purposes" (44)—the discomfort with the ideas of "force" and "displacing another's will," desire, and voice remained sticking points. Many of the women clung to an idealized and, from my perspective, disturbing perception of women as people who were not, and should not be, forceful. The women made a distinction between assertiveness and aggression, dismissing aggression as too hard (read too *male*), thus they rejected aggression in favour of assertiveness, which they said was more polite, softer, less abrasive, more conventionally feminine. I shared with them a portion of dialogue in which former White House news reporter Helen

Thomas forcefully questioned then White House press secretary Scott McClellan following his statement that the United States was in Afghanistan and Iraq "by invitation" (20). The students who tended to be more politically critical were able to understand her aggressive questioning, and this seemed to signal a shift in perception for some of them. For others, this shift did not happen until we read Jo Fisher's *The Mothers of the Disappeared*, about the *madres* who aggressively organized and confronted the atrocities of the Argentine government during the years when thousands of citizens were being "disappeared." The methods of the *madres* were nonviolent yet highly effective. This example illustrated the potential for aggression to be forceful as well as creative and constructive.

The struggle with aggression seemed to me to be one of the more critical struggles in the course. The initial dissonance between the knowledge and experience of the women students and the theoretical perspectives and activist stances presented by authors like Dana Jack, Terry Tempest Williams, bell hooks, Jo Fisher, and Sharon Welch was formidable. And it is possible that their resistance to the idea and practice of aggression in women may have played a role in what appeared at times to be somewhat undeveloped political sensibilities in many of the students. Based on their early resistance to opening their perspectives on aggression, I clearly saw movement by the end of the course, signalling an appreciation for creative aggression in women. And of course, the section on indirect aggression illuminated the common uses of aggression by women and offered critique of this form of sanctioned yet ultimately ineffective aggression.

While the work in the class clearly illuminates some of the difficulty the women students have being in touch with their own anger, a reading by bell hooks, an African American writer, about her encounter with institutional racism and personal prejudice evoked in many of the white students what Francis Seeburger refers to as an "anger of defensiveness" (44). Megan Boler describes this form of anger as arising from "a defense of one's own investments in the values of the dominant culture" (191).

The reading evoking this reaction was the chapter "Killing Rage," from *Killing Rage: Ending Racism*. In this chapter, hooks describes a day of travelling with her friend, K, another African American woman. During this time frame, hooks and K meet with repeated racist responses from a cab driver, airline employees, flight attendants, and white male travellers. hooks's anger culminates shortly after boarding their plane, where she and K have booked first-class seating. A white male passenger had also been given the seating assigned to K. When he brought this to the attention of the flight attendant, she called K over the loudspeaker and told her she must take a different seat. Meanwhile in coach, a white male passenger had taken the wrong seat, and when the African American female passenger with that seat number arrived to take her seat, the white male passenger was not asked to leave. The woman volunteered to take another seat. At this point, hooks noted, she was furious and admitted to feeling a "killing rage" directed most immediately at the white male passenger who had taken K's seat. "I wanted to stab him softly, to shoot him with a gun I wished I had in my purse. And as I watched his pain, I would say tenderly, 'racism hurts'" (11). The remainder of hooks's chapter is an exploration and a defence of Black rage, noting its necessity as a tool for challenging racism.

In discussing this reading, many of the students reacted strongly in defence of the white man seated next to hooks. They did not understand why hooks was so angry at this particular white man, whom they felt had done nothing wrong except take his legitimate seat. This defensiveness impugned their ability to value most of the other comments hooks made in her chapter. They felt that hooks was overreacting and guilty of racism herself. Four or five of the women, who were Women's Studies majors and who had studied systemic oppression, defended hooks, pointing out the institutionalized circumstances and pattern of personal prejudices that had evoked her anger. But other students resisted acknowledging the legitimacy of those arguments. We discussed this reading for two weeks, and a few students wrote strong reactions in their response papers. I wrote back to these students, questioning their positions and attempting to clarify hooks's position. I shared Seeburger's distinction about defensive anger with the class and suggested it was at work in the reactions of several of us. One student, Miranda, was particularly vehement in her negative assessment of hooks's rage, both during class discussions and in her writing. But several weeks later she reflected on hooks's chapter in a new way. She wrote about the difficulty she had been having with hooks's perspective, when in a surprising twist, she used it as a lens to examine her own behaviour toward an African American co-worker. The young man had been wrongly accused of something at work by their boss. Miranda knew he was innocent of the charge levelled against him but did not speak up in his defence. She found herself looking at her behaviour through hooks's eyes. She acknowledged that racism had played a part in the accusation against this young man and in her silent response. She realized that her co-worker might well feel toward her the way hooks felt toward her white seatmate. This was a breakthrough for her. The initial dissonance from the reading was very difficult but ultimately led Miranda to a deeper understanding of the legacy of institutional racism and its impact on her own racial identity development.

Perhaps I should not have been surprised by the defensive reaction of so many students. I expected students who chose a Women's Studies class to have a more critical perspective on the larger culture, and indeed those women who were Women's Studies majors had that orientation. But most of the students in the class represented a broad range of disciplines and were not necessarily accustomed to critical analysis of policies and institutional structures. So the anger of defensiveness that Seeburger identifies was useful in understanding their reactions. Also, upon further reflection I have come to understand the potential presence of an additional dynamic, a general discomfort with being the recipient or target of another's anger. If individuals learn to feel that anger separates us from others, and if girls and women are often encouraged to interpret anger in that way, our own anger or another's anger toward us is likely to be dismissed, repressed, avoided, denied. So while I fully believe the students' anger at bell hooks was defensive and a protection of white privilege, I also think it may be tied into a more gendered fear of *anyone*'s anger, including their own, which, of course, ultimately serves to reinforce male privilege, white privilege, and so on.

The experience with this class led me to better prepare students for future discussion of this reading by reminding them of the perspectives and actions of dominants and subordinates (Miller 1991) that we discuss during the first portion of the course. Also, I now present Seeburger's ideas of defensive anger as well as definitions of institutional racism and Peggy McIntosh's article on white privilege prior to having them engage with hooks. This approach seems to enable students to hear and better understand the rage hooks shares in her essay and her defence of it as an essential component of action for social change.

Gender: A Challenge to the Professor

In early April of this past spring semester I received a lengthy email from a student. Zach wrote to explain to me some of the discomfort he was having in the Women and Anger class discussions and why he had not been participating more fully in those discussions. A portion of that email follows:

I would love to share personal information and stories but it gets confusing for me since I identify totally different than I was socialized. I think a lot of my anxiety about the class is also because as a group we are usually all categorized as women, and even though it may appear to be that way it isn't the case. Most of our discussion questions leave me thinking that I could answer them in two different ways—one being when I thought I identified with the gender I was socialized as, and the other being how I would answer them now based on my identity. These are things that are really difficult to get around when trying to speak about things without giving the class that information about myself, so it's much easier for me to stay quiet.

I had two immediate reactions to the email: gratitude and a desire to learn more. I emailed Zach and thanked him for his courage and honesty. I also asked if he would be willing to meet and talk with me about this as I was not sure how to make things more comfortable for him. When we first met in my office in April, following this email message, he was using his female assigned name and at that time did not request that I call him anything other than this name. I continued to refer to him by his assigned female name until my most recent email from him, in which he informed me that he had come to prefer being called Zach and having the male pronouns used in reference to him.

My meeting with Zach following that first email was close to an hour. I again thanked him for being willing to share his discomfort in class with me and for being open to discussing his situation with me. I asked if he had any resources to suggest for me to read or view in order to learn more about the experience of transgender people. We discussed an imminent speaking engagement on campus by Dean Spade, a professor, attorney, and transgender activist, and I shared with Zach my plans to attend Spade's presentation. I also informed him of my plans for the closing weeks of the semester to see if he had any thoughts on what I might need to do differently to be more inclusive in language or topics. While underscoring that his point was not to criticize the course or me, he told me that, at the least, some of the assumptions I was making about the female identification of my students was problematic. His critique was gently delivered but nonetheless forceful. Zach's communication with me illuminated the limitations of the knowledge created by my positionality and the potential costs to students of this limitation.

Since that conversation I have done quite a bit of reading and thinking about this vacuum in my knowledge. I have tried to understand why I was surprised by Zach's initial email and how exactly the course structure and material might be uncomfortable for transgender students, especially the female-to-male students. Because Zach seemed to present more as a female, I did not even consider that this might not be how he saw himself in the world. And it pushed me to think about the students who have female names but who present themselves in a traditionally more masculine way. In the past I did not presume them to be transgender, and, unlike Zach, they never corrected me or challenged me to think of and/or see them as such. So it is certainly possible they were not transgender or struggling with or challenging gender. But the fact is I did not consider it. Maher and Thompson Tetreault note in their chapter—aptly titled "Breaking Through Illusion"—that "the diversity of the classroom environments we have studied has shown us that position, perhaps more than any other single factor, influences the construction of knowledge, and that positional factors reflect relationships of power both within and outside the classroom itself" (22). This lack of knowledge on my part led to a lack of understanding of what it means to be transgender and to an inability to pick up on cues that could have challenged certain of my assumptions. Perhaps because the topic was women and anger and in this most recent class all the students appeared to be female, whether or not they presented themselves in conventionally female ways, I simply presumed that all felt, to at least a certain degree, comfortably familiar with the experiences and constraints of female identity. My conversations with Zach have illuminated the danger and damage of those assumptions. Something as simple as not referring to everyone in the class as a woman or asking people in the first class meeting what their preferred pronoun is can feel welcoming to students who are transgender or struggling with gender, as Zach noted he was at the beginning of the semester. It can also signal to all students that everyone's knowledge and experience will be welcome and useful as we explore the theoretical perspectives on gender and gender relations in the course.

Zach's initial email and subsequent communications illuminate the great value of positive aggression. As Dana Jack notes, "positive aggression, like all aggression, displaces another's will, but positive aggression uses force to gain equality and full participation in relationships ... Its hallmark is constructive change" (1999, 238). Zach's ability to bring his will clearly and directly into a relationship that is structurally unequal is inspiring and humbling. The inspiration stems from the inherent risk involved in bringing one's thoughts and feelings into relationship. One can always be rejected, and, especially where there is inequality of power, one can be punished. The humility arises in being reminded that there are holes in my knowledge. This example also reveals the ways in which something as apparently simple as speaking the truth of one's experience, expressing one's discomfort, communicating one's anger, can have far-reaching consequences. It is, for example, already changing the way I think about my students and how to teach them.

Conclusion

The students' initial understanding of anger and aggression was quite similar to the understanding of the women educators I interviewed, most of whom described an uncomfortable and unwelcome relationship with both. The women teachers struggled with questions of when and how to address issues that evoke anger for them both personally and professionally (Dorney, 2010). The similarities I found between the two groups, whose ages varied considerably, were somewhat surprising—I had hoped that the efforts of the women's movements and the increased number of women in more powerful positions in the workforce would have resulted in young women feeling more equal in relationships and more entitled to bring their will into dialogue with the will of others. Based on the discussions and writings of the students in the Women and Anger classes, I have learned that many young women are still held captive by conventional gender expectations that influence their relationships and their engagement in public life.

Nina serves as one illustration of this. In the initial weeks of the course I noted that Nina was highly articulate in expressing her political anger. She could speak without hesitation about her frustration with American politics and what she saw as the political right's agenda to dismantle women's reproductive freedom. I thought of her as a powerful young woman who was not afraid to express herself. As the course developed it became clear that even Nina had inherited the onerous directives of the "Over-Eye" when it came to her personal relationships with men. In her final paper she wrote:

> It is almost impossible for me to express my anger in a natural way, not disguised; I do not want to bring on confrontation, because I am truly afraid the loss of the relationship may be my fault. Instead, all this pent up emotion over the years has resulted in anxious behaviors and panic attacks …

> I believe that in order to be successful in bringing about social change, I must look further into my personal relationships and understand my emotions more in depth. I believe I will not be able to give my all in demonstrations and through political and social change if I [do] not truly know my inner relationship with anger and aggression.

Nina has come to see in her own life the connection between the personal and the political, and hopefully, she is on her way to making them more congruent for herself. But her words also illustrate the deep-seated nature of cultural messages about anger and aggression for girls and women, especially in relationship to men. And they suggest that if we are truly serious about educating girls and women to listen to and appreciate themselves and claim their power both individually and collectively, a class on anger and aggression can be a small contribution toward that end. Isabelle's written reflection six months after the course confirms this as one of the outcomes:

> Many of the books selected for the class … have meaningful messages that tend to linger in my mind … Even in the heat of argument induced anger (or

politically induced anger, etc.), I have found that many of the concepts that these books discuss happen to appear in my mind, in my internal dialogue, and allow a sense of on-the-spot analyzation of thoughts, and, ultimately, a potentially healthier outlook on how to, for example, utilize the concept of positive aggression, directly communicate how I feel, and attempt to appropriately conclude the argument, though settling for nothing less than what I feel is right, or equal.

Overall, many of the readings and teachings in Women and Anger have offered encouraging words to inspire and propel me to be in touch with myself, my inner voice, and to express myself ... and that when expressed in a positive, non-violent way, our voices may truly transcend the stereotypical, negative aggression-laced definition of the word anger and transform it into a tool to benefit ourselves and our relationships.

As Isabelle writes about transcending and transforming, I think also of Zach, who reminds me to be humble in the presence of my students' knowledge. Certainly one benefit of the critique he offers as a transgender person is to challenge the conventional power dynamics of male and female. Such power dynamics fuel the "Over-Eye" and signal "appropriate" behaviour and ways of thinking about anger and aggression for both men and women. The study of women and anger is therefore not just about claiming one's voice as a woman. At its heart, it is about the analysis of power. As students come to know their anger and capacity for aggression, they can develop their opportunities to bring themselves more fully into personal and civic relationships. Their opportunities to hear and respond creatively and positively to the anger evoked from such realities as race, class, and gender privilege can unfold. And their voices, rather than being static or constrained, can fashion bold narratives of continually emerging selves that resonate with their deepest knowledge.

I am deeply grateful to all the students who have journeyed through the Women and Anger course with me. I hope my learning does justice to their honesty, courage, and wisdom.

Notes
1 For additional information on the silencing of girls' and women's anger see Belenky et al.; Barrows; Bernardez; Brown; Brown and Gilligan; Dorney; Gilligan; Jack; Lerner; and Miller.
2 For a more extended discussion of the research on girls, women, and anger, see Dorney, "Interviewing Women Teachers."

Works Cited

Barrows, Anita. "The Light of Outrage: Women, Anger, and Buddhist Practice." In *Buddhist Women on the Edge*. Ed. Marianne Dresser. Berkeley: North Atlantic, 1996. 51–56.

Belenky, Mary, et al. *Women's Ways of Knowing*. New York: Basic Books, 1986.

Bernardez, Theresa. "Women and Anger: Cultural Prohibitions and the Feminine Ideal." Stone Center Working Paper Series #31. Wellesley: Wellesley Center for Research on Women (1988). 1–10.

Boler, Megan. *Feeling Power: Emotions and Education*. New York: Routledge, 1999.

Brown, Lyn Mikel. *Raising Their Voices: The Politics of Girls' Anger*. Cambridge, MA: Harvard University Press, 1998.

Brown, Lyn M., and Carol Gilligan. *Meeting at the Crossroads*. Cambridge, MA: Harvard University Press, 1992. http://dx.doi.org/10.4159/harvard.9780674731837

Dorney, Judith. "Thinking Back Through [My] Mother: Reclaiming Anger, Advocacy, and Pleasure in Teaching." In *Wise Women: Reflections of Teachers at Mid-Life*. Ed. Phyllis Freeman and Jan Schmidt. New York: Routledge, 2000. 231–39.

———. "Interviewing Women Teachers About Anger in the Workplace: Some Implications for Teacher Education." *Vitae Scholasticae* 27.2 (2010): 142–60.

Gilligan, Carol. *In A Different Voice*. Cambridge, MA: Harvard University Press, 1982.

———. "Joining the Resistance: Psychology, Politics, Girls, and Women." *Michigan Quarterly Review* 29 (1990): 501–36.

Greene, Maxine. "In Search of a Critical Pedagogy." *The Critical Pedagogy Reader*. Ed. Antonia Darder, Marta Baltodano, and Rodolpho D. Torres. New York: Routledge, 2003. 97–112.

hooks, bell. "Killing Rage: Militant Resistance." *Killing Rage: Ending Racism*. New York: Henry Holt, 1995. 8–20.

Jack, Dana. *Silencing the Self: Women and Depression*. New York: Harper Collins, 1993.

———. *Behind the Mask: Destruction and Creativity in Women's Aggression*. Cambridge, MA: Harvard University Press, 1999.

Jagger, Alison. "Love and Knowledge: Emotion in Feminist Epistemology." *Gender/Body/Knowledge: Feminist Reconstructions of Being and Knowing*. Ed. A. Jagger and S. Bordo. New Brunswick: Rutgers University Press, 1989. 145–71. http://dx.doi.org/10.1080/00201748908602185

Lerner, Harriet. *The Dance of Anger*. New York: Harper & Row, 1985.

Lorde, Audre. "Uses of the Erotic." *Sister Outsider*. Trumansburg: Crossing Feminist, 1984. 53–59.

Maher, Frances A., and Mary Kay Thompson Tetreault. *The Feminist Classroom: Dynamics of Gender, Race, and Privilege*. Lanham: Rowman and Littlefield, 2001.

McIntosh, Peggy. "White Privilege: Unpacking the Invisible Knapsak." Unpublished article. 1989. www.areteadventures.com/articles/white_privilege

Miller, Jean Baker. *Toward a New Psychology of Women*. Boston: Beacon Press, 1976.

———. "The Construction of Anger in Women and Men." In *Women's Growth in Connection*. Ed. J. Jordan, A. Kaplan, J.B. Miller, et al. New York: Guilford, 1991. 181–96.

Miller, Jean B., and J. Surrey. "Revisioning Women's Anger: The Personal and the Global." In *Women's Growth in Diversity*. Ed. Judith Jordan. New York: Guilford, 1997. 199–216.

Piercy, Marge. *Circles on the Water*. New York: A.A. Knopf, 1988.

Seeburger, Francis. *Emotional Literacy: Keeping Your Heart*. New York: Cross-road, 1997.

Spellman, Elizabeth. "Anger and Insubordination." In *Women, Knowledge, and Reality: Explorations in Feminist Philosophy*. Ed. Ann Garry and Marilyn Pearsall. Boston: Unwin Hyman, 1989. 263–73.

Thomas, Helen. "Lap Dogs of the Press." *Nation* (27 March 2006): 18–20.

Welch, Sharon. *A Feminist Ethic of Risk*. Minneapolis: Fortress, 2000.

CHAPTER EIGHT

Beyond the Trolley Problem: Narrative Pedagogy in the Philosophy Classroom

Anna Gotlib

The learning process is something you can incite, literally incite, like a riot.
—Audre Lorde, 2007, 98

As a discipline, philosophy, including moral philosophy, is often considered, especially by beginning students, to be a non-gendered recitation of "great historical figures" and their ideas, or else a ritual of fascinating, but abstract, hypotheticals that appear to be largely removed from "practical" concerns. When biomedicine is added in the form of medical ethics, student expectations often shift from obscure moral debates to received lists of clearly articulated ethical principles and generalizable case studies that would reliably help them decide *what to do*. In both cases, left out by the instructor—and subsequently assumed to be absent or unimportant by the students—is the morally vital role of gender and of racial, social, and other contextualities.

This essay challenges this abstracted approach to teaching and learning philosophy—especially moral philosophy and medical ethics—as intellectually and pedagogically impoverished. Instead, it defends contextually richer narrative pedagogies that borrow deeply from feminist theory by shifting the discourse away from a search for objective principles and generic "moral agents" to focus on the moral sensibility and intelligibility of non-ideally situated individuals. By introducing moral dilemmas narratively—through the sharing of lived stories rather than disembodied, degendered hypothet-icals—narrative pedagogy encourages students to move beyond notions of a necessarily impartial moral theory and consider the more nuanced and difficult questions about what might make certain stories (and storytellers) seem more valued—and valuable. Examining these stories attunes the stu-dents to thinking about how gender, recognition, and other determinants of social power can impact moral judgments—and lives. The essay thus theorizes, and offers examples of, the ways in which narrative methodolo-gies present promising alternatives to traditional pedagogical approaches to philosophy by creating the necessary openings for students to restructure moral landscapes as more diverse, dynamic, and inclusive spaces.

I begin by briefly considering what a "typical" undergraduate ethics classroom looks like. Then I consider the additional pedagogical challenges a medical ethics course presents and suggest that in this new context, the more traditional, "top-down" approaches to teaching and learning largely fail. Third, I introduce the alternative of narrative pedagogy, arguing that by borrowing from the feminist traditions of inclusivity and intersecting subjectivities, and by paying attention to voice and differences in power, it offers much more nuanced and effective methodologies for addressing the kinds of complex, multifaceted moral dilemmas often found in bioethical discourse. I conclude with some thoughts about the relationship between the production of knowledge within the classroom and its effects beyond the pedagogical setting.

The Ethics Classroom: A Brief Look Inside

It would be quite easy to draw a caricature of the stiff, strict philosophy instructor and passive (possibly bored) students. I will not do so here. Such a picture might be useful in locating some weaknesses of "traditional" edu-cation, but it would also be, at best, outdated and not sufficiently reflective of what one actually finds. Indeed, many instructors no longer embody the rigid stereotype at all, but appear to be friendly, open, and even chatty with their students, both in and outside the classroom. So, one might wonder—where is the problem?

The problem has much less to do with personal pedagogical style than with the substance of what is taught. Here, there are two worries, which often overlap. The first relates to *how* the material is introduced to (espe-cially beginning) students; the second, and perhaps the more important one, relates to *what* is presented as the central domain of philosophical ethics.

First, the "how." It would, of course, be irresponsible and inaccurate to paint all instructors of ethics with the same brush—after all, teaching styles and methodologies tend to vary rather widely not just across institutions but within them. So I preface what follows with the caveat that the claims that I offer here are based on personal experiences, observations, and the insights of others and in no way ought to be viewed as the result of scientific research on teaching methodologies. That said, I believe that my more general observations of certain tendencies within the American ethics classroom give rise to some legitimate concerns.

One could say that the first worry is grounded in something like a uniformity of presentation: especially in introductory courses, ethical theories are often marched out, one by one, and presented as (often) deductive, systematic calculi, inevitably leading students, from first principles, to specific sorts of answers to very specific kinds of inquiries. Thus, students are told that deontology demands that the proper motivations (and not outcomes) matter; consequentialism requires the best possible outcomes for the greater number; and so on. As a consequence of these more hierarchical theories, virtue ethics, feminist ethics, casuistry, care ethics, and others are too often either left out in whole or in part, or they are offered as responses to the more "standard" principlist approaches. These less "standard" theories are thus defined and evaluated in terms of how well they address the worries of, say, deontology or consequentialism, or they are diminished as theories for supposedly failing to rise to the requisite levels of action-guiding principles and laws. The result is often puzzlement on the part of the students: Why are any of these theories important? Is it always the case that some theories are too abstract, while others are too "soft" and unclear in their approach to moral problems? And if so, why is there not something better that bridges the gaps between them? Can ethics offer anything to our actual lived experiences except disagreement, vagueness, a lack of guidance?

Thus perhaps one of the more unfortunate consequences of this pedagogical approach is that students simply fail to see the relevance—theoretical or practical—of the theories they memorize for examinations and dutifully describe in papers. Theoretically, they are left with insoluble contradictions and arguments that seem at best circular and at worst removed from anything resembling a consistent set of instructions. Practically, they do not find the demanding, often inflexible principles—or vague notions of virtue or care—to be particularly action-guiding.

Second, the "what." As I noted above, the fact is that in many classrooms, moral theory is presented as either a list of "positions" or a debate among "great men," pitting Plato against Aristotle against Hume against Kant, and so on; only then, if time allows, does the instructor turn to critiques from women, minorities, and non-Western philosophers. Regardless of the approach taken, the result is that moral theory is presented—often to beginning students—as what Margaret Urban Walker calls a "theoretical-juridical" model, or top-down ethical principlism.

On this model, the tasks of moral theory are divided among unyielding principles, the judges who (equipped with the knowledge of these principles and what it means to obey them) make sure they are uniformly followed, and those whose moral duty it is to do the principles' bidding (Walker). Excluded are (among other things) personal relationships, normative warrant of impersonal moral commands, one's sense of oneself as a moral actor, the context of a given moment, and specific demands and valences of facts in specific situations. As Walker puts it, such an approach to normative moral theory is predicated on a metaethics that insists on

> a consistent (and usually very compact) set of law-like moral principles or procedures for decision that is intended to yield by deduction or instantiation (with the support of adequate collateral information) some determinate judgment for an agent in a given situation about what it is right, or at least morally justifiable, to do. (43)

These choices for representing philosophical ethics raise three important questions. First, ought we teach our students that moral theory is constituted entirely of impersonal duties and requirements? Ought we adopt Kant's famous claim that only a categorical imperative, free from any and all empirical or otherwise contextual influences, can properly be called a moral principle, so that only a person who acts from her duty to follow such a principle—rather than from inclination, love, desire, or other motivations not grounded in the demands of the categorical imperative—is the truly meritorious, rational, *moral agent*? (Kant).

Also problematic here is something that at first seems to be beside the point: What good is this duty-bound dedication to principles? As Lawrence C. Becker notes, there is in this principlist, or theoretical-juridical, view of morality a problem of

> reconciling impartiality with close personal relationships, as well as with eudaimonistic conceptions of human good, moral virtue, and the good life. It looks as though "partiality" is a constitutive feature of intimate relationships, friendships, familial ties, and our behavior in social groups from neighborhoods to nations. (699)

In other words, what is missing is the warrant for *why* we, as moral actors, would be merely duty-bound, or would work solely toward utilitarian or contractarian outcomes, as a part of our desire to lead worthwhile, decent lives. Given the requirements of juridical moral thought, we are left wondering what there is to admire about such a life, why such a life is worth having, and why disinterested detachment from everything one cares about—that is, detachment from all that makes the moral life not just worthwhile but possible—is the sole path to robust moral agency. After all, would not a desirable life that is (morally) good for many individual, unique reasons be quite distinct from one that is comprised solely out of universalizable moral *oughts*? Indeed, it seems that although duties and laws might very well be part of moral practices, the "ought" of morality cannot be grounded entirely in bare, unyielding principles.

Second, ought we be teaching students that moral practice is, at its best and most rigorous, detached impartiality? It goes almost without saying that personal relationships, friendships, loves, preferences, and the like are powerful forces in our lives. Yet utilitarian calculus, insistent rights-based arguments, and the laws of Kantian imperatives all call on our students to assess moral claims in ways that prefer the principles, that maximize the good for all, that defer to disembodied rights—in other words, that are detached from any concerns for actual, lived lives. Given the theoretical-juridical view presented in so many courses, the work of morality seems to guard precisely against such context-specific (and person-specific) approaches to moral claims.[1]

Third and finally, ought we be suggesting that morality is just substituted impartiality? When I encourage students to think through the question of *what to do* in a difficult moral situation, their reasoning is influenced, at least to some extent, by their points of view, their interests, their situatedness, and so on. Their self-interest, the things that matter to them, and their subjective perspectives are all part of who they are and thus ought to be part of how they approach moral decisions and moral decision-making.

Yet surely, moral decision-making exclusively from narrow points of view is not an adequate approach to moral work. In fact, that approach is exactly what we, in teaching ethics, are attempting to challenge. To engage in moral deliberation (rather than in the gratification of personal needs and inclinations), the students must consider the interests of others, sometimes including those "others" with whom they have no direct relationship. Thus, instructors need to guide them to some way that will compensate for our most common weaknesses as flawed human beings.

One solution—offered by the proponents of the theoretical-juridical model and embraced by a number of ethics instructors—asks the students to do one of two things. *Either* place themselves as perspectival substitutes for others, and then, from a personally disinterested perspective that switches between the points of view of those others, balance the conflicting interests. *Or* assume what Thomas Nagel has called a view from "nowhere in particular" (Nagel, 1979); this would require them to be the perfectly unbiased spectators whose position is external to everyone's interests—a position of ultimate impartiality and ultimate detachment.

A famous example of the latter approach is a hypothetical, called "the trolley problem," first introduced by the philosopher Philippa Foot (1967).[2] The trolley problem goes something like this: Person X could act (or not act) in a way that will benefit a large number of people. However, as a result of so acting, he will unjustly harm (or kill) another person Y. The moral question, then, is under what circumstances would it be just for person X to violate the rights of person Y in order to benefit the larger group?

It is quite curious that this thought experiment (and all of its many variations) has come to be so central for confronting difficult, complicated dilemmas in ethical theory, for it appears that the insistence on abstract, detached rule-following above all else leads us neither to a fair assessment of another's point of view, nor to the ideal of unbiased spectatorship. Instead, it drains any semblance of moral significance from moral work. For example, in attempting to determine how, and whether, a physician ought to communicate bad news to an elderly, slightly demented patient over the objections of her family, the juridical approach offers us the options of either (1) placing ourselves in the patient's, the physician's, and the family's shoes, and then, in a disinterested, legalistic way, "balancing" their various duties and responsibilities; or (2) trolley-like, placing oneself outside the situation altogether, and deciding from "a view from nowhere."

Both approaches are quite common in classrooms, yet neither gets at what is morally significant about a decision such as this: What is central is not merely what any similarly situated physician would do for any similarly situated patient, but what this particular physician might decide, given this particular patient and her family. Indeed, the moral goodness of the decision is largely defined, and motivated by, the friendship, love, and other non-universalizable, non-impartial facts that the detached and disinterested observer cannot access. But such moral and epistemic access requires precisely the kind of enmeshment with others that the theoretical-juridical model forbids. It seems that when we separate the value of moral decision-making from the subjectivity of the moral actors, we lose both the motivation to act morally and the significance of so doing—and so do our students (Stocker).

The Medical Ethics Classroom: Some Further Complications
The worries born of the theoretical-juridical approach to ethics only intensify when transplanted into an introductory medical ethics setting. Courses

on this topic are growing in popularity and are increasingly viewed as pedagogically vital intersections of science, politics, and philosophy. The theoretical-juridical turn in ethics has long been mirrored by the "principlist" turn in medical ethics, pioneered by Tom Beauchamp and James Childress in *Principles of Biomedical Ethics*. Beauchamp and Childress, who have refined much of their original theory, propose four main mid-level moral principles as necessary grounds of bioethical deliberation: autonomy, beneficence, nonmaleficence, and justice (57–112).

The result has been that most instruction in medical ethics has been structured around these principles, which now frame both the sorts of questions that are asked and the kinds of deliberative practices in which students are asked to engage. As Joan McCarthy notes,

> what is special about these principles is their supposed universal or objective nature. Beyond tradition, individual vagaries, and culture, Beauchamp and Childress claim that these principles have been drawn from a "common morality," the set of norms that "all morally serious persons share" ... According to them: "The common morality contains moral norms that bind all persons in all places; no norms are more basic in the moral life" and they refer to the notion of international human rights as an example of such universal norms ... Having grounded their four principles, they justify their particular choice by pointing out that these four have been presupposed by traditional ethical theories and medical codes throughout history. (McCarthy, 66, as quoted in Beauchamp and Childress, 3)

How this works in the classroom is something like as follows: A student is asked to determine whether she ought to provide a patient with all the information about the side-effects of a treatment for a serious illness. Should the student, in the role of the physician, do so, knowing that the patient might be distressed or choose to cease treatment altogether? And what guidance do we offer her in her deliberative process?

Assuming that principlism is the default position, the first step is to determine the applicable moral rule—"respect patient autonomy"—which suggests a more specific rule: "tell the truth" (McCarthy, 66). But here, the student may well encounter a conflict between the duty of telling the truth and the duty of non-maleficence, given that harm—in the form of treatment refusal or extreme emotional distress—might result from informing the patient that she might lose her hair, her appetite, her sex drive, and perhaps her energy as a result of her treatment. This conflict between principles is common and, since no principle is *prima facie* prior to any others, largely unresolved.

This is why the student might continue the second step, which involves a move borrowed from John Rawls—reflective equilibrium, or the weighing and balancing of principles relative to the particular contexts on which one finds oneself, as well as the general background theories of human nature (McCarthy, 66). Beauchamp and Childress describe the principles as only *prima facie* rather than absolute, suggesting that they may well be modified in certain contexts or within the space of certain dilemmas (66). Thus, the student who would tell the patient about the side-effects of a treatment might argue that the principles may be overridden, or modified, by the effects such truth-telling would have on her psychologically and by how this might impact the entire course of her treatment—and thus by the quality of her life.

Here one might wonder why I am suggesting that the problems endemic to the theoretical-juridical approach to ethics become much more pronounced in a medical ethics classroom—after all, the inflexible, law-like maxims of the applicable moral principles are sometimes softened and made to bend to the context and priorities of a given case. But the worry is this: aside from the usual concerns about the inflexible opaqueness of top-down principlist methodologies—for example, why do the principles include "justice" and "autonomy" and not "compassion" or "fairness"—this specifically bioethical principlism, mediated by reflective equilibrium,

> does not give much guidance on how to reconcile …. priorities or how to frame questions in terms of specific kinds of relations, practices, and institutional structures … The finer analysis of ethical notions alone, though essential, does not adequately meet this need, nor is the injunction to attend to "context" a sufficient guide without some theoretical guidance about which features of context are ripe with possibilities for supporting or compromising moral values. *Which* features of situations provide the *morally relevant context* is itself a question for empirically enriched ethical theory that draws on factual information of many types. (Lindemann, Verkerk, and Walker, 9–10)

It seems that when we tell our students that they ought to be able to simply intuitively "reconcile" a number of principles, empirical data, and broader "ethical notions," we are advising them to simply apply the "theory" to whatever "facts" are in front of them, without the benefit of greater context and without deeper understanding of existing relationships or of the roles of local social practices. It is as if we are telling them that "theory" and "facts" will somehow simply come together if we only deliberate sufficiently and earnestly. But by so doing, we are teaching them a rather flawed—and dangerous—lesson not only about how difficult bioethical decisions are made but also about how they *ought* to be made. And in both cases, we are leading them astray.

This leads to a threefold pedagogical dilemma. First, an overuse of the principlist approach to medical ethics remains, possibly motivated by a desire to avoid outright relativism, and this forces students into a hierarchical, juridical approach to difficult, nuanced decisions. Abstract, principle-based hypotheticals such as the trolley problem are useful for helping students visualize an ethical dilemma in its broadest terms, but they are also limiting when it comes to exploring the available moral options. They are also pointedly non-action-guiding, especially when the principles themselves conflict. Second, while principles are presented, there is nevertheless a distinct lack of moral guidance by the modified principlist approach of Beauchamp and Childress (among others); as a consequence, students are left with general directions but without a means to understand and respond to the varying features—or moral valences—within varying, and challenging, contexts. In fact, a serious problem that might well confront both instructors and students when they turn to the reflective equilibrium methodologies of this modified approach is the puzzle of why, while it is not clear that "the four principles are any longer in play in an ongoing process of reflective equilibrium … they seem to stay in place come what may" (Lindemann, Verkerk, and Walker, 11). Third and finally, even if modified, ethical principlism tends to be silent on how, when, and why to apply the various principles on which its methodology is based—yet principles are "not self-applying" (10). In fact, "we have learned the precepts and what they mean in particular communities of judgment from their typical application within those communities to particular situations" (10). This suggests that the principles themselves may have a significantly lesser role in the non-ideal world of medical ethics pedagogy and practice, or that we require theoretical and methodological modifications of principlism beyond those made by Beauchamp and Childress. While I take certain *prima facie* principles to serve important functions in the teaching of ethical practices, and am not quite ready to give up entirely on their pedagogical application, I now turn to the latter, and I think better, option—to a kind of narrative naturalization of the medical ethics classroom.

Narrative Pedagogy and the Naturalizing of Bioethical Dilemmas

There are many ways to define, and engage in, a narrative approach to teaching; that said, the background theoretical assumptions of such approaches rely heavily on narrative conceptions of who we are and how we evaluate ourselves and one another morally. By a "narrative approach," I mean a focus on the significance of context, situatedness, and, importantly, the communication of the stories people tell about themselves and others as they navigate the ethical universe. A number of feminist (and other) narrative ethicists have outlined a variety of conceptions of the narrative project, arguing that storytelling is not a static account of events; rather, it is a dynamic, identity-forming, and epistemically and morally constitutive practice. Hilde Lindemann notes that

> narrativists have claimed, among other things, that stories of one kind or another are required: (1) to teach us our duties, (2) to guide morally good action, (3) to motivate morally good action, (4) to justify action on moral grounds, (5) to cultivate our moral sensibilities, (6) to enhance our moral perception, (7) to make actions of persons morally intelligible, and (8) to reinvent ourselves as better persons. (as quoted in Nelson, 36)

Joan McCarthy offers a more general overview of the narrative turn in ethics with the following summary of its assumptions:

1 Every moral situation is unique and unrepeatable and its meaning cannot be fully captured by appealing to law like universal principles.
2 In any given ... situation, any decision or course of action is justified in terms of its fit with the individual life story or stories ...
3 The objective of the task of justification in 2 is not necessarily to unify moral beliefs and commitments, but is to open up dialogue, challenge received views and norms, and explore tensions between individual and shared meanings. (67)

What these assumptions look like when they take shape in ethical discourse introduces a number of complex and multifaceted issues that are mostly beyond the scope of this essay. For my purposes here, I consider what a narrative turn means for bioethical practice and, subsequently, for a narrative approach to medical ethics pedagogy.

Relating the narrative methodologies more specifically to the bioethical discourse, Rita Charon has argued that instead of simply examining a patient's chart and treating his symptoms based on strictly ordered biomedical principles, she, as a physician, is a much better steward of not only his health but also his person if she treats their encounter as an ongoing narrative—one that includes the full story of his life and the role of the illness within it. She claims that it is not enough to know the symptoms;

it is also important to know what they make of the patient, what they do to him, how he fought them, what he takes his own recovery (or its lack) to *mean*—and whether he will be the person he once was. These storylines about the patient, told by the patient and by others to the physician, "[create] for ourselves a medical transference that … will deepen my investment in his future, a great and lasting curiosity about his life" (265).

Charon, as a physician and a narrativist, approaches illness not as a hierarchical list of conditions and side-effects—in the language of ethical analysis, not as a principlist set of *prima facie* "oughts" and "oughtnots"—but as a potentially life-shattering event, told by a specific voice, that is part of an ongoing story of a unique and contextualized life. This kind of encounter, which takes seriously the person behind the condition, makes all the difference to the patient. This kind of interaction, which pays attention to the narrative structure of experience, alters the moral relationship between physician and patient and gives form and meaning to the shattering experience of illness.

What does all this mean for pedagogy in a medical ethics classroom? Quite simply, a pedagogy that is grounded in narrative, naturalized ethics is more effective at capturing the students' moral imaginations; it also offers a more nuanced, inclusive lens through which to view the larger moral and biomedical discourses. I now turn to a defence, and explanation, of this view.

Although it is difficult to offer many generalizations about narrative pedagogy, several tendencies seem clear. First, narrative pedagogy is fundamentally non-hierarchical and inclusive; it pays close attention to individual situations, particularities, and oppressions. Second, this focus translates into teaching practices that pay close heed to "situated learning"—the understanding that knowledge, especially the kind of knowledge that has to do with ethical norms, is not an amorphous, detached, and unassailable structure to memorize, but rather a contextual and socially constructed process that is effected by both power and voice. That is, knowledge, rather than being found, is largely *created* through teaching and learning.[3] Pedagogy, therefore, is not the mere transmission of laws, facts, and "neutral" principles, but a wholly immersed practice of constructing, deconstructing, and, above all, collaborating, both with one's subject matter and with one's students. Third, knowledge is often naturalized within narrative pedagogy; it admits and in fact welcomes empirical, scientific, and cultural contributions—indeed, stories—in order to put pressure on and to amend ethical "ideals" and "neutral" theoretical presuppositions. Above all, narrative teaching involves a dialogue among the material, the instructor, and the students that, like the stories themselves, moves forward, backward, and sideways, and that at its best strives to bring students, instructor, and moral dilemmas together in mutual intelligibility (Lindemann Nelson, 1999). This dialogue, I will argue, owes much of its motivation and methodology to feminist theory and pedagogy.

Narrative Pedagogy as Feminist Pedagogy

Throughout this paper, my claims about the roles and philosophical commitments of narrative pedagogy have noted the strong affinity between narrative pedagogy and feminist pedagogy and feminist theory, broadly construed. The next few pages explain how this is so.

While my goal here is not to trace the development of philosophical feminist theory, in order to more clearly see its role within narrative medical ethics pedagogy, it is useful to consider some of its foundational beliefs. Ever since Carol Gilligan noted that women tend to favour a situated, contextualized approach to moral problems over a deductive, universalized one, feminist theorists have argued for moral work that incorporates the psychological, emotional, and physical conditions of *actual* participants in *actual* situations, rather than those of idealized participants in idealized ones (Gilligan; Noddings; Sherwin; Walker). To a large extent, feminist ethical theory can be understood as both a response *to* and a movement *against* the ahistoricism of more abstract, universalist ethical theories such as utilitarianism and Kantianism, both of which view the moral agent as an autonomous, calculating, rational actor deliberating out of a calculus of utility, or duty, or some other distinctly disembodied and decontextualized principle from which all moral decision-making is supposed to descend. Feminist ethicists contend that principlist theorizing has neglected the centrality of situatedness, power differentials, and, importantly, the voices of women, whose lived experiences have simply not been part of ongoing moral debates. Largely discounted by the more traditional moral theorists has been any notion of community, of non-ideal moral actors in non-ideal environments, and of one's personal relationships with others. Often, the default "autonomous agent" has been represented as an otherwise unencumbered man coming to a decision that is not otherwise burdened by the messy contextuality of an actual, lived life. The result has been not only a simplification of what it might mean to be an agent in the non-ideal circumstances of a complicated, social, embodied world, but also the wholesale absence of other kinds of (non-ideal) agents—or, at least the disinclination to call them "rational" (see Brennan; Baier; Held).

The feminist turn in ethical theory, in biomedicine and elsewhere, has led to the inclusion of women, people of colour queer communities, economically underprivileged individuals, and many others. Put another way, feminism within pedagogy has introduced to moral philosophy, and made central its dilemmas, the situatedness of the individual and the intersectionalities of oppression; in doing so, it has brought together in mutual relevance actual non-ideal agents, whose complex positions within existing institutional and social power structures have now become a matter of moral discourse, perhaps for the first time. Worries about what constitutes meaningful philosophical debate—what questions ought to be posed, by whom, and what kinds of responses, and responders, ought to be granted uptake—are thus no longer matters of solely or primarily juridical, theoretical hierarchies of reasons. Instead, they are approached through the lived experiences and embodied voices of students and instructors, whose stories ground evolving moral understandings not as abstractions but as the opposite of abstractions.

Because many of these non-standard agents were engaged with the world in ways not included in traditional unitary, autonomous rational agent scenarios, and were instead participants in what can be generalized as the relational, interdependent work of caregiving, community building, and other activities often defined in terms of relationships with others, their mere entry into the discourse began to change it: feminist moral theory, reified through feminist pedagogy, allowed the voices of women and minorities, and thus their lived experiences, to be heard within the spaces of moral deliberation. Understood broadly, these practices can be viewed as a response to a history of silencing and to the oppression that such silencing underwrites. As Samantha Brennan has noted, "feminist ethics seeks to overcome the limits of narrow, male-centred ethics by constructing moral theories which can make sense of the experiences of women as moral agents ... Feminist ethics has become associated with an ethics of lived, concrete experiences which takes most seriously women's experiences of morality" (861). And this difficult yet necessary process of "making (moral) sense" of often disparate stories of experiences has formed the basis of narrative approaches to ethics and medical ethics—and pedagogy.

The influence of feminist theory within academic philosophy and pedagogy has certainly strengthened over the years. Yet the more male-centred, singularly defined traditions of (especially analytic) philosophy have largely retained their hold, both in research and in pedagogy. Without committing to any essentialist claims about gender, a firewall of male dominance, both numerically and within the hierarchy of philosophical approaches, has sparked a lively and somewhat dispiriting debate about why there are so few women researchers and instructors in professional philosophy (compared to other humanities and the sciences). Some have suggested that Gilligan's "different voice" analysis largely explains the silencing of feminist, narrativist, and other non-dominant voices by those who are neither accustomed nor disposed to hearing their "differences." More recently, others have offered what strikes me as an even more devastating diagnosis (Antony; Buckwalter and Stich). Louise Antony, for example, has argued that women in academic philosophy face not simply a matter of difference but indeed "the perfect storm":

> The discipline of philosophy marks the site of a unique convergence, intensification, and interaction of discriminatory forces—just as a geographical site can serve as the point of convergence, intensification, and interaction of meteorological forces ... The Perfect Storm model predicts that women who act like men will precisely not therefore be perceived or treated like men: the woman who interrupts frequently may be sanctioned more quickly or more heavily than the man who acts the same way. Variance in discourse style, then, would not explain the variance in professional success for women. On the Perfect Storm view the normative atmosphere has some effect on every woman regardless of her intrinsic temperament. (233–39)

Sally Haslanger famously noted that

> there is a deep well of rage inside of me. Rage about how I as an individual have been treated in philosophy; rage about how others I know have been treated; and rage about the conditions that I'm sure affect many women and minorities in philosophy, and have caused many others to leave. (210)

Thus even though some progress has been made, if we are to take these worries as serious pedagogical ones (as I believe we must), it seems to me that philosophers who work in the medical narrative traditions that borrow quite heavily from the foundational work of feminist theory ought to have two goals. The first is what I call an *internal* goal—internal in the sense that it addresses the substance that is taught as philosophy. By this, I mean that through the narrative technique of taking individual and collective stories as fundamental to moral deliberations about what to do, we redefine both in the minds of our colleagues but especially in the minds of our students, what moral philosophy (including medical ethics) is—and importantly, what it can be if *all* of its voices are truly heard. This process calls for a broad reconceptualization of not just how one thinks of one's subject matter, but specifically, how one incorporates this more inclusive conception of, say, medical ethics into one's teaching practices. Thus, in addition to more standard normative fare, one might introduce a not insignificant number of non-traditional texts by female theorists, works of fiction, non-Western sources, words of patients and doctors, as well as poetry from a variety of voices. This *internal* goal also calls for a more generous outlook on what the instructor takes as "philosophical thinking" within the classroom. It can no longer be the case, for instance, that only certain terms, or ways of speaking, or approaches to a problem, will be deemed properly "philosophical." Just as the practitioners of narrative medicine, such as Rita Charon, largely reject the acontextuality of the medical chart in favour of the particular illness experiences as told by their patients, so should the narratively oriented instructor of medical ethics move her students beyond traditional theories, beyond mere formulations of dilemmas, beyond the trolley problem as the totality of philosophical deliberation. Applied to the field of medical ethics, what emerges out of this rejection of juridical, individualist, ahistorical approach to doing ethics is akin to what Susan Sherwin called an attention to context, relationships, character, and power.

The second goal is an *external* one—external in the sense that it addresses the pedagogical practices of the teaching of philosophical medical ethics. As Lynne Webb, Myria Allen, and Kandi Walker argue in "Feminist Pedagogy: Identifying Basic Principles," feminist pedagogy can be understood as a combination of several practices:

> reformation of the relationship between professor and student, empowerment, building community, privileging the individual voice, respect personal experience in its diversity, and challenging traditional views of theory and instruction[... contributing] to the creation of a collaborative learning experience that is the goal of contemporary feminist pedagogy. (68)

Especially important to this *external* goal is to challenge through one's teaching the silencing practices of traditional philosophy: one ought to involve all of one's students, and not just those whose voices are usually heard; one should give equal credence to the responses of those whose experiences and views may challenge prevailing opinions and theoretical constructs; finally, one must offer oneself as an example of what narrative, feminist philosophy might look like by placing oneself in the role of not just a leader, but a collaborator, one who is not merely a source of knowledge but also a participant in the practices of moral understanding. Indeed, whenever possible and appropriate, one should attempt to situate one's pedagogical voice in such a way that it is open to student input, criticism, and difference, rather than adopting the position of an unassailable objective deliberator from nowhere (Antony, 249–50).

This attention to voice, the valuing of personal experience and testimony as distinctly moral, the emphasis on mutual intelligibility over theory-building, and the revision of the teaching role from instructor-as-oracle to instructor as an expert co-investigator are practices that are often evident within narrative and feminist pedagogy. Indeed, a narrative classroom is in many ways a feminist classroom, one in which "participatory ... processes help learners develop independence. It is an active, collaborative classroom where risk-taking is encouraged; where intellectual excitement abounds; and where power is viewed as energy, capacity, and potential, rather than domination" (Christie, 148).

What this looks like in the medical ethics classroom often differs from instructor to instructor. That said, narratively taught courses tend to include examinations of hypotheticals that mirror Charon's approach rather than Beauchamp and Childress's:

> A principal task of feminist medical ethics is to develop conceptual models for restructuring the power associated with healing by distributing medical knowledge in ways that allow persons maximum control over their own health. It is important to clarify ways in which dependence can be reduced, caring can be offered without paternalism, and health services can be obtained within a context worthy of trust. A clear understanding of the dynamics of the power structures now inhibiting these processes is an important aspect of our ethical analysis. We must look at the structures of medicine and medical interaction when attempting to understand the details of any particular medical experience ... We look to feminist medical ethics to provide a more comprehensive, and fairer, approach to medical ethics than has been evident to date. (Sherwin, 70)

The students are thus asked to dig deeper, to find motivations and reasons for actions that include, instead of negating, personal contexts and power differentials that might not be readily visible from a mere recitation of facts or principles.[4] For example, when discussing the deeply divisive issue of organ allocation, instead of presenting abstract cases (of "patient X" versus "patient Y") that encourage one in the direction of generalized solutions, the students might be asked to examine a case in a way that engages third-, second-, and first-person narratives of particular patients and particular medical professionals, taking into account cultural context, scientific findings, social and political environments, and power inequalities—as well as ethical principles. This kind of a naturalized approach opens up the possibility for the students to experiment with a broader, more inclusive reflective equilibrium in their reasoning; their task is thus made more challenging, but in many ways more rewarding. In this widening space of reasons, they might begin to see that neither the instructor, nor a particular principle, nor a unique fact, nor even a single story serves as the one true key to the right moral solution. Indeed, they might even begin to suspect that the notion of a "single correct moral solution" to biomedical dilemmas—and, perhaps, to many others—is neither the proper goal nor a particularly desirable one.

Of course, this is not at all to say that there ought not be a focus on better answers, on stronger analyses, on more nuanced distinctions. It is, however, to suggest that in the case of, for example, serious and ongoing pain, instead of looking to strictly utilitarian, deontological—or top-down—methodologies, the students might be encouraged by a feminist-narrativist instructor to consider the direction taken by Margaret Farley, who argued for a more inclusive and philosophically generous approach that calls on us to consider social contexts, situatedness, and responsibilities, while never forgetting the virtues of compassion and mercy, when difficult, life-changing decisions are being made. Thus, her suggestion is that instead of relying on medical paternalism, or on a singular Kantian emphasis on patient autonomy, or on seeking the sole correct solution to questions of intractable pain and other morally vexing biomedical dilemmas, we look to a kind of compassionate respect for those for whom we care, as well as for those doing the difficult work of caregiving. This, then, becomes the deliberative focus within the classroom (Farley). Specifically, we might point the students to her claim that

> suffering in some form, great or small, overwhelming or overcome, has the power to grasp us when we see it in others. It has the power to hold us so that we cannot avoid the reality of the sufferers or the reality of ourselves. Insofar as we genuinely behold it, it awakens in us a moral response—to alleviate it, ameliorate it, prevent it in others, or if none of this is possible, to companion and literally "bear with" the sufferer, in love and respect. (41)

Pedagogically, this means that we open our students to a moral world—and, importantly, to moral practices—where the waters run deeper and where they do not have to choose between compassion and justice, between reason and emotion, or between theory and lived experience. Instead, with Farley (and others) we can introduce them to "compassionate respect," which calls on "care to be respectful of embodied autonomy as well as every level of need in the person to whom care is owed" (43).

As a result, the students may see that the practice of medical ethics—and they do begin to consider it a practice, rather than a puzzle to be completed and set aside—is much more difficult than they imagined; furthermore, its moral dilemmas call on all of their faculties: reasoning, feeling, intuiting, speaking, and especially listening. They listen to one another and to the text; they listen to the instructor; and they also learn to hear between the lines. To question why certain narratives are not heard and why some stories seem to count more than others. To interrogate why, for example, the voices of the disabled in defining disability have until rather recently been granted less uptake then those who are in charge of making policies that circumscribe their lives. To wonder why the principles of atomistic patient autonomy so often seem to override the needs and desires of groups, families, or even entire communities. Once the necessary narrative spaces are opened up within the classroom, these morally significant pedagogical moments can point the students toward the realization that our moral lives, rather then being bound by pure theoretical impartiality, are lived within multifaceted communities of practice, which must be intelligible and accountable to one another. As Tracy Penny Light notes in this book, in a feminist classroom, students have the opportunity to learn in a way that not only reifies intersectionalities and makes relevant the roles of place, voice, and circumstances in ethical discourse, but also creates possibilities for genuine consciousness-raising, moving the students toward a deeper and more complex place of moral reasoning. And while the result might offer a less firm epistemic and ethical footing with fewer philosophically (and clinically) tidy answers, a richer and deeper appreciation of moral nuance and complexity that becomes possible seems infinitely more valuable to students within, but especially beyond, the classroom.

Conclusion: Pedagogy as Production of Knowledge

The teaching of ethics—and medical ethics—is, above all, a process of showing how to engage in moral deliberation with similar and different others. In this way, pedagogy is a means of producing certain kinds of knowledge and certain kinds of knowers. I conclude with a few thoughts about the importance of what kinds of knowers we produce.

In this essay, I have argued that the more traditional approaches to teaching ethics and medical ethics are theoretically and practically wanting, and I have claimed that teaching practices oriented toward a narrative methodology extend and deepen not only moral theory itself but also its application by students in difficult, complicated situations. I have also suggested that a narrative methodology actively employs many of the techniques and motivations of feminist theory, leading to students who are more finely attuned to inequalities in power—to the importance of context, and generally, to difference. It seems, therefore, that the reasons to consider narrative pedagogy would include not only the *internal* benefits of more profound and comprehensive learning, but also the *external* benefits—the attunement of the people who walk out of our classrooms after the final chapters are read and exams taken. And I believe these students can view the future ethical challenges before them either as interesting puzzles to solve for the "correct" answer or as complex processes of narratively driven, collaborative, and inclusive deliberations that aim for mutually accountable moral understanding—something that no trolley problem can effectively provide. Indeed, I suggest that the future medical professionals who leave our ethics classrooms can learn to be better attuned to the narrative structure of experience—their patients' as well as their own. This more fluid and dynamic view of moral practice, medical and otherwise, "calls attention to the essentially interpersonal nature of morality and moral thinking ... it engages the moral imagination and other moral faculties" (Lindemann, Verkerk, and Walker, 239). And this lesson seems not at all insignificant.

Notes

1 See Llewellyn and Llewellyn on the limitations of individualism in the learning process and the importance of the acknowledgement and practices of relational pedagogy (this anthology).

2 The Trolley Problem is a thought experiment, often employed in moral philosophy (and other) courses, that was first introduced by Philippa Foot in her 1967 paper "The Problem of Abortion and the Doctrine of Double Effect," and later expanded by, among others, Judith Jarvis Thomson in "Killing, Letting Die, and the Trolley Problem" (1976) and "The Trolley Problem" (1985). Although Foot's original version was more complex and involved a judge or a magistrate trying to prevent bloodshed, the current, and most commonly used, version of the hypothetical stipulates that a runaway trolley is quickly moving down the railway tracks, headed toward five people who are tied up and unable to move. The decision-maker is standing next to a lever which, if pulled, will switch the trolley to a different set of tracks. However, there is also a single person on this alternative set of tracks, and the decision-maker cannot move the lever in a way that would save the lives of everyone there. There seem to be two options: (1) Do nothing, allowing the trolley to kill the five people on the main track; or (2) Pull the lever and divert the trolley onto the side track, thereby killing one person. The students are then asked what they would do, and why. In discussing this hypothetical, they are introduced to a number of traditional approaches to moral justification, such as utilitarianism, deontology, the doctrine of double effect, and so on. The significance of this particular hypothetical is not only its many variations and critiques within professional philosophy and philosophical pedagogy, but the pedagogical and normative

power granted to its ahistorical, mostly acontextual, juridical nature. Through its use, students are taught to "think philosophically" and to reason through their decisions, giving rational justifications for each step, as well as for its consequences (or else for why the consequences ought to matter less than motivations, say). This paper is meant as a criticism of the kind of context-free, juridical approach to questions of morality that the trolley problem represents, and it specifically challenges the ongoing pedagogical practices within academic philosophy that uncritically privilege the teaching of ethics and medical ethics in this traditional, rigid manner.

3 For a discussion of a powerfully contextual learning process, see Linda Briskin's discussion of activist feminist pedagogies (AFP), which allow students to thinking critically about, and experience first-hand, the interactions among community involvement, activism, power, oppression, and agency (this anthology).

4 See Susan V. Iverson for a broader discussion of feminist pedagogy that includes self-scrutiny (or, as she puts it, "reflexivity") about one's work, its meaning, and how through it, knowledge is constructed by the student (this anthology).

Works Cited

Antony, Louise. "Different Voices or Perfect Storm: Why Are There So Few Women in Philosophy?" *Journal of Social Philosophy* 43.3 (2012): 227–255. http://dx.doi.org/10.1111/j.1467-9833.2012.01567.x

Baier, A.C. "The Need for More Than Justice." In Marsha Hanen and Kai Nielsen, eds. *Science, Morality, and Feminist Theory. Canadian Journal of Philosophy* (suppl. volume 13) (1987): 41–56.

Beauchamp, T., and J. Childress. *Principles of Biomedical Ethics*. New York: Oxford University Press, 1979.

———. *Principles of Biomedical Ethics*, 5th ed. Oxford: Oxford University Press, 2001.

Becker, Lawrence C. "Impartiality and Ethical Theory." *Ethics* 101.4 (1991): 698–700. http://dx.doi.org/10.1086/293339

Brennan, Samantha. "Recent Work in Feminist Ethics." *Ethics* 109.4 (1999): 858–893. http://dx.doi.org/10.1086/233951

Buckwalter, W., and S. Stich. "Gender and Philosophical Intuition" (September 26, 2010). Available at SSRN: http://ssrn.com/abstract=1683066 or http://dx.doi.org/10.2139/ssrn.1683066

Charon, Rita. "Narrative Medicine: Attention, Representation, Affiliation." *Narrative* 13.3 (2005): 261–270. http://dx.doi.org/10.1353/nar.2005.0017

Christie, A.A. "Using E-mail Within a Classroom Based on Feminist Pedagogy." *Journal of Research on Computing in Education* 30 (1997): 146–176.

Farley, Margaret A. *Compassionate Respect: A Feminist Approach to Medical Ethics*. Notre Dame: Paulist Press, 2002.

Foot, Philippa. "The Problem of Abortion and the Doctrine of Double Effect." *Oxford Review* 5 (1967): 5–15.

———. *Virtues and Vices.* Oxford: Basil Blackwell, 1978.

Gilligan, Carol. *In a Different Voice.* Cambridge, MA: Harvard University Press, 1982.

Haslanger, S. "Changing the Ideology and Culture of Philosophy: Not by Reason (Alone)." *Hypatia* 23.2 (2008): 210–223. http://dx.doi.org/10.1111/j.1527-2001.2008.tb01195.x

Held, Virginia. "Non-Contractual Society: A Feminist View." *Canadian Journal of Philosophy* 17 (suppl. 1; 1987): 111–37.

Kant, Immanuel. *Groundwork of the Metaphysics of Morals.* Ed. Mary Gregor. Cambridge: Cambridge University Press, 1998.

Lindemann Nelson, Hilde. "Context: Backward, Sideways, and Forward." *HEC Forum* 11.1 (March 1999): 16–26. http://dx.doi.org/10.1023/A:1008844116526 .Medline:11184839

———. *Damaged Identities, Narrative Repair.* Ithaca: Cornell University Press, 2001.

Lindemann, Hilde, Marian Verkerk, and Margaret Urban Walker, eds. *Naturalized Bioethics: Toward Responsible Knowing and Practice.* New York: Cambridge University Press, 2009. http://dx.doi.org/10.1017/CBO9781139167499

Lorde, Audre. *Sister Outsider: Essays and Speeches.* Berkeley: Crossing Press, 2007.

McCarthy, J. "Principlism or Narrative Ethics: Must We Choose Between Them?" *Medical Humanities* 29.2 (December 2003): 65–71. http://dx.doi.org/10 .1136/mh.29.2.65. Medline:15884187

Nagel, T. *Mortal Questions.* Cambridge: Cambridge University Press, 1979.

Noddings, Nel. *Caring: A Feminine Approach to Ethics and Moral Education.* Berkeley: University of California Press, 1984.

Sherwin, Susan. "Feminist and Medical Ethics: Two Different Approaches to Contextual Ethics." *Hypatia* 4.2 (1989): 57–72. http://dx.doi.org/10.1111/j .1527-2001.1989.tb00573.x. Medline:11650331

Stocker, Michael. "How Emotions Reveal Value and Help Cure the Schizophrenia of Modern Ethical Theories." *How Should One Live? – Essays on the Virtues.* Ed. Roger Crisp. New York: Oxford University Press, 1998. http:// dx.doi.org/10.1093/0198752342.003.0011

Thomson, Judith Jarvis. "Killing, Letting Die, and the Trolley Problem." *Monist* 59.2 (April 1976): 204–217. http://dx.doi.org/10.5840/monist197659224. Medline:11662247

Thomson, Judith Jarvis. "The Trolley Problem." *Yale Law Journal* 94.6 (1985): 1395–1415. http://dx.doi.org/10.2307/796133

Walker, Margaret Urban. *Moral Understandings: A Feminist Study in Ethics*, 2nd ed. Oxford: Oxford University Press, 2007.

Webb, Lynne M., Myria W. Allen, and Kandi L. Walker. "Feminist Pedagogy: Identifying Basic Principles." *Academic Exchange Quarterly*, 22 March 2002.

CHAPTER NINE

The Power of the Imagination-Intellect in Teaching Feminist Research

Susan V. Iverson

A feminist pedagogy demands that we become personal with the material studied. Growing scholarship attests to the value and importance of reflection and self-awareness in the learning process (Chapman; hooks; Ollis; Rose; Villaverde; Warren). In Women's Studies and in many other disciplines, from Geography to Social Work, from Teacher Education to Psychology, students are often assigned to reveal their life histories and share them through reflective writing; and to become aware of ideological commitments and articulate how these shape our work and who we are (or will be) in the world (Allen and Farnsworth; Boske 2011; Browne; deRoche and deRoche; Engin; Fenwick; Kirsch and Ritchie; Middleton).

This sort of personal and reflective writing has also become increasingly common in qualitative and feminist approaches to research, as a mechanism to negotiate the challenges involved in using the self as an instrument of inquiry (Borg; DeLyser; Griffiths 1994; Jenkins; Lather; Poulin; Wolf). The feminist researcher serves as an instrument in the research process and is called upon to acknowledge her subjectivities. In my graduate research classes, students are typically assigned to maintain a reflective journal. Too often, though, they maintain an aesthetic distance; they gaze at the "object" under study, unaware that each of us is part of and can be found in that which we study (Gerstl-Pepin and Patrizio; Pillow). Having observed this in my teaching of graduate qualitative and feminist research classes, I was left asking: To what extent does such self-examination lead students to act differently as researchers, to think more critically, to disrupt the "objective stance" of dominant positivist research approaches? And I wondered if, or in what ways, this "subjectivity audit" or "taming" of self (Peshkin) might (unwittingly) sustain a distrust of subjective experience in the research process and possibly contribute to critiques of feminist studies as inherently biased. Self-reflection may be only transactional, required for the grade (Francis); students could fail to push "beyond the safe space of [one's] habitual existence" (James, 162).

In this chapter, I argue for a need to (re)conceptualize this self-examination. Rather than "auditing" for bias and "bracketing" assumptions (Gearing), I suggest ways we might expand the possibilities of knowledge creation. Drawing on what Weems calls the imagination-intellect, I posit that the researcher's imaginative, creative, and somatic self must be cultivated and deployed. Through innovative pedagogical approaches, faculty can cultivate and deploy aesthetic appreciation, oral expression, written reflection, and performance (Weems), to contest dominant (objective) conceptions of the knowledge production process.

Feminist Pedagogy

Feminist pedagogy is a teaching and learning process that guides educators' classroom practices "by providing criteria to evaluate specific educational strategies and techniques in terms of the desired course goals or outcomes" (Shrewsbury, 6). Aimed at interrogating and disrupting "traditional" conceptions of power, authority, and knowledge production and transmission, a feminist pedagogy engages students in understanding how they learn, how to examine the contexts within which social problems are framed, and how to view social issues from a variety of perspectives (Ropers-Huilman). The feminist classroom aims to empower students by engaging them in "a social action process that promotes participation of people, organizations, and communities in gaining control over their lives in their community and larger society" (Stein, 7).

I believe that students are (or should be) active participants in the classroom, not passive recipients; they should engage critically with the teacher and the content (hooks). The aim is not for students to parrot back "received knowledge" (Belenky, Clinchy, Goldberger, and Tarule) demonstrating successful transmission from the instructor to the student. Rather, a feminist pedagogy demands that students take personally the material studied; it calls on teachers-as-students and students-as-teachers to engage actively with the learning process, continually reflecting on themselves and the world, thus establishing an authentic form of thought and action (Cook and Fonow; hooks). Through personalization, theory becomes part of one's lived experience. Rather than an academic lesson absorbed (at most) at a cognitive level, course content becomes theory-in-use to uncover certain kinds of realities, to develop tactics and strategies of struggle with the topics being surveyed, and to empower individuals to see themselves as agents of social change. In this way, students are able to identify strategies and their own agency for working toward gender equity (Bricker-Jenkins and Hooyman; Ollis; Villaverde).

An interest in personal experience and the intersection of the personal and the political evolved from the women's consciousness-raising (CR) groups of the late 1960s and early 1970s (Deats and Lenker). CR was an essential part of the overall feminist strategy; it was a mechanism by which to gain awareness and a means through which to organize and act (Sarachild 1978). Yet as Women's Studies programs gained a foothold in the academy, a decline in CR groups was observed (Henderson-King and Stewart). Thus, the importance of personal experience to women, the incorporation of that experience in the classroom as a means of making education more relevant, and the goals of activism and social change coalesce within feminist pedagogy.

Reflexivity

Feminist pedagogy recognizes the value of "integrating the personal and the intellectual along with political analysis" (Henderson-King and Stewart, 391). Various instructional strategies are used to draw out the student's personal experience, to provide opportunities for students to situate themselves within the course content and reflect on the ways in which lived experience is shaped by social processes and structures (Naples and Bojar). My focus, more specifically, is on reflexivity.

Reflexivity is more than reflection. Elizabeth Chiseri-Strater notes that while reflection is an exercise in thinking about self, to be reflexive demands "some self-conscious awareness of the process of self-scrutiny" (130; see also Allen and Farnsworth; Kobayashi); it is to have "an ongoing conversation about the experience while simultaneously living in the moment" (Hertz, viii). As a pedagogical tool, reflexivity can foster "the ability to recognize multiple truths and ways of knowing" (MacDermid et al., 32). It challenges knowers to reflect on their thoughts, beliefs, and interests, to pose questions of self and others, and to "push at the boundaries of their self-awareness" (Thompson, 10). This "radical" tool can challenge students to face "the political dimensions of fieldwork and construction of knowledge" (Hertz, viii).

Ample critique has been levelled at the notion or exercise of reflexivity. Some observe that students are resistant to the reflexive process, viewing it as little more than "navel gazing" (Gerstl-Pepin and Patrizio, 301). Others identify that students "assume if they engage in a series of 'reflexive' techniques ... for the purpose of exposing the 'context' of production of their research ... they can be assured that 'reflexivity' has occurred" (Pillow, 186). The "game" of self-reflexivity has even been described as "tiresome," as detached from material realities and nothing more than "language games" played for "amusement" by scholars (Patai, 66). Heshusius cautions that the focus has shifted away from being as objective as possible toward "anxiety about how to manage subjectivity as rigorously as possible" (16). So how does one engage in reflexive practice, and—perhaps equally challenging— how does (or can) an educator teach reflexivity?

Teaching Reflexivity: Approaches and Challenges
Educators deploy various approaches to teach reflexivity (Barry et al.; deRoche and deRoche; de Santis and Serafini, in this book; Jenkins; Poulin; Watt). Dominant among these, however, are written exercises, which are seen as an opportunity for reflection and inner dialogue (Holly; Richardson; Watt). Engin writes about her use of a research diary as an "integral" tool for "scaffolding" her research knowledge and her development as a researcher (303). In the context of a qualitative research course, Gerstl-Pepin and Patrizio write of a research journal as a repository for personal reflection. They argue that the journal can then serve as a catalyst for discussion that leads to "epistemological awareness" (300) as the journal author realizes how her own knowledge is formed. Altrichter, Posch, and Somekh discuss the role of journal writing in an action research project as fundamental to the research process, for "it makes visible both the successful and (apparently) unsuccessful routes of learning and discovery so that they can be revisited and subject to analysis" (12). Borg writes of his own experiences keeping a research journal and outlines the benefits of such a journal in terms of both process (e.g., resolving fieldwork anxiety) and product (e.g., establishing an archive of decisions and events that guided subsequent action).

Specific to my context—teaching graduate qualitative and feminist research classes—the researcher as "instrument" is central; through reflexive practices, students reflect on "themselves, their work, and themselves in their work" (DeLyser, 241). I have assigned journal writing for years but do not feel that doing so in and of itself disrupts the objective stronghold. Students, in an effort to "discover" their "true" selves, search perhaps unwittingly for the "right" way to be reflexive. The "research diary" (Engin), then, can become a storehouse of bias. Some students are eager to get on with figuring out the "right way" to do research. They have the requisite entry on situating self, ready to insert into their research proposal. Others studiously deposit narratives in their journals; however, "making positions transparent does not make them unproblematic" (Spivak, 276). Van Maanen notes that "confessions, endlessly replayed, begin to lose their novelty and power to inform" (99n12). If my aim is to rupture this epistemological certainty—not only conceptually but also in preparing students for the "messiness" of fieldwork (Billo and Hiemstra)—then the teaching of reflexivity must be interrogated for its use as a methodological tool that "qualitative researchers can and should use to both explore and expose the politics of representation" (Pillow, 176).

I also suggest uprooting reflexivity from its over-adherence to "writing as thinking" (Menary). I am not discounting the evidence-based use of writing—as Menary attests, "writing transforms our cognitive abilities" (621)—nor will I stop assigning journal writing. I am instead arguing that the goals of reflexivity (through journaling) are perhaps not fully achieved when the emphasis is on "cognitive abilities"; our (largely) writing-based strategies may (unwittingly) reify rationality and risk privileging a disembodied, distanced knowledge, as we strive for the "management of subjectivity" (Heshusius, 18). We need to (re)conceptualize self-examination to enable knowing that which "one cannot account for" (Heshusius, 17). Guided by Weems's work on imagination-intellect, I believe that knowing what one cannot account for can be imagined.

Imagination-Intellect

Weems asserts that all ideas are first imagined: "it is not possible to formulate an idea without reflection, or to develop an idea without imagination" (1). For reflexivity to activate, for that metacognitive activity of thinking about our thinking to initiate, we must release ourselves from our everyday world and "dream" (St. Pierre). Foucault refers to this as "the space of our primary perception" (as quoted in St. Pierre, 182). Inspired by Weems, Gitlin posits that it is through imagination "that we are able to see the way everyday images saturate our body, mind, and soul at the same time that we can envision alternatives to those images" (16). This imaginative space keeps "interpretation in play" (St. Pierre, 183).

Ultimately, I believe, reflexivity should not be an end in itself. As Chapman argues, we start by "imagining" and in turn "*embody* knowledges ... rather than simply learning or generating things *as abstractions*" (734; italics in original). Our awareness cannot remain in theoretical abstractions, but must translate into action. Giroux extends this imaginative (dream) space beyond the classroom "to create public spaces ... to energize [people] to do something differently" (77). He adds that it is "in that moment

[we] link critical imagination with the possibility of activism" (77). Such an imaginative exercise can feel abstract. Here is where Weems is instructive. She advances the theoretical possibility of a more reflexive pedagogy; she also delineates specific areas and examples for how to enact an aesthetic, somatic, embodied, imaginative reflexivity. Weems turns to "lived experience" and "the arts" as means to gain "new understanding about yourself and/or the world" (2). She advances that the aesthetic, creative, expressive, and dramatic invite ontological opportunities to blur the boundaries between artist and scholar, between "performing" and "doing" research.

More specifically, Weems delineates five areas that are the core of imagination-intellectual development. First, aesthetic appreciation: "students need to view art, listen to music, attend dance programs, read and discuss poems, plays, short stories, and novels ... [and] develop a socially unbiased creative-critical eye" (5). Second, oral expression: students should become "personally engaged with language through *improvisational* storytelling, rapping, flowing, hip hop, improvisational skits, debate, and public speaking" (5; italics in original). Third, written expression: students should be encouraged "to explore language through the creation of poetry, short fiction, plays, reflecting their own lived experience, and by responding as readers to the creative work of an intercultural selection" (5). Fourth, performance: students should cultivate their "ability to communicate effectively through the memorization and dramatic presentation of original work, the work of published authors, and/or a hybrid mix" (5). This, Weems notes, is different from (2) in that it is improvisational; also, this fourth area of performance takes more time to prepare and is more polished. The fifth and final area is social consciousness: students are encouraged to develop "an awareness of their social position in society enabling them to honor diversity, and to put social justice including the importance of a true participatory democracy at the forefront" (5). This fifth area resonates with the feminist approach in its move beyond a way of thinking to a way of acting. Weems concludes that a "creative-critical, social consciousness shapes an imagination-intellect capable of envisioning, and *actively working toward* a better, more humane world" (5–6; my emphasis). Through various strategies, inclusive of written expression (not exclusively so), students are challenged to "see anew in ways that are not totally saturated with the known" (Gitlin, 17).

Theory to Practice

In this section, I describe ways that educators can incorporate creative and imaginative expressions into their teaching in an effort to cultivate "an increasingly imagination-intellectually astute student population well-equipped to love the pursuit of knowledge, to question, to criticize, to affect positive social change" (Weems, 3).

Several years ago I started playing music at the beginning of each class as the students and I were getting settled, or during class breaks. I was being purposeful about the selections, though I did not articulate this to students or incorporate the music into class discussion; rather, the songs were backdrop. Then, one year, when co-teaching a course on citizenship with a colleague, we purposefully selected and played pieces of music that we felt represented various notions of citizenship (see Iverson and James). This experience fuelled me to think more deeply about how to incorporate music in particular, and aesthetics in general, into my classroom.

Inspired by Denzin's reference to qualitative research as analogous to blues music—which is full of breaks and ruptures, rather than smoothly evolving—I have used music to illustrate concepts or stances in research. For instance, playing a YouTube clip of a band tuning can spur discussion about the necessary messiness of research; the notion of being "well orchestrated" in research design emerges from a tuning process that every researcher must complete. Later, I compare the clip of a band tuning with a piece that deliberately uses dissonance. Both have notes that seem out of tune; yet in the former, we view the tuning as a process moving toward concordance. With the latter, a composer (or researcher) has deliberately used discordance. Students are then more in tune (pun intended) with discord in their research process, and differentiate that which is part of their "tuning" from that which is discordant by design.

I have also played various renditions of the same song to illustrate multiple perspectives and divergent interpretations. For instance, playing "The Star Spangled Banner" as performed by a symphony, and then the Jimi Hendrix rendition, affords lively discussion about interpretive judgments. Similarly, Ella Fitzgerald's "One Note Samba" scat varies from Stan Getz's jazz rendition, and both are distinct from a YouTube banjo interpretation. Listening to these multiple versions of the same song contributes to students' ability to disrupt notions of a fixed self; this disruption is useful not only in their self-reflexivity but also as they embark on data analysis.

Music is not the only aesthetic avenue. Greene turns to artmaking as a pedagogical approach that can inspire people to "imagine a better state of things" (52). Browdy de Hernandez (in this book) uses film to elicit "activist compassion" in her students. Boske ("Sense-Making") uses artmaking with her students to help them "give *form to feeling*" (4; italics in original). With guidance from community artist mentors, students are challenged to visually articulate both their lived experience and their understanding of the experience of disenfranchised populations. They express their "sense-making" through photography, poetry, music, collage, and short films (see also Boske, "Imaginative Thinking"; Nash).

As noted above, oral expression is differentiated from performance by its emphasis on improvisation; however, these two areas overlap, since the polished performance can emerge from the rehearsed improvisation. Oral expression is the process of engaging in the spoken word. By definition, students' class participation is typically evident through oral expression; what I offer here are strategies for eliciting oral expression beyond *just speaking up* in class.

Regular reflective journaling, typically completed as a written assignment, was assigned by Boske ("Audio and Video") as audio and video reflections. Students, Boske reports, grappled with the need to "sound right," "not offend their peers with real thoughts," and "make their reflections sound good" (75); yet, later observed, "the words [would] just [be] rolling off my tongue when I spoke. I wouldn't do that in a written reflection. I would have caught myself" (78). Boske notes that this form of expression creates spaces for students to "express levels of anxiety" and "broaden understanding of self" (79). I have seen this with those of my graduate research students who use interviewing methods in their data collection. When they complete an initial interview, they are more captivated (or distracted) by their own voice on the audio recording than by what the participants are saying. Boske observes that as students gain insight into the "influence of identity, emotions, and lived experiences," they hear their voice as a source of agency and empowerment (80). Students then can be assigned to interview one another and learn about the experience of being interviewed. This exercise also demands that students "stand back and look at ourselves" epistemologically (Jenkins, 26).

Gershon ("Embodied Knowledge") too attests to the relationship between sound and meaning, and that the sense-making benefits are not only for the person producing the sound (the speaker) but also for the listener. Thus, educators should think not only of how students can make noise, but also about the interactional dimension of sound. Francis writes of the need for students "to develop a voice" (229). Acknowledging the limitations of a reflective journal, Francis advocates the use of a "critical friend" with whom one can "stimulate, clarify, and extend thinking" (234) through dialogues and role plays to imagine other ways of being. Educators could use the "fishbowl technique," which involves placing a dyad or small group in an inner circle to debate, discuss, tell stories, or share experiences, while an outer circle observes. The individuals can move in and out as they feel "called" by the ideas or conversation.

Reflexive practice is overwhelmingly visible through written expression. In this section I offer suggestions for how to use creative work to dislodge the dominance a particular form of journal writing that conforms to the rules of scholarly writing. Quaye reflects that as a graduate student in research classes, he was taught how "to write in the detached impersonal style ... that is the accepted way of presenting research within academe" (7). He adds that the "academic writing voice" is not "explicitly" taught but "just *is*" how "one will naturally learn to write" (7; italics in original). So we must extend what counts, not only to elicit students' imaginative selves, but also in an effort to disrupt conventional ways of thinking about, doing, and writing research.

Gilligan and colleagues' "On the Listening Guide" offers one possible approach to data analysis. Students can be assigned to "listen for the plot" in their stories and to hear how they speak about themselves. To counter the epistemological tendency to distance themselves "in an objectifying way" (Gilligan et al., 162), they can be assigned to construct "I poems" from their journals, by underlining first person "I" statements and reconstructing them poetically.

Students can also be assigned to develop scripts of their experiences. This enables them to convey what is important as they (re)arrange and (re)state events to prepare for a narrative climax. Iverson and Filipan suggest various ways that educators might assign students to write scripts and dialogues (real and imagined) that "may lead students to enhanced self awareness [and to] finding and empowering one's voice" (104). They also share the ways they used scriptwriting in their doctoral studies, in an effort to "find our voice" in a "research-intensive environment that rewards objectivity rather than self-examination" (106). Filipan, in a self-assigned exercise aimed at helping her gain insight into her relationship with research, scripted a dialogue between herself and Research, a man whom she *loves* but isn't *in love with*. Through this exercise, she was able to confront her ambiguous feelings about research, which led to deeper insight about its place in her life. Iverson, when assigned to develop an intellectual autobiography in a doctoral research class, found scriptwriting an appealing format; through it, she introduced several characters, leaving the story "ambiguously authored" (Wright, as quoted in Reinharz, 130). Scripting her autobiography through multiple voices best represented how her identity is more complex than unified; it also enabled her to get outside the object of study while still occupying it—the inevitable challenge of reflexivity (Bochner and Ellis).

Having students script their experiences can serve as a precursor to staging their identity performances. The use of drama in education may help students make sense of their educational experiences and find meaning in them (Dowdy and Kaplan). Kurahashi found that when they enacted monologues and dialogues about family histories, the participants engaged in deeper self-reflection. Assigning students to perform a text, whether an assigned reading in class, data collected in the research process, or one's own reflective journal, can "release the power of imagination" (23). Performance allows "participants to shift positions, which invites multiple perspectives and points of view to be represented" (Belliveau, 139). Students' role playing allows them to perform a character who says things they feel nervous about saying; it also permits them to flout the rules and do the unexpected in a serious, academic space, and invites creative and playful transgressions of social norms (Griffiths 2007).

Performance may involve "no movement, talk, or props"—what Vacca and Vacca refer to as "snapshot drama" (189). Some describe this as creating "living pictures" to invite "interpretation of an event in front of an audience" (Barnes, Brinster, and Fahey, 26). Students work in groups to interpret and represent a passage of text by creating a living image using only their bodies. This affords students an opportunity to work collaboratively to make sense of text, generate ideas about possible representations of that text, and strive to capture their understandings through performance art.

In addition to textual performance and personal narrative performance (Langellier), students could perform a song. As an extension of aesthetic appreciation (e.g., listening to a song), educators might assign students to perform musically (see Iverson and James). Students could also be assigned to dance. A notable example is the annual "Dance Your PhD" competition, sponsored by *Science* magazine and the AAAS (*Science*'s publisher), in which doctoral students (in physics, chemistry, biology, and social sciences) are challenged to choreograph and perform their dissertation. The goal is for students to turn their graduate work into an interpretive dance that anyone can understand; they are judged on the dances' scientific and artistic creativity. Sound too can be choreographed, as Gershon ("Making Sense") has demonstrated through his "sound installations," in which he sustains original audio data (typically converted to transcripts) and installs it in a gallery as audio performance. In these various ways, students are challenged to consider the subject of self, or their own data, as text to be performed, whether through theatre, sound, or dance.

Weems identifies social consciousness as the fifth area—a distinct one—of imagination-intellect. I view it as closely linked to the other four, which collectively contribute to the development of critical social consciousness. The fifth area, though, uniquely emphasizes social justice and action—that through awareness of one's social position in society, one will (must) *be* differently in the world. The development of a critical social consciousness is facilitated in many ways; however, experiential learning—more specifically, critical service learning—has been identified as a key mechanism (Allan and Iverson). Critical service learning helps students develop a deeper understanding of social issues and increases their self-awareness (Rhoads); it also affords the opportunity to challenge assumptions related to social power that can contribute to cognitive dissonance, setting the stage for critical consciousness (Dorney, in this book; Rosenberger). In a qualitative study of how pre-service teachers' involvement with critical service learning impacted their thinking, James and Iverson found that a critical approach complicated students' thinking about social problems and pushed them to consider the importance of social action.

Some (e.g., Hopkinson and Hogg; Machtmas et al.) have used service learning in teaching qualitative research methods and demonstrate how it helps improve students' research skills. Service learning, like feminist and qualitative research, emphasizes and promotes reflexivity; *critical* service learning, which is more aligned with the tenets of feminist research with its emphasis on social change, challenges students (researchers) to put social justice at the forefront. Reflexive practice is no longer an end in itself; rather, achieving reflexivity enables the researcher to work toward a better community (or world). Ollis, in her discussion of the process by which individuals learn to become activists, describes the centrality of critical pedagogy, embodied feelings and emotions, and reflexivity to the development of an epistemology of activism. In particular, she notes that reflexivity, fostered through discussion with other activists, through reading and writing, and through observing other activists' poor and skilful practices, "allows [activists] to hone their knowledge and skill, creating an environment of constant renewal of praxis" (216). Weems's delineation of various ways to develop imagination-intellect extends Ollis's reflexive praxis to include the aesthetic and creative, yielding embodied knowledge and agency in learning.

Conclusion

Imagination-intellect invites ways "one can engage the mind, body, and soul in an attempt to move to [what Weems calls] the 'not yet'" (Gitlin, 17). But it is not without its challenges. Students may feel that such engagement "confirms" their belief that the subjective, reflexive, creative self is not "real" research or is biased. For instance, when I assigned readings such as an autoethnographic performance text (see Weems et al.), students would argue that it was not research. Quaye tried to merge his Ghanaian/American life experience with the academic community's values. More often, his home cultural values were situated *against* or *in contrast to* academe, rather than merging with it.

Using pedagogical strategies that draw out the imagination is unconventional but does not in itself disrupt or dislodge the dominant positivist orientation. Feminists have reclaimed subjectivity as "valid and legitimate knowledge" (Hollway, 133); such knowledge, though, remains contested. Few dissertation committees, for example, will embrace the imaginative and creative over the intellect.

A feminist pedagogy enables educators and researchers to disrupt the mind/body dichotomy that situates that which is embodied in opposition (and subordinate) to that which is rational, and to trouble conceptions of power and authority and of knowledge production and transmission. Furthermore, a feminist pedagogy demands that students become personal with that which is studied (and researched); through that personalization, they are then more likely to view themselves as agents of change. Reflexive practice is central to this personalizing, yet approaches to draw out reflexivity tend to be dominated by written expression.

Imagination-intellect invites us to broaden the way we *think* about practices that elicit reflexivity. Yet by definition, imagination and intellect could be viewed as dichotomous. The hyphen that joins these two states of being illustrates how they are inextricably linked; I argue, however, that we must continue to ask questions about this polarity. Gershon ("Embodied Knowledge"), for instance, critiques the continued privileging of mind over body in the elevating of vision over other senses (see also Gotlib, in this book). He argues for pedagogy (and research) to elicit "non-ocular, sensual meaning-making" (71). Ken too argues against the continued privileging of the visual, in ways that yield "neglect of other senses" (17). In an exploration of race–class–gender relationships, Ken posits that we need to draw on a full sensory experience: "What do they smell like? How do they feel? How do their flavors come together in the mouth? Are they harmonic or dissonant?" (17). Until such questions do not appear fantastical, we must continue to imagine.

A cautionary note: I am not suggesting some causal relationship—that through use of particular (feminist) pedagogical strategies students will demonstrate deeper and critical self-reflexivity. Students must be willing to look at the self, in those deep inner spaces that some individuals are unable to go. Without an epistemological readiness to encounter the unfamiliar and to turn "a critical gaze on one's own values, assumptions, experiences, and opinions and questioning the moral validity of the state of affairs in the world" (Kumagai and Lypson, 786), no pedagogical techniques will yield (lasting) change. Furthermore, cultivating the development of imagination-intellect, such as incorporating performance and aesthetic appreciation into one's teaching, without the feminist pedagogical emphasis on social action, will not necessarily translate into a different way of being and acting civically. Rather, I suggest that the instructional strategies described here can invite people to be more curious and imaginative about the self, and to consider our social performances and to script and rehearse possibilities for other performances. By drawing on imagination-intellect in conjunction with feminist pedagogy, educators can expand the field of possibilities for cultivating reflexivity. This, in turn, can crystallize agency into action.

Works Cited

Allan, E.J., and S.V. Iverson. "Cultivating Critical Consciousness: Service-Learning in Higher Education." *Inquiry: Critical Thinking Across the Disciplines* 23.2 (2004): 51–61.

Allen, Katherine R., and Elizabeth B. Farnsworth. "Reflexivity in Teaching about Families." *Family Relations* 42.3 (1993): 351–56. http://dx.doi.org/10.2307/585566

Altrichter, H., P. Posch, and B. Somekh. *Teachers Investigate Their Work: An Introduction to the Methods of Action Research.* London: Routledge, 1993.

Barrett, Betty J. "Is 'Safety' Dangerous? A Critical Examination of the Classroom as Safe Space." *Canadian Journal for the Scholarship of Teaching and Learning* 1.1 (2010): 1–12. http://dx.doi.org/10.5206/cjsotl-rcacea.2010.1.9 http://ir.lib.uwo.ca/cjsotl_rcacea/vol1/iss1/9

Barnes, Natalie S., Pamela Ann Brinster, and Patrick Fahey. "Exploring Tableau Vivant." *Gifted Child Today* 28.1 (2005): 24–29, 65.

Barry, Christine A., N. Britten, N. Barber, and C. Bradley. "Using Reflexivity to Optimize Teamwork in Qualitative Research." *Qualitative Health Research* 9.1 (1999): 26–44. http://dx.doi.org/10.1177/104973299129121677

Belenky, Mary F., Blythe M. Clinchy, Nancy R. Goldberger, and Jill Mattuck Tarule. *Women's Ways of Knowing: The Development of Self, Voice, and Mind,* 2nd ed. New York: Basic Books, 1997.

Belliveau, George. "An Arts-Based Approach to Teach Social Justice: Drama as a Way to Address Bullying in Schools." *International Journal of Arts Education* 3.2 (2005): 136–65. http://ed.arte.gov.tw

Billo, Emily, and Nancy Hiemstra. "Mediating Messiness: Expanding Ideas of Flexibility, Reflexivity, and Embodiment in Fieldwork." *Gender, Place, and Culture* 20.3 (2012): 313–28. http://dx.doi.org/10.1080/0966369X.2012.674929

Bochner, Arthur P., and Carolyn Ellis. "Personal Narrative as a Social Approach to Interpersonal Communication." *Communication Theory* 2.2 (1992): 165–72. http://dx.doi.org/10.1111/j.1468-2885.1992.tb00036.x

Borg, Simon. "The Research Journal: A Tool for Promoting and Understanding Researcher Development." *Language Teaching Research* 5.2 (2001): 156–77. http://dx.doi.org/10.1177/136216880100500204

Boske, Christa. "Imaginative Thinking: Addressing Social Justice Issues Through Movie-Maker." *Multicultural Education and Technology Journal* 3.3 (2009): 213–26. http://dx.doi.org/10.1108/17504970910984880

———. "Audio and Video Reflections to Promote Social Justice." *Multicultural Education and Technology Journal* 5.1 (2011): 70–85. http://dx.doi. org/ 10.1108/17504971111121937

———. "Sense-Making Reflective Practice: Preparing School Leaders for Non-Text-Based Misundertandings." *Journal of Curriculum Theorizing* 27.2 (2011): 82–100.

Bricker-Jenkins, Mary, and Nancy Hooyman. "Feminist Pedagogy in Education for Social Change." *Feminist Teacher* 2.2 (1987): 36–42.

Browne, Kath. "Placing the Personal in Pedagogy: Engaged Pedagogy in 'Feminist' Geographical Teaching." *Journal of Geography in Higher Education* 29.3 (2005): 339–54. http://dx.doi.org/10.1080/03098260500290900

Chapman, Chris. "Resonance, Intersectionality, and Reflexivity in Critical Pedagogy (and Research Methodology)." *Social Work Education* 30.7 (2011): 723–44. http://dx.doi.org/10.1080/02615479.2010.520120

Chiseri-Strater, Elizabeth. "Turning in upon Ourselves: Positionality, Subjectivity, and Reflexivity in Case Study and Ethnographic Research." *Ethics and Representation in Qualitative Studies of Literacy*. Ed. Peter Mortense and Gesa Kirsch. Urbana: National Council of Teachers of English, 1996. 115–33

Cook, Judith, and Mary Margaret Fonow. "A Passion for Knowledge: The Teaching of Feminist Methodology." In *Handbook of Feminist Research: Theory and Praxis,* ed. Cook, Fonow, and Chakravarti, 2007. 705–11.

Deats, Sara M., and Lagretta T. Lenker, eds. *Gender and the Academe: Feminist Pedagogy and Politics*. Lanham: Rowman and Littlefield, 1994.

DeLyser, Dydia. "Teaching Qualitative Research." *Journal of Geography in Higher Education* 32.2 (2008): 233–44. http://dx.doi.org/10.1080/03098260701514074

Denzin, Norman. "Aesthetics and the Practices of Qualitative Inquiry." *Qualitative Inquiry* 6.2 (2000): 256–65. http://dx.doi.org/10.1177/107780040000600208

deRoche, Constance P., and John E. deRoche. "As I Say, as I Do: Teaching Reflexivity Through Reflexive Subject." *Anthropology and Education Quarterly* 21.2 (1990): 128–33. http://dx.doi.org/10.1525/aeq.1990.21.2.04x0252r

Dowdy, Joanne Kilgour, and Sarah Kaplan, eds. *Teaching Drama in the Classroom*. Rotterdam: Sense Publishers, 2011. 49–54. http://dx.doi.org/10.1007/ 978-94-6091-537-6

Engin, Marion. "Research Diary: A Tool for Scaffolding." *International Journal of Qualitative Methods* 10.3 (2011): 296–306.

THE POWER OF THE IMAGINATION-INTELLECT IN TEACHING 193

Fenwick, Tara. "Ethical Dilemmas of Critical Management Education: Within Classrooms and Beyond." *Management Learning* 36.1 (2005): 31–48. http://dx.doi.org/10.1177/1350507605049899

Francis, Dawn. "The Reflective Journal: A Window to Preserve Teachers' Practical Knowledge." *Teaching and Teacher Education* 11.3 (1995): 229–41. http://dx.doi.org/10.1016/0742-051X(94)00031-Z

Gearing, Robin Edward. "Bracketing in Research: A Typology." *Qualitative Health Research* 14.10 (2004): 1429–452. http://dx.doi.org/10.1177/1049732304270394

Gershon, Walter. "Embodied Knowledge: Sounds as Educational Systems." *Journal of Curriculum Theorizing* 27.2 (2011): 66–81.

———. *Making Sense of Science: Teaching and Studenting in Four Urban Classrooms, A Sound Installation*. Akron: Akron Art Museum, 2012. http://akron artmuseum.org/pastexhibitions/details.php?unid=2878

Gerstl-Pepin, Cynthia, and Kami Patrizio. "Learning from Dumbledore's Penseive: Metaphor as an Aid in Teaching Reflexivity in Qualitative Research." *Qualitative Research* 9.3 (2009): 299–308. http://dx.doi.org/10.1177/1468794109105029

Gilligan, Carol, Renee Spencer, M. Katherine Weinberg, and Tatiana Bertsch. "On the Listening Guide: A Voice-Centered Relational Method." *Qualitative Research in Psychology: Expanding Perspectives in Methodology and Design*. Ed. Paul M. Camic, Jean E. Rhodes, and Lucy Yardley. Washington: American Psychological Association, 2003. 157–72. http://dx.doi.org/10.1037/10595-009

Giroux, Henry A. "Cultural Studies, Public Pedagogy, and the Responsibility of Intellectuals." *Communication and Critical/Cultural Studies* 1.2 (2004): 59–79. http://dx.doi.org/10.1080/1479142042000180926

Gitlin, Andrew. "Inquiry, Imagination, and the Search for a Deep Politic." *Educational Researcher* 34.3 (2005): 15–24. http://dx.doi.org/10.3102/0013189X034003015

Gouldner, Alvin W. *The Coming Crisis of Western Sociology*. New York: Basic Books, 1970.

Greene, Maxine. *Releasing the Imagination: Essays on Education, the Arts, and Social Change*. San Francisco: Jossey-Bass, 1995.

Griffiths, Morwenna. "Autobiography, Feminism, and the Practice of Action Research." *Educational Action Research* 2.1 (1994): 71–82. http://dx.doi.org/10.1080/09650799400200005

———. "Keeping Authenticity in Play—or Being Naughty to Be Good." *Feminist Politics: Identity, Difference, and Agency*. Ed. Deborah Orr. Lanham: Rowman and Littlefield, 2007. 119–40.

Henderson-King, Donna, and Abigail J. Stewart. "Educational Experiences and Shifts in Group Consciousness: Studying Women." *Personality and Social Psychology Bulletin* 25.3 (1999): 390–99. http://dx.doi.org/10.1177/0146167299025003010

Heshusius, Lous. "Freeing Ourselves from Objectivity: Managing Subjectivity or Turning Toward a Participatory Mode of Consciousness?" *Educational Researcher* 23.3 (1994): 15–22. http://dx.doi.org/10.3102/00131 89X023003015

Hertz, Rosanna, ed. *Reflexivity and Voice*. Thousand Oaks: Sage, 1997.

Hollway, Wendy. *Subjectivity and Method in Psychology: Gender, Meaning, and Science*. London: Sage, 1989

Holly, Mary Lou. "Reflective Writing and the Spirit of Inquiry." *Cambridge Journal of Education* 19.1 (1989): 71–80. http://dx.doi.org/10.1080/0305764890190109

hooks, bell. *Teaching to Transgress: Education as the Practice of Freedom*. New York: Routledge, 1994.

Hopkinson, Gillian C., and Margaret K. Hogg. "Teaching and Learning about Qualitative Research in the Social Sciences: An Experiential Learning Approach Amongst Marketing Students." *Journal of Further and Higher Education* 28.3 (2004): 307–20. http://dx.doi.org/10.1080/0309877042000241779

Iverson, Susan V., and Rhonda Filipan. "Scripting Success: Using Dialogue Writing to Help Students Find Their Voice." *Teaching Drama in the Classroom*. Ed. Joanne K. Dowdy and Sarah Kaplan. Amsterdam: Sense Publishers, 2011. 123–29. http://dx.doi.org/10.1007/978-94-6091-537-6_26

Iverson, Susan V., and Jennifer H. James. "Songs of Citizenship: The Use of Music in the Classroom." *Teaching Drama in the Classroom*. Ed. Joanne K. Dowdy and Sarah Kaplan. Amsterdam: Sense Publishers, 2011. 49–54. Print. http://dx.doi.org/10.1007/978-94-6091-537-6_11

James, Jennifer H. "Autobiography, Teacher Education, and (the Possibility of) Social Justice." *Journal of Curriculum and Pedagogy* 4.2 (2008): 161–76. http://dx.doi.org/10.1080/15505170.2007.10411662

James, Jennifer H., and Susan V. Iverson. "Striving for Critical Citizenship in a Teacher Education Program: Problems and Possibilities." *Michigan Journal of Community Service Learning* 16.1 (2009): 33–46.

Jenkins, Richard. "Social Skills, Social Research Skills, Sociological Skills: Teaching Reflexivity?" *Teaching Sociology* 23.1 (1995): 16–27. http://dx.doi.org/10.2307/1319369

Ken, Ivy. "Race-Class-Gender Theory: An Image(ry) Problem." *Gender Issues* 24.1 (2007): 1–20. http://dx.doi.org/10.1007/s12147-007-9005-9

Kirsch, Gesa E., and Joy Ritchie. "S. "Beyond the Personal: Theorizing a Politics of Location in Composition Research." *College Composition and Communication* 46.1 (1995): 7–29. http://dx.doi.org/10.2307/358867

Kobayashi, Audrey. "GPC Ten Years On: Is Self-Reflexivity Enough?" *Gender, Place, and Culture* 10.4 (2003): 345–49. http://dx.doi.org/10.1080/0966369032000153313

Kumagai, Arno, and Monica L. Lypson. "Beyond Cultural Competence: Critical Consciousness, Social Justice, and Multicultural Education." *Academic Medicine* 84.6 (2009): 782–87. http://dx.doi.org/10.1097/ACM.0b013e3181a42398

Kurahashi, Yuko. "Theatre as Healing Space: Ping Chong's *Children of War*." *Studies in Theatre and Performance* 24.1 (2004): 23–36. http://dx.doi.org/10.1386/stap.24.1.23/0

Langellier, Kristin M. "Personal Narrative, Performance, Performativity: Two or Three Things I Know for Sure." *Text and Performance Quarterly* 19.2 (1999): 125–44. http://dx.doi.org/10.1080/10462939909366255

Lather, Patti. *Getting Smart: Feminist Research and Pedagogy with/in the Post-modern.* New York: Routledge, 1991.

MacDermid, Shelley M., Joan A. Jurich, Judith A. Myers-Walls, et al. "Feminist Teaching: Effective Education." *Family Relations* 41.1 (1992): 31–38. http://dx.doi.org/10.2307/585389

Machtmas, Krisanna, Earl Johnson, Janet Fox, et al. "Teaching Qualitative Research Methods Through Service-Learning." *Qualitative Report* 14.1 (2009): 155–64. http://www.nova.edu/ssss/QR/QR14-1/machtmes.pdf

Maher, Francis A., and Mary Kay Tetreault. *The Feminist Classroom: Dynamics of Gender, Race, and Privilege.* New York: Basic Books, 1994.

Matthews, Jonathan C. "Somatic Knowing and Education." *Educational Forum* 62.3 (1998): 236–42. http://dx.doi.org/10.1080/00131729808984349

Menary, Richard. "Writing as Thinking." *Language Sciences* 29.5 (2007): 621–23. http://dx.doi.org/10.1016/j.langsci.2007.01.005

Middleton, S. *Educating Feminists: Life History and Pedagogy.* New York: Teachers College Press, 1993.

Naples, Nancy A., and Karen Bojar, eds. *Teaching Feminist Activism: Strategies from the Field.* New York: Routledge, 2002. Print.

Nash, Jennifer C. "Re-Thinking Intersectionality." *Feminist Review* 89.1 (2008): 1–15. http://dx.doi.org/10.1057/fr.2008.4

Ollis, Tracey. *A Critical Pedagogy of Embodied Education: Learning to Become an Activist.* New York: Palgrave Macmillan, 2012. Print. http://dx.doi.org/10.1057/9781137016447

Patai, Daphe. "(Response) When Method Becomes Power." In *Power and Method: Political Activism and Educational Research.* Ed. Andrew Gitlin. London and New York: Routledge, 1994. 61–73.

Peshkin, Alan. "In Search of Subjectivity—One's Own." *Educational Researcher* 17.7 (1988): 17–21.

Pillow, Wanda. "Confession, Catharsis, or Cure? Rethinking the Uses of Reflexivity as Methodological Power in Qualitative Research." *Qualitative Studies in Education* 16.2 (2003): 175–96. http://dx.doi.org/10.1080/0951839032000060635

Poulin, Karen L. "Teaching Qualitative Research: Lessons from Practice." *Counseling Psychologist* 35.3 (2007): 431–58. http://dx.doi.org/10.1177/0011000006294813

Quaye, Stephen J. "Voice of the Researcher: Extending the Limits of What Counts as Research." *Journal of Research Practice* 3.1 (2007): 1–13.

Reinharz, Shulamit. *Feminist Methods in Social Research.* New York: Oxford University Press, 1992.

Rhoads, Robert A. *Community Service and Higher Learning: Explorations of the Caring Self.* Albany: SUNY Press, 1997.

Richardson, Laurel. "Getting Personal: Writing Stories." *International Journal of Qualitative Studies in Education* 14.1 (2001): 33–38. http://dx.doi.org/10.1080/09518390010007647

Ropers-Huilman, Becky. *Feminist Teaching in Theory and Practice: Situating Power and Knowledge in Poststructural Classrooms.* New York: Teachers College Press, 1998.

Rose, Gillian. "Situating Knowledges: Positionality, Reflexivities and Other Tactics." *Progress in Human Geography* 21.3 (1997): 305–20. http://dx.doi .org/10.1191/030913297673302122

Rosenberger, Carolyn. "Beyond Empathy: Developing Critical Consciousness Through Service-Learning." *Integrating Service-Learning and Multicultural Education in Colleges and Universities.* Ed. Carolyn R. O'Grady. Mahwah: Lawrence Erlbaum, 2000. 23–43.

St. Pierre, Elizabeth Adams. "Methodology in the Fold and the Irruption of Transgressive Data." *International Journal of Qualitative Studies in Education* 10.2 (1997): 175–89. http://dx.doi.org/10.1080/095183997237278

Sarachild, Kathie. "Consciousness-Raising: A Radical Weapon." In *Feminist Revolution.* Ed. Kathie Sarachild. New York: Random House, 1978. 144–50.

Shrewsbury, Carolyn M. "What Is Feminist Pedagogy?" *Women's Studies Quarterly* 15.3–4 (1987): 6–14.

Spivak, Gayatri C. "Can the Subaltern Speak?" *Marxism and the Interpretation of Culture.* Ed. Cary Nelson and Lawrence Grossberg. Urbana: University of Illinois Press, 1988. 271–313.

Stein, Jane. *Empowerment and Women's Health: Theory, Methods, and Practice.* New York: Zed Books, 1997.

Thompson, Linda. "Feminist Methodology for Family Studies." *Journal of Marriage and the Family* 54.1 (1992): 3–18. http://dx.doi.org/10.2307/353271

Vacca, Richard T., and JoAnne L. Vacca. *Content Area Reading: Literacy and Learning across the Curriculum.* Boston: Pearson, 2005.

Van Maanen, John. *Tales of the Field: On Writing Ethnography.* Chicago: University of Chicago Press, 1989.

Villaverde, Leia. *Feminist Theories and Education.* New York: Peter Lang, 2008.

Warren, John T. "Reflexive Teaching: Toward Critical Autoethnographic Practices of/in/on Pedagogy." *Cultural Studies, Critical Methodologies* 11.2 (2011): 139–44. http://dx.doi.org/10.1177/1532708611401332

Watt, Diane. "On Becoming a Qualitative Researcher: The Value of Reflexivity." *Qualitative Report* 12.1 (2007): 82–101. http://www.nova.edu/ssss/QR/QR12-1/watt.pdf

Weems, Mary E. *Public Education and the Imagination Intellect: I Speak from the Wound in My Mouth.* New York: Lang, 2003.

Weems, Mary E., Carolyne J. White, Patricia A. McHatton, et al. "Heartbeats: Exploring the Power of Qualitative Research Expressed as Autoethnographic Performance Texts." *Qualitative Inquiry* 15.5 (2009): 843–58. http://dx.doi .org/10.1177/1077800409333155

Wolf, Diane, ed. *Fieldwork Dilemmas in Fieldwork.* Boulder: Westview Press, 1996.

CHAPTER TEN

From Muzzu-Kummik-Quae to Jeanette Corbiere Lavell and Back Again: Indigenous and Feminist Approaches to the First-Year Course in Canadian History

Katrina Srigley

*When I'm teaching the young women I have to bring them along,
eh. Come along, come along. The teachings are waiting. Come
along. Sometimes I have to give them a little push into the lodge, eh
[laughter]*

—Grandmother Elder Lorraine Whiteduck Liberty[1]

In her essence as the land and as relationship between, to, and of mothers
and mothering in the past and today, Muzzu-Kummik-Quae or Mother
Earth is a key concept in "Mewnzha, mewnzha, mewnzha"—long, long,
long ago for Anishnaabe (Ojibway) peoples. She points to the centrality of women and femininity, of the land, to the foundational stories of
Anishnaabe history (Beaucage; Johnston; Roy, Roy, and Corbiere; Simpson 2011; Simpson 2013). Teaching and living as we do on the traditional
territory of the Nbisiing Anishinabeg (Nipissing First Nation), we have
brought Muzzu-Kummik-Quae in to our first-year Canadian history classroom at Nipissing University in North Bay, Ontario. In her appearance,
Muzzu-Kummik-Quae is not just *in* the story, but *of* the story we tell. She

represents a way of understanding the past that is circular, emanating from Indigenous femininity, and rooted in the land, which is a starting point for students to reflect on the different stories of this country and the various ways these stories are shared and understood. Weaving these understandings with Euro-Canadian understandings of the past, as linear, understood through continuity and change, and as driven by people, places, and things in the past, we are working to create a space where various ways of understanding and knowing about the past come together.[2] To use Marie Battiste's words, we are mobilizing and reaching "*beyond* the two distinct systems of knowledge" to introduce students to and strengthen their understandings of the fundamentals of different histories (103).[3] In doing this, we, much like Tracy Penny Light, Jane Nicholas, Jamelee Baroud, and others in this volume, understand our classroom as a context for learning as well as for social justice and empowerment.

Over ten years of teaching in undergraduate and graduate history classrooms, I have come to better understand my impact on students, including their engagement with the world around them and the knowledge and skills they bring to their post-university lives. What happens in university classrooms matters.[4] I have also experienced the challenging dissonance between my training as a feminist historian and educator in "critical disciplinary history" and the on-the-ground realities of teaching at universities, particularly in first-year survey courses (Barton and Levstik; hooks; Lévesque; Osborne 2000; Osborne 2003; Bowen Raddeker; Sandwell; Seixas, "'Students' Understanding"; Stearns, Seixas, and Wineburg). There is a difficult push-and-pull relationship at the heart of these courses. While they provide the opportunity to teach disciplinary fundamentals and to interact with (mostly) energized and excited students, they also involve teaching larger groups, time-consuming course administration, and, to a much great extent than in upper-year courses, disciplinary pressure to cover "essential" information. These courses are often assigned to vulnerable faculty in non-tenured contract positions—faculty who "survive" by teaching the English Canadian story of European settlement and colonization, whatever their innovative pedagogical ideas, their energy for and immersion in their field, and their own sense of boredom during their lectures about Confederation. With time and greater job security, perhaps they will extend their discussion to the different stories of Turtle Island, or to the experiences of Loyalist women, and do their best to cover working-class perspectives as they fly over industrialization; but even in such an amended form, the first-year course remains driven by a Eurocentric national story, a line from Cabot to Chrétien, that does nothing to shift the narrative framework that suppresses the history and world views of Indigenous peoples, heralds the liberal-order narrative of progress, and limits attention to the violence of inequality in Canada's past.[5] The dominant story of contact, settlement, and nationhood has become so naturalized that most Canadians—citizens, politicians, and teachers—do not understand how it undergirds colonialism and stands in the way of historical understanding.

At the end of my sixth year of teaching, I realized I was teaching a course that did little more than "add and stir" different experiences and perspectives. To make change, I turned to my training in feminist history and the work I was doing in partnership with Anishnaabe and Ininew (Cree) women in my community.[6]

Using my journey in our first-year course in Canadian History as a case study, this essay examines how we might alter the Eurocentric trajectory of first-year history classrooms by putting into practice the challenges of feminist pedagogy and Indigenous methodologies. Here I share how I came to sit with Nokomis and teach from Muzzu-Kummik-Quae to Jeanette Corbiere Lavell and back again. To do so, I consider three key areas of pedagogical practice: first, my teaching context, particularly the dynamics of power that inform it and the ways in which I have worked to challenge them; second, curriculum, including what I teach and how I teach it; and, finally, modes of evaluation. I argue that making these types of changes in our classrooms would enrich historical education and, more importantly, contribute to the healing of relationships, of communities and identities, destroyed by the history of colonialism.[7]

Indigenous Feminism and Historical Pedagogy

While the intersections of feminist and Indigenous methodologies may seem unlikely starting points for historiographical and pedagogical change, their synergies make for powerful scholarly practice inside and outside Canadian history classrooms. It is clear that feminism has a complicated relationship with Indigenous histories. Almost twenty years ago, Patricia Monture-Angus pointed to the connections she saw between the politics and practice of second-wave feminism and legacies of colonialism. In *Thunder in My Soul,* and in later publications, Monture-Angus spoke about the limits of sisterhood and feminism for her as a Haudenosaunee (Mohawk) woman. She argued that the very structure of the feminist movement was incompatible with her understanding of the world and the changes needed to create social equality. "In my experience," she wrote, "the woman's movement must come to terms with Aboriginal women's diversity *as we define it*" (178). As Sherene Razack explains in a recent issue of *Canadian Women and the Law,* which is dedicated to Monture-Angus, Monture-Angus identified as a feminist anti-colonial activist for whom "equality with men was not a high enough standard" (ii). This epistemological argument and its application are as relevant to the history classroom as they are for the feminist movement. Scholars and activists must be willing to identify, critically reflect on, and challenge normative ways of knowing in their research and teaching (Cole; Kovach; Tuhiwai Smith; Wilson).

Indigenous feminists see critical reasons to bring these methodologies together (Green; Smith; Suzack et al.). As so many scholars in this book make clear, feminists have long recognized learning contexts as spaces of struggle and change. This is as true for Indigenous as it is for non-Indigenous women. In history classrooms, we need more Indigenous women's history attentive to the centrality and power of women and the "critical importance of gender" in the Indigenous societies of Turtle Island (Huhndorf and Suzack, 2). This is history that places the stories of Muzzu-Kummik-Quae and Jeannette Corbiere Lavell centrally and that uncovers the intertwined violence of patriarchy and colonialism. It was this intersection that fundamentally compromised traditional and (some would argue) inherently feminist gender roles and relations that existed long before the arrival of Europeans. When we neglect this history, we are free to understand Indigenous women and their experiences as "historical abstractions" and to ignore the fact that the world confronting Indigenous women today is one of the greatest social justice issues of our time (Razack). The Canadian Research Institute for the Advancement of Women reports that 48 to 90 percent of Indigenous women will experience violence in their lives. The stories of more than 1300 missing and murdered Indigenous women in Canada make this reality all too clear. When history classrooms become sites to honour Nokomis and the knowledge she carries, when they expose the squaw/princess binary, they confront the inequalities that shape the histories and lives of women in this country.

As the conversations developed in this book make clear, intersectionality is a key element of feminist pedagogies (Dorney; Llewellyn and Llewellyn; Penny Light). This analytical concept encourages us to see and understand individuals and communities within a broader web of relationships, both material and subjective, in the past and the present. Indigenous methodologies widen and deepen the function of intersectionality by framing intersections as relationships. This is not unlike Kristina and Jennifer Llewellyn's point that community gives relationships greater significance and longevity. Indigenous methodologies also draw land and animals, both inanimate and animate, as well as spiritual understandings, into the circle for reflection. In ways critical for history classrooms, intersectionality also focuses students and teachers on the connection between the present and the past in their learning contexts. Whose history is being

taught, and why? That the epistemological traditions of Western European society came to dominate those of the Indigenous societies of Turtle
Island through violent means, and that the ideologies and structures of
this unequal relationship persist today, is inseparable from the story of
this country, including who is present and has power in today's university classrooms. Students are struck with anger, confusion, and a genuine
sense of enlightenment when they realize that history has a history and
that what they learn and how they learn it have historical determinants.
Thus, intersectionality offers tools for the kind of structural change called
for by historical and feminist pedagogy. It addresses the need for deeper
understandings of experiences and inequalities, for sensitivity to multiple
perspectives and world views, and for a complication of binaries, such as
empowered/victimized.

My Teaching Context

*A lot of people come to university to get smart. Education is the new
buffalo. But, I say that it is important to stay smart while you are getting smart, and I learned that one from old Nanabush. It was summer-
time, and Nanabush was in the forest, feeling pretty hungry but also
kind of lazy. He got to thinking that all his problems could be solved if
only he were smarter. "Owah," said Nanabush. "If I were only smarter,
I wouldn't have to spend all this time hunting. I bet those animals
would come right to my lodge." ... So Nanabush thought about how he
could get smart, and when he couldn't come up with any ideas, he went
to see old Nokomis.*

—"Please Be Careful When You're Getting Smart,"
Storyteller Leanne Simpson (33)[8]

Taking myself out of the university to learn has been one of the great
rewards of working in partnership. Guided by the teachings intrinsic to the
territory on which I live and work, as well as my disciplinary training, my
intellectual and physical journey has taught me the meaning and importance of relationships in all their complex expressions—among people, the
land, and their stories. The survey course has been one of the spaces where
I have come to understand this and to learn what it means to spend time
with Nokomis:

"Nokomis, I think my life would be so easy and so much better if I were
smarter," said Nanabush. "Ehn, you're right. Smart people do have a good
life. It's true," replied Nokomis. "Do you know how I could get smart,
Nokomis? Because if I were smarter, everything would be a lot less work ..."

"Hmmm," said Nokomis. "I do know this place in the forest, and in this special place is a bush, and on that bush are some very special berries, smart berries. One handful, and you start to get smarter, immediately." "Oh, Nokomis," said Nanabush. "This is exactly what I need. Take me, take me, TAAAKE MEEEE!" (Simpson, 34)

Of course, it is one thing to grasp the importance of learning from the elders—from the stories and their carriers—and another to actually do so, particularly when you are a Euro-Canadian academic working in a Euro-Canadian institution. Building relationships, like change itself, involves time and commitment. When I found myself walking toward Grand Elder Peter Beaucage's Canadore College office, a syllabus in my right hand and tobacco tie in my left, I had been engaged with and living on the territory of Nbisiing Anishinabeg for six years.[9] My learning started inside the university, where I requested guidance from the Office of Aboriginal Initiatives; after that, working with a community member and university employee, I began to spend more time in the community. I applied for and was awarded a $5,000 Internal Research Grant to build relationships.[10] I attended public events, such as the annual powwow. With time, I was invited to community gatherings and teachings, many of which were Peter Beaucage's circles. As part of this process, I had to accept a level of the unknown (perhaps I would be accepted, perhaps I would not) uncommon in the Euro-Canadian academic world, and to listen more than talk (also uncommon). I learned when it was appropriate to head to Peter's office on my own. No one told me I had "passed"—I just arrived at a point in experience and relationship when I knew I was making my request in ways that supported the principles of *bimaadiziwin*, of doing things in a good way.

When I arrived at Peter's office during the summer of 2012, he listened patiently as I outlined my intention to change the way I taught first-year Canadian history and my hope to involve elders so that we could make Anishnaabe history from the Anishnaabe perspective part of that space. Peter smiled and, as is his way, patiently circled me back to where I should have started: "Tell me who you are, Katrina." Right. Bashfully, I said: "Katrina *nindizhinikaaz. Niin wabskyekwe.* Toronto *donjiba.* North Bay *dondaa.*" After a conversation about my Euro-Canadian ancestors and the land on which I grew up in the Toronto area, we arrived back at the course. Yes, he would be involved, but I needed to visit Nokomis—in this case, Lorraine Whiteduck Liberty, who is elder-in-residence at Canadore College. What emerged over several meetings with Lorraine was her offer to participate in the course, to share her knowledge or arrange to bring knowledge keepers to lectures at appropriate times throughout the year.

As I developed these relationships, my position as a university professor shifted in meaningful ways, fostering, as Tracy Penny Light suggests here, "multiple authorities." The notion that the professor holds all relevant knowledge is a key fallacy of undergraduate classrooms. No amount of critical pedagogical practice can completely disrupt this power (Ellsworth, 101), but that power can be destabilized. It was through meetings with Peter and Lorraine that I became conscious of the power of the syllabus.[11] It is remarkable how the rigid, linear format of syllabi structures knowledge delivery. These messages, though, can be reshaped in several ways. When I included the names of Peter and Lorraine on the syllabus beside (rather than below) my name, relationships shifted in meaningful ways. In doing so, I acknowledged the expertise that elders bring to the classroom and, in keeping with the principles of *bimaadiziwin*, made clear that the relationship between elders and the course would be significant and ongoing. Over the course in the first year (2012–13), Peter and Lorraine spent time with us six times. They set the extent and nature of their participation. This involved giving up control of content and time. While this challenged my desire to control teaching contexts, I now understand it as part of the process of pedagogical and epistemological change. It forced me out of the constraints of linear narratives by, for instance, circling me back to Anishnaabe creation stories in the context of nineteenth-century trade or territorial sovereignty. It forced me to give things time to unfold.

Most powerfully, the presence of elders in classroom space creates the potential for important learning outcomes for students. It validates the intellectual traditions of Indigenous students, for whom elders are knowledge keepers in their communities, highlighting their role as teachers and experts. It allows elders to provide Indigenous students with "a serious understanding about where they live," where they come from, and where they might go next (Bird and Gray, 4). In mainstream classrooms, knowledge is almost always "conceptualized, vetted, and delivered" by Euro-Canadian professors (Ball, 457). By restructuring how and by whom content is shared, and by having an open curriculum, we encourage students to question the "privilege of knowledge" (Ball, 468; Gehl). Perhaps most importantly, for Indigenous students, it increases the cultural relevance of the classroom, validating the cultural knowledge they bring to this space (Ball, 457). In the words of one student who participated in university classrooms that involved elders: "We can't learn everything from our books. We have to learn from our Elders too ... So it's like applying two worlds as one" (Ball, 460). In equally important ways, when elders share knowledge they introduce non-Indigenous students to epistemological traditions central to understanding Canada past and present. Many students have little sense of the fact that the tradition of recording and sharing stories of the past is age-old among Indigenous peoples, and even fewer understand how these teaching systems, and the historical traditions and core values on which they are based, provide an essential intellectual context for Canadian history. All of us must listen to the elders. "Their words are strong. If we listen hard, if we listen in a good way, their words will stay with us for a long time" (Kulchyski, McCaskill, and Newhouse, xxiv; Snowball).

In a great deal of literature on classroom pedagogy, teachers are understood quite simply and homogenously as empowerers of students. Yet as Jennifer Gore points out, discussions of pedagogy, of classrooms as contexts for empowerment, consistently fail to consider the complexities of that empowerment. Gore reminds us that power is a slippery, inconsistent, and contradictory force, "existing only in action" and ever changing depending on context. As such, teachers are not necessarily empowered or students necessarily disempowered (59–61).

Dominant narratives are not just discipline specific. They are institutional and administrative, shaped by departmental culture and the motivations, interests, and pedagogical practices of colleagues. With survey courses, pedagogy is subject to group discussion far more often than is the case with upper-year courses. The first-year course is typically understood as having a dual purpose: to lay the knowledge groundwork *and* the skill base for future courses. The former goal has traditionally been viewed as more pressing than the latter. To ensure that students have basic knowledge and a sense of the national story, and are able to show (through their marks) that they understand this framework, survey history courses often repeat the content of high school history. Increasingly, the first-year course must also act as a net that captures students, funnelling them into majors through which departments receive money, attention, and applause from administration. Even without considering significant changes in content and approach, finding a balance between these objectives is tremendously difficult, especially for beginning teachers. Will such changes be recognized as innovative and as complimentary to enrolment goals? What toll might it take on the professor professionally and personally?

Job security is crucial to (dis)empowerment for faculty. A willingness to challenge the status quo is at the heart of social justice and Indigenous feminist education, so we cannot ignore that some faculty can be tremendously vulnerable if they challenge departmental culture or receive negative student reviews. I am a tenured Associate Professor. I work in a department in which I enjoy significant autonomy in course design and delivery, at a university that sells itself as an undergraduate institution committed to Indigenous learners. I am privileged with job security and institutional support. Within some fairly broad pedagogical constraints, I can design the first-year course as I see fit and make an argument for innovation and change. Whether or not the course continues will have less to do with the department and the university administration than with my students. How do they respond to the course in their evaluations? Does enrolment increase or decrease in the following year? Setting aside the recognized limitations of student evaluations, there seems no better evidence of success in university than a high student approval rating. We often fail to consider this context of student empowerment when reflecting on the social justice achievements of our classrooms. As we make even greater changes to the normative narrative of Canada's past, it remains to be seen whether we will need to challenge the power of the student body.

As feminist scholars have long established, identities play an important role in classroom dynamics. As Nicholas and Baroud highlight in their discussion of Humanities 101, understanding who your students are and reflecting on how your course impacts them is a crucial aspect of feminist pedagogies. For some, the exercise of knowing and reflecting on the student body sounds troublingly unempirical. It need not be. In Ontario, all universities collect publicly accessible data on full- and part-time students. Some of the most recent surveys (2010–11) have focused on first-year students. Three such surveys have been conducted by Common Universities Data Ontario, Multi-Year Accountability Agreements, and the Canadian University Survey Consortium. Through these, universities gather information about individual students, including gender and minority status as well as whether they are first-generation university students, identify as Indigenous, or have a disability. While the accuracy of the data is necessarily impacted by the methodology used, these instruments do provide a window on university populations and allow for comparison with other universities. At Nipissing University, the data collected for first-year students in 2010–11 indicated that close to 71 percent of first-year students were women and that the vast majority were English speaking. This was in keeping with patterns at other Ontario universities. However, Nipissing University differs from other locations in its higher percentage of first-generation students, Indigenous students, and students with disabilities and lower percentage of minority and immigrant students. While this information provides me with an important sense of the students likely to appear in my classrooms, a second and equally important tool for understanding students is spending time observing the class, during lectures but also before and after. This ethnographic exercise adds important contextual information to otherwise general numbers. What groups exist? Which groups or individuals dominate? Are some being silenced, or are they choosing silence?[12] As Mimi Orner points out, this reflection must be holistic, including the entire classroom context. "Everyone is someone else's other." If we only reflect on the place of the most marginalized students, we do nothing to disrupt the power dynamics inherent in their oppression. We leave the position of the most powerful students and the professor intact (85). Also the reflective process must be ongoing, for contexts change with the audience and the content and nature of delivery. Feminist pedagogies focus teachers on classroom power dynamics. This includes relationships between the teacher and students, among students, and between the teacher and her/his colleagues, as well as the cultural, economic, and political dynamics of the university and community that surrounds it. Such reflections are necessarily uneven, but they acknowledge that power—indeed, the world we live in—is not static, but shifting and complicated.

At Nipissing University, there is a great deal of respect for the authority of professors and much less entitlement than I have experienced in other contexts. This may be explained by the number of first-generation students unfamiliar with university culture and its power structures and class dynamics. It may also relate to the university's culture of accessibility and friendliness, which, along with the identity of the professor, plays itself out in interesting ways. As a female professor, I am expected to be friendly and warm, supportive and even mothering to my students. Perceived violations of this relationship dynamic and can result in charges of favouritism and anti-feminist dismissive language such as "she's just a feminist." Establishing and maintaining authority, even in the Nipissing context, is not as easy for female as for male professors. It requires maintaining authority through expert status and assertiveness, qualities often antithetical to the goals of feminist and Indigenous pedagogies. In the undergraduate classroom, these factors affect everyone, but they empower unequally. In this I share experiences with other students in my classroom.

Indigenous methodologies focus on the impact of colonialism in teaching contexts. For Indigenous students, this means acknowledging their unique history of subordination. Too often, Indigenous students are understood to be equally disempowered or, even more erroneously, empowered in our classrooms. There is *nothing* free about the education that Indigenous students receive in Canada (Kirkness 1999). Teaching Indigenous students also means a commitment to contribute to "cultural survival" (Regnier, 76), a process that can start with recognition that we are "all treaty people" (Switzer). Most students have not reflected on this fact. Few have considered how formal education has long been "one of the main ways of subjugating Indigenous peoples" to the culture of the colonizers (Ball, 457). The field of history is particularly fraught. "What counts as history [does] not often correspond with the ways that traditional indigenous communities make meaning out of the past," and the stories chosen do little to disrupt the celebratory nation-building narrative (Marker, 97). Nonetheless, and perhaps even because of the highly charged nature of history classrooms, they are crucial sites to confront "the weight of Canadian history" that stands in the way of "transformative change" (Regnier, 71). In the words of Maori scholar Linda Tuhiwai Smith, "history is power" (28–39). When we acknowledge this, when we teach our students how to study and use history in this spirit, our classrooms become places to work for meaningful change to the most damaged yet most promising relationships in Canada today. Positioning students in my classroom, both the most powerful and vulnerable, to take up these teachings in the best possible ways means recognizing how inequalities converge in their lives and offering them opportunities to learn from and about different perspectives.

Curriculum—Indigenizing and Feminizing what I Teach

And so Nanbush and Nokomis began to walk down the path to find the smart berries. They walked and walked, and finally they came to a plant with tiny red berries on it. Are these the berries? Are these the smart berries, Nokomis? Are they? Are they? Are they? Gaawiin ... those aren't the smart berries. (Simpson, 34–35)

In recent years, angst about the historical knowledge of Canadians has gained considerable traction, especially since the federal government's changes to citizenship tests, which do much to celebrate Canada's military past and weaken understandings of the ways in which the Canadian nation-state has failed citizens and non-citizens alike. At the heart of this controversy is one question: What do Canadians need to know about the country's past to be "true" Canadians? (See also Wilson this book.) What is valuable knowledge, and what is trivial and unimportant? (Jones and Perry). As the Historical Thinking Movement has clearly established, the goal of the history classroom should not be defined by a student's ability to regurgitate content, whether that be the number of Canadians who served in the Great War or the date when some Canadian women gained the federal franchise (Friesen; Ashby, Gordon, and Lee; Osborne; Bowen Raddeker; Seixas; Seixas and Clark). Instead, students should develop the skills to engage with this content, understand it as part of a contested body of knowledge, and be able to apply that knowledge in their thinking about the past and the present. This includes recognizing multiple world views and knowledge frameworks, as well as being able to read, question, and compare information and communicate their findings in writing and orally. These types of skills lead to higher rates of democracy, so that citizens are better equipped to challenge inequality. While this is certainly an important pedagogical shift for history classrooms, it is important to remember that content matters. If it did not matter, then what we teach or do not teach would be irrelevant. On the contrary, the knowledge we share about the past in the classroom becomes more powerful through the process of sharing and learning. To change the social justice potential of the first-year course, I had to change the curriculum.

> After walking for a long time past heart berry, blood berry, and blue berry bushes, Nokomis stopped walking. "We're here," she announced. Nanabush looked around for the big, delicious berries. "Where are they, Nokomis?" "They are here, Nanbush, on the ground." These don't look like berries." "These are the smart berries." Those don't smell like berries." "These are the smart berries. One handful and you'll start getting smarter almost immediately." "Nahow," said Nanabush, taking a big handful and putting them into his mouth. AAAAAAHHHHHHH, BLECK, YUCK! These aren't berries, Nokomis! These are *waawaashkesh*, poop!" "See, Nanabush, you are getting smarter already." (Simpson, 34–35)

Abandoning the course textbook was one of the earliest shifts we made to our curriculum. We recognized that it is impossible to teach from different epistemological traditions when one tradition is given power through a single text. Within textbooks, efforts to integrate more Indigenous and women's knowledge, perspectives, and experiences have often led to caption boxes or additional sections that do not alter the European, male, liberal narrative framework that propels history forward (Kirkness 1977). Olive Dickason and Arthur Ray offer important exceptions, though they do not focus on women or femininity. This structuring of knowledge creates a strange disconnect between women's history and Indigenous history, as if the experiences and histories of Indigenous and non-Indigenous women do not intersect and femininity is somehow oppositional to Indigeniety. My work in partnership with Anishnaabekwe has shown me that their histories have been shaped by intersections between colonialism and patriarchy—intersections that have had an impact on Euro-Canadian women (Srigley). Certainly, as Marie Battiste points out, "decolonization belongs to everyone," and ongoing divisions limit change (9). Despite this, the textbook and the survey course are so tightly bound that we were not sure how we or the students would fair. We chose to list several different textbooks in the syllabus, those written from Anishnaabe and Euro-Canadian perspectives that survey Turtle Island/Canadian history, as well as those attentive to the history of women and the working class. For many students, having no textbook appeared to leave them afloat without a means to reach land. Though I have rarely had a sense that the vast majority of students read the assigned textbooks, they clearly found it comforting to have a source to consult that tells *the* story. In the end, we resisted the easy route and directed them to the recommended texts on hold. When the "single text book" is removed from the equation, many students are moved outside their comfort zone and the course becomes what it tries to teach.

All the time that I have studied history, Confederation and John A. Macdonald have figured in the narrative. They are crucial signposts of pride, and of political and economic beginnings and endings. It seems that Confederation, with its Quebec City and Charlottetown conferences, a hard-working Macdonald, and drinking and dancing, is one of the harder stories to shake up. We divide the survey course in Canadian History here. The modern nation began here. Our research and academic jobs are typically defined in this manner. How could we not relate this story to students? Twenty-five years later, I remember the pride I felt when I correctly identified the face of John A. Macdonald pinned at the back of my grade eight classroom, alongside numerous other "great" Canadians taken from the covers of *Maclean's*. There was not an Indigenous person among them. Mother Teresa had a spot, I believe. It was in this classroom that I first realized I loved history, particularly the permission it gave me to listen to stories and use my imagination. Notwithstanding these romanticized reminiscences, as I applied Indigenous feminist methodologies to my teaching, the dangers of classifying significant national knowledge become clearer than ever.[13]

For Indigenous peoples—for the many and varied nations across Turtle Island—Confederation was an ominous development. In an abandonment of the spirit of the Royal Proclamation of 1763, which had acknowledged the right to self-determination on First Nations land (Dickason, 162–66), not one First Nation was invited to talks of union. That First Nations had not been considered became even clearer under the British North America Act, which formalized Confederation and assigned jurisdiction of Indigenous peoples to the federal government through the Canadian Parliament. It also listed vast stretches of Rupert's Land, British Columbia, and the Northwest Territories for entry into Confederation with no consultation with the people to whom this land belonged (Miller, 129). Indeed, the desire to take control of these regions for their raw materials and as a market for goods produced in eastern Canada was "one of the driving forces behind Confederation" (Ray, 194). The ensuing "Canadian invasion" did not mean national progress for Indigenous peoples. Instead, it led to the gradual entrenchment of racist and assimilative policies. It led to genocide (Daschuk). Between 1867 and 1876, the relationship between Indigenous peoples and the Canadian state disintegrated further. This reality shaped the new nation as well as First Nations, irrevocably and violently.

Instead of dividing the class content at Confederation, I chose 1850 as a transitional date. There are multiple reasons why that year works well in my classroom. It was the year the British government signed the Robinson Superior and Robinson Huron Treaties with Anishnaabe communities around the Great Lakes from Lake Huron to west of Lake Superior, including the territory of Nbisiing Anishinabeg. As two of the most important treaties signed in nineteenth-century Canada West (Ontario), they have national significance, but more importantly, they are relevant to the land and people local to Nipissing University. By choosing that year, I was also changing how local history factored into the content of my course. While I used this opportunity to teach students about treaty relationships in a general sense, I also shared stories from the historiography that forefronted the Anishnaabe perspective. For instance, students learned that mining activity on the part of the colonial government north of Lake Superior encouraged Anishnaabe leaders to sign the treaty. When Anishnaabe leaders from the region travelled to Toronto to demand a share of the revenue generated on their lands, they received no response. They later took the matter into their own hands by shutting down the Quebec and Lake Superior Mining Company by force, which drew British troops to the area. When efforts to build or force conversations failed, the Anishnaabe sought a more formal treaty relationship, one that would delineate the lands over which they would remain sovereign. From the Anishnaabe perspective, these were not lands granted to them but lands they were not willing to share with settlers (Dickason, 231–32). This is an important counternarrative to that of victim and conqueror. It has great contemporary relevance in an era of seemingly unrestricted resource development.

What happens when we take students from celebration to tragedy, from drinks, dancing, and national pride to the violence of colonialism? When the pivotal year is shifted to 1850, students are exposed to a different narrative of their country's past and learn that history is about perspective and intellectual traditions. This develops a sense that world view matters; it also leads to greater empathy for and understanding of relationships in Canada today. Some students reject the revision outright. In seminars and course evaluations they lament the "negativity" of their history and the feeling that they as Euro-Canadians are implicated in the colonial project. It is notable, though, that these responses are far less frequent than those which express thankfulness, anger about injustice, and a desire to participate in change. Learning this history is a hard process. Thanks particularly to my colleague Catherine Murton Stoehr, I have learned to acknowledge rather than dismiss this feeling in my students, and to encourage them to do something about their discomfort. For most students, the course makes them pause and reflect. Initially startled by a different story, they are surprised (positively) when I point out to them that they already know the history of the founding fathers and Confederation. Hadn't they all heard about Macdonald's drinking before? And if they have forgotten that history, they will find row after row of books in the virtual and actual library to refresh their memory. For them, the idea that they are not blank slates to be filled with knowledge is powerful. In the end, when I arrived at the story of Confederation in second term, I also learned something important. In this learning context, it was okay for Macdonald to have a place in the narratives I was teaching. I did not need to erase him to teach the history of colonialism because the most powerful lessons about epistemology and world view were well under way.

Evaluating Our Students

Besides contexts and content, modes of evaluation remain central to change in history classrooms. Students need to engage in analysis, to actively think about how the past led to the present, in order to develop skills for participation in democratic society (Barton and Levstik). They need to position themselves in the narrative of Canada's past. Through evaluation, it is possible to shift the ways in which students engage with historical sources, communicate with one another and with elders and professors, and participate in change.

Where discussion and debate are possible, participation is a standard element of evaluation in history courses. Despite pressure to eliminate seminars from large first-year classes, at Nipissing University the History Department remains committed to these learning contexts. As I have long explained to my students, we emphasize participation in seminars because the ability to express and defend ideas is crucial to the field of History and, more importantly for most students, to success in the workplace. While this is certainly true for many jobs and many students, this style of evaluation privileges students with existing skills, as well as an interest in and familiarity with sharing their views publicly. So it is important to reflect on whose interests are served when students speak. When we require our students to speak in class, do we "welcome selective inhabitants of the margin in order to better exclude the margin" without ultimately changing the structure of the interaction (Orner, 87; Spivak, 107; hooks)?

We need to rethink our understanding of silence in history classrooms, especially when it comes to participation. What does the requirement to speak mean to students for whom silence, particularly in the presence of a respected person, is culturally required? For many Anishnaabe students, silence is a sign of respect rather than disengagement. Creating different contexts for communicating develops a wider array of skills and gives more students the opportunity to be involved and engaged in the classroom. This can happen in a variety of ways. Two examples are shifting evaluation to acknowledge active listening and including small-group discussion as part of classroom time. A talking circle is another example.[14] In a talking circle there is no discussion leader, which offers a sense of shared responsibility and authority for the discussion. People take turns speaking in a manner rather different from a discussion-style seminar. The presence of a talking stone or another talking object has a remarkable impact on the dynamics of the group. Participants tend to listen more completely, more people participate, and a different level of conversation develops.

Allowing students to see themselves in the history they are studying is certainly at the heart of both Indigenous and feminist pedagogies, and this can be well supported through evaluation. To see history through ourselves is to recognize how we are placed in and relate to our world. Epistemologically individual histories rooted in land and family are the essential starting point for Indigenous histories. It is with this in mind that I developed a course assignment called "My History." In this assignment, each student composes and relates a five-minute story that connects them to Canada's history. These oral presentations are made over the course of the school year at the beginning of seminars. The story can occur in their lifetime or in the lifetime of one of their ancestors. We ask the students to focus on one particular theme or issue. When I designed this assignment I had no idea how students would respond. I wanted to include a component of the course that was oral to allow students who communicate more comfortably in this manner the opportunity to do so. The results have been remarkable.[15] The vast majority of students take the assignment very seriously and include audio and visual sources, material culture, and documentary research. In remarkable ways, historical sources that previously seemed inaccessible and incomprehensible to them as first-year students became clear when situated in their own contexts and related to their own lives and families. This has strengthened their understanding of the nature and extent of historical sources. Also, the sense of community among the students is strengthened as people hear others' stories. This builds empathy. Greater empathy leads to greater openness to different perspectives, and, as Llewelyn and Llewelyn establish, "restorative justice." It is one thing to hear a professor speak about residential school policy and quite another to hear what impact that policy has had on the person next to you, her parents, aunties and uncles, grandparents and elders. This listening makes history real, tangible, and meaningful for students. It also helps emphasize that history is not one story, but multiple stories structured by different frameworks.

The process of assigning historical significance is another area of evaluation that can be powerfully shifted. Peter Seixas's concept of historical thinking highlights the importance of reflecting on the relationship between historians and what they teach. His first concept, historical significance, typically ascribed to events, people, or places considered important or worth studying, has multiple origins. As Seixas (2009) notes, "historical significance does not inhere in the past itself, but rather, is created out of the relationship between the historian and the past" (28). Historical significance is also created in the relationship between the student and the historical issue. What historical events, issues or people are students likely to give historical significance? Why? As Ken Osborne (2012) points out, thinking in these terms validates the knowledge and experiences students bring to the classroom, empowering them by highlighting their abilities and showing them how to apply their knowledge and experiences to the discipline of History. Indigenous feminist pedagogies take this further, encouraging historians to think about the identities students bring to their classrooms and the impact that classroom contexts may have on them, on both the relationships inherent in this space and the stories shared. Moreover, they highlight that significance is created by reflecting on the history of the land on which you live, work, and study. When I teach my students about Jeanette Corbiere Lavell and others who challenged the sexist provisions of the Indian Act that forced Indigenous women who married white men to give up their status, I assign significance to Indigenous women in our past. Furthermore, Corbiere Lavell is from nearby Wikwemikong First Nation. Her history is local—an aspect important in Indigenous feminist methodologies, and one that, as Linda Briskin outlines in this volume, is also important for "empower[ing] students as change agents." It is also national and international, as Sandra Lovelace's case before the UN helped ensure that the changes Corbiere Lavell called for were made under Bill C-31 in 1985 (Srigley). When I tell these stories I circle back to Muzzu-Kummik-Quae, drawing links to the foundational roles of women and femininity in Anishnaabe culture, to the central place of women. Intentionally, I do not embed Lavell and Lovelace in the second-wave feminist movement. Sharing these women's stories in this way provides the opportunity to build on the historical understandings and knowledge of some students and challenge others to learn new knowledge and develop new skills in a respectful and meaningful way.

Conclusion

It takes time, eh. But we're doing a good thing. It's the right way. We'll figure it out.
                                   —Grandmother Elder Lorraine Whiteduck Liberty.[16]

This year, as before, Lorraine was recognized as the grandmother elder of our course. We spent time together over the course of the year, but she did not come to visit the classroom as much as in the past. In May 2013, Peter retired from Canadore College. I sat with him in circle yesterday, learning history from the Anishnaabe perspective. He is making teaching in his community a priority and is not spending as much time in institutional settings.[17] As Department Chair, I found myself preoccupied with departmental reviews and the demoralizing process of prioritization. I am no longer a vulnerable contract faculty member, but I am pulled away from meaningful work in the present university climate. It makes me angry. It worries me. Lorraine assures me that participants in circles change and what is important is rooting them in place. She thinks this is our most important achievement.

As I come to the end of this discussion, I reflect on what we have rooted in place in the first-year course. The roots of our circle are in the relationships established between us, elders, professors, and students. I continue to learn from Lorraine and Peter and bring that learning to my teaching. Some of my students now feel comfortable approaching Lorraine at university functions and visiting the Office of Aboriginal Initiatives. These are critical elements of pedagogical shifts that resulted from engaging with Indigenous feminist methodologies. Through them I have reflected on the university, department, and classroom, the land on which the university sits and the community of people that surrounds and sustains it to change my teaching context. By involving elders in our course, we challenged disciplinary convention and knowledge hierarchies. Disciplinary skills are essential, but content matters. It is through content that societies have always controlled or shaped the future. Together we have also changed how we evaluate our students. This includes reflecting on the role of participation and silence in course evaluation, but also working to move the discipline in pedagogical and epistemological directions that complicate significance and abandon standard expectations, lines, and directions.

Change in our first-year course is ongoing. There is plenty more to do, but I share our work so that others can take these ideas up in their learning spaces. It seems that today, more than ever, before historians have to legitimize their discipline, academics their production of deliverables, humanities their value to the world relative to business, science, and technology. These conversations are exhausting. Yet by developing the skills necessary to understand our past, other people, and the world around us, to challenge power dynamics and inequality, to realize social justice goals, to challenge racism and empower, History classrooms have revolutionary potential. It is time to understand histories in this manner. It is time to start teaching from Muzzu-Kummik-Quae to Jeanette Corbiere Lavell and back again.

Notes

1 Grandmother Elder Lorraine Whiteduck Liberty shared these words with us during our roundtable at the Berkshire Conference on the History of Women, "Roads of Colonization: Journeys and Contested Spaces in Indigenous Women's Lives," Toronto, 26 May 2014. I start with this quote to acknowledge my learning as part of this process, as well as the integral relationship between education, Nokomis (grandmother in Anishnaabemowin) and Mother Earth in the history of Anishnaabe peoples.

2 While this essay explores my journey teaching and learning in History 1405, Power and Resistance in Canada's Past, the course has developed in community with my colleagues Dr. Catherine Murton Stoehr and Dr. James Murton, elders Lorraine Whiteduck Liberty and Peter Beaucage, and our students. When I teach this course, I give all lectures and run one seminar. Dr. Stoehr runs the remaining seminars. We develop the syllabus, readings, and assignments together.

3 Emphasis in original.

4 Much like Nicholas and Baroud, I acknowledge the challenge of keeping this in focus in our present climate (Coates & Morrison; Côté & Allahar).

5 I use Indigenous in this article to refer to all (Status and non-Status) First Nations, Inuit, and Métis peoples.

6 My training as a feminist historian is rooted in Toronto and shaped by relationships with and the scholarship of many people, including Franca Iacovetta, Bettina Bradbury, Kate McPherson, Cecilia Morgan, Carolyn Strange, and Natalie Zemon Davis. In North Bay, I have had the privilege of learning with and from many women, including Glenna Beaucage, Patty Chabbert, Marianna Couchie, Erin Dokis, Dawn Lamothe, Virginia Goulais, Laurie McLaren, Lorraine Sutherland, and Lorraine Whiteduck Liberty. Anti-colonial and anti-racist pedagogies and theories have also informed my work, particularly those of Gayatri Spivak, bell hooks, Angela Davis, and Audre Lorde. I recognize that anti-racist pedagogies often fail to consider the unique inequalities experienced by Indigenous peoples.

7 It is important to acknowledge that educators, particularly those who are themselves Indigenous, have had their "backs to [this] plough" (Maracle, *Bobbie Lee,* 241) for a long time. See, for example, the work of Marie Battiste, Marlene Brant Castellano, Lynn Gehl, Verna Kirkness and Lorna Williams. This work is also going on in other history classrooms. See, for example, http://noneedtoraiseyourhand.wordpress.com/2014/03/28/on -teaching-aboriginal-history-to-non-aboriginal-students; Thrush, "Teaching Colonialism"; and Podruchny, "Indigenous History in the Classroom."

8 I have right justified the Anishnaabe teachings I am sharing to recognize the east, beginnings and endings, as I work to draw different teachings together.

9 Canadore College shares space with Nipissing University.

10 It is important to acknowledge that Nipissing University awarded me a grant to build relationships. They also gave me permission to give all of the money as an honorarium to a community partner who supported my efforts. This certainly pushes the boundaries of "normal" expectations around grants and associated funds.

11 Peter, Lorraine, and I use first names with one another, and, in recognition of this aspect of our relationship, I use them here. Our students refer to them as Grandfather and Grandmother/Nokomis or use their first names.

12 In her interview for the What I Learned in Class Today Project, Benita Bunjun calls this process "vibe watching." Visit http://www.whatIlearnedinclasstoday .com.

13 Timothy Stanley makes similar observations in his work.

14 I have had the privilege of learning about talking circles from Anishnaabe elders. There are important starting points available online. Visit http://www .circle-space.org/2009/10/16/using-talking-circles-to-promote-social-justice.

15 After the second year of this assignment, Dr. Stoehr made a video of some of the most powerful stories. Visit http://www.nipissingu.ca/academics/ faculties/arts-science/history/Pages/We-Made-a-Movie.aspx.

16 Personal conversation, 26 May 2014.

17 Beaucage, "The History of Nipissing First Nation."

Works Cited

Ashby, Rosalyn, Peter Gordon, and Peter Lee, eds. "Understanding History: Recent Research in History Education." *International Review of History Education* 4 (2005). http://dx.doi.org/10.4324/9780203340929

Ball, Jessica. "As If Indigenous Knowledge and Communities Mattered: Transformative Education in First Nations Communities in Canada." *American Indian Quarterly* 28.3–4 (2004): 454–79. http://dx.doi.org/10.1353/aiq.2004.0090

Barton, K.C., and L.S. Levstik. *Teaching History for the Common Good.* Mahwah: Lawrence Erlbaum, 2004.

Battiste, Marie. *Decolonizing Education: Nourishing the Learning Spirit.* Saskatoon: Purich Press, 2013.

Beaucage, Peter. "The History of Nipissing First Nation." Garden Village, Ontario. 25 June 2014.

Bird, Louis, and Elaine Gray. *The Spirit Lives in the Mind: Omuskego Stories, Lives, and Dreams.* Montreal and Kingston: McGill-Queen's University Press, 2007.

Bowen Raddeker, Hélène. *Sceptical History: Postmodernism, Feminism and the Practice of History.* New York: Routledge, 2007.

Brant Castellano, Marlene, Linda Archibald, and Mike DeGagné. *From Truth to Reconciliation: Transforming the Legacy of Residential Schools.* Ottawa: Aboriginal Healing Foundation, 2008.

Bunjun, Benita. "What I Learned in Class Today." http://www.whatIlearnedinclasstoday.com

Canadian Research Institute for the Advancement of Women and Girls. "Violence Against Women and Girls" (2012). http://www.criaw-icref.ca/ViolenceagainstWomenandGirls

Cole, Peter. *Coyote and Raven Go Canoeing: Coming Home to the Village.* Montreal and Kingston: McGill-Queen's University Press, 2006.

Coates, Ken and Bill Morrison. "Unemployed, Unhappy, and Drowning in Debt." *The Walrus* (October 2012): 30–50.

Côté, James, and Anton L. Allahar. *Ivory Tower Blues: A University System in Crisis.* Toronto: University of Toronto Press, 2007.

Daschuk, James. *Clearing the Plains: Disease, Politics of Starvation, and the Loss of Aboriginal Life.* Regina: University of Regina Press, 2013.

Davis, Angela. *Women, Race, and Class.* New York: Vintage Books, 1983.

Dickason, Olive Patricia. *Canada's First Nations: A History of Founding Peoples from Earliest Times,* 3rd ed. Toronto: Oxford University Press, 2002.

Ellsworth, Elizabeth. "Why Doesn't This Feel Empowering? Working Through the Repressive Myths of Critical Pedagogy." *Feminism and Critical Pedagogy.* Ed. Carmen Luke and Jennifer Gore. New York: Routledge, 1992. 90–119.

Friesen, Gerald. "The Shape of Historical Thinking in a Canadian History Survey Course in University." *New Possibilities for the Past: Shaping History Education in Canada.* Ed. Penney Clark. Vancouver: UBC Press, 2011. 210–23.

Gehl, Lynn. "From Cognitive Imperialism to Indigenizing 'The Learning Wigwam.'" *World Indigenous Nations Higher Education Consortium Journal* (2010): 11–25.

Gore, Jennifer. "What We Can Do for You! What Can 'We' Do For 'You'? Struggling over Empowerment in Critical and Feminist Pedagogy." *Feminisms and Critical Pedagogy.* Ed. Carmen Luke and Jennifer Gore. New York: Routledge, 1992. 54–73.

Green, Joyce, ed. *Making Space for Indigenous Feminism.* Halifax: Fernwood, 2007.

hooks, bell. *Talking Back: Thinking Feminist, Thinking Black.* Boston: South End Press, 1989.

Huhndorf, Shari M., and Cheryl Suzack. "Indigenous Feminism: Theorizing the Issues." *Indigenous Women and Feminism: Politics, Activism, Culture*. Ed. Cheryl Suzack et al. Vancouver: UBC Press, 2010. 1–20.

Johnston, Basil. *Honour Mother Earth=mino audjauhdauh Mizzu Kummik Quae*. Cape Croker: Kegedonce Press, 2003.

Jones, Esyllt, and Adele Perry. *People's Citizenship Guide: A Response to Conservative Canada*. Winnipeg: Arbeiter Ring, 2011.

Kirkness, Verna. "Prejudice about Indians in Textbooks." *Journal of Reading* 20.7 (1977): 595–600.

———. "Aboriginal Education in Canada: A Retrospective and Prospective." *Journal of American Indian Education* 39.1 (1999): 14–30.

———. *Creating Space: My Life and Work in Indigenous Education*. Winnipeg: University of Manitoba Press, 2013.

Kovach, Margaret. *Indigenous Methodologies: Characteristics, Conversations, and Contexts*. Toronto: University of Toronto Press, 2009.

Kulchyski, Peter, Don McCaskill, and David Newhouse, eds. *In the Words of Elders: Aboriginal Cultures in Transition*. Toronto: University of Toronto Press, 1999.

Lévesque, Stéphane. *Thinking Historically: Educating Students for the Twenty-First Century*. Toronto: University of Toronto Press, 2008.

Lorde, Audre. *Sister Outsider: Essays and Speeches*. Freedom: Crossing Press, 1984.

Maracle, Lee. *Bobbie Lee: Indian Rebel*. Toronto: Women's Press, 1990.

Marker, Michael. "Teaching History from an Indigenous Perspective: Four Winding Paths up the Mountain." In *New Possibilities for the Past: Shaping History Education in Canada*. Ed. Penney Clark. Vancouver: UBC Press, 2011. 97–112.

Miller, J.R. *Compact, Contract, Covenant: Aboriginal Treaty-Making in Canada*. Toronto: University of Toronto Press, 2009.

Monture-Angus, Patricia. *Thunder in My Soul: A Mohawk Woman Speaks*. Halifax: Fernwood, 1995.

Orner, Mimi. "Interrupting the Calls for Student Voice in 'Liberatory' Education: A Feminist Poststructuralist Perspective." In *Feminisms and Critical Pedagogy*. Ed. Carmen Luke and Jennifer Gore. New York: Routledge, 1992. 74–89.

Osborne, Ken. "'Education Is the Best National Insurance': Citizenship Education in Schools, Past and Present." *Canadian and International Education / Education Canadienne et Internationale* 25 (1996): 31–58.

———. "'Our History Syllabus Has Us Gasping': History in Canadian Schools, Past, Present and Future." *Canadian Historical Review* 81 (2000): 404–35. http://dx.doi.org/10.3138/CHR.81.3.404

———. "Teaching History in Schools: A Canadian Debate." *Journal of Curriculum Studies* 35.5 (2003): 585–626. http://dx.doi.org/10.1080/0022027032000063544

———. "A History Teacher Looks Back." *Canadian Historical Review* 93.1 (March 2012): 108–37. http://dx.doi.org/10.3138/chr.93.1.108

Podruchny, Carolyn. "Indigenous History in the Classroom: Four Principles, Four Questions." http://activehistory.ca/2013/11/indigenous-history-in-the-classroom-four-principles-four-questions

Ray, Arthur. *I Have Lived Here Since the World Began: An Illustrated History of Canada's Native People.* Toronto: Key Porter, 1996.

Razack, Sherene. "Equality Is Not a High Enough Standard: Patricia Monture, 1958–2010." *Canadian Journal of Women and the Law* 26.1 (2014): i–iii. http://dx.doi.org/10.3138/cjwl.26.1.00i

Regnier, Robert. "Warrior as Pedagogue, Pedagogue as Warrior: Reflecting on Aboriginal Anti-Racist Pedagogy." In *Anti-Racism, Feminism, and Critical Approaches to Education.* Ed. Roxana Ng, Pat Staton, and Joyce Scane. Toronto: OISE Press, 1995. 67–86.

Roy, Kate, Evelyn Roy, and Alan Corbiere, eds. *Gechi-piitzijib Dbaajmowag: The Stories of Our Elders.* West Bay: Ojibwe Cultural Foundation, 2011.

Sandwell, Ruth, ed. *To the Past: History Education, Public Memory, and Citizenship in Canada.* Toronto: University of Toronto Press, 2006.

Seixas, Peter. "Students' Understanding of History Significance." *Theory and Research in Social Education* 22.3 (1994): 281–304. http://dx.doi.org/10.1080/00933104.1994.10505726

———. *Theorizing Historical Consciousness.* Toronto: University of Toronto Press, 2004.

———. "A Modest Proposal for Change in Canadian History Education." *Teaching History* 137 (December 2009): 26–39.

Seixas, Peter, and Penney Clark. "Murals as Monuments: Students' Ideas About Depictions of Civilization in British Columbia." *American Journal of Education* 110.2 (2004): 146–71. http://dx.doi.org/10.1086/380573

Simpson, Leanne. *Dancing on Our Turtle's Back: Stories of Nishnaabeg Re-Creation, Resurgence, and a New Emergence.* Winnipeg: Arbieter Ring, 2011.

———. *The Gift Is in the Making: Anishnaabeg Stories.* Retold by Leanne Simpson. Winnipeg: Highwater Press, 2013.

Smith, Andrea. "Indigenous Feminism Without Apology." http://unsettlingamerica.wordpress.com/2011/09/08/indigenous-feminism-without-apology

Snowball, Andrew. "Aboriginal Education for Non-Aboriginal Students." MSW thesis, University of Toronto, 2009.

Spivak, Gayatri. *In Other Worlds: Essays in Cultural Politics.* New York: Methuen, 1987.

Srigley, Katrina. "I Am a Proud Anishnaabekwe: Issues of Identity and Status in Northern Ontario After Bill C-31." *Finding a Way to the Heart: Feminist Writings on Aboriginal and Women's History in Canada.* Ed. Robin Jarvis Brownlee and Valerie J. Korinek. Winnipeg: University of Manitoba Press, 2012. 241–66.

Stanley, Timothy. "Why I Killed Canadian History: Towards an Anti-Racist History in Canada." *Histoire Sociale / Social History* 33.65 (2000): 79–103.

Stearns, Peter N., Peter Seixas, and Sam Wineburg, eds. *Knowing Teaching and Learning History: National and International Perspectives*. New York: NYU Press, 2000.

Suzack, Cheryl, Shari M. Huhndorf, Jeanne Perreault, et al., eds. *Indigenous Women and Feminism: Politics, Activism and Culture*. Vancouver: UBC Press, 2010.

Switzer, Maurice. *We Are All Treaty People*. North Bay: Union of Ontario Indians, 2011.

Thrush, Coll. "Teaching Colonialism, Complexity, and Survivance: A Pedagogical Journey." Unpublished paper presentation, Fairhaven College, Washington State, 20 April 2011. http://vimeo.com/23286334

Tuhiwai Smith, Linda. *Decolonizing Methodologies: Research and Indigenous Peoples*. Otago: University of Otago Press, 1999.

Wilson, Shawn. *Research Is Ceremony: Indigenous Research Methods*. Halifax: Fernwood, 2008.

CHAPTER ELEVEN

Don't Mention the "F" Word: Using Images of Transgressive Texts to Teach Gendered History

Jacqueline Z. Wilson

Introduction

The increasing use of Student Evaluation of Teaching (SET) surveys by university administrators to assess teacher performance presents special problems for female academics, especially those who teach feminist or gender-focused topics. I teach History courses comprising just such aspects. My problems are compounded by the fact that I work in a rural university whose student cohort tends toward a socially conservative outlook.

This essay summarizes these multilayered issues and presents an outline of a lecture aimed at introducing students to feminism (the forbidden "f" word) and feminist concepts by stealth, as it were, through the use of photographs taken during my fieldwork research in historical prisons across Australia. I begin with images and discussion of historical prison architecture; then I take students "inside" the prisons via examples of inmate graffiti, in the hope of generating insight into the experiences of inmates. Graffiti created by inmates both male and, crucially, female, affords students glimpses into the concerns and daily sensibilities of both groups. In the process, students come to understand the need for a gendered approach to the topic, and some of the problems associated with SET surveys are resolved.

Student Evaluation of Teaching Surveys and the Feminist Academic

In August 2012, Melbourne's *Sunday Age* reported that the National Tertiary Education Union (NTEU) had been fielding "dozens of complaints" from those of its members employed at the Australian National University (ANU), regarding the university's new practice of factoring SET survey results into its performance reviews of teaching staff (Thomson). ANU has long been acknowledged as Australia's most prestigious university—the leading institution among the "Group of Eight" that set the quality benchmark, in both research and teaching, for all others in Australia. According to the NTEU, many staff members contend that the notion of evaluating teaching performance even partly on the basis of their ability to "make their students happy" must inevitably undermine the rigour, intellectual integrity, and capacity to challenge "fledgling thinkers" upon which ANU has built its teaching reputation. Further, they argue, the data gained from such "satisfaction" surveys is intrinsically skewed and unrepresentative, due to the relatively low numbers who respond and the likelihood that such surveys are filled in by disproportionately high numbers of students disaffected by unexpectedly challenging course content and/or rigour of assessment (Thomson).

The *Age* report notes that "satisfaction" surveys have been filled out by ANU students for some years; they have prompted concern now only because of the new use to which they are being put (Thomson). It is unclear, at this writing, to what extent the fears of ANU's teaching staff will prove justified, but for many academics observing from within less exalted Australian institutions, the issue is all too familiar: SET survey data are routinely put to a variety of uses related to career advancement, course viability, and so on. The mere fact that such practices have been adopted at ANU ("of all places") serves only to confirm the ubiquity and intractability, across the tertiary sector, of the managerialist paradigm that attempts to quantify all aspects of academic work while rendering students as education "customers" (Wilson et al., 537, 540, 541, 542).

If these developments at ANU are of concern to teaching academics at other universities, there is reason for them to be of particular concern—perhaps even alarm—for women in the academy. It has been shown that many universities constitute insidiously gendered workplaces for both research- and teaching-based staff—insidious because of the largely cryptic nature of the gender imbalances prevailing in supposedly enlightened institutions that by and large purport to uphold egalitarian values and practices (535–37, 541–42). It has been shown, for instance, that opportunities for promotion, especially to higher-level positions, are more readily available to male than to female academics, due to systemic advantaging of work practices, employment structures, and modes of work evaluation more suited to men (537). SET, in particular, fosters this "hidden" disadvantaging of female teaching staff:

> SET ... is particularly inappropriate and potentially unfair to teachers in the Humanities and Social Sciences ... It is in these areas that students are most likely to find their core beliefs and concepts actively challenged by "thought-provoking" material and lesson content, while also being confronted with open-ended and/or imprecisely defined lines of enquiry. Hence their subjective sense of progress in learning and overall satisfaction with the learning experience are hardly amenable to reliable quantification. Yet it is in precisely these areas that women teachers predominate. It is evident, therefore, that women are especially disadvantaged by SET. (538)

Nor is the female teacher concerned purely with a simple dichotomy between endorsement and disapproval; as Alison Bartlett points out, gender expectations can feature negatively in SET results that look, on their face, to be positive, in the form of qualitative comments that characterize the teacher in approving but stereotypically feminine terms such as "a lovely person," and "nice" (195).

If the female Humanities or Social Sciences teacher is beset more than most by the subjective reactions of students to "challenging" course content, then for those women attempting to introduce the historical, philosophical, and/or sociological concepts of Gender Studies and feminism, the potential problems become greater still. Even students whose disposition leaves them relatively even-handed in many other areas of thought may find the requirement to examine and question their and their peers' gender perceptions/assumptions both highly personal and highly confronting (Copp and Kleinman, 101–3). And, as Bulbeck has shown, a significant number of students whose intellectual and cultural background might be thought to have prepared them for conceptual encounters with feminism do not see it as especially relevant, due to a lack of "big issues" regarding gender.

To these problematic factors may be added, as something of a final layer of difficulty, the plight of the female teaching a gender-focused course in a university located in a rural city, where the prevailing demographic of undergraduate enrolments tends to be socially (and often politically) conservative. In such an environment, the teacher who attempts to introduce feminism *qua* feminism in the classroom can expect to be challenged directly (and with, at times, marked vehemence) and must also deal with the very real possibility that students' resistance may be sufficient to prevent them from engaging with and absorbing what they need in order to satisfactorily complete the course. The first aspect can make teaching overly taxing, even unpleasant; the second is, of course, anathema to any teacher who cares about the effectiveness of their work and their students' learning. The fact that both possibilities can translate into poor SET results adds insult to injury—an unnecessarily stressful and pedagogically useless negative that ultimately does nothing but provide an overlay of career anxiety.

The Rural University

The above scenario, of teaching what may be perceived as radical content to a broadly conservative rural cohort, provides the basis for Bartlett's article on students' gendered expectations in the learning environment (196); it happens also to be my situation. I run a course for student teachers on History Curriculum and the teaching of History, in the School of Education at a rural university located in a regional centre ninety minutes' drive from the state capital. The student body by and large reflects the surrounding area's population, in terms of relatively conservative social values, numerically stronger church attendance than for equivalent groups in major urban centres, and lifelong immersion in a culture structured very much along "traditional" gendered lines. It is also markedly homogenous ethnically: white, mostly of Anglo-Irish background, and thus tending to resemble an Australian demographic of past eras, prior to the advent of multiculturalism in the 1970s. This has implications for students' capacity to respond insightfully to a range of differences encountered—that is, not merely to ethnic diversity—because of the "normalization" of whiteness when it is the sole or predominant ethnicity (Frankenburg, 64–65). Further, and in various ways this is a compounding factor, a significant number of them have come to tertiary education from families with no history of university attendance and minimal aspirations in that regard; they therefore bring to class little of the intellectual and cultural capital needed to meet and deal constructively with radical, and radically novel (for them), ideas.

But it is not only encounters with the radical for which such lacks leave students ill-equipped; much that is generally considered common knowledge is new to them. Thus, surveys I have undertaken with them reveal that their knowledge and understanding of history prior to starting my course tend to be both factually and conceptually narrow, confined largely to an amalgam of "iconic" events and sweeping, markedly superficial interpretations, often assertively presented and clearly more influenced by reductionist tabloid nationalism than by measured reflection or intellectual rigour.[1] The popular conception of Australian history to which many of them adhere, as reflected both in the media and in much of the curriculum in schools, focuses very heavily on a few "key" episodes and individuals. As these are central to Australian social memory and hence to national identity, it is apposite to briefly consider a small selection of them here.

History and National Identity

Typical, first, is the mid-nineteenth-century Victorian gold rush, which in 1854 incorporated a dispute over government fees for mining rights that led to a miners' rebellion and culminated in a brief, one-sided battle with troops at a makeshift barricaded encampment immortalized ever since in schoolchildren's minds as the "Eureka Stockade." Eureka was the only armed civil rebellion in Australia's history and is to this day extolled in the public memory as a pioneering step toward democracy in a colonial society then still half a century from the self-determination that would come with Federation.

A few decades on, in the late 1800s, we encounter arguably the most recognizable figure in Australia's history, a bushranger (roadside bandit) named Edward "Ned" Kelly. Kelly is an admittedly interesting character, the moral nature of whose crimes (and even, in some circles, his guilt in committing them) is still debated with at times surprising vehemence. For his last stand against surrounding police he equipped himself with a home-made suit of bulletproof armour beaten from ploughshares, complete with fully enclosed helmet, which cemented a unique visual image in the Australian psyche. Although his career was marked by much violence, and he was hanged for killing a police officer, his personal courage gave to Australian English a colloquialism, "as game as Ned Kelly." His escapades included a Robin Hood component, in that he gained contemporary renown for such "political" acts as ordering the managers of banks he was robbing to gather and destroy all mortgage records held on the local debt-ridden small-holding farmers.

It is in the early twentieth century, with Australia's military involvement in the First World War, that Australian history becomes most ineradicably bound up with populist national identity. In April 1915, a combined British, Canadian, Australian, and New Zealand operation was launched to invade Germany's ally Turkey at a coastal location in the Dardanelles known to the anglophone Allies by its Greek name, Gallipoli. The Australian and New Zealand forces were mobilized as a combined unit under the acronym ANZAC (for Australian and New Zealand Army Corps). The Gallipoli campaign ultimately failed in its objective, but during the months of trench warfare that preceded the Allied withdrawal a series of dispatches were sent home from the invasion beaches by Charles Bean, the official Australian war historian, for the domestic market. Bean's and others' encomiastic accounts of the Australian soldiers' casual bravery, comradeship, athleticism, rugged individualism, and irreverence for authority were published in a bestselling anthology, *The Anzac Book,* and gave rise to an indelible image, in the minds of the general population, of an archetypal warrior—the "digger"—that supposedly exemplified all the heroic virtues Australians identified as peculiarly their own. This image would be subsequently enhanced and consolidated during the Second World War, to form the core of the national myth known as the "Anzac legend."

A central aspect of the historical events noted above—Eureka, the Kelly "outbreak," and Gallipoli—is that their construction within the conventional framework of the national narrative renders them almost entirely masculine. The Eureka story, as told and retold in schools and popular historical accounts, is very much an affair of the men of the goldfields, led by men; that women played significant roles on the goldfields in general, and in the Eureka episode in particular, is far from apparent unless one makes far greater efforts of inquiry than can reasonably be expected of schoolchildren (Wright). The traditional Kelly story "naturally" focuses on Ned; recent historical works demonstrating the central part played by women in his life and his outlaw career remain all but unknown among the wider population beyond the realm of academic historians (Lake; Aveling and Damousi, xiv, 194; Wilson 2005). Gallipoli and the Anzac legend are the most problematic of all: as historian Marilyn Lake has pointed out, the national mythologizing of Gallipoli means it has come to serve as "Australia's creation story" (11). Its front-and-centre placement in the nation's historical sensibility, at the expense of many alternative, more inclusive stories, has had the overall effect of "militarizing" Australian history. Such militarization, Lake observes, is inherently masculinist (11). Thus an inherently anti-feminist conception of the nation's fundamental character has been enshrined in the national psyche and effectively legitimized.

Almost a century after Gallipoli, and notwithstanding the efforts of a number of modern historians, most Australians remain unaware that Bean's accounts of the Anzacs' exploits were heavily edited for public consumption, resulting in a national icon that, while not wholly fictitious, certainly strayed far outside the simple, and inevitably at times unedifying, human realities of ordinary Australian men immersed in the horrific experiences of war (Ingliss, 35; Damousi, 261; Thomson, 25). Of course, such revisionist awareness would require an abandonment of some of the deeply internalized, identity-forming concepts on which nationalistic patriotism is based. It almost goes without saying that few of the students who attend my lectures are among those who have taken such a path; by far the majority hold, and when challenged profess, a wholehearted and unexamined allegiance to the Anzac legend. Because of the above conditions and limitations, I have learned to make no initial mention of "gender" or "feminism" in the lectures in which such concepts are central. My strategy is, rather, to approach the core concepts via a series of stages. The first is to establish my credentials.

Don't Mention the "F" Word

Students who arrive at an institution of higher learning with little or no prior concept of what such learning entails are in my experience unlikely to recognize or respect the expertise of a female teacher (Bartlett; Wilson et al.). It therefore falls to me to persuade them that (a) I have something to say; (b) what I say is credible; and (c) it will be to their benefit to take it on board (at least as the basis for informed discussion; needless to say, I do not expect every utterance I make to be regarded as the last word on the subject) (see also Silva Flores, in this book).

The first lecture begins with a general talk on the nature of history. This I describe as an "ongoing interrogation" of the past; such a pursuit is characterized not so much by the compilation of compendia of "facts" and neatly linear narratives, as by ongoing contention, debate, and at times passionate dispute regarding meaning. The students are introduced to the key questions of the historian: What stories are to be told? Whose stories are they? Who should tell them? Whose voices are to be heard, and whose excluded? At that point I pause, and to ensure their own connection to these concepts I point out that such questions apply to them, and to their stories, as much as to the events and persons they might regard as legitimately "historical."

They hear, too, that as future educators they will inevitably have to engage with the professional issues arising from the *political* nature of such questions: in the last decade an intense, and at times highly rancorous, public debate has developed over the nature of white/Aboriginal relations throughout Australia's history since the first British settlement in 1788. That debate has been conducted at times with such indecorous and visceral fervour that it has been dubbed the "History Wars" (MacIntyre and Clark). A side note here that I can utilize in the ongoing quest for credibility and hence rapport is to mention to students my own tiny, passing role in the History Wars: some years ago a research paper of mine was singled out by a right-wing tabloid newspaper columnist as an example of "bad history" purely on the basis of the title (!) (Wilson 2008; Devine).

Architecture as History

Having established in their minds something of a general concept of history as discipline, vocation, and gladiatorial arena, I shift the lecture's focus to the particular. The students are told that, through a series of photographs I have taken in the course of my fieldwork, we will now consider the architecture of a selection of Australia's oldest public buildings, products of a wave of colonial construction in the early to mid-nineteenth century. These buildings I prefigure as relics of a "Britishness" that formerly pervaded the colony's culture, society, and landscape; they stood not merely as functional, habitable structures, but also as contemporary monuments to Empire. Given the students' backgrounds, such notions tend to have strong resonance. What they are not told immediately is that the buildings in questions are former prisons.

The castellated neo-Gothic facade shown in Figure 11.1 is the first image I present. It is the front entrance of Pentridge Prison, which was built in the 1850s and occupies sixty acres in the northern suburbs of Melbourne. For almost 140 years, before closing in 1997, it was the State of Victoria's main maximum security prison. The neo-Gothic style is typical of public architecture of the period, and prisons were no exception to the trend. The prominent sign above the entrance identifying it as a prison invariably prompts audible surprised reactions from the students, and from that moment they are strongly engaged with the topic. I segue from Pentridge to a sampling of genuine European castles, then return from the global to the parochial with an image of the front entrance of one of the local independent schools, which, like the prison, sports an ornately castellated facade. Inevitably, some of the students have attended this school, and almost all are familiar with it; the juxtaposition of school and jail is intended both to amuse and to emphasize the ubiquity of the neo-Gothic architectural style. The topic of historical architecture has now been established in their minds as personally relevant, of national significance, and potentially surprising.

A further series of images follows, depicting prisons large and small across the continent. I note that Australia has a relationship to its institutions of incarceration almost unique among the nations of the world, due to its origins as a penal colony. (An easy laugh here is to remind them that "we're all descended from convicts—except for those who aren't.") The theme I am now openly pursuing relates directly to Australian identity and its connection with the ordinary individual. The audience is thus urged to begin thinking about the institutions they are viewing not merely as edifices to be contemplated with a detached aesthetic, but centrally as places of habitation, of mass confinement.

My "patter" while showing these images includes references to a variety of secondary sources on prison architecture, the nature of incarceration, Australian colonial history, and so on. My intention here is not to inform my audiences of sources so much as to continually reinforce the connection

FIGURE 11.1
Pentridge Prison

Photo credit: Jacqueline Wilson.

between what they are seeing and the broader body of "traditional" historical literature. This serves both to legitimize the topic as more than just an academic eccentricity and to reaffirm my own credentials. It is, in other words, to some extent a performance of self-conscious erudition.

At about this time I introduce the work of the historian E.P. Thompson, who famously advocated, and dedicated himself to doing, what he called "history from below"—that is, history based on the experiences of the masses at the lower strata of society rather than on the doings of the great and powerful. In the light of Thompson's ethos, it is now natural to ask whether an examination of the external architecture of a prison is able to provide us with "the full story." In order to understand, as fully as possible, the world of the prison, we need somehow to gain insight into the experience of those individuals who give the prison meaning: the inmates. In other words, I say, it is time to go *inside* the prison.

Inmates' Voices: Male
In defining prisons and other radically sequestered establishments, sociologist Erving Goffman speaks of a special category of institution, "a place of residence and work where a large number of like-situated individuals, cut off from the wider society for an appreciable period of time, together lead an enclosed, formally administered round of life" (xiii). This type of establishment Goffman defines as the "total institution": "Their encompassing or total character is symbolized by the barrier to social intercourse with the outside and to departure that is often built right into the physical plant, such as locked doors, high walls, barbed wire [et cetera]" (4).

Although images of the prison's intra-mural structure can provide hints of the inmate's experience, they remain hints; from a view of a cell interior, for instance, we may infer something of what it might be like to be locked up, but the insight remains bound to our own (imagined) reaction to such an experience. Once inside, we must look in a slightly different direction, and with what might be thought of as an "eye" for the inhabitants' "voices." It is not an obvious artifact of confinement or restraint, per se, that provides us with the first clue to their world, but something far more banal.

Figure 11.2 shows the open, communal facility in an indoor exercise yard of the Melbourne City Watch House (a large nineteenth-century holding jail decommissioned in 1992 with the closure of the Old Magistrates Court complex, to which it was attached). I joke that this is my "Ned Kelly" picture, owing to the appliance's superficial resemblance to a famous series of highly stylized paintings of the iconic outlaw, by artist Sidney Nolan. Having thus got another easy laugh, I enlarge the image and invite the audience to examine the flusher-box more closely. It becomes apparent that it is covered with graffiti, simple "tags" comprising names and in many cases dates, scratched into the enamel over decades (the earliest visible is 1970) by countless inmates as they stood using the facility. This, then, is my students' introduction to the day-to-day experience of the inmate. We go on to view a wide selection of inmate graffiti—initially all created

FIGURE 11.2
Prison urinal

Photo credit: Jacqueline Wilson.

by men—which I present with accompanying explication of the range of probable motivations that produced them and that are peculiar to prison life. A small sample of those viewed will serve here to illustrate this range.

Just as the total institution has a special, and especially oppressive, character that sets it apart from all other social environments, so the ongoing experience of the inmate immersed in that institution is unlike any experience of normal life outside. The inmate's sensibility tends to be dominated by a drastically reduced spectrum of intensified affect and thought, based around a small number of broad issues.

The first, and perhaps most obvious, is a sense of profound isolation and separation from those they care about on the outside—that is, loneliness. This is allied with feelings of societal abandonment, leading to an erosion of whatever sense of personal social worth the inmate had. Hence the impulse to record on available surfaces, such as the flusher box, what amounts to a simple affirmation of personal presence—a proclamation that "I was here."

Second, there is for the inmate a recurring and urgent need to hold at bay the feeling of interminable "dead and heavy-hanging time" (Goffman, 67). The boredom of prison is a special kind of torment and weighs especially heavily on many inmates due to their lack of the mental defences that come with education and literacy (Wilson 2008, 85). Much of the graffiti found in prisons seems to fit the category that Goffman characterizes, in his study of total institutions, as "removal activities." As he puts it, "every total institution can be seen as a kind of dead sea in which little islands of vivid, encapturing activity appear ... Removal activities [are] voluntary unserious pursuits ... [designed to] mercifully kill [time]" (69). Figure 11.3, a detail from an extensive work encompassing a cell in Fremantle Gaol, is typical of the kind of graffiti that results from such need.

While such leavening interludes are sometimes possible, most inmates spend much of their time pondering far more serious matters. Almost constant, at least in the background, and overriding all else much of the time, is a preoccupation with survival. As one inmate has put it: "Everywhere, every minute—like the air that you breathe—there is a threat of violence lurking beneath the surface ... It permeates every second of everyone's existence [and] there is no let up from it—ever" (as quoted in Heilpern, 100). From such a fearful ambience arises an obsessive fixation on personal power and dominance and on the perceived power of others. Thus declarations of hatred and vengeful intent, invariably couched in the most rancorous tones, abound in the prison (Figure 11.4).

Added to these central concerns is the problem of sex. This might be assumed to be most naturally linked to the first point noted above, that is, loneliness; however, the nature of the incarceration experience means that sex tends to be bound up at least as much with the drive for personal power as it is with a desire for companionate pleasure. Thus sexual expression in prison—whether acted out or simply depicted graphically—very often takes grotesquely violent forms, as in Figure 11.5.

FIGURE 11.3
"Ferret" cartoon

Photo credit: Jacqueline Wilson.

FIGURE 11.4
"You Die Dog"

Photo credit: Jacqueline Wilson.

FIGURE 11.5
"How to Become a Pig"

Photo credit: Jacqueline Wilson.

But even when sex is explicitly linked to loneliness and separation from those outside, its graphic expression can often reveal the profoundly masculinist nature of the prison, and with it tones of overt misogyny (Figure 11.6).

Given the unmitigated viciousness of much that they have viewed thus far, and the raw and brutish sexism with which the graffitist of Figure 11.6 expresses his "affection," it is a much smaller leap now for the students to

FIGURE 11.6
"When I Get Out"

Photo credit: Jacqueline Wilson.

begin some examination of gender. For the first time in the lecture I make
mention of women, pointing out that it is not only men who are imprisoned
and that the very jail in which this repellent declaration was rendered—the
Melbourne City Watch House—had a section for female inmates. There

exists, therefore, the need to undertake some sort of *gendered* study of the prison environment.

Inmates' Voices: Female

It turns out that the layout of the exercise yard in the women's section was very similar to that of the men, complete with a lavatory in the corner. And like the men, the women whiled away the minutes drawing or scratching a record of what was on their minds. But unlike the men, the women were deemed to need a little more privacy, and thus were afforded a door (Figure 11.7). It is on this fixture that they left much of the textual evidence of their time there. We pass, then, to a selection of graffiti created by the women held in the Watch House.

As the holding facility for the Old Magistrates Court, the Melbourne City Watch House at some stage contained virtually every prisoner destined for any kind of hearing in that court, as well as those who, having had their hearing, were destined for delivery to long-term prison. Because of the Magistrates Court's dual function as both the lowest level of criminal court, able to impose sentences of up to two years, and also the venue for committal to trial for more serious crimes in higher courts, the Watch House cells saw a full cross-section of offenders. Many of them were destined for incarceration in one of the state's maximum security prisons, or they were already doing time and had been brought to Melbourne for further hearings.

Of the dozens of Australian historical prisons at which I have done fieldwork, the Watch House is the only one in which female inmate graffiti is extant and accessible in abundance. Its historical value as a primary source is therefore high, but also somewhat compromised by the fact that it constitutes a single sample created by a transient population, and thus may not be entirely typical of what women write and draw on available surfaces while in prison. What we can infer with some certainty, however, is that incarcerated women shared much of the range of motivations we have already observed in the men—albeit often expressed somewhat differently. On the lavatory door, and on walls and other doors and surfaces in various locations about the jail, but especially in the exercise yard, we find declarations of piteous isolation and loneliness; complaints aplenty about the seemingly endless tedium of imprisonment (even in the Watch House, where one's stay was generally brief); and, most prolific of all but in some cases not entirely obvious, a variety of survival-based declarations and messages. A significant difference from their male equivalents is that these categories tend to blend together (for reasons we will discuss shortly), and that the fourth category of affect visible among the men—i.e., violently aggressive

FIGURE 11.7
Green door

Photo credit: Jacqueline Wilson.

lust—is not visible at all. The women were not inhibited about announcing their romantic desires toward and alliances with one another and with men outside, but nothing remotely equivalent to the sentiment of Figure 11.6 is visible anywhere in the women's section. What *is* visible, in stark contrast to

FIGURE 11.8
Detail of green door

Photo credit: Jacqueline Wilson.

the men's graffiti, is a free and apparently heartfelt use of the word "love"—
whether signifying romantic attachment or platonic alliance.

There is apparent among the women's graffiti a far stronger tendency
toward "networking": the seeking, establishment, confirmation, and
resumption of acquaintances and alliances. Aside from confirming to some
degree a feminine stereotype noted of women outside jail, this trend provides a clue to an important peculiarity about the Watch House in regard to
its female inmates, one that also shows up the ways in which the categories
of motivation for their graffiti are far less clearly demarked than among the
men. Once convicted and sentenced to a custodial term, for both men and
women the Melbourne City Watch House was the last port of call before
being taken to long-term prison. The men rarely knew which prison of a
number around the state they would be assigned to. The women, however,
usually knew exactly where they would be going. Due to the relatively low
numbers of female offenders compared to men, for most of its history the
State of Victoria has only required one maximum security female prison,

and in the latter decades of the Watch House, that was H.M. Women's Prison Fairlea, in Melbourne's northeastern suburbs. Fairlea (closed in 1996) held at most a little over 100 inmates, which made for an effectively village-sized, face-to-face "community" of convicted females. This in turn meant that certain imperatives had to be met *before* the inevitable journey to one's final destination. As ethnographer Barbara Denton explains: "Experienced prisoners ... knew the best way to function in prison: 'If you want to survive in prison, you find yourself a close friend, and you look after each other,' [former inmate] Betsy explained. Her networking had commenced in the police cells. 'The first thing I do when I'm arrested is find myself a mate, someone to watch my back'" (137).

As I have argued elsewhere, the female section of the Watch House may thus be viewed as an "ante-room" of the main women's prison, and the various graffitied surfaces as a "communal notice board" on which were posted announcements of friendships/alliances (including apparent romantic attachments) ensuring mutual protection against future aggressors (Wilson 2008, 96–97). For the first-time inmate or (especially) those from locations outside Melbourne, a first step might be to announce what would hopefully be seen as a stance of solidarity—thus declarations that, for instance, "ALL COPS ARE CUNTS," or more specifically "BENDIGO [a Victorian regional centre] COPS ARE CUNTS," or "COPS IN SHEPP[arton, a country town] ARE DEAD SET CUNTS, DOGS, PIGS." Apparently simple expressions of vengeful rancour of the kind already discussed also served as "a statement about the graffitist as a potential ally against the common enemy" (98).

An aspect of both male and female inmate graffiti I have observed is an impulse to "diarize" personal events—an extension, one might speculate, of the existential "tag." But whereas the men were more likely to do it as a "private" record in their cells (sometimes hidden entirely from view behind a fitting or bed), the women produced theirs for public view in the common areas and were far more likely to record the key events of their criminal careers (Figure 11.9).

These self-styled "rap sheets," in which the author recounts a sometimes long array of serious charges/convictions, were unlike anything I saw among the male graffiti in any prison I studied. I interpret them as a further variation of the power/survival imperative, whereby the graffitist eschews the need or opportunity to protect herself via alliances and instead proclaims herself "dangerous." In this way we see once more the blurring of the boundaries between the inmates' likely motivations, compared to those of the men.

Not all of the women's graffiti, of course, is calculated networking or shoring up of one's status. Aside from the sample of graffiti I am presenting,

FIGURE 11.9
"Rap sheet"

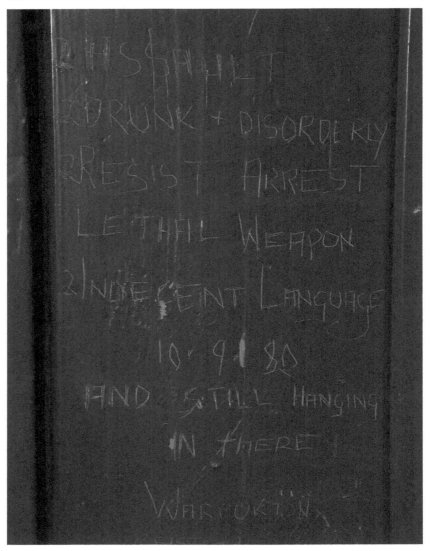

Photo credit: Jacqueline Wilson.

there is, I can now tell my students, ample evidence that women's experience of incarceration is signally different from that of men and for various reasons can be worse. Some of these messages of *prima facie* distress and/or fury at their plight, and their manifest hatred of (typically) the police, really are products of unalloyed anguish. I now read out a passage from feminist lawyer Amanda George, who points out that there are times when "the woman [in prison] is completely powerless. There is no real accountability in prisons. It is a closed hypermale military environment demanding a slavish submission to hierarchy and authority" (214).

A key term here, I tell the students, is "hypermale military environment," with all that it implies for women. The students have now received sufficient visual information on the nature and products of such environments, and have been cogently challenged in sufficient of their core gender assumptions, to assimilate and constructively process such terminology without any of the reflexive (and aggressive) skepticism I could have expected had I introduced such concepts too early.

Feminist theorist bell hooks speaks of the "transformative" potential of acquiring the capacity for critical thinking through education (3). In particular, she utilizes visual media, in the form of cinema, to promote such constructive scrutiny and questioning. It is with just such goals in mind that I employ the visual material described here—which, although static images, nevertheless resonate with students as emotive, relevant, and highly novel yet intrinsically linked with settings made quasi-familiar by popular culture media such as cinema. hooks is centrally concerned with the life-changing transformations that empower individuals to overcome oppressive socioeconomic, ethnic, and/or gender-based circumstances; but I suggest that a transformation of potentially equal importance occurs when learners discover their capacity to recognize, question, and fearlessly critique their own assumptions (see Penny Light, in this book). I am able to say with confidence that many of my students do undergo just such a transformation, as evinced by positive feedback via SET and unsolicited comments, by the markedly open and engaged content of subsequent class discussion, and by the quality of assessment tasks submitted.

You May Now Use the "F" Word
The slide show finished, in the lecture's last minutes I return to E.P. Thompson, whom I have earlier extolled as a pioneer in the type of history I try to do; but I now point out that even he has attracted wide criticism for his broad omission of women from history. In this (regrettably) he did no more than reflect a wholesale disregard for women across many academic disciplines, not least history. In the fields of criminology and sociology of deviance—allied areas of obvious relevance to a historian of incarceration—women offenders were ignored almost entirely as a group, and when anyone did deign to comment on them, they were subject to absurd stereotyping—that is, until the late 1960s, when Frances Heidensohn produced

her pivotal gendered work on crime and justice (Miller, 133–34). I am now able to use the words "gender" and "feminism," and posit the need for studies in these fields, with confidence that they will elicit no uncomfortable shifting in seats or querulous murmurings in the lecture theatre.

Since I was given access to the Melbourne City Watch House and photographed its interior some years ago, it has been opened for tours. It stands adjacent to the Old Melbourne Gaol, long one of Melbourne's most visited tourist sites. Both sites are overseen by the Victorian branch of the National Trust of Australia, and as with most historic sites, much of their custom is derived from school tours. As a coda to the above lecture, I journey to Melbourne with my students (who are, of course, future schoolteachers) for an excursion to the Watch House, where the management kindly allow me to conduct the tour. The effect of having first viewed the images and received the theoretical background to the study, then walking about in the space itself, taking their own photographs, discussing, making the connection between the classroom and the tangible primary source itself, is for some students nothing less than profound.

Time permitting, we also take in the Old Melbourne Gaol next door, which is where Ned Kelly was hanged. His execution is a standard feature of tours. But it is also where Ned Kelly's mother, Ellen, was imprisoned for three years (she was there when her son died). Here I permit myself a final flourish to cement my own credentials, for (as I tell the students) I happen to have authored the entry on Ellen for the *Australian Dictionary of Biography,* and thus have something to say about the relatively unknown *female* history of one of the most masculine stories in the Australian cultural memory. Their reaction to this news—which they might once have received as a challenge to one of their own formative national myths—is nothing less than intense curiosity, and demonstrates that they have come to regard it as not merely unremarkable, but a benefit, to be taught gendered history by a (female) feminist lecturer. Such a response more than adequately meets the goals I have set out to achieve as a teacher.

Note

1 The surveys are part of an ongoing three-year ethics-approved study I am conducting into students' prior historical knowledge and experience of learning history in school. The data showed that of approximately 100 students participating, over 80 percent reported they could not remember what history they were taught at school. Their invited qualitative comments indicated a range of historical awareness very much in accord with that described in the text.

Works Cited

Aveling, Marian, and Joy Damousi, eds. *Stepping Out of History: Documents of Women at Work in Australia*. Sydney: Allen & Unwin, 1991.

Bartlett, Alison. "'She Seems Nice': Teaching Evaluations and Gender Trouble." *Feminist Teacher* 15.3 (2005): 195–202.

Bulbeck, Chilla. "'You Learn about Feminists but They're All Like Years Old': Young Women's Views of Feminism and Women's History." *Outskirts* 25 (2011).

Copp, Martha, and Sherryl Kleinman. "Practising What We Teach: Feminist Strategies for Teaching about Sexism." *Feminist Teacher* 18.2 (2008): 101–24. http://dx.doi.org/10.1353/ftr.2008.0007

Damousi, Joy. "Socialist Women and Gendered Space: Anti-Conscription and Anti-War Campaigns 1914–1918." *Gender and War: Australians at War in the Twentieth Century*. Cambridge: Cambridge University Press, 1995.

Denton, Barbara. *Dealing: Women in the Drug Economy*. Sydney: University of New South Wales Press, 2001.

Devine, Miranda. "Windschuttle Takes on the Historians." *Herald Sun* [Melbourne], 20 June 2004.

Frankenburg, Ruth. "Whiteness and Americanness: Examining Constructions of Race, Culture, and Nation in White Women's Life Narratives." In *Race*, ed. Steven Gregory and Roger Sanjek. New Brunswick, NJ: Rutgers University Press, 1994. 62–77.

George, Amanda. "Strip Searches: Sexual Assault by the State." In *Without Consent: Confronting Adult Sexual Violence: Proceedings of Conference 27–29 October 1992*. Ed. Patricia Weiser Easteal. Canberra: Australian Institute of Criminology, Conference Proceedings No. 20 (1993).

Goffman, Erving. *Asylums: Essays on the Social Situation of Mental Patients and Other Inmates*. Garden City, NY: Anchor Books, 1961.

Heidensohn, Frances. "The Deviance of Women: A Critique and an Enquiry." *British Journal of Sociology* 19.2 (1968): 160–75. http://dx.doi.org/10 .2307/588692

Heilpern, David M. *Fear or Favour: Sexual Assault of Young Prisoners*. Lismore: Southern Cross University Press, 1998.

hooks, bell. "Cultural Criticism and Transformation" [interview transcript]. Media Education Foundation (2005). 2 January 2013.

Ingliss, Kenneth. "The Anjac Tradition." *Meanjin* 3 (1965).

Lake, Marilyn. "Fight Free of Anzac, Lest We Forget Other Stories." *The Age* [Melbourne], 23 April 2009, 11. Melbourne.

Macintyre, Stuart, and Anna Clark. *The History Wars*. Melbourne: Melbourne University Press, 2004.

Manne, Robert. *In Denial: The Stolen Generations and the Right*. Melbourne: Schwartz, 2001.

Miller, Jodi. "Commentary on Heidensohn's 'The Deviance of Women': Continuity and Change over Four Decades of Research on Gender, Crime, and

Social Control." *British Journal of Sociology* 61 (S1; 2010): 133–39. http://dx.doi.org/10.1111/j.1468-4446.2009.01268.x

Thompson, E.P. *The Making of the English Working Class*. London: Victor Gollancz, 1963.

Thomson, Alastair. *Anzac Memories: Living with the Legend*. Melbourne: Oxford University Press, 1994.

Thomson, Phillip. "Unsatisfied Students Mark Down Teachers at ANU." *Sunday Age* [Melbourne], 12 August 2012.

Wilson, Jacqueline. "Kelly, Ellen (1832–1923)." *Australian Dictionary of Biography*. National Centre of Biography, Australian National University. 2005.

———. "Pecking Orders: Power Relationships and Gender in Australian Prison Graffiti." *Ethnography* 9.1 (March 2008): 99–121. http:// dx.doi.org/10.1177/1466138108088951

———. *Prison: Cultural Memory and Dark Tourism*. New York: Peter Lang, 2008.

Wilson, Jacqueline, Genee Marks, Lynne Noone, et al. "Retaining a Foothold on the Slippery Paths of Academia: University Women, Indirect Discrimination, and the Academic Marketplace." *Gender and Education* 22.5 (2010): 535–45. http://dx.doi.org/10.1080/09540250903354404

Wright, Clare. *The Forgotten Rebels of Eureka*. Melbourne: Text, 2014.

CHAPTER TWELVE

Rethinking "Students These Days": Feminist Pedagogy and the Construction of Students

Jane Nicholas and Jamilee Baroud

In this essay, we begin to unpack the category of "students" by contrasting pedagogical practices in regular university classes where students register, pay tuition for, and get credit toward a degree and experiences teaching women's history in Lakehead University's non-credit outreach program, Humanities 101, which is based on in partnerships with various social service agencies that refer students to the course. We hope to show that implicit practices of shaming are often wedded to our perceptions of students and how we narrate the characteristics of "the student body." In addressing shame we aim to build on Sandra Lee Bartky's work on the widespread, institutionalized, and often subtle practices of shaming female students inside the classroom. As Bartky suggests, these practices are so deeply engrained as standard practices in higher education that they are almost invisible ("Shame and Gender," 93–98). We argue here that when we narrate studenthood in the singular, especially when discussing so-called Millennials, we implicitly reinforce constructions of the institution that shape students as young, white, heterosexual, middle class, and masculine. Perhaps more damagingly, we may miss the significant challenges and disruptions in students' lives that impact academic progress. In the end, we offer here ideals, ideas, and questions about our roles as feminist instructors in higher education and by arguing that feminist pedagogy must engage in critical dialogues regarding students' complex identities. In all of this, we echo many of the concerns raised in other essays in this collection that point to the strong trend among Canadian universities toward corporate neoliberal models, which make engaging with feminist pedagogies increasingly difficult (in particular, see Briskin, Srigley, and Llewellyn and Llewellyn).

We come to this essay from very different perspectives. Jane is a tenured professor of predominantly WASP background; Jamilee is a Ph.D. student from a Canadian-Lebanese family. Our educational histories and those of our immediate families are more complex than these categories might suggest; we write together because of our mutual concerns about girls and women in education in the twenty-first century. Jane's experiences here with Humanities 101 and Jamilee's ongoing research on girls and their educational experiences with the "hidden curriculum" bring us together (Baroud).

Feminist Pedagogy in Higher Education

Feminist pedagogy emerged as a critical field in the 1980s. It was intent on rethinking teaching and learning and on decentring androcentric theories, models, curricula, and practices. Feminist pedagogy is much less interested in "grand theorizing" (Gore, 337) and much more inclined to emphasis "actual classrooms and classroom practices" (338). This does not mean that theory is absent; rather, feminist pedagogues have focused on praxis, the act of integrating theory with practice in a reflexive manner. Since the 1990s, feminist pedagogy has offered sophisticated analyses of education, practices for overcoming oppression, and frank debates on pedagogy and practice (Webb, Allen, and Walker). Briskin and Coulter offer a critical and concise definition of feminist pedagogy: for them, it "acknowledges that the classroom is a site of gender, race, and class inequalities, and simultaneously a site of political struggle and change. It recognizes that teaching and learning have the potential to be about liberation" (251). Closely tied to feminist movements, feminist pedagogy is engaged in a wider aim of social justice and liberation (Briskin). As Louise Morley suggests,

> feminist pedagogy for empowerment crystallizes around a common purpose to change gender relations in a society characterized by power inequalities. Changes start in the micro politics of the classroom. Mechanisms for achieving feminist pedagogy's aims are the validation and sharing of women's experiences, democratized organizational arrangements and use of the group for support and development. Underpinning these approaches is the desire to counter women's internalized oppression and the recognition that confidence and self-esteem are gendered attributes. (33)

In a highly influential book called *Teaching to Transgress,* bell hooks argues for an engaged feminist pedagogy working from Paulo Freire's classic *Pedagogy of the Oppressed.* Freire's work has achieved an almost cult-like status, but here we want to draw attention to his concerns about dehumanization and oppression. Freire wrote that "dehumanization, although a concrete historical fact, is *not* a given destiny but the result of an unjust order that engenders violence in the oppressors, which in turn dehumanizes the oppressed" (44). Adding a much-needed feminist voice to Freire's work, hooks argues that we should view theory as liberatory practice (hooks; Freire). In a much-quoted passage, she writes about theory's significance for explaining personal experiences with structural violence: "I came to theory because I was hurting—the pain within me was so intense that I could not go on living. I came to theory desperate, wanting to comprehend—to grasp what was happening around and within me. Most importantly, I wanted to make the hurt go away. I saw in theory then a location for healing" (59). In this essay, we want to pick up on some of the themes developed with feminist pedagogy, especially humanization and intellectual engagement as liberatory practices, to explore the problems inherent in flattening the category of "student" and simplistically narrating them as a problematic generation.

"Students These Days"

The dominant narrative of "students these days" circulates unofficially in conversations on and off campus. This narrative laments students' lack of interest, their inability to work and to meet faculty expectations, and their sense of entitlement and privilege. This is part of a wider national discussion propelled by critical books like *Ivory Tower Blues* and by receptive media that broadly disseminate elements of the debate on the current state of higher education in Canada (Côté and Allahar). These discussions are important and do reflect serious issues in higher education. They also reveal university teachers' care and devotion to good teaching, if also more subtly their fatigue, stress, and too-heavy workloads as a result of larger classes, increased expectations to conduct research, and high service demands. It is not the teaching precisely that is our concern here, but rather the broader discourse that frames our collective discussions. We all seem to have had the same students, but what is striking is how similar the students all seem—how homogenous, how flat. In particular, there is a sharp disjuncture between what we teach (the complexity of people's lives in the past and present) and how we see the students.

Defining students generationally—as the commonly used term Millennials does—homogenizes students based on assumptions related to their access to advanced technologies as well as to cultures of parenting within which they have been "protected from realities in their immediate lives" (Côté and Allahar, 102). Côté and Allahar also point to issues in consumer culture as a result of which, supposedly, the Millennial generation think of education in crassly consumer terms: money paid = degree. If students have been raised as consumers, then certainly the assumptions regarding what this means need careful analysis. Moreover, consumer culture is nothing new, and this is hardly the first generation to be raised as consumers (see Monod; Belisle 2011; Comacchio). As recent historical work has shown, representations of consumers (a highly feminized image in itself) have presented them as irrational and unthinking. The historical truth is far more complicated and is tightly woven into assumptions of gender and gender roles as well as class. As Belisle concludes, so-called irrational female shoppers "were not only articulations of anxieties about urbanization, industrialization, and capitalism, so were they attempts to enforce feminine docility." Representations of materialistic women have worked to shore up male authority (606). The stereotype of the crazed, unthinking female shopper has persisted, despite research showing that when it comes to consumption, women's *and* men's decision-making processes are sophisticated (Parr). It is important to understand that women and girls may articulate their identities through consumption; but it is *more* important to understand that they are acting agents and subjects who organize their consumption based on cultural regulations and sanctions (Lewis). Work that has focused on the contemporary period has revealed that consumers are able to think critically and carefully about their consumer practices (e.g., see McRobbie). Furthermore, reducing issues to ones of consumerism falsely makes real material issues such as massive debt and limited job prospects seem frivolous.[1] Also, assumptions that "mom" and "dad" are footing the bill do not align with the diversity of students; indeed, many students balance work and school, and a fair number of the "mature" students returning to school after many years in the workforce have dependents themselves. Moreover, ideals and consumerism do not have to be at odds. But the complexity of students' lives gets lost when they are framed universally as entitled, consumerist, and unthinking.

If history provides insight into the larger structures and discourses framing current anxieties, new books like *Sisters or Strangers?*, edited by Marlene Epp, Franca Iacovetta, and Frances Swyripa, remind us to ask important questions about how people are categorized. Writing from a perspective that sees gender as relational, the editors ask important questions about the intersecting categories of race, ethnicity, class, age, marital status, and experience. Reflecting on these shifts in the historiography exemplified by *Sisters or Strangers?* made us wonder if pedagogically, we have accepted the multiple, fractured, and complex identities of students in our class-rooms. As Epp, Iacovetta, and Swyripa write in the introduction to their book, "being female and members of a specific racial, ethnic, or class group affected what women could or could not do, how they saw themselves (and others), and how others in turn saw them" (3). According to social con-structivist feminists, sex does not neutrally or naturally exist, and the body does not neutrally or naturally exist; gender is constructed, and bodies are always socially inscribed. This analysis of performativity does not assume that sex and gender are specific to biology or behaviour; nor does it assume that gender is self-consciously performed. "From within this strand of fem-inist theorizing, what women do and what they are, are indeed what they can be, is neither the expression of an essential autonomous or semi-au-tonomous subject, nor just a reflection of their oppression by the powerful forces of capitalist patriarchy, but is the product of the intersection of a number of powerful, historically and socially located, strands of thought/ groupings of belief" (Frost, 31). Theories of performativity posit that "tech-niques of the body" (Myers, 820), such as gender performance, are real-ized, refined, and maintained through historical sediments and practices. As Simone de Beauvoir's now classic argument goes, women are made, not born; this means that women's and girls' subjectivities are formed and maintained through a performative pedagogy that pervades every aspect of life as girls are expected to work on or refashion themselves routinely in the interest of prescribed ideals (Bernstein). Within the confines of school, girls in particular are subjected to a "powerful disciplinary pedagogy" (Bartky 1996, 1) that teaches them they are the other and are *destined* for lesser lives. The educational system is extremely significant in the construction of girl-hood, for its discourses define, describe, and restrain how girls should act and look (Cote & Allahar; Mitchell & Reid-Walsh). Thus the school is the stage on which a particular performance of identity is created (Mitchell & Reid-Walsh)—a space where performative pedagogy prevails, encouraging judgment as girls become valued solely for their performance, their pro-ductivity, and their "socialization to act in stereotypically feminine ways" (as Hill suggests in Coleman, 71). This system of control as a performative pedagogy is a culture "that lends itself to alienation of the self as people are constantly required to make themselves different and distinct through 'micro-practices of representation' judgement and comparison: for exam-ple, through academic performance, or what they eat, or how they exercise, or what they weigh" (Evans et al., 82).

Performative pedagogy thus reproduces certain types of identities and bodies while simultaneously constraining and rejecting others. These per-formances are endorsed and legitimized within the culture of performativ-ity—more specifically, "trainability"—that prevails in schools (Evans et al.,

399). As the social pressure increases on them during adolescence, many girls become more self-conscious and less satisfied with their self-image; they lose their voices and their identities as their behaviours are continuously defined, regulated, and normalized within a culture of performative pedagogy (Evans et al.).

As teachers, from the perspective of feminist, performative pedagogies, we must ask ourselves deceptively simple questions: How do we see our students? How do we interpret their behaviour? Ultimately, these simple questions reveal that our own particular ways of narrating students deeply structures how we see them, interact with them, and (perhaps most damagingly) teach them. We see them as students first and people second; as Millennials first and as students facing enormous debt loads and diminished job prospects second; as a generation of cheaters and plagiarizers first and as students in a failed system that refuses to recognize and trust their abilities and intelligence second; as privileged students for having a seat in the class first and as individuals facing complex life circumstances and balancing family, health, disease, poverty, violence, and/or multiple social dislocations second.

The creation of the category of students is tied to power differentials between students and professors, and a certain politics of disclosure frames what students can and cannot reveal about themselves. Despite the recent efforts of national, provincial, and local campaigns to normalize experiences with mental illness, addiction, poverty, and violence, issues of shame remain. Yet what we see in classes is often framed by the widespread discourse that suggests the "Millennials" are a problem of privilege, that they are weakening the institutional structures of the universities and rapidly degrading academic standards (Côté and Allahar). Our concern is that this seemingly neutral descriptor of students in the twenty-first century may flatten differences in historical access to education and its legacies as well as erase ongoing issues related to class, race, and gender. Universities are places of remarkable privilege—a privilege born out of a history of implicit and explicit violence that has produced a hierarchy as a result of which the white middle class has come to be dominant and privileged within institutions of higher education. Although universities have ostensibly opened themselves to a wider segment of the population, the legacies of exclusion still need to be reckoned with.

Education in Canadian History

Learning is part of all societies, but formal schooling and the accompanying institutions are not. Education throughout the nineteenth and twentieth centuries meant very different things to children and adults depending on their class, race, gender, and place (Axelrod). As a result of the Indian Act, the education of Indigenous people fell to the federal government. By the late nineteenth century, residential schools for Aboriginal students had evolved into close partnerships between the federal government and various religious orders, as education remained expensive and churches helped offset costs (Dickason). The explicit policy of assimilation ended in 1910. Education by way of residential schools for Aboriginal children was about cultural genocide, and the curriculum specifically prepared them for labour: boys were trained for agricultural work as well as some trades and crafts, while girls' education focused on preparing them for domestic work (Miller, 10; Dickason, 315). Indigenous children were seen as incapable of intellectual work. Many of the experiences of these children reveal an education shaped by violence: the forcible cutting of hair, the banning of Indigenous languages and cultures, and widespread physical, emotional, and sexual abuse. Residential schools are not, however, something "of the past"; they shaped Aboriginal education throughout the twentieth century, and their legacy remains in what is commonly referred to as "intergenerational impact."[2] The recent Truth and Reconciliation Committee has noted that impact on the present day's high rates of poverty, addiction, and incarceration among Aboriginal peoples as well as on suicide rates and personal and family dysfunction. Aboriginal students educated on reserves are funded at a lesser rate, and educational facilities are far from accepted norms; these things have led to education rates in Indigenous communities that average seven years of formal education—the same average that was achieved a century ago for non-Indigenous children (Henderson, 225). Despite significant resistance (sometimes by students themselves), the racial bias in education remains (Reimer; Stonechild). In framing the current generation of students as ones protected from the reality of their lives, we perpetuate the idea of white, middle-class students. Aboriginal experiences in education reveal little protection from reality.

In the early to mid-nineteenth century, formal schooling for non-Indigenous people was often limited to middle-class children, and usually, only boys were educated past rudimentary lessons. Curriculum was also shaped by class, gender, and race. A full-scale, nuanced history of education in Canada is not possible in this brief article, but a few key points provide some necessary context. By the 1860s, schooling had become a responsibility of the state (typically the provincial government), and most children had at least a couple of years of formal education. Family labour demands—paid and unpaid—for many children meant that school attendance was erratic and limited. Compulsory education was still controversial, and despite the work of school reformers, "free" schools were not equally accessible and consistent formal education was beyond the means of many families (Conrad and Finkel, 13). Even by 1911, when most children had close to eight years of education, discrepancies for working-class, racialized, and immigrant children were notable (Cuthbert Brandt et al., 195). The actual education of children varied based on class and gender, and this trend was especially notable with the hardening typology of people based on class, race, and gender in the last three decades of the nineteenth century. Girls were separated from boys, and racially integrated classes were segregated (Cuthbert Brant et al., 196; Barman). Increasingly powerful professionals, such as physicians, along with social reformers, warned about over-educating women, which might weaken "the race" (Mitchinson). Mariana Valverde notes that "the slippery term 'race' allowed Anglo-Saxons to think of themselves as both a specific race and as the vanguard of the human race as a whole. The ambiguity of the term hence allowed white Anglo-Saxon supremacy to be justified without argument or evidence: it was obvious that as Anglo-Saxons progressed or declined, so would the world" (109–10). Such attitudes inflected the curriculum and pedagogy and worked to define levels of and claims to citizenship (Stanley).

Formal schooling had become a common feature in the lives of Canadian children by the 1920s (Sutherland, 212). Class, gender, race, ethnicity, and context shaped the amount of time spent in school as well as the experience of children within it. Oral histories of English Canadian students attending school from the 1920s to the 1950s reveal that many children entered schools with excitement mixed with trepidation; some, though, were simply fearful (Sutherland). Gabrielle Roy's fictionalized memoir *Children of My Heart* (1979) recounts the fear with which many immigrant children came to her classes.[3] And although high school or secondary schooling was born in the nineteenth century, it was only in the 1920s that a majority of adolescents actually attended one (Comacchio, 100). Rural children still often missed significant portions of school if they were needed on the farm. Despite rules for compulsory education in most provinces and truant officers to enforce them, material conditions (among other factors) limited access to formal school for many children, especially during the Great Depression, when children's labour was essential to many families' survival (Comacchio; Sutherland, 221; Campbell).

The post–Second World War period saw significant change but also the persistence of old patterns. Increased rates of primary and secondary education were the norm, but working-class and Aboriginal students remained disadvantaged in access to education. Girls and young women found their educational choices and career options broadening but still bound by traditional gender stereotypes as well as by the assumption that they were destined for marriage and motherhood (Comacchio). Perhaps the most significant change in terms of this essay's discussion was the increased access to post-secondary institutions. University education largely remained exclusive to middle- and upper-class students until the postwar period, although gender and racial barriers had been cracked in the late nineteenth century (Cuthbert Brandt et al.). The government's postwar programs to assist veterans made higher education more accessible to more people (Owram). Recent research by Patricia Jasen has revealed the ongoing concern over student mental health in higher education in the postwar years, as well as student efforts to transform health services in this period. This suggests that today's issues have a much longer history than is usually immagined, and one that should inform current discussions (Jasen).

This very brief overview of some elements of the history of education in Canada serves two purposes here: first, as a reminder that the structure and legacies of formal schooling in Canada have been intimately shaped by discourses of race, class, sexuality, and gender; and second, as an illustration that discussions of education and pedagogy are always knitted to these categories. The legacies of residential schools are palpable and obvious. As Briskin and Coulter note, other issues of access remain for immigrant women, women in poverty, and women in abusive relationships. Provincial social services can also hinder access to higher education (248). And here, gendered disparities in poverty and experiences of violence are important to recognize. Queer students face significant challenges in educational structures that are heteronormative, and Luhmann has pointedly called for us to think of queering our pedagogy for all students. She writes that queering pedagogy "is an inquiry into the conditions that make learning possible or prevent learning" (130). Queer pedagogy is important in the classroom because if differences of race, class, and gender identities, as well as prejudice, class privilege, and heterosexism, are not acknowledged in schools, educators may fail to investigate how knowledge and power relations are produced and reinforced through these various interconnections. As Kevin Kumashiro maintains, "ironically, our efforts to challenge one form of oppression often unintentionally contribute to other forms of oppression, and our efforts to embrace one form of difference often exclude and silence others" (1).

Shaming "Students"

Shame, according to Bartky, requires an audience—one that can be internalized—that witnesses the passing of judgment and the creation of oneself as a lesser object (1996, 227–29). Identity can thus be defined as combining how we are represented by others and with how that positioning affects how we represent ourselves (Hall). Bartky's essay goes over now common understandings of the gender dynamics of the classroom: women are quieter in the classroom, get called upon less, and get asked simplistic questions (men are chosen to answer analytical ones). Men are encouraged and coached more by instructors, receive more praise for their responses, and are interrupted less. (This is reflected in and reproduced by graduate studies [Iacovetta].) Women of colour, Bartky reminds us, are doubly discriminated against, with instructors reading students' behaviour in light of racial stereotypes. Class also often shapes how students perform—literally act—in the classroom. The "invisible pedagogy" is a "manipulative strategy to achieve a more effective form of control" (Davis, 76) based predominantly on educational assumptions that begin very early and shape students throughout their education. The invisible pedagogy implies that "lower-class children are presumed to have an intellectual or linguistic deficit; girls are expected to do poorly in math and science; and Blacks and Hispanics are expected to be poor learners and eventually drop out of school" (76).

White, middle-class privilege shapes who feels comfortable with and interacts with other people in the classroom. The shamed may perform differently in light of years of classroom difference: they may be quieter, speak with hesitation, use self-effacing phrases to make their contributions seem lesser, and apologize for the quality of their work (Bartky 1990, 88–92). Bartky points out that ultimately, "shame is profoundly disempowering" (1996, 237).

Could academic disempowerment based on shame masquerade as lack of interest or entitlement? Certainly, disappointment in the "new" generation of students is nothing new, and historians have long lamented students' loss of historical sense and ability to retain knowledge. In "Crazy for History," Sam Wineburg reveals that generations of students since the early twentieth century have repeatedly disappointed their teachers and examiners by failing to demonstrate an acceptable sense of the facts of the past. There have long been complaints of students' lack of seriousness of intent and purpose compared to earlier generations (Wineburg). We absolutely have to get students to face the issue of privilege, and there are many privileged students in my classrooms, but we cannot assume to know who holds privilege based on how students look and perform in class. In challenging students to face the issue, we must continually engage in our own assessment of our privilege as professors and instructors. In describing privilege as running with the wind at your back, Kimmel writes that "confronting privilege makes one extremely uncomfortable—a productive and healthy discomfort, to be sure, but discomfort just the same" (xi). Shaming reminds us of what comes too close and of what is too distant—of moments, events, and attributes that remind us of things we'd forgotten or thought we'd left behind and of things we can't or don't understand. Standing in front of a class—regardless of its composition—is a potential lesson in confronting privilege as well as an opportunity to turn around and address the wind.

Humanities 101

Humanities 101 is a non-credit course offered at Lakehead University based on the model founded by Earl Shorris's "Clemente course" in the 1990s, which subsequently spread throughout North America. The first program in Canada was offered by the University of British Columbia. Shorris developed his course in reaction to an interview with a female prisoner in Bedford Hills. In responding to his question "Why do you think people are poor?," Viniece (Niecie) Walker replied that people needed "a moral alternative to the street." Walker contended that to leave poverty, the poor needed to be able to reflect, as a bridge to entering a political world—that is, a world of engagement with other people at all levels (Shorris, 50). For Shorris and Walker, engagement with the humanities was essential in building this engagement. We would argue, further, that women's history, using multiple categories of analysis to explore gender, class, race, age, and sexuality, is fundamental if students are to understand the politics of exclusion that make political engagement a site of privilege.

At Lakehead University, Dr. Christina van Barneveld started the course in 2005. All students are referred to the program by a local social service agency; these agencies range from mental health services to women's shelters to addiction recovery centres. The Humanities 101 program at Lakehead partners with a host of social service agencies (http://humanities101 .lakeheadu.ca). Besides offering a fifteen-week course in which volunteer professors give one or two lectures to the class, the program provides an orientation session to the university, a pathways session that allows students to explore their options for education after Humanities 101 concludes, and a graduation. The pathways session includes information on university and college applications and on how to complete high school. Students are also offered information on financing school, as well as help gaining access to their educational records.

Humanities 101 typically enrols between twenty-five and thirty students; usually, between twenty and twenty-five graduate. In addition to the course, which is offered without tuition fees, students are offered dinner in advance of the lectures as well as funds for child care or elder care, school supplies, and bus passes to help offset domestic responsibilities, issues of food insecurity and poverty, and, more generally, the true costs of education. Access to universities has broadened over the past sixty years, but structural inequalities still seriously limit opportunity.

The Humanities 101 classroom is very different from a typical university classroom. The students are highly mobile. They walk in and out of class as need be and ask very different questions. Some are more willing to challenge theories and histories based on their life experiences, but many are very quiet. What I [Jane], as a professor, know about the students is different as well: I am far more willing to keep in mind that most of these students are first-generation learners from remarkably diverse backgrounds; some are new immigrants, many more than in my university classroom are Aboriginal, and many are poor. Many of them have had negative experiences in educational institutions, and from the anecdotal evidence, a fair few have had negative experiences in history class. After I have lectured about women's history in Humanities 101, it is not unusual for students (both male and female) to ask me why history isn't taught like this in elementary or high school. What they have connected with is the analysis of people's lives at the intersection of categories of identity. Some are for the first time seeing *themselves* in a history class. To be able to see yourself and claim a history is a powerful moment.

Some of the differences in Humanities 101 are based largely on expectations and on how the classroom space is shaped. These are pedagogical differences. The student body in Humanities 101 may be different—students are fighting poverty, mental illness, addiction, and domestic violence—yet it also may *not* be. Recognition of the complex life experiences of the Humanities 101 students is what frames the absence of shame. Cammileah [pseudonym], was enrolled in one session of Lakehead University's HUM 101 class. At the conclusion of the course, she reflected back on her experience:

> To be honest, when I first heard of Humanities 101, learning was not first on my list of priorities. I was thinking it would be a good "free" meal and I would not have to eat alone. I had just come out of a very long and abusive marriage and was not used to being out at night let alone being around so many strangers in a higher education setting. It was overwhelming, but Christina, Nadine and all the other professors made us feel so welcome that I found that, for at least some of the time I was in the classroom, I was able to focus on what was being taught instead of being in a constant struggle

and feeling that horrible overwhelming feeling you get when you are trying to get your life back. I found myself looking forward to the lectures every week ... When I was younger, I was not fortunate enough to have any teachers who had the passion the way these people do ... I know that I will continue to keep my mind open to what this world has to offer. Being involved in the course helped me realize that I am worthwhile. As hard as life is for me right now, I know that it will eventually get better. I feel myself starting to get out of "survival" mode and into the next phase of my life. (https://www.lake headu.ca/academics/other-programs/humanities101/student-experiences/profiles/node/20412)

Cammileah's story highlights broader social factors in higher education. The alarming rates of domestic violence that Canadian female university students reported in the Canadian National Survey (1998)—35 percent of female students reported a physical assault by a male partner in the previous twelve months, and 45 percent reported an act of sexual abuse since leaving high school—should give us pause in narrating the universality of privilege among Millennials. Scholars have also noted that men are able to mistreat, harass, and embarrass their female peers in school with little institutional punishment or consequences (Zaslow, 16). In addition, battering, date rape, street violence, and homophobic violence negatively shape students' lives. There are scandalously high rates of First Nations children living in poverty and of Aboriginal students facing racism in schools (Urban Aboriginal Task Force: Thunder Bay Final Report). Rising student debt loads and the increasing numbers of students seeking mental health services should also crack the discourse of almost universal student privilege. When we narrate students and read their actions and behaviours in the context of privilege and entitlement, we may miss important signals of violence, both personal and structural.

What we find most radical about Bartky's essay and its possibility for teaching is her argument that subjectivity is not "brought ready-made to the classroom: The classroom is also a site of its constitution" (1990, 90). If anything, this argument should remind us that the classroom is a multiple space reflecting our society, the culture of our institution, our students, and perhaps most scarily of all, ourselves as teachers. If we do not find the students we prefer in our classroom, what does this say about us as teachers or the institutions in which we work? What does it say about what and how we teach them if we recognize our role in constituting them as students? We write this recognizing the deep structural problems of large classes, the increasing demands for research and service, and the general sense of what Tomkins has insightfully called "the Pedagogy of the Distressed." We must certainly work to push back against the corporatization of the university and the profit-driven models that place all of us in a stressful and demeaning system. Yet I still want to argue that we need to keep our humanity and see the humanity in our students in this broken system. In his essay in *Harper's*, Shorris wrote: "I resolved to do no harm. There was no need for the course to have a 'sink or swim' character; it could aim to keep as many afloat as possible" (52). Floating doesn't have to be interpreted as the lowering of academic standards. Keeping them afloat means that students need to see themselves and their own histories in courses we teach, but it also means constantly reflecting on the histories we tell of our students and the ways we tell them to ensure they are humane. To be told you don't have a history—even when this is by subtle absence as opposed to a firm declaration—is to participate in a deep shaming of students. Keeping them afloat is also a reminder that part of our job as teachers is to make the academy a humane space, and that may mean teaching students *to be* students, not by shaming but by engaging in open and frank discussions of our implicit expectations. (On relational aspects of teaching, see Gotlib, in this book.) And it may also mean recognizing that the conventions of today's classroom have a history enmeshed with past educational practices that privileged white, middle-class, male students. Assuming that students come to class ready-made as students who understand the expectations of university education (including all of the informal but essential performative aspects) leads to practices of shaming. (See also Gullage, in this book.) Deep intellectual engagement is not icing; it is not something to be layered onto someone who has it all together and is ready to wholeheartedly dedicate herself to academic study. It strikes us that the expectation of that role is one that speaks to white, middle-class, masculine privilege. Intellectual engagement is an essential component of humanity. And sincere intellectual engagement is ultimately a practice of respect.

To be sure, Humanities 101 is not perfect, and it is important to acknowledge the gulf that exists between the space of this classroom and a regular university one. Academic rigour often gets sacrificed in making a safe space in the institution, but this itself should give us pause to rethink the practices of "rigorous" scholarship and how they might be made more humane. Further, in Humanities 101 there are no mandatory assignments—often a touchpoint of conflict in the academy—and there are no teacher evaluations, so our perception of the course is left unchecked by student voices. Yet we firmly believe that once the pedagogies of shame so imbricated into teaching and the narration of students are undone, the two spaces of these different classrooms can fruitfully inform each other. After she directed the program for a year, Jane's teaching changed profoundly; she recognized that teaching is about *teaching*—not expecting students to come into the classroom fully formed, but recognizing that it is a place, as Bartky suggests, in the construction of subjectivity. We help create people as "students." When we exclude unconventional students by continuing practices of shaming, we impoverish ourselves as instructors as well as the academy. We need to carefully engage with students' own narrations of their biographies, and we need to acknowledge the complex histories they bring into the classroom even if we don't know them. And we must take care in employing "students" as a category in our discussions about people, if we are first to do no harm.

Notes

1 For instance, in Jean M. Twenge's *Generation Me,* Twenge carefully compares the cultural characteristics and attitudes of young adults in modern society with those of previous generations. According to Twenge, Generation Me has unrealistic goals associated with careers and incomes. They have a desire to become wealthy, yet they are not equipped with the proper tools to achieve that goal. They are taught from a young age that you can become "whatever you want to be" and that "nothing is impossible" (77). Generation Me is able to acknowledge money and value it, however, they are unable to earn it.

2 For a full list of the types of symptoms of intergenerational impact, see http://www.wherearethechildren.ca/en/exhibit/impacts.html.

3 Roy's fictionalized memoir is surely problematic in its use of ethnic stereotypes to describe children and their families. Nonetheless, her work intimately reveals some of the social dislocations of newcomers to Canada in relation to formal education.

Works Cited

Axelrod, Paul. *The Promise of Schooling: Education in Canada, 1800–1914.* Toronto: University of Toronto Press, 1997.

Barman, Jean. "Separate and Unequal: Indian and White Girls at All Hallows School, 1884–1920." In *Rethinking Canada: The Promise of Women's History.* Ed. Veronica Strong-Boag and Anita Clair Feldman. Toronto: Copp Clark Pitman, 1991.

Baroud, Jamilee. "Gendered Media Representations of Sexiness and Their Effects on Girls' Educational Experiences" M.Ed. Thesis, Lakehead University, 2014.

Bartky, Sandra Lee. "Shame and Gender." *Femininity and Domination: Studies in the Phenomenology of Oppression.* New York: Routledge, 1990.

———. "The Pedagogy of Shame." In *Feminisms and Pedagogies of Everyday Life.* Albany: SUNY Press, 1996.

Belisle, Donica. "Crazy for Bargains: Inventing the Irrational Female Shopper in Modernizing English Canada." *Canadian Historical Review* 92.4 (2011): 581–606. http://dx.doi.org/10.3138/chr.92.4.581
———. *Retail Nation: Department Stores and the Making of Modern Canada.* Vancouver: UBC Press, 2011.
Bernstein, Basil. "From Pedagogies to Knowledges." *Toward a Sociology of Pedagogy: The Contribution of Basil Bernstein to Research.* Vol. 23. New York: Peter Lang, 2001. 363–84.
Briskin, Linda. *Feminist Pedagogy: Teaching and Learning Liberation.* Ottawa: CRIAW, 1990.
Briskin, Linda, and Rebecca Priegert Coulter. "Feminist Pedagogy: Challenging the Normative." *Canadian Journal of Education* 17.3 (1992): 247–63. http://dx.doi.org/10.2307/1495295
Coleman, John C. *The School Years: Current Issues in the Socialization of Young People.* 2nd ed. London: Routledge, 1992.
Côté, James E., and Anton L. Allahar. *Critical Youth Studies: A Canadian Focus.* Toronto: Pearson Prentice Hall, 2006.
Campbell, Lara. *Respectable Citizens: Gender, Family, and Unemployment in Ontario's Great Depression.* Toronto: University of Toronto Press, 2009.
Comacchio, Cynthia. *The Dominion of Youth: Adolescence and the Making of Modern Canada, 1920 to 1950.* Waterloo: Wilfrid Laurier University Press, 2006.
Conrad, Margaret, and Alvin Finkel. *History of the Canadian Peoples: 1867 to the Present.* Toronto: Pearson, 2005.
Côté, James E., and Anton Allahar. *Ivory Tower Blues: A University System in Crisis.* Toronto: University of Toronto Press, 2007.
Cuthbert Brandt, Gail, Naomi Black, Paula Bourne, and Magda Fahrni. *Canadian Women: A History.* Toronto: Nelson, 2011.
Davis, N.J. *Youth Crisis: Growing Up in the High-Risk Society.* Westport: Greenwood, 1999.
Dickason, Olive Patricia. *Canada's First Nations: A History of Founding Peoples from Earliest Times.* Toronto: Oxford University Press, 2002.
Epp, Marlene, Franca Iacovetta, and Frances Swyripa. *Sisters or Strangers? Immigrant, Ethnic and Racialized Women in Canadian History.* Toronto: University of Toronto Press, 2004.
Evans, John, Brian Rich, Emma Davies, et al. *Education, Disordered Eating, and Obesity Discourse: Fat Fabrications.* London: Routledge, 2008.
Freire, Paolo. *Pedagogy of the Oppressed.* New York: Continuum, 2006.
Frost, Liz. *Young Women and the Body: A Feminist Sociology.* Houndmills: Palgrave, 2001. http://dx.doi.org/10.1057/9780333985410
Gore, J. "What We Can Do for—You? Struggling over Empowerment in Critical and Feminist Pedagogies." In *The Critical Pedagogy Reader.* New York: Routledge, 2003.

Hall, Stuart. *Representation: Cultural Representations and Signifying Practices*. London: Sage, 1997.

Henderson, J.Y. "Treaties and Indian Education." In *First Nations Education in Canada: The Circle Unfolds*. Ed. M. Battiste and J. Barman. Vancouver: UBC Press, 1995.

hooks, bell. *Teaching to Transgress: Education as the Practice of Freedom*. New York: Routledge, 1994.

Iacovetta, Franca. "Towards a More Humane Academy? Some Observations from a Canadian Feminist Historian." *Journal of Women's History* 18.1 (2006): 141–46. http://dx.doi.org/10.1353/jowh.2006.0015

Jasen, Patricia. "Student Activism, Mental Health, and English-Canadian Universities in the 1960s." *Canadian Historical Review* 92.3 (2011): 455–80. http://dx.doi.org/10.3138/chr.92.3.455

Kimmell, Michael S. "Preface." In *Privilege: A Reader*. Ed. Michael S. Kimmel and Abby L. Ferber. Boulder: Westview, 2003.

Kumashiro, K. *Troubling Intersections of Race and Sexuality: Queer Students of Color and Anti-Oppressive Education*. Lanham: Rowman & Littlefield, 2001.

Lewis, A.L. *Gender Politics and MTV: Voicing the Difference*. Philadelphia: Temple University Press, 1990.

Luhmann, Susanne. "Queering/Querying Pedagogy: Or, Pedagogy Is a Pretty Queer Thing." In *Queer Theory in Education*. Ed. William F. Pinar. New York: Routledge, 1998.

McRobbie, Angela. *Feminism and Youth Culture: From Jackie to Just Seventeen*. London: Macmillan, 1987.

Miller, J.R. *Shingwauk's Vision: A History of Native Residential Schools*. Toronto: University of Toronto Press, 1996.

Mitchell, Claudia, and Jacqueline Reid-Walsh. *Girl Culture: An Encyclopedia*. Vol. 1. Westport: Greenwood, 2008.

Mitchinson, Wendy. *The Nature of Their Bodies: Women and Their Doctors in Victorian Canada*. Toronto: University of Toronto Press, 1991.

Monod, David. *Store Wars: Shopkeepers and the Culture of Mass Marketing, 1890–1939*. Toronto: University of Toronto Press, 1996.

Morley, L. *Feminist Academics: Creative Agents for Change*. London: Taylor and Francis, 1995.

Myers, Natasha. "Pedagogy and Performativity Rendering Laboratory Lives in the Documentary Naturally Obsessed: The Making of a Scientist." *Isis* 101.4 (2010): 817–828. http://dx.doi.org/10.1086/657480

Owram, Doug. *Born at the Right Time: A History of the Baby Boom Generation*. Toronto: University of Toronto Press, 1996.

Parr, Joy. *Domestic Goods: The Material, the Moral, and the Economic in the Postwar Years*. Toronto: University of Toronto Press, 1999.

Reimer, Karl. "What Other Canadian Kids Have: The Fight for a New School in Attawapiskat." *Native Studies Review* 19.1 (2010): 119–36.

Roy, Gabrielle. *Children of My Heart*. Toronto: McClelland & Stewart, 1979.

Shorris, Earl. "As a Weapon in the Hands of the Restless Poor." *Harper's,* September 1997.

Stanley, Tim. *Contesting White Supremacy: School Segregation, Anti-Racism, and the Making of Chinese Canadians*. Vancouver: University of British Columbia Press, 2011.

Stonechild, Blair. *The New Buffalo: The Struggle for Aboriginal Post-Secondary Education*. Winnipeg: University of Manitoba Press, 2006.

Sutherland, Neil. *Growing Up: Childhood in English Canada from the Great War to the Age of Television*. Toronto: University of Toronto Press, 1997.

Tompkins, Jane. "Pedagogy of the Distressed." *College English* 52.6 (1990): 653–60. http://dx.doi.org/10.2307/378032

Urban Aboriginal Task Force: Thunder Bay Final Report, February 2007.

Valverde, Mariana. *The Age of Light, Soap, and Water: Moral Reform in English Canada, 1885–1925*. Toronto: University of Toronto Press, 2008.

Webb, Lynne M., Myria W. Allen, and Kandi L. Walker. "Feminist Pedagogy: Identifying Basic Principles." *Academic Exchange Quarterly* 6.1 (2002): 67–72.

Wineburg, Sam. "Crazy for History." *Journal of American History* 90.4 (2004): 1401–14. http://dx.doi.org/10.2307/3660360

Zaslow, Emilie. *Feminism, Inc.: Coming of Age in Girl Power Media Culture*. New York: Palgrave Macmillan, 2009. http://dx.doi.org/10.1057/9780230101531. http://www.wherearethechildren.ca/en/exhibit/impacts.html

Feminist Pedagogies of Activist Compassion: Engaging the Literature and Film of Female Genital Cutting in the Undergraduate Classroom

Jennifer Browdy de Hernandez

Feminist pedagogy works deliberately to break down the walls between the classroom and the real world, and in my courses on global literature by women, I often share stories by contemporary women who are struggling with issues that my students find shocking and upsetting—violence, cultural oppression, lack of opportunities, and inequality. Students sometimes ask me why I teach such "depressing" books. The beginning of an answer to this question comes in the theory of "*conocimiento*" developed by Chicana feminist theorist Gloria Anzaldúa. In her essay "Now let us shift ... the path of *conocimiento*...inner work, public acts," Anzaldúa describes *conocimiento* as a multi-stage process of coming to awareness, and then taking action based on that new awareness, in which the stages are not chronological or mutually exclusive, and where the process itself is more important than any given goal—in fact, it's a never-ending process rather than a goal-oriented one. The seven stages of *conocimiento* are:[1]

1 The shock that jars you into openness to a new perspective
2 *Nepantla*, the in-between stage where you consider new perspectives

3 *Coatlicue*: doubt, despair, self-loathing, paralysis
4 A call to action sends you looking for ways to act productively in the world
5 Crafting a new personal narrative that reflects your new understanding of the world
6 Taking your new story out in public, testing it in dialogue with others
7 Forming holistic alliances with others based on your sense of commonality and compassion.

Anzaldúa emphasizes that "in a day's time you may go through all seven stages, though you may dwell in one for months" and that "you're never only in one space, but partially in one, partially in another, with *nepantla* occurring most often as its own space and as the transition between each of the others" (546).

The wrenching stories of survivors of female genital mutilation (FGM) that I share with students in my "African Women Writing Resistance" course have the power to initiate the first stage of *conocimiento,* the powerful emotional shock that comes from being exposed to a new and very different, unfamiliar view of reality. Such shocks, Anzaldúa says, are necessary to growth; they are moments of "awakening that cause you to question who you are, what the world is about" (547). The "depressing" moments in the books we read in my Women Writing Resistance classes offer many opportunities for these kinds of productive shocks, which can take us further along the process of coming to awareness or *conocimiento.* Anzaldúa has observed that it is only by going through what she calls the "*Coatlicue* state" (*Coatlicue* being a reference to a dark, "hellish" Meso-American goddess who can drag one down to the underworld of "despair, self-loathing and hopelessness" (545) that we can find an effective path of action. Such a journey, though challenging in every way, is ultimately healing and empowering. "Delving more fully into your pain, anger, despair, depression will move you through them to the other side," Anzaldúa says, "where you can use their energy to heal. Depression is useful—it signals that you need to make changes in your life, it challenges your tendency to withdraw, it reminds you to take action" (553).

As many global feminists have learned the hard way, what looks like cultural oppression to one woman may feel like a valuable cultural tradition to another. Before we can think about taking action on a complex issue like female genital mutilation, we have to take the time to learn about it from the women on the frontlines, those who are in favour of the practice as well as those who are opposed to it. Our first task is simply to listen carefully, with open minds and hearts.

When we tune in to the stories of women survivors of FGM, we learn quickly that this issue affects millions of girls and women, mostly from African countries but also in Muslim communities in Indonesia and elsewhere in the African and Muslim diaspora. Every year an estimated two million girls, from infants to teens, have their clitoris and labia cut and their vaginal openings sewn, most often by traditional female excisers with no formal medical training, who generally use simple implements like razors or even thorns, and who provide no anaesthesia or modern post-op hygiene.[2] The lifelong impacts of this practice are often severe, ranging from the numbing of the genital area to hemorrhaging and severe pain during intercourse to dysfunction of the vaginal canal during birthing.[3] Faced with this upsetting information, students in my classes want to know two things above all: Why have they never heard about FGM before? And what can they do to help the movement to abolish it?

The answers to these questions take us right into the heart of the complexity of our current moment in the global feminist movement. We have come a long way in a short time from the triumphal tone of Robin Morgan's 1996 anthology *Sisterhood Is Global.* Morgan's idea of women's solidarity was predicated on the premise that women in societies that were more progressive, in feminist terms, should ally themselves with women around the world and use their privileges to push for universal women's equality and human rights. But this approach has produced a backlash that has taken the wind out of the sails of the ideal of a global feminist sisterhood: women in other countries have rejected the leadership of North American and European feminists, basically telling these would-be sisters to "mind your own business; our issues are none of your concern."[4] Some students, learning about FGM for the first time, may agree, saying in so many words: "the removal of millions of little girls' genital organs is deeply upsetting, but it's their cultural practice, what right do I have to get involved?"

As a feminist, I believe in the ideal of global sisterhood and in the responsibility of those with more privilege to reach out and help those who are more oppressed. As Virginia Woolf put it: "As a woman, I have no country. As a woman, I want no country. As a woman, my country is the whole world" (109). To which Audre Lorde later added, "I am not free while any woman is unfree, even if her shackles are very different from my own" (132–33). I have increasingly come to see the value of looking at global feminist issues through the broader lens of human rights doctrine, particularly in the wake of the UN Millennium Development Goals of 2000, which placed special emphasis on the rights of women and girls to education, employment, and social empowerment. The well-being of women worldwide should be the concern of *all* feminists, regardless of their social location, and discussion of women's issues across cultural and geographic boundaries should be a part of the feminist curriculum at every level, but especially in higher education.

That said, where does this leave me as an undergraduate teacher of comparative literature, faced with a roomful of shocked young American women who are getting their first introduction to the controversial issue of female genital mutilation? How do I channel their concern for their sisters around the world into productive action that can really make a difference? Can the literature of FGM be a vehicle for effective human rights advocacy?

If I didn't believe that narrative could make a difference to the real lives of women on the ground, I would have thrown in the towel as a teacher of literature long ago. But it's clear to me that narratives are indeed one of the most powerful tools of resistance we humans possess. From the slave narratives of the nineteenth-century abolition movement, to the *testimonios* of twentieth-century Latin American resisters like Rigoberta Menchu, to contemporary anti-FGM testimonials by African women like Waris Dirie, Fadumo Korn and Khady Koïta, it has been wrenching stories, told with graphic detail and deeply felt emotional resonance, that have penetrated the inertia of bystanders and ignited serious, sweeping movements for change. Today these stories are as likely to be told through cinematic narrative as through words on a page, so I often bring relevant films into the classroom as well.

In teaching FGM to undergraduates, I have found it most effective to combine a strongly written testimonial, such as Fadumo Korn's *Born in the Big Rains* or Khady Koita's *Bloodstains,* with the powerful feature film *Moolaadé,* by the great Senegalese filmmaker Ousmane Sembène, together with some carefully chosen shorter critical works that situate these primary texts in the context of the international debates over the cultural legitimacy of FGM and the role of outsiders in anti-FGM advocacy. My goal in assembling such a unit as part of my African Women Writing Resistance course is to expose students to a wide range of viewpoints on this controversial issue and give them enough information to make up their own minds about whether the human rights of girls are violated when they are genitally cut as infants or children, and if so, what role cultural outsiders such as ourselves can play in standing in solidarity with women from within those cultures who are resisting the practice.

Reading the first-hand accounts by survivors of FGM can be a painful experience. Here is how Khady Koïta of Senegal describes what was done to her with a razor when she was seven years old:

> Two women caught and dragged me in. The one behind me grabbed my head and, with all the strength in her knees, crushed my shoulders to the

ground; the other clutched my thighs to force the legs apart ... Using her fingers, the exciser grasps the clitoris and stretches that minute fragment of flesh as far as it will go. She then—if all goes well—whacks it off like a piece of zebu meat. Often, she can't hack it off in one go so she's obliged to saw. To this day, I can hear myself howling. (11)

And here is Fadumo Korn of Somalia, remembering virtually the same experience:

The first cut was ice cold.

A deep blue pain.

A lightning bolt to the head.

The voice of my mother, calling: "Don't scream like that. Don't shame me. Be a big girl!"

This *cold*.

Blood on my backside, ice cold blood.

I bucked under an all-consuming, devouring pain.

A shriek to the ends of the world wanted to escape but stuck in my throat. It couldn't get out.

The world stopped spinning.

Everything went numb.

And soft.

Oh, so soft and light and beautiful. A cocoon of fine sand, taking my body up and carrying me off, hugging me, protecting me.

When I came to, I felt nothing. I heard scraping, scratching, noises and voices. I was floating and looking on from overhead, seeing myself on the ground, on the upside-down tub, stiff as a board, my mother and Aunt Asha holding me tight, putting a block of wood in my mouth, and an old woman squatting between my legs, carrying out her barbaric craft.

At some point I could breathe again. I screamed: "Mommy, help me!"

But it didn't stop. It didn't stop for a very long time. (Korn, 38)

For both Koita and Korn, the physical and psychological trauma brought on by the after-effects of the cutting were lifelong, and we can multiply their stories by millions to get a full sense of the impact of this cultural practice on women worldwide. According to the World Health Organization, which has condemned the practice as having no positive health benefits and many negative effects on girls and women, at least two million African girls are at risk for FGM each year, and an estimated 125 million girls and women worldwide are living with the consequences of FGM.[5] To me it is clear that this is a human rights violation on a vast scale, targeted at a specific, biologically defined group: women.[6]

But it is important to note that FGM is not an institution like slavery that is imposed on women and girls by an oppressive outside power. Rather, it is a practice perpetuated by loving mothers and grandmothers, some of whose daughters and granddaughters are in fact eager to participate in what they understand to be an essential rite of passage into womanhood. As Tobe Levin observes, the question for us as bystanders who are cultural outsiders is "how to approach an issue viewed as urgent by only a tiny transnational minority. For make no mistake," Levin cautions, "an enormous and powerful majority tenaciously defends the practice" (Levin and Asaah, xv).

If we were just to go by the published documents on FGM, whether fiction, personal narratives, poetry, or research-based journalistic and scholarly articles, we might have trouble believing that the majority of people concerned with the issue of FGM are in favour of it, since almost all the published work views FGM as a human rights violation to be eradicated. Defenders of FGM are more likely to make their arguments locally and orally, on the ground where the cutting occurs. One published source that does an excellent job at presenting the pro- *and* anti-FGM arguments is Fuambai Ahmadu's "Rites and Wrongs: An Insider/Outsider Reflects on Power and Excision." Ahmadu, raised in the United States by Sierra Leonean parents, was a college senior when she was taken back to Sierra Leone with her sister to be initiated into the Kono women's secret society, the Bundu. In Sierra Leone, according to World Health Organization statistics, 90 percent or more of women undergo removal of the clitoris as one of many rituals required of girls seeking to join the Bundu. Ahmadu, who now holds a graduate degree in cultural anthropology, describes her FGM experience incorporating both the anthropologist's attention to detail and the testifier's first-hand point of view:

> I was hoisted up by four or five ... stocky women. I looked down: a large leaf had been laid on the ground directly underneath my buttocks. I looked up again. Terror finally overcame me as the women's faces, now dozens, now hundreds, moved in closer all around my near naked body suspended in mid-air. They grabbed my legs and arms apart. The women's screams, the sounds of drums and then a sharp blade cut deep into my flesh on one side and then on the other. As I cried out in unimaginable agony, I felt warm

blood ooze down between my thighs. Perhaps for the first time since I was an infant, I vomited. (293)

Despite her own "agony," Ahmadu, in her culturally detailed and nuanced insider/outsider description of the ritual practice of FGM, shows how the practice can also be, paradoxically, empowering to the women who uphold it. Kono women view their Bundu membership strategically, Ahmadu says: "women claim sole credit for everything from procreation to the creation of culture, society and its institutions" (106), and the most important rite of initiation into this sisterhood is the genital cutting that makes a girl a marriageable woman. Ahmadu ends her essay by arguing for medicalization of the procedure as a way to reduce "the immediate physical pain and risk of infection."[7] She also suggests that a "ritual without cutting model," which "positively values many cultural aspects and beliefs underlying female genital operations and initiation while attempting to eliminate the actual physical cutting," might be "a reasonable middle ground" (108).[8]

Ahmadu's essay opens a window into the intra-cultural debates taking place around the practice of FGM, and allows students to move beyond a simple binary framework of response. Clearly it's important to guard against what Joseph A. Massad has aptly characterized as "a Western nativism armed with Rousseauian zeal intent on forcing people into freedom, indeed one that considers assimilating the world into its own norms as ipso facto liberation and progress and a step toward universalizing a superior notion of the human" (251).[9] Sembène's magnificently *Moolaadé* (2004) demonstrates the complexity of the struggles within communities where traditionalists are pitted against younger women and men who are open to the possibility of change. The fact that this film was made by a man, and a greatly respected African elder at that (Sembène, who died in 2007 at the age of 84, was arguably the most prominent internationally recognized francophone African filmmaker of his generation), models the intergenerational, male/female alliances that must occur to create the necessary momentum for change.

The film is presented largely from the point of view of a mother, Collé, who invokes the ancient tribal custom of giving sanctuary (*moolaadé*) to a group of little girls who decide to run away from the excisor. Collé lost her first two children due to her own botched circumcision, and her third and only child, her daughter Amsatou, survived only because Collé found a midwife who "tore her apart" in order to deliver the baby. Collé has refused to let Amsatou undergo FGM, and in the course of the film she stands up to social pressure and personal violence in her determination to be a bulwark for other girls in her village as well.

Moolaadé especially celebrates the courage of men and women in the transitional generation: Amsatou's fiancé Ibrahima, a chief's son who has been educated in France, who stands up to his powerful father in insisting that he will marry Amsatou even though she has not been cut; Collé's husband Ciré, who finally breaks with his dominating older brother and sides with his wife, saying "it takes more than a pair of balls to make a man"; and Collé herself, who is honoured by the other women as "a warrior, more valiant than men," for refusing to conform to tradition even in the face of fierce pressure, including the lash of a whip. Importantly, Sembène shows us that both men and women need to be engaged in the work of change: it will take both Ciré and Collé, along with Ibrahima and Amsatou, to make the decisions needed to reject a harmful traditional practice.

Moolaadé also clearly demonstrates that change must come from within African societies themselves; it cannot be imposed from outside. The one outsider in Sembene's narrative, a travelling peddler from the city, meets a violent end because he is suspected of challenging local traditions. This is important for students to realize, since they often tend to imagine that quick interventions from outside—say, governments becoming signatories to human rights conventions—could put a stop to FGM once and for all. But as Nicholas Kristof and Sheryl WuDunn observe, "The impulse of Westerners to hold conferences and change laws has, on one issue after another, proved remarkably ineffective" (228). Here we come back to the desire of most students in my classes to contribute to the FGM abolition movement. Above all, students learning about FGM for the first time want to know what they can *do.*

In a college classroom, what we can do, for starters, is engage openly and honestly with the texts we're reading, and with one another. I use response journals to initiate a dialogic encounter in which we are able to interrogate both the texts we're reading and our own reactions to them. Students often work on their response journals collaboratively, posting them online and commenting on one another's ideas, which allows for the discussion of the text to start even before we've entered the classroom. In the response journals, students engage in what Anzaldúa calls the work of the *nepantlera*, taking their ideas public and testing them out in dialogue with others. "*Nepantla*" is a Nahuatl[10] term meaning "the space in-between"; in Anzaldúa's usage, it is a "zone of possibility," a "liminal ... site of transformation, the place where different perspectives come into conflict and where you question basic ideas, tenets, and identities inherited from your family, your education and your different cultures" (548). Though by no means comfortable, *nepantla* is an ideal state for growth, exchange, and dialogue; it is the kind of space I am always trying to create in my classroom, and it begins in a tangible way in the response journal exchanges, along with the many other discussions students have with one another, in the dorms or at home with their families and friends, in which they test out and refine new ideas.

Coming to voice is a critical first step in becoming an effective change agent, and it may be the most important step students can take during their undergraduate years. It's modelled beautifully by the FGM accounts we read in "African Women Writing Resistance," where the testifiers have had to overcome great challenges to find the courage and make the necessary alliances that allow us to hear their stories. As Audre Lorde says in her seminal essay "The Transformation of Silence into Language and Action":

> We have been socialized to respect fear more than our own needs for language ... and while we wait in silence for that final luxury of fearlessness, the weight of that silence will choke us.

> The fact that we are here and that I speak these words is an attempt to break that silence and bridge some of those differences between us, for it is not difference which immobilizes us, but silence. And there are so many silences to be broken. (44)

This lesson often hits home with students as we discuss anti-FGM testimonials that clearly demonstrate the power of speaking out. In her response to Lorde's essay, posted online for other students to read and respond to, one student wrote:

> Like everyone else it seems, I was most moved by this essay. Of course the issue of speaking out is important to me, because for the longest time I had no voice at all. I sometimes think I didn't even have an inner voice. And then suddenly I had a raging voice and it took me a long and painful time to learn how to express that. And I do know that we can learn to speak when we feel fear like when we're hungry, tired or frustrated. It's critical, in fact, that we learn to do this. How will you even find the words to express yourself if you have no voice with which to talk?[11]

In the classroom (as well as online), discussions of charged material like anti-FGM narratives can sometimes become heated. One student may want to raise money for anti-FGM advocacy groups, while another will see this as a kind of old-school charitable benevolence and make the case that Americans should not get involved in the internal politics of other cultures. Another student may remain detached and unmoved by the emotional content of a given narrative, preferring to focus on the intellectual question of how the text was constructed. In the classroom, I see all of these points of view as valid opportunities for exchange and growth. The important thing is to insist that students treat one another with the respect and attention they themselves would like to receive, and that no one voice or opinion dominates the discussion. My role as the facilitator of such a discussion is very much that of the Anzaldúan *nepantlera,* inhabiting the space in between the sometimes conflicting viewpoints of students, and in so doing enacting my own form of *conocimiento,* as the students' viewpoints inform my own, often leading me to see familiar material in a new and different light.

All of my Women Writing Resistance courses include a major research project as the principal assignment, besides the primary readings and response journals. I ask students to start from a question they have about one of our primary texts, or about an issue that is at least tangentially related to a primary text, and to research this issue in depth, presenting their findings in class as well as writing them up as the final paper. To some students, this may not feel sufficiently like action, but it is important to emphasize that informing oneself and one's community is an essential first step in the process of coming to awareness, which can culminate in one's becoming an agent of change. Students often find that my classes are the starting points of much more work around a given issue, which may become the topic of their senior thesis, or the focus of extracurricular activity, such as founding an Amnesty International chapter on campus, creating and distributing a campus publication related to social justice issues, or starting a campaign to pressure the campus food service to provide beverages produced by non-exploiting companies. The form of action is actually less important, at this point in students' lives, than the realization that they have the power to transform their passions and convictions into concrete positive actions.

Besides the examples of the texts and films themselves, we also discuss political advocacy and education as important vehicles for social change. I often point to the Senegal-based NGO Tostan as a model of a successful approach to anti-FGM solidarity by a cultural outsider. Tostan was started by an American woman, Molly Melchin, who had married a Senegalese man and recognized the importance of education in the struggle to eradicate the practice of FGM. Tostan trains local community activists, speaking the local dialects, to go into village communities and open up spaces for dialogue, learning, and reflection. "Hard-line efforts by abolitionists to coerce women to reject the practice and to stigmatize those who uphold their ancestral traditions as 'illiterate,' 'backward,' and against 'women's rights' and 'progress' are unacceptable," Fuambai Ahmadu states unequivocally. Instead, the approach favoured by Tostan—respectfully presenting the facts to people and letting them make up their own minds—is the best way to work toward the gradual shift of the practice of FGM away from harmful cutting. "In the event that I ever have a daughter," Ahmadu says, "I would like her to be well-informed about the socio-cultural and historical significance of the operation as well as its purported medical risks so that she can make up her own mind" (310).

Tostan educates communities and individuals about the dangers of FGM until they are ready and willing to outlaw the practice themselves, offering classes that meet three times a week for two or three hours, over a period of three years. This is no quick fix, but a slow, mind-altering process of community reflection that aims to proceed with what Gayatri Spivak calls "great tact," which is what "is called for if the effort is to draw forth consent rather than obedience" (558). Since 2002, nearly 3,000 Senegalese villages have participated in the Tostan program and voluntarily announced that they would no longer genitally cut their girls.

Advocacy against FGM is taking place not just in small villages in Africa, but also among African immigrant communities in some of the biggest and most cosmopolitan cities of the West. In *Bloodstains: A Child of Africa Reclaims Her Human Rights*, Khady Koïta documents her transition from a happy, bright child growing up in a small Senegalese town, to a genitally mutilated child bride who is married at age 13 to a cousin 20 years her senior and sent to live with him in Paris, to an empowered, trail-blazing activist. Koïta's story is important because unlike Fadumo Korn, she is not the daughter of social elites, nor has she gained wealth and fame on her own, like anti-FGM activists Waris Dirie or Ayaan Hirsi Ali. She is very much an ordinary African woman, dealing with the ordinary pressures that so many African women face: the sudden removal of her clitoris at age seven, with the attendant pain and trauma; marriage as a child to a stranger; the abrupt shift to a life as an immigrant woman in a foreign culture. Koïta's husband proves to be physically and emotionally abusive, and much of her narrative is dedicated to documenting her transition from a cowed, fearful teen mother, crowded into a small apartment with a rapidly growing family (including, eventually, a co-wife) to an independent woman who educates herself, finds work, and gets herself and her children out of the reach of her abusive husband. Koïta finds support from French neighbours, other African women immigrants, and generous French social services and charitable organizations, showing once again that the struggle for empowerment is always enhanced by collaborative allies.

Koïta's story ends on a strong note, as she becomes the president of the European Network for the Eradication and Prevention of Female Genital Mutilation (Euro-Net-FGM). At the end of her testimonial, Koïta eloquently describes her own journey as "an obstinate march that led me from the shadow of the mango tree to the light of international sorority, from an intimate and secret mutilation to the blaze of a public campaign trail" (212).

Testifiers like Koïta, Ahmadu, and Korn invite us to join them on their "obstinate march" toward the full enjoyment of their rights as global citizens. Through testimonial narratives, cultural outsiders can gain insight into the personal dimensions of the human rights violations that are presented at an impersonal remove in the Universal Declaration of Human Rights. Human rights conventions are essential as legislative policy guidelines and ethical prescriptions, but just like abstract feminist theory, they can be too far removed from the reality of people's lived experience. I continue to rely on the power of stories, told with drama and passion by narrators with first-hand experience of FGM, to take us to the painful heart of the issue and force us to confront it in personal terms. I share Elizabeth Ammons's belief that "the tremendous value of the humanities and especially the study of literature resides in the power of texts to teach us about ourselves, individually and corporately, including the systems of injustice that we as human beings create. But the value of the humanities also resides in the power of words to inspire us, to transform us, to give us strength and courage for the difficult task of *re*-creating the world (14). Ammons goes on to argue in favour of an engaged pedagogical practice that is not afraid to reimagine literary study "as a progressive cultural force capable not simply of providing critique but also of offering hope and inspiration in the real-world activist struggle for social justice" (21).

It is my hope that students' encounter with anti-FGM texts in my African Women Writing Resistance classes will inspire them to dig deeply into the work of *conocimiento:* in Anzaldúa's words, to "dedicate yourself, not to surface solutions that benefit only one group, but to a more informed service to humanity" (574). When students understand how much they have to learn from these women's stories, and also how much they have to offer these women, a circle of reciprocity is created, from which we can enact the seventh and final stage of the journey of *conocimiento,* "spiritual activism." Affirming the importance of "mobilizing, organizing, sharing information, knowledge, insights and resources with other groups" (571), spiritual activism encourages the kind of collaborative alliance building that can manifest not only the dream of global sisterhood, but also, perhaps, the ambitious goal of universal human rights.

Notes

1 I am paraphrasing and condensing Anzaldúa's much lengthier description of the seven stages in her essay.

2 Extensive, up-to-date information about the practice of FGM from a women's health perspective can be found at the World Health Organization website: http://www.who.int/topics/female_genital_mutilation/en. Information presented from an anti-FGM advocacy point of view, setting FGM in the context of human rights, can be found at the website of the End FGM European Campaign, affiliated with Amnesty International: http://www.endfgm.eu/en/female-genital-mutilation/what-is-fgm/what-is-fgm.

3 The question often comes up, but how is this different from the widely practised circumcision of infant boys, which is often advocated as beneficial to men's health? FGM is very different from male circumcision. The removal of a boy's foreskin does not negatively impact his sexual pleasure as a man, nor does it affect his ability to urinate. The wound generally heals within a few days, with no lasting repercussions. The situation for girls is quite different. Even aside from the psychological trauma that can result from the severe pain and sense of powerlessness, the immediate and lifelong physical consequences are dramatic: it is not uncommon for girls to die of hemorrhaging or infection after undergoing FGM, and survivors often have ongoing problems with urination and menstruation, pain and bleeding during sexual intercourse, and serious complications in childbirth that can lead to newborn deformity and death. These chronic complications, affecting millions of girls and women annually throughout Africa and the African and Muslim diaspora, have led WHO to take a strong stand against FGM, arguing that the practice has no health benefits for girls and women—quite different from WHO's stance on male circumcision.

4 A good overview of North American, European, and African literary engagement with the topic of FGM is provided in the essay "Excision and African Literature: An Activist Annotated Bibliographical Excursion" by Pierrette Herzberger-Fofana (in *Empathy and Rage,* ed. Levin and Asaah, 142–55), which traces the literary outlines of the abolition movement. Herzberger-Fofana also documents the backlash that has sprung up among traditionalists in African and Muslim communities, who argue that to abandon the practice would be to accede to the cultural imperialism of the West, as well as among African women, who may agree that the practice is harmful but resent Western feminists' sometimes self-righteous interventions and the tendency of the Western media to sensationalize FGM because it deals with women's sexual organs.

5 The World Health Organization provides extensive information and statistics about FGM on its website: see http://www.who.int/topics/female_genital_mutilation/en/.

6 The human rights framework can provide a valuable reference point for students. Article 3 of UDHR states unequivocally that "everyone has the right to life, liberty and security of person." Article 2 of the Convention on the

Elimination of All Forms of Discrimination Against Women (CEDAW) calls on states "to take all appropriate measures, including legislation, to modify or abolish existing laws, regulations, customs and practices which constitute discrimination against women." Article 24(3) of the Convention on the Rights of the Child (CRC) directs states to "take all effective and appropriate measures with a view to establishing traditional practices prejudicial to the health of children." Article 19(1) of the CRC also insists that states "protect the child from all forms of physical or mental violence, injury or abuse." See the Amnesty International website for more information: http://www.amnestyusa.org/our-work/issues/women-s-rights/violence-against-women/violence-against-women-information.

7 WHO takes the position that there is no medical rationale for FGM: "FGM has no health benefits, and it harms girls and women in many ways. It involves removing and damaging healthy and normal female genital tissue, and interferes with the natural functions of girls' and women's bodies ... WHO is particularly concerned about the increasing trend for medically trained personnel to perform FGM. WHO strongly urges health professionals not to perform such procedures" (WHO Female Genital Mutilation Fact Sheet, http://www.who.int/mediacentre/factsheets/fs241/en).

8 The American Academy of Pediatrics has recently suggested that "American doctors be given permission to perform a ceremonial pinprick or 'nick' on girls" whose parents request the procedure, arguing that it might "keep their families from sending them overseas for the full circumcision" (Belluck). Current federal law prohibits "any nonmedical procedure performed on the genitals of a girl in the United States," which some doctors say "has had the unintended consequence of driving some families to take their daughters to other countries to undergo mutilation" (Belluck).

9 One way to undermine the possible "superiority" of the West in regard to initiation rituals is to demystify FGM by contextualizing it as one among many initiation rituals or beautifying practices worldwide that can have harmful physical repercussions. For example, hazing practices by athletic teams, fraternities and sororities, the military, and gangs all involve putting aspirants through painful and humiliating rituals that, once survived, guarantee one's place as a member of the group. FGM's role in making girls into women can also be discussed in terms of international beauty standards for women, which can lead to harmful practices like self-starvation, skin bleaching, or plastic surgery procedures, including, in the West, the ever more popular vaginoplasty. The important difference is that for the most part, participation in these rituals is voluntary, while in most cases of FGM, the practice is forced on little girls who have no agency to resist.

10 Nahuatl is an ancient Meso-American language still spoken by many Indigenous people in central Mexico.

11 Reprinted with permission from a response journal excerpt by sophomore Tiffany Albright (Bard College at Simon's Rock A.A. graduate, 2008), from *Women Writing Activism*, Fall 2007.

Works Cited

Ahmadu, Fuambai. "Rite and Wrongs: An Insider/Outsider Reflects on Power and Excision." In *Female "Circumcision" in Africa: Culture, Controversy, and Change*. Boulder: Lynne Rienner, 2000. 283–312.

Ammons, Elizabeth. *Brave New Words: How Literature Will Save the Planet*. Iowa City: University of Iowa Press, 2010.

Anzaldúa, Gloria. "Now Let Us Shift ... the Path of *Conocimiento* Inner Work, Public Acts." In *This Bridge We Call Home*. Ed. Gloria Anzaldúa and Analouise Keating. New York: Routledge, 2001. 540–78.

Belluck, Pam. "Group Backs Ritual 'Nick' as Female Circumcision Option." *New York Times*, 7 May 2010.

Herzberger-Fofana, Pierrette. "Excision and African Literature: An Activist Annotated Bibliographical Excursion." In *Empathy and Rage*, ed. Levin and Asaah, 142–55.

Koïta, Khady, with Marie-Thérèse Cuny. *Bloodstains: A Child of Africa Reclaims Her Human Rights*. Trans. Tobe Levin. Frankfurt am Main: UnCUT/VOICES Press, 2010.

Korn, Fadumo, and Tobe Levin. *Born in the Big Rains: A Memoir of Somalia and Survival*. New York: Feminist Press, 2004.

Kristof, Nicholas D., and Sheryl WuDunn. *Half the Sky: Turning Oppression into Opportunity for Women Worldwide*. New York: Knopf, 2009.

Levin, Tobe, and Augustine H. Asaah, eds. *Empathy and Rage: Female Genital Mutilation in African Literature*. Oxford: Ayebia Clark, 2009. 1–14.

Lorde, Audre. *Sister Outsider*. Freedom: Crossing Press, 1984.

Massad, Joseph A. "Sexuality, Literature, and Human Rights in Translation." In *Teaching World Literature*. Ed. David Damrosch. New York: Modern Language Association of America, 2009. 246–57.

Moolaadé. Dir. Ousmane Semène. 2004.

Morgan, Robin. *Sisterhood Is Global*. New York: Feminist Press, 1996.

Spivak, Gayatri Chakravorty. "Righting Wrongs." *South Atlantic Quarterly* 103.2–3 (2004): 523–81. http://dx.doi.org/10.1215/00382876-103-2-3-523

Weingarten, Kaethe. *Common Shock: Witnessing Violence Every Day—How We Are Harmed, How We Can Heal*. New York: Dutton, 2003.

Woolf, Virginia. *Three Guineas*. Harcourt, 1966.

CHAPTER FOURTEEN

"I Can't Believe I've Never Seen That Before!": Feminism, the "Sexualization of Culture," and Empowerment in the Classroom

Tracy Penny Light

There is a widespread assumption that simply because my generation of women has the good fortune to live in a world touched by the feminist movement, that means everything we do is magically imbued with its agenda. It doesn't work that way. "Raunchy" and "liberated" are not synonyms. It is worth asking ourselves if this bawdy world of boobs and gams we have resurrected reflects how far we've come, or how far we have left to go.

—Ariel Levy, 5

Ariel Levy's lament in *Female Chauvinist Pigs* was an early commentary on what she and other feminists viewed as a disconnect between the ways young women were performing their femininity in the twenty-first century and the hard-won rights accorded to women as a result of second-wave feminist activism (Levin and Kilbourne; McRobbie). Since then, the ubiquitous use of technology has reinforced these ideas by making more visible and accessible post-feminist ideas that raise questions about the value of feminism in a technologically mediated world. As Kingston notes, this seems to reinforce the notion of an "enlightened sexism ... based on the presumption that women and men are now 'equal' which allows women to embrace formerly retrograde concepts such as 'hypergirliness' and seeing 'being decorative' [as] the highest form of power" (52). My purpose here is not really to take up whether these ideas are good or bad, but rather to explore the ways in which teaching critical media literacy can foster greater questioning of the world and our place in it, as well as the ways it can encourage empowerment in the classroom. Rather than trying to account for, or even ignore, the fact that many of my students believe that feminism is no longer necessary, I aim to destabilize students' post-feminist views of the world by engaging them in an active critique of the culture that surrounds them. When they can "see" what they have not recognized before in the media, they are able to consider ways to reformulate, push back against, or even accept the representations of femininity that constantly surround them.[1] At the end of the day, this process allows students to "chart their own way through their attachments to feminism," which at times may not align with my own (Luhmann, 80). I see this as part of the feminist pedagogical process—indeed, as part of the relationship between teacher and student in the feminist classroom.

For many of my students, feminism is a dirty word that they are vehemently opposed to claiming as part of their own identities, and this idea is often reinforced in the wider culture in which they live (Bobba). They believe they live in a liberated world wherein they can wear what they like and perform their femininity as individuals because they have achieved equality with men. And to some extent, this is true and they can often perform their identities however they choose. But this sense of liberation usually comes without any critical questioning about why they are able to do so, the privilege that is associated with these performances, and the messages that are present in our world that may shape their understanding of it. The classroom is a space where that critical questioning can occur. In this chapter, I focus on my Gender, Sexuality, and History in Film course as an example of the ways in which feminist pedagogy can open up space for students to develop the capacity to critically interrogate media so that they can more easily "see" the messages they are surrounded by and thereby more effectively wrestle with them and make change in the world.

Feminist Pedagogy in the Classroom

In 1992 Linda Briskin and Rebecca Coulter noted that "feminism recognizes education both as a site for *struggle* and as a tool for *change making*" (249). For me, this quote, now more than twenty years old, reflects how I view my own pedagogical goals. I focus my teaching around a desire to empower learners to struggle with course material so that they develop an ability to challenge traditional assumptions, ask critical questions about the world around them, and make connections (transfer their knowledge between and among contexts), particularly with a view to making change by encouraging their development as responsible citizens. The principles of feminist pedagogy outlined in 2002 by Lynne Webb, Myria Allen and Kandi Walker (reformation of the relationship between professor and student, empowerment, building community, privileging voice, respecting the diversity of personal experience, and challenging traditional pedagogical notions) along with the ideas of critical pedagogy developed by Paulo Freire and others (Freire; Giroux; McLaren and Kincheloe), have shaped my overall objectives for teaching. Reflecting Amy Gullage's and Jacqueline Z. Wilson's explorations of power in this book, when I teach my course Gender, Sexuality and History in Film, I aim to problematize and conceptualize issues of power, domination, and liberation in visual culture and to contexualize these historically as I open up space for learners to think through these issues for themselves. The desire to engage learners in discussions about the power of visual culture and the media extends beyond one particular course, however, and has tended to permeate most of my teaching in the recent past.

Feminism in a "Postfeminist Media Culture" Classroom

What does it mean for students today to participate in a feminist classroom, particularly when we are living in what Gill has termed a "postfeminist media culture" (249)? The answer to this question is certainly complex. Today's learners[2] are definitely different—they live in a world that is technologically mediated and, as such, are shaped by the information and images that surround them. A 2010 study by the Kaiser Foundation in the United States, which surveyed eight-to-eighteen-year-olds, found that young people were spending, on average, seven and a half hours each day exploring media content and that they were increasingly multi-tasking while doing so. This was an increase of nearly one hour from five years previously. The same study noted that "the development of mobile media has allowed—indeed, encouraged—young people to find even more opportunities throughout the day for using media, actually expanding the number of hours when they can consume media, often while on the go" (Rideout, Foehr, and Roberts, 2). The numbers are similar for Canadian youth.[3] The Kaiser Foundation study also found that despite the increased ability to access information, anytime, anywhere, the use of all types of media increased except for reading. As a historian, this troubles me: I worry that this lessening practice with text may result in learners becoming less able to comprehend complex ideas in writing. But at the same time, it presents an opportunity for us as educators to explore new ways of teaching/learning that incorporate visual culture more than in the past.

Indeed, rather than lament this shift in the way learners access and use information, I have chosen to harness technology as a means to engage them in new and interesting ways. Instead of discouraging new information technologies in the classroom, I actively encourage their use. This is particularly helpful to me as an instructor, because it assigns students some of the responsibility for gathering examples of the types of imagery we are discussing. Students happily partake in these activities because it allows them to weigh in on classroom discussions as they bring in their examples. Often, learners access similar types of advertisements or films that they have watched. But they often also bring varied and diverse examples, and this provides many opportunities for discussion. This reformulates the relationship between teacher and student by shifting the onus from me, to bring in all of the examples, to the students, who now have the power to do so themselves. At the same time, it presents them with a voice in what they see and discuss. In addition, their examples point to the diversity of students' experiences as students; they find themselves empowered by their own experiences and knowledge of the course topics. While they may not voice their own examples and experiences as "feminist," this approach does open up space for conversations about what feminism is and how it is still meaningful today. As Joan Scott notes, "seeing is the origin of knowing" (776). The acknowledgement of what students see is an important first step in having them tap into their own experiences so that they can begin to understand that their positionality shapes their view of the world.

Why today's students often assume that feminism is irrelevant (McRobbie; Levy) is an important question. This postfeminist thinking is "an active process by which feminist gains of the 1970s and 80s come to be undermined. It proposes that through an array of machinations, elements of contemporary popular culture are perniciously effective in regard to this undoing of feminism, while simultaneously appearing to be engaging in a well-informed and even well-intended response to feminism" (McRobbie, 255). It is perhaps not a bad thing that young women (and men) view the world as an egalitarian place where they will have equal opportunities for employment, consumption, and roles in society. Yet many scholars have decried this shift, viewing it as it a historical move away from earlier waves of feminist activism, as a "backlash" (Faludi) against feminism, or as a way to selectively use feminism to obtain "particular kinds of freedom, empowerment, and choice 'in exchange for' or 'as a kind of substitute for' real feminist politics and transformation" (McRobbie, as quoted in Gill, 63–64). This poses an interesting challenge for those of us teaching who do still see the value of feminism and who want to see our students identify as such.

But as a historian, I also recognize that our students are operating within a particular system—their "social positions are relational" (Gill, 67). In other words, valuing their perspectives as constructions of the world in which they live and as an integral part of the experiences they have had prior to coming to learn with us (Scott) is an essential element in the feminist classroom that can assist them as they move toward developing the skills necessary to ask critical questions of the world.

Pedagogy, the "Sexualization of Culture," and "Seeing"
In seeking to teach students the critical abilities that will allow them to better understand "the multiple positioning that constitutes everyday life and the power relations that are central to it" (Phoenix and Pattynama, as quoted in Gill, 67), we must provide them with opportunities to "see" for themselves "the complex, irreducible, varied and variable effects which ensue when multiple axes of differentiation—economic, political, cultural, psychic, subjective and experiential—intersect in historically specific contexts. The concept emphasizes that different dimensions of social life cannot be separated out into discrete and pure strands" (Brah and Phoenix, as quoted in Gill, 67). Privileging the individual voice as a way of getting at experience and, therefore, as a way of knowing is important for feminist pedagogy and deep learning (Kuh), for it encourages the recognition of authority in self and others and views knowledge as constructed and culture bound. Of course, this is also how most historians view historical thinking or "doing history" (Penny Light 2008).

When multiple authorities are fostered in the classroom, power shifts to students. They can interact and ask questions, their feedback is actively sought and incorporated, and the teacher works to make herself less intimidating and more approachable. In my experience, particularly with issues related to the construction of the body, this type of approach is important in order to capture the multiplicity of views (and biases) that students bring to their understanding of the topic. In my course, we interrogate films and images from the postwar period to the present, paying particular attention to who created them and for what purpose, and querying the messages they send the viewer. Asking questions of visual culture can allow students to identify where preconceived notions come from and "unpack" them as they conduct their own study of the history of the body. The "I've never *seen* that before" experience of most students points to the ways this pedagogy can foster their ability to articulate their own identities around the body. For instance, in exploring the ways that advertisers construct femininity and the body, students consider historical representations of women in advertising (Penny Light 2013), the recent Dove Campaign for Real Beauty, and

Jean Kilbourne's documentary about the portrayal of women in advertising, *Killing Us Softly*. This activity allows them to critically explore how traditional ideals of femininity are reinvented in different eras. On first blush, they view the Dove Campaign as liberating and feminist in nature. However, the act of situating the historical ads among the contemporary ones and then considering the role of consumer capitalism in Dove's attempt to democratize beauty (Persis Murray, 83) leads them to be more critical of the contemporary branding of femininity, rather than simply accepting the idea of liberation being sold in constructions of the body in the media they encounter daily. This is often an unsettling realization, for they want to believe (unsurprisingly) that they are living in a world in which feminism is no longer necessary—indeed, their identities have developed in terms of that assumption. The idea that they have been shaped by a "branding strategy [that] perpetuates an oppressive ideology of 'real beauty' requiring a behaviour ('self-esteem') that underscores neoliberal self-improvement benefitting the corporation [Dove's] power" (Persis Murray, 98) is shocking to most of them.

Providing students with an opportunity to feel angered and to voice their concerns about such advertising as well as their support of it, is an important pedagogical strategy that allows them to share their own perspectives (voice). It also builds community and celebrates the diversity of experiences and perspectives within the classroom. This leads to the realization that it is important to remember that "women's [and men's] complex and multiple identities [are] experienced *in* and *through* the discourses that define feminine [and masculine] gender identity, sexuality, ethnicity, class [and] culture." This means "that an understanding of women [and men] and the concept[s] of femininity [and masculinity] cannot be articulated in universal principles, but must come from women's [and men's] individual voices articulated from specific social and cultural locations" (Luke, "Feminist Pedagogy," 33). Hence, in feminisms generally and in feminist pedagogy specifically, the importance of the "positionality" of voice and the intersectionality of experience is paramount. Rosalind Gill has noted the need to face up to "the complex dynamics *and complicities* at play in the current moment" (67). Nowhere are these complexities more visible than when students are asked to interrogate the sexualization of visual culture across different time periods. This interrogation challenges traditional pedagogical notions that promote knowledge transmission from teacher to student by empowering learners to actively participate in the learning process as they explore the complexities for themselves.

Empowerment: Challenging Traditional Pedagogical Notions

Overall, this course is designed to challenge the ways that students "see" the world. It does so by empowering them to participate actively in the learning process in ways that reflect egalitarian and democratic ideals. Besides providing space for them to interrogate a variety of visual representations of gender and sexuality in historical context, I encourage students to participate in consciousness-raising activities that allow them to develop and extend their own critical thinking around the history of the body in visual culture and to understand where ideas about gender and sexuality, which have become normative, come from. In many ways, this is not dissimilar to Maggie Labinski's desire to open up space for discussions of sex in her classroom (see Labinski, in this book).

A key barrier in traditional pedagogical notions is the idea that the teacher knows all and is able to transmit the "truth" to students. By contrast, critical feminist pedagogy establishes "a norm of inquiring curiosity" (Webb, Allen and Walker, 68) where the professor acts as an intermediary between the student and the topic rather than as the fountainhead of truth. Approaching teaching and learning from a feminist perspective can empower students to find answers for themselves, to explore the context in which knowledge is created and becomes normative, and to challenge those ideas. "By focusing on empowerment, [critical] feminist pedagogy embodies a concept of power as energy, capacity, and potential rather than domination ... Under conceptions of power as capacity, the goal is to increase the power of all actors, not to limit the power of some" (Shrewsbury as quoted in Webb, Allen, and Walker, 69). This view of the learning process is consonant with the "decentering, antihierarchical perspective of feminism" (Woodbridge as quoted in Webb, Allen, and Walker, 69) and helps lay the foundation for educating civically engaged and critically responsible citizens capable of transforming our world. But it is important to remember that even when the teacher desires to empower students "wherein all participants allegedly have equal speaking status and equally valued cultural and linguistic resources with which to make knowledge claims" (Luke 1996, 297), not all students are always empowered, and some may not want to participate at all.

Today's educational culture does not typically require reflective, critical thought on the part of learners; rather, it calls for the demonstration of knowledge (the "right" answers). Given this cultural gap, feminist pedagogues need to brace themselves for challenges from students. Even when those challenges do not exist, we need to "acknowledge that our agency has limits, that we might 'get it wrong' in assuming we know what would be empowering for others, and that no matter what our aims or how we go about 'empowering,' our efforts will be partial and inconsistent" (Gore, 63). It is also important to remember that even when attempting "to transform top-down transmission models of knowledge by reconceptualizing the teacher role," it is important not to give "up authority over and claims to knowledge altogether" (Luke 1996, 297). In other words, teachers need to provide a framework for beginning these discussions, which means that we are in an authority position as we choose which theories/methods to employ.

Opening up dialogue is important, but as we empower student voices in knowledge construction we need to be cognizant that, as Luke points out, multiple voices cannot be articulated in universal principles (290). We need to be careful not to encourage discussion that reflects a "single-con-sciousness"—all students do not share the same experiences of media, for instance. And "rendering differences as equal but situated unifies them into a principle of sameness that contradicts feminism's commitment to differ-ence(s) of identity, location, history, and experience" (290). So, while the teacher needs to guide the learning process, it seems to me that the most effective way to empower students is to be conscious of the markers we put in place to shape the student's understanding. Paying particular attention to the themes identified for discussion (the theoretical and methodological approaches we employ) and how those are shaped by experience provides a space for debate and difference in terms of interpretation. One might ask students, for instance, what they think interesting themes for debate might be. Thus, after viewing *Killing Us Softly,* students identified female cosmetic surgery as an area worth further study. By employing a commit-ment to difference, teacher and student alike can participate in a process where they embrace "the multiplicity and partiality of all knowledge and the ongoing processes of identity formation and renegotiation" (Orner, 84). The caution that Luke makes, one that I agree is significant, is that it is important to provide students with theoretical interpretations which can help explain "processes of identity production ... the discursive nature of experience and ... the politics of its construction." As Joan Scott notes, "experience is... always already an interpretation *and* something that needs to be interpreted" (797).

In order to engage my students in thinking about these issues, I encour-age them to delve "into their own histories and systems of meaning, [and] to learn about the structural and ideological forces that influence and restrict their lives" (Thompson and Gitlin, 126). I want them to *see* with their own eyes how the normative systems around gender and sexuality have been constructed historically (in other words, to understand context), and to be able to articulate why they see things the way that they do, while at the same time recognizing that "class, gender, sexuality, history, language, culture, 'individual experience' and so on, all contribute to what we understand to be our identities—to what we recognize as our voices" (Orner, 85). Beyond (I hope) encouraging them to consider the ways in which feminism can be useful, even in a post-feminist world, rather than seeing it as the *f* word, this use of reflexivity allows students to make connections between their own experiences (see Bondy and Wilson, in this book) and the learning in my classroom. I hope this means they will become more critical consumers, because this method challenges the view that education is a neutral cognitive process and promotes critical and creative approaches to reality so that learners can participate in the transformation of their world (Webb, Allen, and Walker). For me, this should be the goal of *all* education—we ought to prepare students to think critically and become civically engaged and responsible citizens; we ought to empower them to value their own and others' ideas about the world while recognizing how those ideas are culturally and historically specific. This is, of course, a social constructionist approach that explores how gender and sexuality (and, by connection, the body) have been constructed in visual culture and how those constructions shift and change over time. As such, one cannot avoid considering the role of critical theory, particularly post-structuralism, in the curriculum.

Theorists like Carmen Luke and Jennifer Gore have pointed out the challenges with rethinking traditional pedagogies, particularly when using the term "empowerment." Gore notes that critical and feminist discourses can be "dangerous" because their "normalizing tendencies [might allow them to] serve as instruments of domination, despite the intentions of their creators" (54). She problematizes the idea of empowerment, particularly in terms of the role of the teacher as the agent of power. As she notes, claims whereby teachers are called to be agents of change can "attribute extraordinary abilities to the teacher" (57), which it may not be possible to enact depending on the context in which the teacher is acting (for instance, in her location in a patriarchal institution or, as Kingston articulates, in terms of the ability of mothers to be agents of change for their daughters). In some contexts, the teacher may not be/feel empowered to teach particular material (for instance, to highlight homonegativity at a Catholic institution, or to discuss feminism with her daughter, who says "oh mom, it's not like that anymore"). In such cases, it does not really matter whether the lack of empowerment is real or perceived, since in either case it constrains the kinds of pedagogical approaches that can be implemented. These are important ideas; however, I am pointing to the issue of empowerment not as a problem per se, but rather to highlight how I have developed activities around a few of the principles of feminist pedagogy that I am discussing and how I have tried to address some of the concerns that Gore and others explore in their work. The idea of empowerment itself is a challenge to traditional pedagogical approaches and allows learners to explore their own voice and subjectivity in my course to build respect for diversity. While there are some challenges inherent in this type of teaching methodology, employing a critical feminist pedagogy allows both teacher and students an opportunity to participate in a process whereby change is possible.

Respecting the Diversity of Personal Experience
For change making to be possible there is a need to consciously and cautiously respect the diversity of individual students in our classrooms. As Kingston points out, society today is shaped by an ethos of individualism, and scholars lament the erosion of community participation in civic, professional, and volunteer associations. Allowing students to buy into the culture of individualism—the pervasive sense that "it's all about me"—creates a natural barrier to change making, which we need to expose in our classrooms. It is paradoxical to me that, at a time when students are more connected to the outside world than ever through Facebook, YouTube, and other social networking sites, they are able to be so in a way that seems more isolating than in the past. At their computers, they often develop ideas about themselves and others away from those who may hold different ideas about the world (teachers, politicians, social activists, mothers, etc.). "There's less public space to come together to discuss these things so it's much easier for them to keep [ideas about themselves and their place in the world] to themselves" (Kingston, 53). We need to create spaces, then, to facilitate dialogue and to model the kind of critical thinking and analysis that we'd like to see our students employ when they view the world (as seen in films and images in this course) around them. Again, here, the issue of authority in the classroom is important. bell hooks suggests that teachers must assert their authority against the myth of the egalitarian classroom. Instead of a pedagogy that promises a mythic safe space for "equal talk among equals," hooks suggests a "confrontational" pedagogy, one that can dislodge students' monochromatic world views, which are often racist, sexist, and homophobic (Luke; hooks). Going back to the concerns about the need to transform the educational culture that I mentioned earlier, this points to the need for learning spaces where we pay attention to the multiplicity of experiences and bring those to the surface of discussions of gender, sexuality, and the body. But in working to transform education, we need to be careful not to treat our students as "other." We need to address the ways that social, cultural, and economic differences define students' identities and lives inside *and* outside the classroom while at the same time ensuring that we do not abandon the political and moral responsibility and

authority we have as teachers to work on students' consciousness through critique and analysis (Luke, 291–92).

Conclusion

Feminism is still fundamentally about transformation and enlightenment; therefore, feminist educators still attempt in their teaching to give students access to "better," more inclusive, socially just, and non-exploitative knowledge. But in doing so, feminists like all educators resort to criteria of moral, ethical, and political worth to make value judgments in their teaching: from arbitrating student commentary to evaluating their work, to selecting course readings and classroom materials, to teaching aspects of feminist knowledge as "better" than patriarchal knowledge. We also make theoretical and political value distinctions among feminist theories (Luke, 296). While there are some challenges associated with the kind of critical feminist pedagogy discussed here, such as how we understand empowerment, whose voices are privileged in the classroom, and the normative functions that privilege can serve, as well as the need to avoid seeing our students as "other," I think this approach does provide us with opportunities to facilitate dialogue around the kind of critical thinking we want to foster in our students. At the same time, it is important to remember the gendered politics of speech and silence that exist in the university classroom, for these are central theoretical, political, and practical concerns for feminist educators—*who* articulates what they see and *who* does not says a lot about privilege and power. Here (and traditionally) we have been concerned with the feminine in patriarchal systems of education. Yet I would argue that it is important to consider men and masculinity as well within these discussions. Even though masculinity has traditionally been privileged in terms of experience, silencing these experiences neglects to address the ways that the experience of masculinity may also be disabling. Paying close attention to whom, in the broadest sense, we are educating is critical, because *all* of our students are our hope for change making in the future.

Notes

Thanks to Claire Van Nierop, who so vehemently brought the issue of seeing to my attention.

1 This essay discusses representations of femininity explicitly, although in the classroom, we consider the implications of the sexualization of culture for both women and men.
2 I am referring here to learners who are traditionally aged and who have come to university from high school (or shortly thereafter). While some classrooms

may include non-traditional university learners, my classes have tended to represent that demographic. This is not to suggest that such strategies would not work with different learner demographics, as increasingly, I believe older learners are similarly impacted by the ubiquitous use of technology in society.

3 Young Canadians in a Wired World, Phase III: Talking to Youth and Parents about Life Online. http://mediasmarts.ca/sites/default/files/pdfs/publication-report/summary/YCWWIII-youth-parents-summary.pdf

Works Cited

Bobba, Anuhya. "'Women Against Feminism' Generates Backlash among Students," *USA Today*, 18 July 2014. http://college.usatoday.com/2014/07/18/women-against-feminism-generates-backlash-among-students/

Brah, Avtar, and Ann B. Phoenix. "Ain't I a Woman? Revisiting Intersectionality." *Journal of International Women's Studies* 5.3 (2004): 75–86.

Briskin, Linda, and Rebecca Priegert Coulter. "Feminist Pedagogy: Challenging the Normative." *Canadian Journal of Education* 17.3 (1992): 247–63. http://dx.doi.org/10.2307/1495295

Faludi, Susan. *Backlash: The Undeclared War Against American Women*. New York: Three Rivers Press, 1991.

Freire, Paulo. *Pedagogy of the Oppressed*. New York: Bloomsbury Academic, 2000.

Gill, Rosalind. "Sexism Reloaded, or, It's Time to Get Angry Again!" *Feminist Media Studies* 11.1 (2011): 63–64. http://dx.doi.org/10.1080/14680777.2011.537029

Giroux, Henry A. *On Critical Pedagogy*. New York: Bloomsbury Academic, 2011.

Gore, Jennifer. "What We Can Do for You! What *Can* 'We' Do for 'You'?: Struggling over Empowerment in Critical and Feminist Pedagogy." *Feminisms and Critical Pedagogy*. Ed. Carmen Luke and Jennifer Gore. New York: Routledge, 1992. 54–73.

hooks, bell, *Thinking Back: Thinking Feminist Thinking Black*. Boston: South End Press, 1989.

Kingston, Anne. "Outraged Moms, Trashy Daughters." *Maclean's*, 10 August 2010. http://www.macleans.ca/culture/outraged-moms-trashy-daughters

Kuh, George D. *High-Impact Educational Practices: What They Are, Who Has Access to Them, and Why They Matter*. Washington: Association of American Colleges and Universities, 2008.

Levin, Diane E., and Jean Kilbourne. *So Sexy So Soon: The New Sexualized Childhood and What Parents Can Do to Protect Their Kids*. New York: Ballantine Books, 2008.

Levy, Ariel. *Female Chauvinist Pigs: Women and the Rise of Raunch Culture*. New York: Free Press, 2005.

Luhmann, Susanne. "Pedagogy." *Rethinking Women's and Gender Studies*. Ed. Catherine M. Orr and Ann Braithwaite. New York: Routledge, 65–82.

Luke, Carmen. "Feminist Pedagogy and Critical Media Literacy." *Journal of Communication Inquiry* 18.2 (Summer 1994): 30–47.

———. "Feminist Pedagogy Theory: Reflections on Power and Authority." *Educational Theory* 46.3 (1996): 283–302. http://dx.doi.org/10.1111/j.1741-5446.1996.00283.x

McLaren, Peter, and Joe L. Kincheloe. *Critical Pedagogy: Where Are We Now?* New York: Peter Lang, 2007.

McRobbie, Angela. "Post-Feminism and Popular Culture." *Feminist Media Studies* 4.3 (2004): 255–64. http://dx.doi.org/10.1080/1468077042000309937

———. *The Aftermath of Feminism: Gender, Culture, and Social Change.* London: Sage, 2009.

Orner, Mimi. "Interrupting the Calls for Student Voice in 'Liberatory' Education: A Feminist Poststructuralist Perspective." In *Feminisms and Critical Pedagogy.* Carmen Luke and Jennifer Gore. New York: Routledge, 1992. 74–89.

Penny Light, Tracy. "Making Connections: Developing Students' Historical Thinking with Electronic Portfolios." *Academic Intersections* 2 (Spring 2008).

———. "Consumer Culture and the Medicalization of Gender Roles in Interwar Canada." In *Consuming Modernity: Gendered Behaviour and Consumerism before the Baby Boom.* Ed. Cheryl Warlh and Dan Malleck. Vancouver: UBC Press, 2013. 34–54.

Persis Murray, Dara. "Branding 'Real' Social Change in Dove's Campaign for Real Beauty." *Feminist Media Studies* 13.1 (2013): 83–101. http://dx.doi.org/10.1080/14680777.2011.647963

Phoenix, Ann, and Pamela Pattynama. "Intersectionality." *European Journal of Women's Studies* 13.3 (2006): 187–192. http://dx.doi.org/10.1177/1350506806065751

Rideout, V., U.G. Foehr, D.F. Roberts, et al. *Generation M²: Media in the Lives of 8–18 Year Olds.* Kaiser Family Foundation, January 2010, 2. http://www.kff.org/entmedia/upload/8010.pdf

Scott, Joan. "The Evidence of Experience." *Critical Inquiry* 17.4 (1991): 773–97. http://dx.doi.org/10.1086/448612

Thompson, Audrey, and Andrew Gitlin. "Creating Spaces for Reconstructing Knowledge in Feminist Pedagogy." *Educational Theory* 45.2 (1995): 125–150. http://dx.doi.org/10.1111/j.1741-5446.1995.00125.x

Webb, Lynne M., Myria W. Allen, and Kandi L. Walker. "Feminist Pedagogy: Identifying Basic Principles." *Academic Exchange Quarterly* (Spring 2002): 67–72. http://findarticles.com/p/articles/mi_hb3325/is_1_6/ai_n28914616/?tag=content;col1

CHAPTER FIFTEEN

Jane Sexes It Up ... on Campus? Towards a Pedagogical Practice of Sex

Maggie Labinski

In *Jane Sexes It Up: True Confessions of Feminist Desire,* Merri Lisa Johnson suggests that "the world polices women—even now in this so-called post-feminist era—into silence about sex" (1). More specifically, Johnson argues that feminists have been policed into silence about the positive aspects of sex, about "what we—as women, as feminists—like about sex" (7). The premise of the present chapter is that such statements ring equally, if not especially, true for feminist pedagogues. The "Janes" of the feminist classroom have been allowed to speak around sex—for example, of the erotic and of human sexuality. Similarly, the "Janes" of the feminist classroom have been allowed to speak about the negative manifestations of sex—for example, of sexual harassment and sexism. However, we are policed into silence about sex itself. More pointedly, feminist pedagogues are policed into silence about what we might like about sex.

My goal in what follows is to explore the possibility of a feminist peda-gogical practice that allows sex—allows "intimate erotic activity"—to play a positive role in the classroom (Jackson and Scott, 2). To this end, I will first (1) summarize some of the major trends within feminist scholarship about the role of sex in education. I will argue (2) that most of these studies have not fully addressed the pedagogical benefits of sex. Without denying the need for feminists to continue to explore the oppressive and marginal-izing aspects of sexual activity, I will suggest that there are alternative sexual constructs at work within contemporary collegiate education that might support feminist pedagogy. More specifically, I will describe three sexual irruptions in my own classroom that have challenged me to reconsider some of the most basic principles of my feminist practice—namely, (3) authority, (4) the translation of thought into action, (5) and empowerment. As such, most generally, in what follows I will argue that one of the things I like about sex is its ability to raise questions about how I "do" feminist pedagogy.

I will conclude (6) by calling attention to the dangers of reducing any feminist account about sex to the binary terms of positive or negative, pro- or anti-, "yes" or "no." The reality of sex stands somewhere between the ideal and the deplorable. My hope in giving voice to one of the pedagogical benefits of sex is not to replace a discourse limited to the negative with one equally limited to the positive. On the contrary, my hope is to contribute to a space wherein feminist pedagogues might be encouraged to stand between.

Feminist Pedagogy and Sex
There are two general trends that have tended to characterize feminist scholarship about the role of sex in collegiate education. First, many of these studies have focused on the extent and effects of fundamentally oppressive sex—for example, sexism and sexual harassment (Paludi; Dziech and Weiner). These accounts have paid special attention to the ways in which women and those who identify within the LGBTQI community have been particularly victimized. Most notably, the landmark report by Roberta Hall and Bernice Sandler was one of the first to examine the connection between sexual objectification and the experience of the classroom as a hostile environment.

Second, feminists have also focused on separating the pedagogical possibilities of the "erotic" from the dangers of sex (Jones; McWilliam; Bartlett; Pryer). The premise of these studies is that the erotic itself (e.g., erotic desire) is a valuable pedagogical tool—that is, a "power" uniquely capable of motivating teachers and students alike (Lorde). As Jyl Felman explains, "there is fuel here to be used and accelerated in epistemological pursuit if only we can stop being in denial or so afraid of the power of the erotic to propel us forward into unknown galaxies" (110). So understood, scholars took to developing alternative conceptions of the erotic that might unhinge it from sex and, by extension, inspire the process of education. As bell hooks concludes, "to understand the place of *eros* and eroticism in the classroom, we must move beyond thinking of those forces solely in terms of the sexual" (194–95).

Limits

Without denying the important differences in this body of scholarship, one similarity is clear: feminist pedagogues have not been especially positive about the role of sex in collegiate education. Rather, most of these studies have denounced sex, either in the hope of eradicating sexual abuse or in the hope of transitioning toward a non-sexual version of the erotic. Two important assumptions appear to underlie this conclusion.

First, both scholarly trends have tended to assume that the (by and large) Western world has been and remains a sexually dangerous place (MacKinnon; Dworkin; Buchwald, Fletcher, and Roth). In light of this emphasis, and given the social/political orientation of feminist pedagogy, it is hardly surprising that scholars have been so cautious in their conclusions. When sexual culture appears to be nearly equivalent with rape culture, it is uncertain whether feminist pedagogues can, in good faith, speak positively about sex. In fact, it is uncertain whether feminist pedagogues *should*.[1]

By extension, and secondly, the kind of sexual activity of interest in these studies would seem to be of an especially (if not essentially) dangerous variety—namely, sex between teachers and students. Even those feminist pedagogues who have managed to creatively interpret their own experiences of sex in the classroom do so by reinforcing the notion that there is only one sexual construct on the table. For example, Jyl Felman describes "hugging" her students (123–24). bell hooks speaks of "dancing" with hers (197–98). Angela Trethewey discloses a past "relationship" with her professor (34). Sharon Todd hints of "the breaking of the sexual taboo" with hers (7). Jane Gallop's examples swing both ways, but she remains best known for a "sensational kiss" (1997, 88–92).

However, there are indications that both of these assumptions are limited. To begin, it is not evident that the sexually violent reality of the world implies that *all* sex is dangerous. More pressingly, it is not evident that *all* feminists would argue as such. Instead, feminist scholarship broadly construed is home to a range of perspectives. For example, many who self-identify as "pro-sex" or "sex-positive" have offered compelling arguments in support of the liberating—rather than marginalizing—potential of sex (Vance; Willis; Califia; Johnson). Some have even gone so far as to argue that it is precisely the widespread denial of the positive aspects of sex that feminists must face today. For example, Carole Vance suggests that "to speak only of sexual violence and oppression ignores women's experience with sexual agency and choice and unwittingly increases the sexual terror and despair in which women live" (1).

Furthermore, it is not evident that the only sexual construct that might exist in the context of collegiate education is that between teachers and

students. College campuses are home to multiple sexual constructions—
constructions that, intentionally or not, often make their way into the
classroom. Most notably, there is the sex occurring between students themselves—sex that not only arises within the broader educative setting of the
campus but also occasionally springs from relationships begun in the particularly educative setting of the classroom. More importantly, while this
sex is no doubt privy to its own problematic power dynamics, it is hardly
of the essentially dangerous variety—that is, it is hardly prone to the same
concerns raised by sex between teachers and students.

Therefore, in light of the sexual opportunities opened by "sex-positive"
feminist theory and the existence of such an alternative sexual construct, I
would like to argue that the feminist analysis of sex and education is incomplete. At the very least, these theoretical and practical considerations allow
for the possibility that sex might support rather than thwart the practice of
feminist pedagogy. This possibility would be rooted in a different kind of
feminist assumption—one that claims "we haven't heard enough about sex
rather than too much" (Hollibaugh, 229). Likewise, this possibility would
assume a change in focus—one away from the primacy of the teacher and
toward the students themselves.

But how? How might one attempt the second half of the conversation—
attempt to offer a positive feminist analysis of sex? As Anna Gotlib has suggested in this volume, the tradition of feminisms has long been suspicious
of the totalizing nature of "arguments." Rhetorical forms like description,
narration, and confession tend to be less essentialistic and more reflective
of the diversity and plurality of human experience. This resonates with me.
Especially given the privileged status of my own sexual identity—as both
a "sexual" and a "heterosexual"—I am wary of appearing to offer any universal claims about the benefits of sex in feminist education. Therefore, in
what follows I will avoid the temptation to argue as Merri Lisa Johnson
might have me do—that is, to argue for what *we*, as feminist pedagogues,
might like about sex. Instead, I will simply describe how sex has served my
own practice of feminist pedagogy. More specifically, I will share how sex
raised questions about three aspects of my teaching: the construction of
authority, the translation of thought into social/political action, and the
relationship between empowerment and dialogue. In returning to these
experiences, I do not wish to claim that these are the only ways in which
sex might surface in the feminist classroom. Nor do I wish to claim that
the educative aspects they have brought into relief are the only aspects of
import to feminist pedagogues. My hope is simply to "confess" that, by calling my pedagogy into question, sex not only contributed positively to my
teaching.[2] My hope is to confess that I—if not I alone—liked it.

Authority

One issue that has been of special interest to feminist pedagogues is the structure and navigation of classroom authority. In particular, many studies have argued that "male" or "masculine" models of authority are a roadblock to transformative student learning (Friedman; Gabriel and Smithson; Woodbridge; Shrewsbury). More specifically, those who have understood the goal of feminist education to be the fostering of student agency have suggested that traditional forms of authority—the "dominance" of the professor—are incompatible with the feminist classroom (Caughie and Pearce). To this end, scholars embarked on the task of locating alternative models. For as Frances Maher and Mary Kay Thompson Tetreault suggest, "to uncover diverse sources of authority for learning is to indicate what classrooms transformed by feminism might look like" (130).

The diverse sources exposed in these studies vary. They include appeals to the "feminine" and to "feminism/s" (Grumet; Gallop 1995; Ropers-Huilman; Bauer). However, a common thread running through many feminist reconstructions of authority is an emphasis on the value of extending authority to students. As Shirley Parry explains, "the goal is to give students the means to gain power and control over knowledge and, as a consequence, to have authority in the classroom" (46). This is not to deny the authority of the teacher (Santoro, 313–14). It is, however, to acknowledge the benefits of student agency—the importance of cultivating a space within which students might transform themselves. It is to acknowledge, for example, that the kind of authority that is often most useful for feminist pedagogues is best understood as "authority with" rather than "authority over" (Culley, 214–15).

At first glance, the inclusion of sex in a feminist pedagogical practice would seem antithetical to this discourse. For example, sex between a "grader" and a "graded" has been widely understood as a misuse of authority. The same misuse can be seen in cases of sexual harassment. As the authors of *The Lecherous Professor* suggest, students "who are sexually harassed recognize that the professor's role and authority are major reasons for their own victimization" (Dziech and Weiner, 16). However, as suggested above, these cases are not the only sexual constructs that may exist in the classroom. There is also the sex that students have which each other.

It is not rare for the students who take my courses to enter into sexual relationships. Nor is it rare for them to perform these relationships in front of the class. Conversations with my colleagues suggest that I am not alone in this experience. Many of us have seen students enter class holding hands or kiss before leaving. Many of us have witnessed the shared knowing glances and flirtatious dialogue. To be clear, in my own case these sexual performances are not something that I require in my courses. My syllabi do not demand that students extend their sexual activities into the space of the classroom.

But I *have* found on several occasions that my students' sexual performances raised serious questions about my practice of pedagogical authority—my practice of "authority with." Most generally, these performances often modelled a vivid account of "collaborative" student learning—of what it might look like for students to enter into the process of education "with" each other (rather than "under" me). More specifically, they modelled a kind of collaborative learning that not only included sex but included it in a way that did not appear dangerous or oppressive. On the contrary, these sexual relationships appeared to excite the students and benefit their work. For example, many were more engaged in our class discussions—playing off of the sparks that were flying between them. These students tended to enter class with a newfound enthusiasm. It was as if, to return to Felman's language, a new "fuel" had been discovered and was "accelerating" each of them—"propelling" them forward (110).

However, these pedagogical benefits—the benefits of this sex—also modelled a kind of learning that had nothing to do with me. What I first noticed about these sexual performances was my own annoyance that my students were doing "my" job better that I was. Put simply, my students were "fuelling" one another—"accelerating" their passion for our course—in ways that far surpassed what I was capable of. These sexual performances did not originate with me as "the teacher." They also forbade me any form of entry. Instead, my students were modelling to one another an exciting kind of learning "with" that I (precisely as the teacher) could not be invited into. I could not similarly engage in such a student/student relationship. I could not entice the (other) student in such a way.

As a result, these sexual performances challenged me to confront the limits of my own practice of "authority with" my students. In particular, this sex forced me to acknowledge that I was less than open to my students engaging "with" one another in ways that reinterpreted my role—my position of authority—in their educations. The annoying sensation I felt when faced with these performances was not due to any learning gap—these students were doing exceptionally well! Rather, my annoyance was due to the realization that my students' success was not *because of* but *despite* my presence in the classroom. In other words, by opening this new, sexually powerful—and powerfully sexual—option, the students were initiating a new educative possibility. These relationships not only diversified what it meant to learn within our classroom and whom it meant to learn "with."

Because they were offered and received by the students, these performances stood as an act of "claiming" the classroom space as their own (Rich; Bauer).

It is by raising questions about the kind of authority at work in my classroom that sex contributed to my pedagogical practice. Of course, this sex did not totally resolve my ongoing struggle to have "authority with" my students. However, it did reveal that *my* authority ("with" or otherwise) is not always the point. In particular, my students taught me that their sexual relationships carried pedagogical benefits—benefits that stood distinct from those I might share "with" them. By bringing sex into the classroom, my students taught me that. And, I confess, I liked it.

The Translation of Thought into Action

A second issue that has been of lasting interest to feminist pedagogues is the relationship between theory and action. As Gail Cohee and colleagues explain, feminist pedagogy is "oriented toward social transformation, consciousness-raising, and social activism, that is, the translation of thought into action" (3). This comportment toward action is perhaps the strongest evidence of the connection between feminist pedagogy and the feminist movement/s. While grounded in the classroom, feminist pedagogues remain committed to effecting social/political change in the world.

However, the actualization of this commitment has proven itself to be easier said than done. For example, it is unclear how feminist pedagogues might change even the immediate world of the traditional university— that is, the practices and curricula of traditional education (Schuster and Van Dyne; Dever; Rinehart; Crabtree and Sapp). Even less obvious is how feminist pedagogues might push the theories of the classroom beyond the boundaries of the college campus in order to "let feminist knowledge serve the city" (Gilbert, Holdt, and Christophersen, 320). As a result, scholars have stressed the importance of locating concrete strategies for extending theory into social/political action. For as Suzanna Rose hints, "a raised consciousness does not automatically lead to rabble-rousing" (171).

One way in which feminist pedagogues have attempted to make this commitment more "automatic" is by incorporating activist-based assignments within their course curricula. These alternatives call into question the conservative norms of collegiate assessment; they also direct teachers and students more explicitly toward the community writ large. The summary of and contribution to this scholarship made by Linda Briskin in this book is much more extensive than anything I can offer here. I will simply nod to the ways in which, for example, Community-Based Learning approaches have helped feminists close the gap between "knowing" and "doing" (Gilbert, Holdt, and Christophersen; Rose). These approaches imply alternative assumptions about what constitutes the goal of education. It is a set of assumptions, as Joy James argues, "that only when we act upon the material studied can we say that we know it" (77).

The inclusion of sex in a feminist pedagogical practice would appear to be contrary to this emphasis on social/political action. For one thing, it is not obvious that sex (or sexual desire) encourages much activity at all. As Teresa Ebert suggests, the temptation to linger with one's desires is often all too strong (806). Furthermore, even if sex does prompt action, it is not clear that it can, itself, be construed as anything other than socially/politically dangerous within the classroom. For example, it is often politically dangerous for students to turn down the sexual advances of faculty who might destroy their professional careers. Likewise, it is often politically dangerous for students to have sex with those same faculty and earn a reputation for "sleeping their way to the top." As a result, and following the logic of Larry May, instead of a political activity, sex between teachers and students would seem to be little more than a "coercive choice."

I would like to share one alternative to the contrary—one example where sex helped rather than hindered my students' ability to translate theory into action. It is an example that called into question the extent of my pedagogical commitment to feminist activism. And, it is an example focused exclusively on the sexual lives of my students. Like many of those who teach courses on sex and sexuality, it is not rare for my students to disclose changes in the kinds of sexual decisions they are making in their lives. Students will often intimate in free-writing exercises and class discussions that they are choosing to engage in different sexual actions and choosing to engage sexually with different people. Such disclosure is not something I explicitly require in my courses. I do not demand that students share the particulars of their sexual activities. If anything, I am constantly amazed by (and impressed with) my students' openness in this regard—for example, by their willingness to present their experiences with short- and long-term sexual relationships, masturbation, pornography, etc.

And I have found that many students are willing to go one step further. In particular, many have articulated the changes in their respective sex lives precisely in terms of the theories discussed in our class. In fact, part of what makes these disclosures distinct is how rarely it happens that the revelation is unrelated to our class discussion—to the "thought" at hand. By and large, my students tend to speak about their sexual actions as translations of our course content—for example, content about the limits of heteronormativity, the status of "sex work," or the relationship between power and pleasure.

To be clear, these translations did not just include sex. Rather, they included sex in a way that did not appear limiting or politically "coercive" to the students. In particular, the purpose of most of these disclosures seemed to be to suggest that these new sexual actions were more in keeping with the students' ongoing understandings of their own identities and the work of those identities within their social/political communities.

In the beginning, I found these translations—found this sex—to be quite embarrassing. I was embarrassed, not because my students were sharing the details of their sex lives. Rather, I was embarrassed about how these translations highlighted a (now obvious) gap in my activism-based assignments. For this sex represented a social/political action distinct from those I usually encourage my students to participate in—that is, distinct from the "traditional" forms of social/political activism that I *do* require in my courses. In fact, I was not even all that aware of the force of the disclosures themselves until my students began (with increasing regularity) to ask me if such translations would "count"—that is, count for our assignment/s.

As a teacher of feminist philosophy, I regularly challenge my students to theorize about sex. Furthermore, as a teacher within feminist pedagogy, I regularly demand the practice of theory—the translation of thought into action. However, when it came to "thoughts" about sex, I had in no way connected the dots—the relationship was in no way "automatic." On the contrary, I was genuinely surprised to hear my students reflect a sentiment that suddenly sounded so foreign— that "only when we act upon the material studied can we say that we know it" (James, 77). By extension, this sex demanded that I confront the limits of my commitment to my feminist framework. More specifically, by opening this new sexual option, my students challenged me to question whether I considered their sexual actions to be a "sufficient" form of feminist activism. Perhaps even more importantly, this sex demanded that I confront a suspicion I had not known I carried—a suspicion about my students' ability to decide for themselves what kinds of social actions were authentic or worthwhile ends for their own educations.[3]

I must admit that I have yet to add "sex" to the list of activism options on my course assignments. I do not yet have the courage—or tenure. However, the questions my students' sexual lives have raised have highlighted the implicit—and highly problematic—message of the alternative. It is a message that infers that certain theories are untranslatable or undesirable for translation into action in the context of the feminist classroom. It is a message that suggests that sexual agency no longer falls under the list of social/political goals of the feminist movement/s. By bringing sex into the classroom, my students taught me that. And, I confess, I liked it.

Empowerment

Finally, as Robbin Crabtree and colleagues suggest, feminist pedagogy is "predicated on ideas about empowering individuals" (4). This emphasis reflects the ongoing conversation between feminist pedagogues and other "liberatory" models of education—most notably, those inspired by Paulo Freire. It is not only because so many are disempowered—individually and systemically—that feminist pedagogues have focused on empowerment. It is also because many feminists assume that empowerment is a necessary condition for education to occur. As Carolyn Shrewsbury explains, "to be empowered is to be able to engage in significant learning" (168).

However, the goal of empowerment has proven itself to be as much a source of contention as an obvious ideal. In the context of critical feminism, scholars have been especially vocal about the formal limits of many of the constructions of "empowerment" pedagogy (Weiler; Giroux; Gore 1992; Gore 1993). Most notably, many have argued that the notion of empowerment tends to idealize the role of the teacher. As Jennifer Gore suggests, "strong senses of human agency and optimism pervade claims about the teacher as empower-er in ways which portray the teacher's role as crucial and sometimes even as omnipotent" (1992, 57). For example, Mimi Orner argues that this false "optimism" can be seen in common empowerment strategies such as the call for students to find their voice (75). More pointedly, Orner explains that when "the only call is for student voice ... critical and feminist teachers, we are to assume, have already found and articulated theirs" (87).

One way in which feminist pedagogues have responded to these concerns is by exploring the importance and difficulty of educational dialogue—that is, the empowerment possible in the mutual exchange of teacher and student voices. As Freire explains, teachers cannot "merely co-exist with [their] students. Solidarity requires true communication" (58). Many have worked to recognize the terms of such authentic communication—such "true" dialogue. These are terms, as Elizabeth Ellsworth suggests, that must grapple with the imperfections of human speech and the inevitable partiality of human speakers (115). Furthermore, these are terms that must acknowledge the potential benefits of alternative voices—for example, anger and silence (Culley; Lewis).

Here, too, the inclusion of sex within the classroom would appear to be antithetical to the practice of such empowered dialogue. It is not clear, for example, whether any transparent communication can occur between teachers and students who are having sex. It is not evident whether a student might be able to discern if and when her teacher is speaking *as* a teacher and when s/he is speaking as a sexual peer. As Deirdre Golash explains:

"There is always the issue of what role the words are being spoken in. The power relationship often requires the polite pretense that one considers the less powerful person one's equal ... the peer relationship presupposes a degree of frankness" (451). Insofar as "true" communication would seem nearly impossible in this context, it also seems impossible that such sex might be empowering.

I would like to suggest one example to the contrary. But at this point it seems necessary to risk the dangers of reintroducing the teacher. One of my primary goals, thus far, has been to problematize the assumption that the only kind of sex that can arise within collegiate education—the only kind of sex that can be of interest to feminist pedagogues—is sex between teachers and students. Most generally, this is because the sex that has been the most beneficial to my own practice of feminist pedagogy has had nothing to do with teachers—nothing to do with me—and everything to do with the sexual activities of my students. However, in the interest of full disclosure, I will say that this is also because I believe that feminists have been correct in their conclusions—that is, they have been right to suggest that sex between teachers and students is (at least by and large) of the essentially dangerous variety. But let us assume, for a moment, that even this kind of sex is more complicated than essentialism would suggest. Let us assume, for a moment, that this kind of sex—although risky—could be pedagogically beneficial. What might it look like? What would it *have* to look like? What form would this sex have to take so as to allow for "true" dialogue and, by extension, empower teachers and their students?

It would seem that one option can be found in the work of Audre Lorde. In her foundational study "Uses of the Erotic," Lorde argues for the importance of a particular kind of "empowering" dialogue—that is, erotic dialogue, the sharing of one's erotic experiences with others in community. More specifically, Lorde suggests that this sharing of the erotic—this "looking" at the erotic together—is what differentiates erotic dialogue from erotic abuse. For as she explains, "when we look the other way from our experience, erotic or otherwise, we use rather than share the feelings of those others who participate in the experience with us" (58). Thus, to refuse to look away from the erotic is, according to Lorde, to refuse to abuse the other. It is the transformation of the erotic into ethics.

Following Lorde (albeit into a place I am not sure she would want to go) I would like to propose something similar regarding forms of sexual activity between teachers and students that might also avoid abuse. More specifically, I wonder about the potential benefits of feminist teachers and students engaging in a particular kind of sexual act, a particular kind of sexual dialogue—the act of "looking" at sex together. Are there possibilities hidden within what we might call acts of pedagogical voyeurism? By this I do not mean to suggest that teachers and students should look at the pornographic per se. However, I do wonder about the repercussions—the potentially "abusive" risks—of not looking, of refusing to dialogue.

If we choose to attempt—if we *should* attempt—to be voyeurs with our students, Lorde's insights offer two characteristics that we might strive toward. First, to look at sex with our students would demand that we look honestly (Seymour). Such honesty will likely take a variety of forms. It might, for example, begin with an honest look at human sexuality—a discourse in which feminist pedagogues have been more willing to engage. Such honesty might also include an honest look at sexism and sexual harassment—a conversation for which feminist pedagogues have laid a solid foundation. But such honesty would also require an honest look at the positive aspects of sex—that is, an honest look at the ways in which sex might empower rather than disempower both our students and ourselves.

Second, to be voyeurs with our students would demand that we acknowledge the reality of their lives. It would, in other words, demand that we recognize that our students' lives are a part of our wider social/political and therefore sexual communities. As Alison Pryer suggests, "school is the real world. It is a real living place, a place full of *eros* ... Wild *eros* flows into the cracks in the system, and the cracks are everywhere" (12). To recognize the reality of college life is, in part, to acknowledge the presence of those hegemonic systems and structures from within and without. It is to acknowledge that these structures really intrude on our students as they intrude on our classrooms. It is because our students are fighting the sexual odds that their lives are real. It is because they are fighting the sexual odds that we might look at sex with them. But to recognize the reality of college life is also to recognize the possibility that our students' sexual actions contribute to the task of making our world a sexually better place. It is, in other words, also because our students can improve the sexual experiences of the members of our communities that their lives are real. It is because they are also fighting the "good fight" that they (for lack of a better word) deserve for us to attempt such difficult dialogue.

To be clear, to enter into these acts of voyeurism—to look at sex with our students—cannot fully confront the myriad difficulties raised by traditional constructions of sexual activity between teachers and students. But it might highlight the dangers of the alternative. If and when sex does irrupt in the classroom (however it might irrupt), a simple denial of its existence—a simple looking away—is hardly without its own risks. To deny the dialogue is to risk denying our students—denying their sexual experiences.

To deny the dialogue is to risk denying those sexual experiences that may prove to be pedagogically beneficial in ways we cannot always see ourselves. It is, therefore, the beginning of the second half of the feminist analysis of sex and education that begins when we look. It is the beginning of that half which seeks to discover if and how sex might benefit a feminist pedagogical practice. And, I confess, it is a beginning that I like.

Conclusion

I have argued that the feminist analysis of sex and education is incomplete. While feminist pedagogues have articulated the potential dangers that sex brings to the classroom, we have not yet fully addressed its potential benefits. As such, I have described one way in which sex has enhanced my own feminist practice. In short, sex has raised pointed questions about the limits of my feminist pedagogy. More specifically, sex has prompted me to re-evaluate my understanding of authority, of the translation of thought into action, and of the relationship between empowerment and dialogue.

However, my intention here is not to replace one incomplete discourse with another—to replace an unnecessarily negative understanding of sex with an unnecessarily positive one. As Ann Ferguson suggests, both of these reductions are problematically essentialist (112). Both tell only one side of a complex story. It is because sex is real that it rests somewhere between. My hope is that, in their analyses of sex, feminist pedagogues might be allowed to stand between as well—between positive and negative, pro- and anti-, "yes" and "no." Such a space may be new to feminist pedagogy. But it is hardly new to "Jane."

Notes

1 For one contemporary survey, see NAESV Rape Crisis Center Survey.
2 For an account of the potential dangers inherent in such narrative and "confessional" feminism, see Bernstein, "Confessing Feminist Theory."
3 Some scholars have already well argued for this connection. For example, Jane Gallop explains, "thanks to feminism, not only did I become a better student, but my sex life improved ... For me, that sea of change will always be a central part of what 'women's liberation' means." Gallop, *Feminist Accused*, 4.

Works Cited

Bartlett, Alison "A Passionate Subject: Representations of Desire in Feminist Pedagogy." *Gender and Education* 10.1 (March 1998): 85–92.

Bauer, Dale. "Authority." In *Feminist Pedagogy: Looking Back to Move Forward*. Ed. Robbin D. Crabtree, David Alan Sapp, and Adela C. Licona. Baltimore: Johns Hopkins University Press, 2009. 23–26.

Bernstein, Susan David. "Confessing Feminist Theory: What's I Got to Do with It?" *Hypatia* 7.2 (1992): 120–47.

Buchwald, Emilie, Pamela Fletcher, and Martha Roth, eds. *Transforming a Rape Culture*. Minneapolis: Milkweed, 1993.

Califia Pat. *Public Sex: The Culture of Radical Sex*. San Francisco: Cleis Press, 1994.

Caughie, Pamela L., and Richard Pearce. "Resisting the Dominance of the Professor." In *Feminist Pedagogy: Looking Back to Move Forward*. Ed. Robbin D. Crabtree, David Alan Sapp, and Adela C. Licona. Baltimore: Johns Hopkins University Press, 2009. 27–39.

Cohee, Gail, Elisabeth Däumer, Theresa D. Kemp, et al. "Collectively Speaking." In *The Feminist Teacher Anthology*. Ed. Gail Cohee, Elisabeth Däumer, Theresa D. Kemp, et al. New York: Teachers College Press, 1998. 1–12.

Crabtree, Robbin, and David Alan Sapp. "Theoretical, Political, and Pedagogical Challenges in the Feminist Classroom." *College Teaching* 51.4 (2003): 131–40.

Crabtree, Robbin D., David Alan Sapp, and Adela C. Licona. "The Passion and the Praxis of Feminist Pedagogy." In *Feminist Pedagogy: Looking Back to Move Forward*. Ed. Robbin D. Crabtree, David Alan Sapp, and Adela C. Licona. Baltimore: Johns Hopkins University Press, 2009. 1–22.

Culley, Margo. "Anger and Authority in the Feminist Classroom: A Contradiction in Terms." In *Gendered Subjects: The Dynamics of Feminist Teaching*. Ed. Margo Culley and Catherine Portuges. Boston: Routledge and Kegan Paul, 1985. 209–18.

Dever, Maryanne. "Wrestling with the Devil." In *Meeting the Challenge: Innovative Feminist Pedagogies in Action*. Ed. Maralee Mayberry and Ellen Cronan Rose. New York: Routledge, 1999. 49–62.

Dworkin, Andrea. *Woman Hating*. New York: Plume, 1974.

Dziech, Billie Wright and Linda Weiner. *The Lecherous Professor: Sexual Harassment on Campus*. 2nd ed. Urbana: University of Illinois Press, 1990.

Ebert, Teresa. "For a Red Pedagogy: Feminism, Desire, and Need." *College English* 58.7 (November 1996): 795–819.

Ellsworth, Elizabeth. "Why Doesn't This Feel Empowering?" In *Feminisms and Critical Pedagogy*. Ed. Carmen Luke and Jennifer Gore. New York: Routledge, 1992. 90–119.

Felman, Jyl Lynn. *Never a Dull Moment*. New York: Routledge, 2001.

Ferguson, Ann. "Sex War: The Debate between Radical and Libertarian Feminists." *Signs: Journal of Women in Culture and Society*. 10.1 (1984): 106–12.

Freire, Paulo. *Pedagogy of the Oppressed*. Trans. Myra Bergman Ramos. New York: Continuum, 1999.

Gabriel, Susan, and Isaiah Smithson, eds. *Gender in the Classroom: Power and Pedagogy*. Urbana: University of Illinois Press, 1990.

Gallop, Jane. "The Teacher's Breasts." In *Pedagogy: The Question of Impersonation*. Ed. Jane Gallop. Bloomington: Indiana University Press, 1995. 79–89.

———. *Feminist Accused of Sexual Harassment*. Durham: Duke University Press, 1997.

Gilbert, Melissa Kesler, Carol Holdt, and Kristin Christophersen. "Letting Feminist Knowledge Serve the City." In *Meeting the Challenge: Innovative Feminist Pedagogies in Action*. Ed. Maralee Mayberry and Ellen Cronan Rose. New York: Routledge, 1999. 319–40.

Giroux, Henry A., ed. *Postmodernism, Feminism, and Cultural Politics: Redrawing Educational Boundaries*. New York: SUNY Press, 1991.

Golash, Deirdre. "Power, Sex, and Friendship in Academia." In *The Philosophy of Sex*, 5th ed. Ed. Alan Soble and Nicholas Power. Lanham: Rowman and Littlfield, 2008. 449–58.

Gore, Jennifer. "What We Can Do For You! What *Can* 'We' Do For 'You'." In *Feminisms and Critical Pedagogy*. Ed. Carmen Luke and Jennifer Gore. New York: Routledge, 1992. 54–73.

———. *The Struggle for Pedagogies*. New York: Routledge, 1993.

Grumet, Madeleine. *Bitter Milk: Women and Teaching*. Amherst: University of Massachusetts Press, 1988.

Hall, Roberta M., and Bernice R. Sandler. *Out of the Classroom: A Chilly Climate for Women?* Project on the Status and Education of Women. Washington: Association of American Colleges, 1988.

Hollibaugh, Amber. "Desire for the Future: Radical Hope in Passion and Pleasure." In *Feminism and Sexuality: A Reader*. Ed. Stevi Jackson and Sue Scott. New York: Columbia University Press, 1996. 224–29.

hooks, bell. *Teaching to Transgress*. New York: Routledge, 1994.

Jackson, Stevi, and Sue Scott. "Sexual Skirmishes and Feminist Factions." In *Feminism and Sexuality: A Reader*. Ed. Stevi Jackson and Sue Scott. New York: Columbia University Press, 1996. 1–34.

James, Joy. "Reflections on Teaching." In *The Feminist Teacher Anthology*. Ed. Gail Cohee, Elisabeth Däumer, Theresa D. Kemp, et al. New York: Teachers College Press, 1998. 75–86.

Johnson, Merri Lisa. "Jane Hocus, Jane Focus." In *Jane Sexes It Up: True Confessions of Feminist Desire*. Ed. Merri Lisa Johnson. New York: Thunder's Mouth Press, 2002. 1–12.

Jones, Alison. "Desire, Sexual Harassment, and Pedagogy in the University Classroom." *Theory into Practice* 35.2 (1996): 102–9.

Lewis, Magda Gere. *Without a Word: Teaching Beyond Women's Silence*. New York: Routledge, 1993.

Lorde, Audre. "Uses of the Erotic." In *Sister Outsider*. Berkeley: Crossing Press, 2007. 53–59.

MacKinnon, Catharine. *Sexual Harassment of Working Women*. New Haven: Yale University Press, 1979.

Maher, Frances, and Mary Kay Thompson Tetreault. *The Feminist Classroom*. New York: Basic Books, 1994.

May, Larry. *Masculinity and Morality*. Ithaca: Cornell University Press, 1998.

McWilliam, Erica. "Touchy Subjects: A Risky Inquiry into Pedagogical Pleasure." *British Educational Research Journal* 22.3 (June 1996): 305–17.

NAESV Rape Crisis Center Survey, 2012 http://www.ncdsv.org/images/NAESV_ RapeCrisisCenterSurvey_2012.pdf

Orner, Mimi. "Interrupting the Calls for Student Voice in 'Liberatory' Education." In *Feminisms and Critical Pedagogy*. Ed. Carmen Luke and Jennifer Gore. New York: Routledge, 1992. 74–89.

Paludi, M.A., ed. *Ivory Power: Sexual Harassment on Campus*, 2nd ed. Albany: SUNY Press, 1990.

Parry, Shirley. "Feminist Pedagogy and Techniques for the Changing Classroom." *Women's Studies Quarterly* 24.3–4 (1996): 45–54.

Pryer, Alison. "'What Spring Does with the Cherry Trees': The Eros of Teaching and Learning." *Teachers and Teaching: Theory and Practice* 7.1 (2001): 75–88.

Rich, Adrienne. "Claiming an Education." In *On Lies, Secrets, and Silence*. New York: W.W. Norton, 1979. 231–36.

Rinehart, Jane. "Feminist Wolves in Sheep's Disguise." In *Meeting the Challenge: Innovative Feminist Pedagogies in Action*. Ed. Maralee Mayberry and Ellen Cronan Rose. New York: Routledge, 1999. 63–98.

Ropers-Huilman, Rebecca. "Scholarship on the Other Side: Power and Caring in Feminist Education." In *Feminist Pedagogy: Looking Back to Move Forward*. Ed. Robbin D. Crabtree, David Alan Sapp, and Adela C. Licona. Baltimore: Johns Hopkins University Press, 2009. 40–58.

Rose, Suzanna. "The Protest as a Teaching Technique for Promoting Feminist Activism." In *Feminist Pedagogy: Looking Back to Move Forward*. Ed. Robbin D. Crabtree, David Alan Sapp, and Adela C. Licona. Baltimore: Johns Hopkins University Press, 2009. 171–75.

Santoro, Doris Gomez. "Women's Proper Place and Student-Centered Pedagogy." *Studies in Philosophy and Education* 27.5 (2008): 313–33.

Schuster, Marilyn, and Susan Van Dyne. "Curriculum Change for the Twenty-First Century." In *Women's Place in the Academy*. Ed. Marilyn R. Schuster and Susan R. Van Dyne. Totowa: Rowman and Allanheld, 1985. 3–12.

Seymour, Nicole. "The Interests of Full Disclosure: Agenda-Setting and the Practical Initiation of the Feminist Classroom." *Feminist Teacher* 17.3 (2007): 187–203.

Shrewsbury, Carolyn. "What Is Feminist Pedagogy?" *Women's Studies Quarterly* 25.1–2 (1997): 166–73.

Stanford Friedman, Susan. "Authority in the Feminist Classroom: A Contradiction in Terms?" In *Gendered Subjects: The Dynamics of Feminist Teaching*. Ed. Margo Culley and Catherine Portuges. Boston: Routledge and Kegan Paul, 1985. 203–8.

Todd, Sharon. "Desiring Desire in Rethinking Pedagogy." In *Learning Desire: Perspectives on Pedagogy, Culture, and the Unsaid*. Ed. Sharon Todd. New York: Routledge, 1997. 1–16.

Trethewey, Angela. "Sexuality, Eros, and Pedagogy: Desiring Laughter in the Classroom." *Women and Language* 27.1 (2004): 34–39.

Vance, Carole S. "Pleasure and Danger: Toward a Politics of Sexuality." In *Pleasure and Danger: Exploring Female Sexuality*. Ed. Carole S. Vance. Boston: Routledge and Kegan Paul, 1984. 1–27.

Willis, Ellen. *No More Nice Girls*. Hanover: Wesleyan University Press, 1992.

Weiler, Kathleen. *Women Teaching for Change*. Westport: Bergin and Garvey, 1988.

Woodbridge, Linda. "The Centrifugal Classroom." In *Gender and Academe: Feminist Pedagogy and Politics*. Ed. Sara Munson Deats and Lagretta Tallent Lenker. Lanham: Rowman and Littlefield, 1994. 133–52.

About the Contributors

Jamilee Baroud is currently a Ph.D. student in the Department of Education with a concentration in Society, Culture, and Literacies at the University of Ottawa. She holds a M.Ed. with a specialization in Women's Studies from Lakehead University. Her research focuses on gendered media representations of sexiness and their effects on girls' educational experiences. Her research interests include feminist pedagogy, media and education, and girlhood studies.

Renée Bondy is a lecturer in the Women's and Gender Studies program at the University of Windsor. A Canadian historian by training, she finds that writing for the popular press allows her to explore her interests in women's history, popular culture, and spirituality. She is a regular contributor to *Herizons* magazine.

Jennifer Browdy de Hernandez, Ph.D., teaches comparative literature and media studies at Bard College at Simon's Rock, in Massachusetts, with a focus on women's narratives of social and ecological justice. She is the founding director of the annual Berkshire Festival of Women's Writers and editor of two anthologies of contemporary African, Latin American, and Caribbean women's writing of resistance. She blogs on social and environmental justice at *Transition Times.*

Linda Briskin is a Professor Emeritus in the Social Science Department and the School of Gender, Sexuality and Women's Studies at York University (Toronto). She has been a feminist and union activist for more than forty years. Her commitment to social justice has framed her scholarship and inspired her teaching. In addition to her ongoing interest in feminist pedagogies, her research interests include equality bargaining, gendering worker militancies, women's organizing inside trade unions, leadership and representation (see http://womenunions.apps01.yorku.ca/), and the impact of austerity measures on equality. She is currently involved in a project to digitize feminist activism in the 1970s and 1980s (www.womens movementcanada.com).

Carm De Santis, Ph.D. (C), is an Adjunct in the Department of Sexuality, Marriage, and Family Studies at St. Jerome's University in the University of Waterloo. She is constantly exploring innovative ways to weave theory and research into practice as an educator, clinician, and researcher. She facilitates courses that focus on systemic thinking, social justice, sexuality, and inclusivity as part of meaningful and therapeutic interventions with people who have intersecting identities. Because learning is not limited to the classroom, she is invigorated by her interactions with students, her interest in the multifaceted nature of human relations and development, and most profoundly by her work with clients. She is a doctoral candidate in Family Relations and Human Development at the University of Guelph, with a focus on the embodiment of pleasure, erotic literacy, and sexual diversity and inclusivity, and she works as a relational/sex therapist in private practice in Guelph.

Judith Dorney is an Associate Professor in the Department of Educational Studies at the State University of New York at New Paltz. Her research explores the development of women teachers, focusing on their understandings and experiences of anger in their work. She is currently engaged in examining how the expression and repression of anger in the workplace contributes to the construction of gender and race for women teachers in schools.

Anna Gotlib is an Assistant Professor of Philosophy and a Pre-law Collegiate Adviser at Brooklyn College CUNY. Before joining the faculty at Brooklyn College, she was an Assistant Professor of Philosophy and director of the Pell Honors Program at Binghamton University (SUNY). Prior to her academic career, she was employed as an attorney who specialized in international law and labour law, and she worked in that capacity in the United States and abroad. Professor Gotlib's areas of research and teaching include bioethics/medical ethics, moral psychology, philosophy of law, and feminist philosophy. Her recent research is in the areas of illness and marginalization, intergenerational justice, motherhood, and memory and identity.

Amy Gullage recently completed a Ph.D. in Curriculum Studies and Teacher Development and the Graduate Collaborative Program in Women and Gender Studies at Ontario Institute for Studies in Education at the University of Toronto. Her dissertation explores how educators understand discourses of corporeality, such as notions of fitness and fatness, and the impact they have on teachers' professional and personal lives. Currently, Gullage is a Projects and Programs Coordinator at the McMaster Institute for Innovation and Excellence in Teaching and Learning at McMaster University.

Susan V. Iverson is an Associate Professor of Higher Education Administration and Student Personnel at Kent State University, Ohio, where she is also an affiliated faculty member with both the Women's Studies and LGBT Studies Programs. Iverson earned her doctorate in higher educational leadership, with a concentration in women's studies, from the University of Maine, where she also served as an instructor in higher educational leadership and women's studies. In 2006, Iverson was honoured with the Outstanding Dissertation Award presented by American Educational Research Association, Postsecondary Education division, for her dissertation "A policy discourse analysis of U.S. land-grant university diversity action plans." Iverson's scholarly interests include the status of women in higher education, multicultural competence, feminist pedagogy, and the use of feminist poststructural research. Iverson co-edited *Reconstructing Policy Analysis in Higher Education: Feminist Poststructural Perspectives* and *Feminist Community Engagement: Achieving Praxis*. Other work has appeared in *Review of Higher Education, Innovative Higher Education, Michigan Journal of Community Service Learning, Journal about Women in Higher Education, Equity and Excellence in Education*, and *Educational Administration Quarterly*.

Maggie Labinski is an Assistant Professor in the Philosophy Department at Fairfield University, Connecticut. She completed her graduate work at Boston College and Loyola University Chicago. Her research focuses on feminist philosophies and medieval philosophy.

Jennifer J. Llewellyn is the Viscount Bennett Professor of Law at the Schulich School of Law at Dalhousie University. Her research is focused in the areas of relational theory, restorative justice, truth commissions, international and domestic human rights law. She has written extensively on the theory and practice of a restorative approach in both transitional contexts and established democracies. Her work is reflected in two recent collections she co-edited: with Jocelyn Downie, *Being Relational: Reflections on*

Relational Theory and Health (2011), and, with Daniel Philpott, *Restorative Justice, Reconciliation and Peacebuilding* (2014).

Kristina R. Llewellyn is Associate Professor of Social Development Studies at Renison University College, University of Waterloo. She is also an associate member of the Department of Sociology and Legal Studies as well as the Women's Studies Program at the University of Waterloo. Llewellyn's areas of teaching and research encompass historical sociology of education, feminist and gender studies, democratic theories of schooling, and qualitative methods, particularly oral history. She is the author of *Democracy's Angels: The Work of Women Teachers* (2012) and co-editor of *The Canadian Oral History Reader* (2015).

Jane Nicholas is Associate Professor in the Department of Sexuality, Marriage and Family Studies at St. Jerome's University in the University of Waterloo. She is the author of *The Modern Girl: Feminine Modernities, the Body and Commodities in the 1920s* (2015) and co-editor with Patrizia Gentile of *Contesting Bodies and Nation in Canadian History* (2013).

Tracy Penny Light is Executive Director of the Centre for Student Engagement and Learning Innovation at Thompson Rivers University, Canada. She was previously Director of Women's Studies and Associate Professor in the Sexuality, Marriage, and Family Studies and History departments at the University of Waterloo, Canada. She is the co-editor of *Bodily Subjects: Essays on Gender and Health, 1800–2000* and is co-author of two books on ePortfolio implementation and practice: *Electronic Portfolios and Student Success* (2010), with Helen L. Chen, and *Documenting Learning with ePortfolios: A Guide for College Instructors* (2012), with Helen L. Chen and John Ittelson.

Toni Serafini is Associate Professor and Chair of the Department of Sexuality, Marriage, and Family Studies (SMF) at St. Jerome's University, in Waterloo, Ontario. She teaches courses in adolescent development; parent, child, and family relationships; relationship formation, maintenance, and conflict/crisis; human sexuality; communication and counselling skills; research methods; practicum capstone; and introductory psychology. Serafini's main research interest is identity formation across the lifespan. She is the co-editor of *Taking Sides: Clashing Views in Adolescence.* To measure identity functions, she developed and validated an instrument that has been translated into several languages and is used internationally, and has examined how identity is shaped through transformative experiences.

She also studies the role of critical self-reflection in teaching and learning, and how self-reflective processes contribute to identity development. Toni is also a practising Couple and Family Therapist.

Jeannette Silva Flores is a Doctoral Researcher in Sociology at the University of Warwick (UK). She did her B.A. in Sociology at the Pontificia Universidad Católica, Chile; her Diploma in Public Opinion at the Universidad Diego Portales, Chile; and her master's in Global Studies at Lund University in Sweden. She has a wide range of research interests within the field of sociology of higher education, and sociology of work and professions. She is also interested in topics such as gender and higher education; feminist theories, methodologies, and activism; and citizenship and migration. Her current doctoral research, titled "Being Feminist, Doing Academia," examines experiences of feminist academics in the UK.

Katrina Srigley is Associate Professor in the Department of History at Nipissing University in North Bay, Canada. Srigley's scholarship forefronts women's collective and individual experiences and explores the dynamics of memory making and storytelling. Her current Social Sciences and Humanities Research Council of Canada–funded project developed in partnership with Nipissing First Nation picks up the themes of storytelling and engaged practice. *Nbisiing Anishinabeg Biimadiziwin: To Understand the Past and Shape the Future* uses oral history and decolonized research practice to examine Indigenous ways of understanding the past and revitalizing and mobilizing Anishinaabe knowledge. She is currently co-authoring a book entitled *Gaa-Bii Kidwaad: The Story of Nipissing.*

Jacqueline Z. Wilson is a Senior Lecturer in the School of Education at Federation University Australia. Her current research and publications focus on historical sites of incarceration and institutionalization and their role in the formalization and emergence of welfare and justice systems, and on Care Leavers participation in higher education. Jacqueline is an award-winning university lecturer and teacher. Her leadership in the area of professional learning and research engages with diverse learners in innovative ways, and has been recognized with a Citation for Outstanding Contributions to Student Learning from the Federal Office of Learning and Teaching in Australia.

Index